Frontiers of the Roman Empire

Ancient Society and History

Frontiers of the

C. R. WHITTAKER

Roman Empire

A Social and Economic Study

The Johns Hopkins University Press
Baltimore and London

Johns Hopkins Paperbacks edition, 1997
06 05 04 03 02 01 00 99 98 97   5 4 3 2 1

The Johns Hopkins University Press
2715 North Charles Street
Baltimore, Maryland 21218-4319
The Johns Hopkins Press Ltd., London

Library of Congress Cataloging-in-Publication Data

Whittaker, C.R.
  [Frontières de l'Empire romain.   English]
  Frontiers of the Roman Empire : a social and economic study / C.R.
Whittaker.
      p.   cm.—(Ancient society and history)
  Includes bibliographical references and index.
  ISBN 0-8018-4677-3
  1. Rome—Boundaries—History.   2. Boundaries.   I. Title.
II. Series.
DG59.A2W5513   1994
937'.06—dc20   93-31342
ISBN 0-8018-5785-6 (pbk.)

A catalog record for this book is available from the British Library.

To Carmen and Ted

How many things by seasons seasoned are
To their right praise and true perfection

Contents

Contents

Illustrations

Preface

The origin of this book lies in a series of four lectures delivered in May 1987 at the Collège de France, and it is due to the iron discipline and infinite patience of my host and friend Christian Goudineau that the book took shape in its French edition, published in 1989.

Since then the book has changed its form but not, I trust, its basic ideas. The theme of the original lectures was social and economic change on the western frontiers of the Roman Empire, and some of those chapters remain more or less as they were first spoken. But the aim has since broadened. I have added a chapter on the ideological aspect of frontiers in Roman thought and two chapters of narrative, intended to help the nonspecialist. The Roman East, which was ignored in the first book, has now found a place, although inevitably the western bias remains prominent. Finally, I have added a chapter on the last days of the Roman frontiers, since the later Roman Empire increasingly occupies my thoughts. If readers find the final effect unbalanced, I can only excuse myself by saying that the later Roman Empire has been much less studied than the earlier Empire.

One hardly needs a reason to write a book on frontiers these days, when the collapse of one frontier—the iron curtain, on the night of 9 November 1989—has had a quite extraordinary knock-on effect in opening up a Pandora's box of frontier problems. What will now be the frontiers of a greater Germany? What will be the frontiers of a lesser Russia or a lesser Yugoslavia? By what criteria will Ukraine maintain its nationhood, where 40 percent of the population is Russian? Can Iraq and Turkey resist the claims of a new Kurdistan? And so on. I am not sure this book will do anything to answer these problems, but it offers one historical perspective among many to correct the myths of the past.

Many persons have helped me produce this book. In particular I am grateful to Greg Woolf and Mike Fulford, who read the first, French version, and to Pol Trousset, Henry Hurst, and Catherine Hills, who did the same for this English edition. They all made many helpful suggestions or corrections, and it is not their fault if errors remain. John Rich, the syndics of Cambridge University Press, and the editors of Ennaudi's *Storia di Roma* have allowed me to use parts of chapters that were originally written for them. Christian Goudineau of the Collège de France and Claude Levêque of the University of Besançon have permitted me to rework and translate the French edition of 1989. Paul Fordham has given his time generously to produce the maps as I wanted them. All maps not otherwise credited were drawn by him. Other acknowledgments and thanks appear with the illustrations, but I must note my particular gratitude to Alice Bennett for her skillful professionalism in the editing stage. Above all it is my wife I have to thank for her help in all those tedious jobs of typing and checking, without which I would have been incapable of finishing the book.

Frontiers of the Roman Empire

Introduction:
The Historiography of Frontiers

One of the most romantic descriptions of Hadrian's Wall in the English language was written by Rudyard Kipling in 1904 in what was intended as a children's book, *Puck of Pook's Hill*, when he imagined what it was like for a Roman soldier arriving at the frontier.

> The road goes on and on—and the wind sings through your helmet plume—past altars to legions and generals forgotten. Just when you think you are at the world's end, you see the smoke from east to west as far as the eye can turn, and then under it, also as far as the eye can stretch ... one long, low, rising and falling, and hiding and showing line of towers. And that is the wall!

Swirling mists, beacon fires, the far distant boundaries of the empire and dark hordes of barbarians beyond in the outer darkness waiting to attack—that was the image held by Kipling and his contemporaries in the last years of the nineteenth century.

> Qui procul hinc?, the legend's writ
> The frontier grave is far away.

1

Those are the words of Kipling's dining club companion Sir Henry Newbolt, in "Lines written on Clifton Chapel," one of the most chauvinistic and best loved poems of the period. Clifton College, I should add, was one of the great English public schools, where gentlemen were bred to govern the British Empire.

Kipling's Roman frontier stories of courage and heroism had an enormous influence on the thought of his generation and those to come. The Roman soldiers in his stories, says his biographer, "resembled subalterns of the Indian army" (Carrington 1970, 447). To understand the historiography of frontiers, therefore, we must have some awareness of the influence of imperialism on British writing. Kipling, the poet of the "White Man's Burden" and other songs of empire, returned to India in 1882 as a young journalist just at the time of the Afghan wars. But despite his fascination with frontier stories like *Kim* and "The Man Who Would be King," he visited the frontier only once (in 1884), to report the ceremonial reception of Amir Abdurrahman Khan. On that occasion he rashly wandered into the Khyber Pass but hastily retreated when, as he says, a tribesman took a shot at him—an experience that led him to give the immortal advice, "Never close with an Afghan. Plug him at a distance" (Carrington 1970, 95).

The episode illustrates in a lighthearted way the attitude of Kipling and the British Victorians. To them frontiers were simply the dividing line between the civilized and the barbarian. A sophisticated theory did not exist. Lord Curzon, himself one of the great empire builders, pointed out in a lecture at Oxford in 1907 that even though four-fifths of all treaties were concerned with frontiers, "you may ransack the catalogues of libraries, you may study the writings of scholars and you will find the subject is almost wholly ignored" (Curzon 1907, 5). This was when Britain controlled over twenty-one thousand miles of frontier in Canada, India, and Africa.

It is this background that has shaped today's Anglo-Saxon views of Roman frontiers. Curzon, who was credited with the most successful attempt made by any administrator to bring stability to the Indian frontier, when he became viceroy in 1899, was later to compare the Indian frontier "point by point with its ancient counterpart and prototype, the Frontier system of Rome" (Davies

1975, 115; Curzon 1907, 54). C. C. Davies, author of the classic Indian study in the 1930s, *The Problem of the North West Frontier, 1890–1908,* also found it proper to pronounce his verdict on Rome. "Rome fell," he said, "because her dykes were not strong enough to hold back the flood of barbarian inroads."[1] This linear description of Roman frontiers, which Davies himself saw to be quite unlike the reality of the Indian North-West Frontier, with its "zone or belt of mountainous country," was adopted by statesmen and modern historians alike in the first half of this century.

Naturally ancient historians were not unaffected. For instance, Rice Holmes, that excellent historian of the Gallic campaigns of Caesar and Augustus, was led to what is now called the "ludicrous misunderstanding" that Augustus's expansionist drive to the Elbe was in defense of the line of the Rhine frontier (Rice Holmes 1928–31, 2:164–65; Wells 1972, 152). French scholars have remarked that the chronic Anglo-Saxon disease in studying Roman North Africa has been to believe that Hadrian's Wall in Britain and the African *fossatum,* two of the great Roman frontier walls, not only were the creation of a single mentality (Hadrian's) but were constructed with the single strategy of forming a barrier line to keep the barbarians out.[2]

The British, however, were not the only imperialists of the nineteenth century. The French too were active players in the game, where the *mirage d'illusions* of the Partie Coloniale fed the insubordinate ambitions of bored military officers (Porch 1986, 8–10). As a colonial power France has been responsible for at least 17 percent of the frontiers in the modern world (Foucher 1986, 11). But one looks in vain for any sophisticated French theories of frontiers during the scramble for Africa or in settling upon the Mekong River as the frontier of Indo-China in 1893. Such theory as there was derived from the jurisprudential discourses of Grotius and Pufendorf and concerned the frontiers between *sovereign* states. Otherwise classical authors—Caesar, Tacitus, and the agronomists—were often inaccurately quoted and inappropriately interpreted to add the authority of antiquity to a concept of natural frontiers, which had in fact gained currency only between the fourteenth and seventeenth centuries with the rise of the absolutist state (Nordman 1979, esp. 81–87; Alliès 1980, 31; cf. Febvre 1922, 326).

By the time the frontiers of the French colonial empire were defined, however, the original, tentative notion that France was an integral territory endowed by nature with special boundaries, such as Richelieu had articulated in pursuit of his political ambitions against Austria,[3] was radically reinforced by the Revolution, with its special stress on natural law, natural rights, and therefore on natural frontiers as the essential elements of the new nation. Linear frontiers acquired concrete reality in the Treaty of 1814, which supposedly restored to France her formal integrity (Foucher 1986, 120–21). *Potamologie*, the myth of river frontiers, both encapsulated France's national ambitions in Europe and became, in the Maghreb, an administrative symbol that perverted territorial and ethnic realities (Nordman 1980, 25–28; Guichonnet and Raffestin 1974, 19).

Colonial ideology of *la mission civilatrice* also invented sharp frontiers between civilization and barbarism. E.F. Gautier, one of the pioneers of Roman African history, had taken part in Captain Dinaux's Saharan expedition in 1905 and was convinced from his vast experience of the desert that the southern boundary of Algeria was a natural "chaine du *limes*" of mountains from the Aures to Tlemcen, where he claimed the Roman frontiers could be traced with great precision. Beyond, he says—and we hear the undertones of his colonial experience—lay "un autre monde" of barbarian nomads uncontrollable and uneconomical (Gautier 1952, 211–12, citing his earlier studies; Porch 1986, 9).

This French concept of natural, linear frontiers probably received encouragement after the First World War from military strategists who believed that a naturally sited blockade could eliminate the horrors of trench warfare. The ancient historian Julien Guey formulated a theory in 1939, just before the outbreak of the Second World War, of an ancient African "*limes* du chameau," where the *fossatum* was implicitly likened to the Maginot Line and camels to tanks (Guey 1939).

The United States was the one place where a more interesting historiography of frontier studies might have been conceived, since the early pioneers had faced something not unlike the experience of the Romans in their expansion westward. In a seminal paper, "The Significance of the Frontier in American History," delivered in 1893, Frederick Jackson Turner was perhaps aware of this comparison when he described the frontier as "the meeting place between savagery and civilisation." Certainly a year later he had enlarged his definition by likening the experience of "the ever retreating Great West" to that of the Greeks as they crossed the Mediterranean, where the frontier meant not only an institution but "a state of mind" that created the constant tendency to expand.[4]

Turner gave birth to the theme, developed in Walter Prescott Webb's *The Great Plains* (1931), of a frontier as "not a line to stop at, but an area inviting entrance," by definition never still—a process, not an area or a boundary (Webb 1953, 2; Powell et al. 1983, 4–5). But the value of the American experience, which had the virtue of clarifying the distinction between state limits and pioneering frontiers, has been diverted into other directions; for both Turner and Webb, like many Americans since, were preoccupied not so much with frontiers as with frontiersmen—the growth of American manhood and its national history.

Turner's vision, moreover, was almost totally ethnocentric, excluding Indians from any role in the frontier's formation or function. It was as though the native population had not been present. "Inherent in the American concept," said Webb, "is the idea of a body of free land which can be had for the taking."[5] The omission flaws the basic description of the process, since it was through interaction, not military advance, that the frontier crystallized, and it was the American whites who to a large extent defined the political development of the Indians.

There is no doubt that American perspectives were also strongly influenced by the massive work of Friedrich Ratzel, "father of the new political geography" and the product of Bismarck's unified German state in the later nineteenth century. Ratzel himself participated in the Franco-Prussian War of 1870–71 and benefited educationally from the new *Kultur* and the holistic, spatial thinking (*Ganzheit*) developed by Alexander von Humboldt, Karl Ritter, and others (Parker 1985, 11; Korinman 1990, 10, 35–37). He also visited America, where he met Turner, and he was strongly impressed by the vast open spaces, the *Lebensraum*, of the West as well as by the superb geometrical organization of that space, which in his opinion provided the essential stimulus for the dynamic growth of the United States—and of all successful states.[6] Ratzel's two major works, *Anthropo-geographie* and *Politische Geographie*, were given a wide American audience in the 1890s—particularly the former, through the translation by his American disciple Ellen Semple, since both saw similarities between the expanding American and German states.[7]

Ratzel's political geography developed the notion of laws of political geography that accounted for successful world states, rooted in the soil and adapted to the environment. Influenced by the social Darwinism of Herbert Spencer and trained as a zoologist, Ratzel conceived of states as biological and physiological "space organisms" with brains, arteries, and so on, that needed to devour the "nutritious food" of expansion into lesser states. You either expanded or declined. Ratzel's theory, conceived in the atmosphere of Prussian ambitions but also much impressed by Turner's writing, regarded stable frontiers as a sign of weakness, since the survival of the fittest came through action (Guichonnet and Raffestin 1974, 30–31; Fouchet 1986, 56). This chimed well with the indigenous American slogan of "Manifest Destiny" popularized by Theodore Roosevelt and the worldview of Alfred Mahan's influential book on American imperialism in the 1890s (Parker 1985, 12). Ratzel, it might be added, was free with historical examples drawn from Roman history, particularly the Roman expansion into its western provinces (citation in Korinman 1990, 47).

When we turn to American ancient historians, therefore, it is difficult to believe that the influential book by Edward Luttwak, *The Grand Strategy of the Roman Empire,* was not in some respects affected by this tradition, whether consciously or unconsciously. His evident admiration for the earliest phase of the Julio-Claudian expansion and for its period of what he calls "forceful suasion" leads him to compare unfavorably the static frontiers of later generations, which he evidently regards as the beginning of the end. This is very much in Turner's and Ratzel's mold of thought, for they regarded the adventures of an expanding frontier as character building and saw consolidation as decline. To Luttwak, as to Turner, the indigenous frontier populations were an enemy to be intimidated but were nowhere part of the equation of frontier formation. No doubt this is because, as one reviewer has said of Luttwak's later book, *Strategy,* he studies strategy as military fighting, not as a political process.[8]

A notable reaction to this general historiographic trend was Lucien Febvre, cofounder of the Annales school of social history in France. Febvre was attracted by the antideterminist, political-geographical schema—the "possibilism"—of Vidal de la Blache, who was writing at the same time as Ratzel. He violently disliked Ratzel's scientific totalitarianism in its subordination of history to geography. But like many Frenchmen, he also regarded Ratzel's geographic preoccupation with state power and deterministic expansion as sinister and dangerously threatening to the unity of the French state as it had evolved historically. The *Politische Geographie,* he declared, was "a kind of manual of German imperialism."[9] Febvre's epoch-making book *La terre et l'evolution humaine* begins by attacking Ratzel on the very first page and ends on the last page with a condemnation of "la psalmodie monotone des vieilles litaines ratzéliennes."

What is interesting is that in his chapter "Le problème des frontières et les régions naturelles d'états" Febvre mentions Ratzel's name only once, when he criticizes him for ignoring the cultural-social dimension in his geographic considerations, since political states and cultures need not share the same confines. (His chosen example is the world of Islam, which is an influential factor, although islamic states are potential rivals) (Febvre 1922, 323–42). This was because Ratzel's expansionist, geopolitical "laws" took no account of the social and economic dynamics of frontier zones, nor did they explain how limits were formed.

For historians, however, Febvre pointed out with customary clarity that the two concepts of a frontier as a fixed military "front" and as a territorial boundary (*fins*) did not merge until the nineteenth century. Nor was the fixed frontier, he argued, an evolution from a cordon sanitaire to a natural barrier line; he saw it as the consequence of the rise of the nation-state, which accentuated the moral differences in nationalities—"Elle se doubla d'une frontière morale." His good sense contrasts strikingly with that of many ancient historians who still accept the Rhine and Danube as Rome's natural frontier and regard the German and British *limites* both as territorial boundaries and as military barricades of the Roman Empire, long before the advent of the nation-state. The concept of natural frontiers, said Febvre, is deeply "encrusted" in us all.[10]

A contemporary of Febvre, Geouffre de Lapradelle, who was professor of international law at Aix-en-Provence, followed up Febvre's insistence that pursuit of "natural frontiers" was in reality a political instrument of imperialism by going on to claim that the *limites* of Rome were a subjective "symbole de crainte ou de domination," an artificial tool of organization and a base of conquest, not delimitation.[11] Despite this, however, and despite recent exposés of the false stereotype that the Greeks and Romans created of a world divided between their own civilization and the "otherness" of the world of "barbarians",[12] many ancient historians have accepted this classical Weltanschauung as a statement of Roman frontier policy. I think that is incorrect.

That does not, of course, mean that the symbolic, sacred character of Roman *limites* was without significance, as I shall argue later, in developing internal concepts of territoriality and *Romanitas* or in encapsulating Roman attitudes toward boundaries. But it is questionable whether we can go as far as the ex cathedra statement of one ancient historian who says, "Not only a waterway . . . not only did a palisade isolate the [barbarians] . . . but the frontier line was at the same time a line of demarcation between two fundamentally different realms of thought" (Alföldi 1952, 1).

The implication that power was restricted by linear boundaries of walls or great rivers is flatly contradicted by historical, geographical studies that, while admitting that the Romans, like the Chinese, may have had an ideological view of a *limite de civilisation,* rightly conclude that the frontiers were imprecise, more zonal than linear, despite the illusion of walls (Guichonnet and Raffestin 1974, 16). One of the most influential statements of this point of view was Owen Lattimore's important study of the frontiers of China, written in 1940, in which he too makes comparisons with Rome. As I shall argue later, his economic and ecological explanation of frontiers may help to explain why Roman frontiers stopped where they did (Lattimore 1940, 1962; I discuss Lattimore's views on pp. 85–86).

There is therefore a plethora of historiographic tendencies to lead or mislead ancient historians in their general conceptualization of Roman frontiers. I stress the word "general," since it does not need me to prove that no two frontiers are ever exactly alike. In the Roman world the greatest of such differences was between the frontiers in the East and in the West. But even in the East—despite the older, more centralized empire of Parthia, succeeded by that of Persia, on the borders of the Roman Empire—there are interesting comparisons to be made with the West, while within the western frontiers it is easy enough to identify differences and specificities. What is lacking, however, is an organizing principle beyond the specialized regional studies, a satisfactory model that includes the interpretation and development that take place on a frontier—as many students of frontier studies have complained.[13] If this book goes some small way toward filling that need it will have been justified.

One

Space, Power, and Society

In Plutarch's *Life of Numa* (16) there is a passage that describes
the building of the temples on the Capitoline Hill, the modern
Campidoglio, in Rome, one of which was the temple to Terminus, the "god of boundaries." In this context Plutarch says:

> It appears that the merit of having drawn up boundaries for the city
> [of Rome] dates back to Numa. It was something Romulus never
> wanted to do, for fear that by measuring up his own territory he would
> give recognition to the property he had taken away from others. If a
> boundary is respected it is a restraint on the use of force; and if it is
> not respected then it is proof of an abuse of power.

I am not concerned here with whether the traditional date given
to the *terminatio* ("drawing up the boundaries") of Roman territory
was correctly attributed to the second king of Rome.[1] My interest
is in the central paradox of Roman history contained in the tension
between the figures of Romulus and Numa: Romulus, the symbolic
figure of Roman expansion, and Numa, the symbol of law and
order and of limits. You find the same paradox in the legend of
the two minor gods associated with Jupiter Optimus Maximus on
the Capitol, Terminus and Iuventas, who represented two aspects
of Jupiter; one as the god of young men of military age, the other

10

as the protector of the private property that was divided up between them. This double face of Jupiter corresponds to polarities that ran deep in Indo-European culture (Dumézil 1966, 203–4).

It is perhaps not surprising, then, to find that the whole subject of Roman frontiers is riddled with paradox. First we find a state that—to use the words of a recent study—was "from the beginning a society of frontiers"; yet it was also a society where it is impossible, despite the best efforts of this same author, to detect anything like a frontier policy before the emperor Augustus (Dyson 1986, 7). Second, we discover a society deeply committed from its very earliest laws to the juridical and sacral definition of boundaries; yet it is virtually impossible at any given time either before or after Augustus to discover where the outer limits of those boundaries were drawn. The reason for these paradoxes lies not in the sparseness of the sources but in our own inadequate understanding of Roman cosmology and science.

Current debate among historical geographers divides structural determinists from behaviorists. The first, who are the product of the positivist revolution and the "science of the spatial," believe that people, no matter who they are, act according to the way the world is. Behaviorists, on the other hand, through their stress on "intentionality," ideology, and cognitive mental maps, believe that people behave according to the way they perceive the world to be (Sacks 1986, 95; Gregory and Urry 1985, 3). There is no doubting the position of the eminent French ancient historian Claude Nicolet, among the first group, when he complains in his recent fascinating book, *Space, Geography, and Politics in the Early Roman Empire*, of those who "put forward a 'natural' difference between the ancient way of thinking and ours." And, he adds, "In the name of anthropological reading of the ancient texts, their conceptions and representations of space have been implacably compared to our own."[2]

Let me therefore also from the start clearly nail my colors to the mast by saying that my own views fall between those of determinists and behavioralists, although they are more in sympathy with the latter. I share the opinion of Henri Lefebvre that social relations project themselves spatially. But, he says, "Space is political *and* ideological. It is a product literally filled with ideology" (Lefebvre 1976, 31; Soja 1985). My particular interest here is how Roman perceptions of cosmology and social space projected themselves onto their concepts of imperial frontiers.

Cosmology

Let us begin with cosmology. Broadly speaking we can say that, however much the Romans may have interested themselves in "chorography" (the Greek word Strabo used for his detailed study of lands, unlike the global study of "geography"), and however much they contributed to the improvement of the subject—which I agree with Nicolet (1991, 66) was not negligible—Roman cartography did not advance any further theoretically than did that of the Greeks and Alexandrians to whom they were indebted.

So for instance, despite the empirical accuracy of the global shape and distances calculated by Eratosthenes in the third century B.C., Romans were quite prepared to embrace subsequent "improvements" (as they thought) in the science of cosmology, which in reality brought not greater but lesser correspondence between ideology and reality. Romans of the second century B.C. honored the more "scientific" reinterpretations by Crates of Mallos, who calculated that only one-quarter of the globe contained the *oikoumene,* that is, the inhabited world. By Plutarch's day in the second century A.D., intellectuals were comfortably prepared to believe that the world looked like a dinner table (*Quaest. conv.* 7.4.704b). By the fifth century A.D. the cartographers of the emperor Theodosius II believed that a map of the *totus orbis* would be more comprehensible if it could be made smaller (*Div. orb. terr.* = *Geog. Lat. Min.* 19 f.) (Arnaud 1989, 11). And by the time of Cosmas Indicopleustes in the sixth century A.D. the map illustrated in his work was "little more than a geometric sketch" (Harley and Woodward 1987, 144).

Such a cosmology of order, harmony, and above all supposedly known "scientific" limits produced two consequences for Roman perceptions of the world. First, there was a tendency to underestimate the distance between center and periphery. All world maps

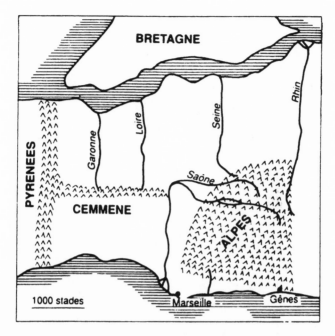

Fig. 1. Following Strabo's description, this is what Gaul looked like to the Romans. From Goudineau 1990, 83; reproduced by the author's permission.

contained a center of practical, empirical certainty and a periphery of ideological or "scientific" certainty. But between the two lay large areas of uncertainty. Although the proportions of the world were distorted by the visible shape of the maps on which it was displayed—a fact to which both Geminos in the late Republic and Ptolemy drew attention (Arnaud 1989, 14–15)—space and time were expressed in terms of accessibility, as they are in many societies (Tuan 1987, 46–47).

For example, in the geographic studies of Strabo, the region between the Pyrenees and the Rhine was perceived as a series of elongated, rectangular blocks from east to west, marked off between rivers running north and south (Strabo 2.5.28; fig. 1).[3] That is an example of the ideology that the cosmos was harmonious and regular. But then came the distortions produced by accessibility. Although the distance between the Pyrenees and the Rhine was

13

elongated by 50 percent, the distance from Marseilles due north to the limit of Oceanus, where Britain lay, was compressed into only half that distance. Because Caesar had reached Britain and claimed the subjection of all the maritime states of Gaul up to Oceanus within three years (*BG* 2.34), the bridge between center and periphery had contracted. But given the harmony of the world order, the time and distance it would take to advance to the eastern shores of Oceanus, which we know both Caesar and Augustus contemplated, must have seemed equally possible from the center (Brunt 1963, 175). From the figures of Pliny the Elder, which derived from the map drawn up by Augustus's assistant Agrippa, those distances too were underestimated by about 50 percent (Moynihan 1986, 152).

The second consequence of the cosmology was that the unknown regions between the known center and the ideological periphery of Oceanus were perceived in terms not of territory but of power. The clearest illustration of this comes from the works collected in the *Geographi Latini minores*[4]—works such as the *Sphaera* or *Cosmographia* of Julius Honorius and the *Cosmographia of Pseudo-Aethicus*—which it is generally agreed derive from the cartographic and chorographic initiatives of Julius Caesar but above all of Augustus (Dalché and Nicolet 1986), whose figure is still illustrated on the medieval mappamundi in Hereford cathedral (fig. 2). In the lists of *provinciae* contained in those works are many that were never Roman "provinces" at all but were regions that extended to the four quarters of the ocean.

So, for instance, under the heading for the southern quarter, *oceanus meridianus*, are listed the *provinciae* of Africa and Mauretania, as we would have expected, but there is also Gaetulia, which was never a formal province but was the name of the terra incognita that lay to the south of the African frontier. Numidia, furthermore, which was part of the Roman provincial organization, is said to extend all the way to the *oceanus aethiopus*, and a precise distance of 480 miles is noted. Under the heading *oceanus orientalis* are listed the *provinciae* of Syria, Commagene, and so forth, which were within the Roman frontiers, but under the same heading we

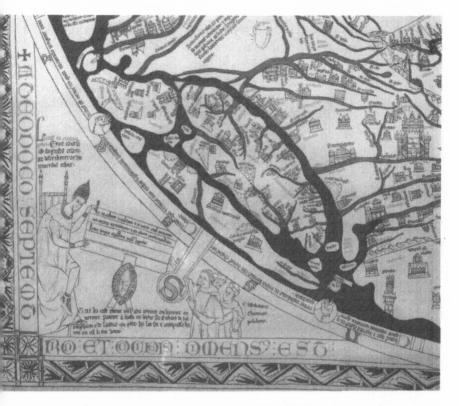

Fig. 2. Detail of the mappamundi (ca. 1300) in Hereford cathedral, portraying Augustus as a medieval monarch commissioning three geographers to survey the world. Photograph by kind permission of the dean and chapter of Hereford cathedral and the Hereford Mappa Mundi Trust.

also find India, which was obviously never a part of the Roman Empire as we normally think of it.

These pseudoprovinces corresponded to areas that the Romans claimed to control but not to organize. In each quarter of the world we also have recorded the *gentes*, the barbarian periphery that ringed the *oikoumene* and "went on as far as Oceanus"—*pergentes usque ad oceanum*. But they lay within, not outside, the *provinciae*. Julius Honorius's cosmographic lists were still current

15

in the sixth century when Cassiodorus gave them as recommended reading for monks, since they contained, as he says (*Inst. div. litt.* 25), "seas, islands, famous mountains, provinces, cities, rivers, tribes . . . so that practically nothing is missing in the book" (*maria, insulas, montes famosos, provincias, civitates, flumina, gentes . . . ut p(a)ene nihil libro ipsi desit*). But one category is missing from these cartographic lists: "frontiers," or *limites,* are never mentioned.

From the structuralist point of view, this Roman world vision corresponds to something Paul Claval has noticed concerning absolutism—which, he says, rests on a concept of belief in power that has a geographical dimension but not necessarily a geographical continuum: "The empire does not have a frontier in the sense that we nowadays use the term; that is, an enclosure separating it from a different state. . . . It is surrounded by barbarians; . . . its expansion stops at the boundaries of the cultivated universe (1978, 109). From a behaviorist point of view, however, it corresponds closely to the cosmology of Strabo, who sums up previous Greek cosmology but adds a new Roman, "scientific," cultural view of barbarians that believed in the possibility of civilizing them (Thollard 1987, 39).

Strabo was a contemporary of the emperor Augustus, and his perception of the *externae gentes* was probably a close reflection of Augustus's own ideology (Lassère 1983). But it is similar to what is implied in the *Cosmographia.* The peoples beyond the provinces are treated by Strabo as part of the empire, to whom *clementia* and *amicitia* are extended but who are not worth the cost of occupation because of the weakness of their economic infrastructure. The most celebrated example was Britain (Strabo 2.5.8). Only the "best and best-known part of the *oikoumene*" was to be occupied and organized, although the rest was certainly open to economic exploitation.

How far this political application of ideology to space had developed before Caesar and Augustus is difficult to determine. Some hint of the geographical distortion of Europe produced by Strabo can also be found in Polybius's description of the region between Narbo and the river Don (Polyb. 3.37.8, 38.2–39; cf. Dion 1977, 233). Polybius, who lived in the second century B.C., also held the opinion that the whole world was "subject" (*hypekoos*) to the Roman *arche* (Polyb. 1.2.7 etc.; *arche* means either "power" or "empire"). Yet at the same time he says that Rome ruled only what he describes as "all the known parts of the inhabited world" (Polyb. 3.1.4 etc.). This resembles Strabo's dualist vision of Roman power extending to both the organized core and the *externae gentes*.

Polybius, so it is argued, was in this way responsible for encouraging two quite contradictory ecumenical views in the late Republic; first, that the empire and the world were coterminous; second, that imperial expansion was still possible. So, to explain the contradiction, it is argued that we have to believe the first view was mere ideological rhetoric, *laus imperii,* and that in reality all Romans knew that military glory was to be won by conquering new territory for the empire—*propagatio imperii* (Richardson 1979).

But the contradiction disappears if we accept the cosmological perspective that there were two parts of the *orbis terrarum imperium*: first, the organized territory of Roman administration, which might be extended, and second, the *externae gentes* who were subjects but not usually worth annexing. This dualist attitude was inherent in the ambiguity of the very term *provincia*; it could be understood as a *forma* with geographical dimensions (Tacitus talks of "reducing Britain to the form of a province" [*redacta in formam provinciae; Agr.* 14]). Or it could refer to space for power without geographic boundaries (Julius Caesar was voted the *provincia* of Transalpine Gaul when it was just a "sphere of command"; Suet. *Jul* 22.1). It follows that when Suetonius said that kings were treated "as the limbs and parts of the empire" (*nec aliter quam membra partisque imperii; Aug.* 48), he meant they were a genuine part of the *imperium,* that is, a part of imperial control—although not of the administered *provincia.*[5]

This ambivalence between frontier and empire, or between an empire of administration and an empire of control, revealed itself very clearly in Rome's early relations with the principalities and empires of the East. Alliances were struck with states that seemed to be outside the empire, but in reality they found themselves expected to submit to Roman jurisdiction. But what is notable is

17

the absence of anything like a strategy of frontiers. The Treaty of Apamea in 188 B.C., for instance, laid down what look like quite specific boundaries between King Antiochus and the Romans along the Taurus Mountains in southeastern Asia Minor (Livy 38.38). But Rome itself did not occupy the space vacated by Antiochus; the boundary was well beyond the formal territories of the allies of Rome, and it is clear from subsequent events that Rome in no way limited its diplomatic interference to the agreed line.[6]

The cosmological inheritance from the Greeks for the Romans in the Republic and the early Empire was therefore of a finite *orbis terrarum–oikoumene,* open and accessible to power but not to territorial control.

Limitatio

The second facet of the Roman mentality that determined Roman attitudes toward frontiers was associated with the science and techniques of divination and mensuration. As is well known, these techniques were deeply embedded in Roman society and derived, so Romans believed, from "a heavenly origin and an eternal practice." Those are the words of Hyginus Gromaticus, one of the Roman *gromatici,* writers on land surveying, whose works have come down to us (Hyg. Grom. *Cons. limit.,* p. 131 Thulin). Whatever the historical, practical, and earthly origins and values of early geometric surveys, *scamnatio* or *limitatio* was never the act of limiting expansion but was "a purifying enclosure of land" whose boundary stones or *termini* were of special symbolic and religious significance for Romans,[7] more so than for the Greeks. The penalty *de termino moto*—that is, for tearing up boundary stones—was far more serious in Roman than in Greek law (Hinrichs 1989, 84).

The art of the land surveyors, those called in republican times *finitores* and in the later period *agrimensores,* was steeped in religious ritual; first the ritual of Latin divination, to which was later added Etruscan augury. The growth of the art represented not a conflict between rational science and magical religion but the practical application of scientific techniques to myth and ritual to render an expanding world more intelligible. Cassiodorus talks of "this *disciplina mirabilis,* which could apply fixed reason to unlimited fields" (Var. 2.52).

All rectangular surveys in history have had a strongly utopian character, used in a period of expanding power and colonial foundations as the dream of a distant administration for organized control. The great American Rectangular Land Survey of the eighteenth century was designed to bring "order upon the land" at a time of particularly fluid frontiers. Frederick Jackson Turner, whose 1893 paper on the American frontier laid the basis for future frontier studies, regarded the Ordinance of 1785, which established the American survey, as fundamental to the welfare of the early settlers (Johnson 1976, preface). Yet at the same time, as we saw earlier, Turner viewed this as not inconsistent with the theory of an open American frontier—"not as a line to stop at but an area inviting entrance."

I hardly need repeat that Caesar and Augustus also had a close and personal interest in the art of *agrimensio,* as is attested in the works of the *gromatici* (Dilke 1971, 37–38). The interest derived partly from their concern to organize land for their colonial foundations, but it was also complementary to the cosmological dreams contained in the *Cosmographiae.* Indeed, Nicolet has recently revived an old hypothesis that the cosmography was specifically part of the grand project of imperial cadastration,[8] from which, as we saw, *fines* and *limites* were conspicuously absent. In short, land cadastration and enclosure, whether in the United States or in the Roman Empire, established ideological and scientific rules of visible, physical boundaries at the precise time when frontiers were most invisible. They were a means of organizing internal control, "pour la bonne gestion" (to follow Claval again), not for the limitation of power in the *oikoumene.*

Enclosing sacral space was therefore not the same as defining a military boundary. The *agrimensores* explained and illustrated this proposition. In several of their examples they made a distinction between the "frontier" limits of a territory—a river, for instance (called *flumen finitimum;* fig. 3), or a mountain range—and the organized, cadastrated land. What we find is that there were two kinds of boundaries: the boundary of assigned lands and the

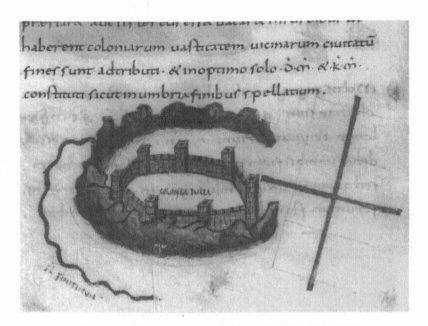

Fig. 3. Illustration of the text of Hyginus Gromaticus describing a *flumen finitimum* in the territory of Colonia Julia (Hispellum) in Spain. The miniature comes from a ninth-century manuscript copied from an earlier illustration. Photograph from MS P. Vat. Lat. 1564, P 88v, by permission of the Biblioteca Apostolica Vaticana.

boundary beyond, enclosing land that is *extra clusa,* so called because "it is shut out beyond the *limites* by a boundary line [*finitima linea*]" (Hyg. Grom., *Cons. limit.* p. 161 Thulin; fig. 4). Significantly, this land beyond was named *arcifinius* because it "protected" (*arceo*) the organized land—or at least that was what the grammarian Varro believed at the time of Caesar, whether rightly or wrongly. The *ager arcifinius* was outside the measured land but often marked by a natural boundary such as a river or a mountain.[9] The Roman mentality, therefore, in this way clearly differentiated between administered and unadministered land. But both were incorporated within the orbit of power and collective ownership of the city-state.

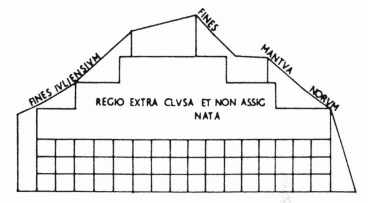

Fig. 4. Centuriation, as described by Hyginus Gromaticus, showing an area *extra clusa*, beyond centuriation. Miniature of Hyginus Gromaticus reproduced from Dilke 1971, 64.

Pomerium

Support for this sort of dualist view of space can be found in the rituals of Rome's boundaries, such as the *suovetaurilia,* or in the ceremony of beating the bounds of town and country, the *amburbium* and *ambarvalia.* The *suovetaurilia,* the sacrifice of three animals dedicated to Mars, began within the civilian boundary of the city (*pomerium*), but the procession (*pompa*) and the actual sacrifice were always in the "military zone" of the Campus Martius or, if the army was on campaign, outside the camp, as we can see depicted on Trajan's Column (fig. 5). The Salii priests, who symbolized military power by their dress, also conducted their ceremonies outside the *pomerium* at points such as the bridges.

The protective character of the formulaic prayer at the *suovetaurilia* is recorded for us by Cato the Elder in the second century B.C.: "Grant that you preserve us and keep us free from all damage and storms" (*Uti . . . calamitates intemperiasque prohibessis defendas; De agr. cult.* 141). The ceremony, however, was not a manifestation of a defensive mentality, since the censor's prayer after the lustration associated with the *suovetaurilia* was "and grant that the Roman people's estate may grow more prosperous and greater" (*ut populi Romani res meliores amplioresque facerent*). Although later, it is true,

21

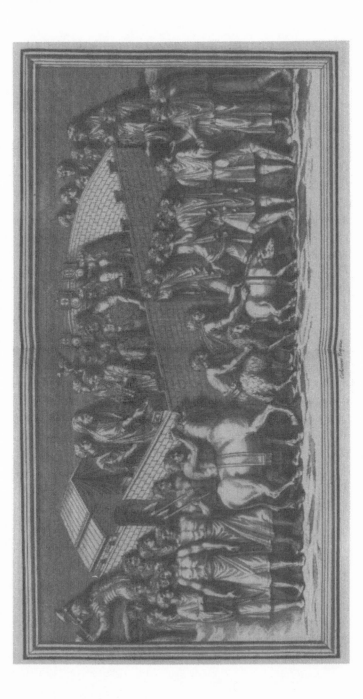

this prayer was modified to say "and keep them safe in perpetuity" (*ut eas perpetuo incolumes servent;* Val. Max. 4.1. 10), we have an example of how the ceremony was applied in practice to the frontiers. In A.D. 35 the Roman general L. Vitellius celebrated the *suovetaurilia* on the banks of the Euphrates as a preliminary to an aggressive attack into Mesopotamia, which could not be regarded as a move to protect the Roman province (Tac. *Ann.* 6.37). Tacitus also says that part of the purification prayers in the *suovetaurilia* were to Jupiter, Juno, Minerva, and "the gods who watch over the empire" (*praesides imperii deos;* Tac. *Hist.* 4.53). The prayer, in other words, was very much associated with the extension and maintenance of Roman power.

There is an interesting illustration of this ceremony on one of the most distant frontiers of the empire, the Antonine Wall at Bridgeness on the Firth of Forth in Scotland. It was perhaps here, says George MacDonald, the great expert on the Antonine Wall, that the frontier wall began to be built, when a distance slab with pictorial relief was set up. One half represents the *suovetaurilia* being celebrated by the legion; the other shows Roman cavalry trampling barbarians. The iconography is, in MacDonald's words, "pregnant with meaning," since it probably shows the ceremony of lustration by the soldiers "*before embarking on a Caledonian campaign*" (my italics). In other words, the ceremony of the boundary was not an admission of the limit (MacDonald 1921, 13 and pl. 1).

The *pomerium* itself is the best known of all Roman definitions of space—a *locus determinatus* (Aul. Gell. 13. 14) whose precise meaning and location in relation to the city walls are much debated. Whatever the original position, whether outside or inside, when Livy wrote everyone must have seen that it extended beyond the

Fig. 5 (opposite). The *suovetaurilia* being celebrated outside the camp, as depicted on Trajan's Column. The emperor himself is inside the camp in "civilian" clothing (*velatus toga*). This drawing was made by M. Fabretti for Dom. Bernard de Montfaucon, who traveled to Italy in the late seventeenth century and collected pictures of Roman monuments, many of which have since deteriorated badly. From *Antiquité explicée et representée en figure* (Paris, 1719), 3:188. Photograph by permission of the Syndics of Cambridge University Library.

moenia or city walls and was marked by fixed *termini* (boundary markers), as Livy described it (1.44).[10] The description of the *pomerium* as a circle (*orbis;* Varro *LL* 5.143), whatever its shape, carried cosmological symbolic significance. It was the separating line between *domi* and *militiae*—that is, between the civil and military sphere—as the story of an inadvertent violation of the line by the presiding consul illustrates; he had left the civilian Senate and forgotten to say the formulaic words as he crossed the *pomerium* to invest himself with military auspices when mustering the centuries in the Campus Martius (Cic. *Nat. deor.* 2.4; Bouché-Leclerq 1882, 225).

The "magic circle" of the sacred *pomerium* was redrawn in every colonial foundation by the *circumdatio* or drawing of the lines around a city and the cutting of the first sod—the *sulcus primigenius*—when the plow was pulled by a bull and a cow. A late writer John Lydus (*De mens.* 4.50) explains the symbolism of the act in relation to the boundaries. The male, he says, was always yoked on the outside of the *sulcus* "toward the countryside" and the female inside "on the side of the city," "so that the men may be feared by outsiders and the women may be fertile within." Birth was naturally a domestic event associated with peace, while death was kept outside. The famous republican inscriptions of the Esquiline record the decree of the urban praetor, "that no one should throw a corpse within the boundary stones" (*coerc(uit) nei quis intra terminos . . . cadaver iniecisse velit; CIL* 6.31614–15).

The *termini* of the *pomerium*, therefore, were in a sense the limits of the organized power of the city, beyond which the fighting men were stationed. In the passage from Plutarch's *Life of Numa* quoted at the beginning of this chapter, the second king brought civil law, whereas Romulus represented the military force of Rome. There we see the two faces of the state in its civil and military aspects.

The *pomerium* was also explicitly linked by Romans to *imperium,* since the right to move forward the civil boundary (*ius proferendi pomerii*) and the right to extend the boundary stones (*propagare terminos urbis*) were permitted only to those who extended the *imperium* itself (Tac. *Ann.* 12.23; Sen., *Brev. vit.* 13.8) and increased the *fines* of the Roman people (*CIL* 6.1231). *Termini* and *fines*, therefore, referred to the limits of internal order, not of military power. *Propagatio terminorum* did not contradict the idea of fixed boundaries. It was a religious formula for the proper advance of the boundaries, establishing a "dynamic stability" in order of the state (Piccaluga 1974, 111, 119).

Another interesting symbolic link with the *pomerium* and the empire has been seen in the Roman concept of *portoria*, a word we are accustomed to think of as "customs dues," which were collected on the frontiers. In reality it had its origin in a strip of land between the ditch (*fossa*) and the berm (*vallum*) of a Roman fortification (*circumductio*)—that is, the *intervallum*, which one paid to cross. Just as the city levied its dues, on the frontiers of empire the provincial border did likewise. But—and this is the important point—the *fines* or boundaries of civil order never corresponded to the point where *portoria* were levied. There was an area between Roman territory stricto sensu and the enemy, which the Romans controlled.[11]

We have seen already how the language of sacral and social space in the city was closely associated with the symbolism of the frontier. This, I believe, is a clue to understanding the posthumous advice given by Augustus in his will to his successor, Tiberius: "He had added the advice that the empire should be kept within its boundary stones" (*addideratque consilium coercendi intra terminos imperii*; Tac. *Ann.* 1.11). The language is strangely evocative of the words used in the urban praetor's decree, just quoted—*coercuit . . . intra terminos*—which aimed to preserve the city unpolluted. Augustus's advice, recorded by Tacitus over a hundred years later, is often cited as the first articulation of Roman defensive frontier policy. But if the linguistic resonance means anything, it could be that Augustus was not talking about limiting Roman power to any military frontier but was making a statement about the domestic space of the organized provinces. He is saying, "Keep the *civil*, provincial boundaries where they are." We know how in the law of *postliminium*, respecting the rights of those who returned from beyond the frontiers as war captives, the term *intra fines* referred to the juridical boundary of civil law.[12]

25

Augustus's testament needs to be read together with a well-known passage from Strabo concerning the division of the provinces by Augustus. Strabo was writing soon after Augustus's death and therefore, presumably, after the *consilium* was published as common knowledge. Augustus, he says, "allocated to himself the part of the territory in need of military guard, that is, the barbarian part, adjoining the tribes who have not yet been subdued" (17.3.25). Although the context is that of the division of the provinces, the Greek word *mepo* ("not yet") is pregnant with meaning. True, Strabo is writing in the context of a period before Augustus's death. But there is no suggestion in anything he says that Augustus ever renounced control or conquest of barbarians beyond the *termini*. The reference to the "barbarian part" links us metaphorically with the bull on the outside of the city's sacred boundary. Strabo notoriously never mentions "frontier" in all his descriptions of the Roman Empire.

Frontiers and Space In Early Roman History

I began this chapter by saying that it is impossible to find any evidence of a Roman frontier policy in the period of the Republic, despite the strong Roman sense of organized social and political space. The nearest Roman sources come to a sense of military frontier is the early view, said to derive from Cato the Elder, that the Alps were "like a wall"—*muri vice*—to protect Italy (Serv. *Ad Aen.* 10.13), which rapidly became a literary topos that was repeated again and again (e.g., Polyb. 3.54.2; Cic. *Prov. cons.* 14.34, Livy 21.35.9, Hdn. 2.11.8, etc.). If so, this was long before any formal organization of Gallia Cisalpina or cadastration of territory north of the Po had taken place. So it was not the territorial boundary of organized space that Cato meant. The concept fits more neatly into the model, discussed by the *agrimensores*, of *mons finitimus* and *ager arcifinius* beyond the organized territory of the *civitas*.[13]

Mountains, like rivers, have never served as military frontiers in history, but as Lucien Febvre noted, "they are promoted to the dignity of a natural frontier" by victorious nations in the process of expansion (1922, 325 ff.; discussed on p. 7–8). Far away in the *ager Romanus* on a clear day the towering Alps must have appeared as a splendid, impressive barrier, even though Hannibal had successfully crossed them with an army. But Livy confirms Febvre's opinion that they really served as a political claim by Rome to exercise power in a territory it did not yet occupy.

The historian Livy gives an excellent example of what that meant in terms of organized space. In 183 B.C. members of a Gallic tribe who had crossed the Alps to settle complained that, although they had surrendered themselves to Roman authority, they had been ordered to leave. The Senate defended the decision, "since they did not have the permission of the Roman magistrate *in charge of that province.*" They were told, therefore, to warn all other Transalpine Gauls that the Alps were "in effect a boundary that could not be crossed" (*prope inexsuperabilem finem;* Livy 39.54.10 ff.) Yet no formal, organized Roman *provincia* existed in northern Italy; there was only a *provincia* of power.

No military frontier or "proto-limes system"[14] was developed by the Romans in the republican provinces, nor was there any sense of spatial limit apart from the civil boundaries detailed in the *forma provinciae,* such as the old Numidian earthworks, the "King's Ditch" (*fossa regia*), in Africa. All that can be traced is a development in the Roman claims of where the immediate natural boundaries of the *ager arcifinius* lay. As earlier with the Alps, so later Caesar made a symbolic claim of power beyond the territorial boundaries of Provincia in southern Gaul as far as the Rhine, which he claimed no German was permitted to cross, even though Rome did not at that moment occupy the land between the province and the river (*BG* 1.43–44). Later, after Caesar's first campaigns, Cicero says that, as once the Alps, so now Oceanus was the limit of Roman *imperium* (Cic. *Prov. cons.* 14.34). The claim was to power, not to territory. When Pompey was asked by the Parthians to recognize the Euphrates as a "boundary of Roman rule" (*horos tōn hegemoniōn;* Plut. *Pomp.* 33.6), he gave a deliberately evasive reply, which Theodore Mommsen long ago rightly interpreted as a declaration that Rome accepted no militant state as its frontier (1976, 5.9.358).

We can, of course, view all this—as some historians have done—as simply part of the rhetoric of Roman imperialism, which it was. But Pompey's and Caesar's claims were consistent with the theory declared by Cicero and Polybius that "the *orbis terrarum* is already contained within our *imperium*" (Cic. *De Rep.* 3.15.24). As we saw earlier, the apparent contradiction between such a cosmological claim and the imperialist boast that both Caesar and Pompey had added to the *termini imperii* (e.g., Cic. *Prov. Cons.* 12.31, 13.33) lay in the ambiguity of words like *provincia* and *imperium* as both organized territory and spatial power. The *externae gentes* were always subject but were only sometimes incorporated within the *fines*, when Rome was forced to do it. This was what Romans traditionally regarded as acting in "good faith" (*fides*) and conducting campaigns according to the ideological rules of *bellum iustum*—a "justified war."

We have come back again to ideology, so let me return to the legend of Romulus and Numa and the gods Iuventas and Terminus with which this chapter began. In the story it is important to recognize that there was no real paradox in uniting the polarities of unlimited expansion and limiting borders. The *terminatio* of *ager Romanus* carried out by Numa concerned the cadastration of the land and the organization of private and public property. It was clearly not a myth that incorporated the notion of restricting Roman expansion, according to the context of the sources. Otherwise the whole of the rest of Roman history would have been a violation of Numa's limits. Rather, it was to give to Roman *propagatio* certain rules of procedure, which the Romans associated with *fides*. Numa's organization of the Capitoline cults associated with Jupiter, according to Plutarch's legend, significantly also included an altar of Fides. In so doing Numa gave to *propagatio terminorum* what has been called a "moral resonance" (Piccaluga 1974, 183–85, 198–99, citing the phrase used by Dumézil).

Dionysius of Halicarnassus, who wrote a history, *The Antiquities of Rome*, recounts another tradition about a later reorganization of the Capitoline cults and tells how Temon and Notes (the Greek forms of Terminus and Iuventas), not wishing to be displaced from their home on the Capitol by Jupiter, gave unfavorable auguries until left alone (*Rom. Ant.*3.69.5–6). So, says Dionysius, "From this event the augurs arrived at the conclusion that never on any occasion would the extent of the Roman state be disturbed and that Rome's prosperity would not be overturned." This cult of Jupiter-Terminus, therefore, which was specifically linked to the "prosperity" of the Roman state, signified Roman concern not only for the maintenance of internal order but for the continuation of expansion. The poet Ovid, a contemporary of Augustus, makes this point when he tells us that the cult of Terminus was located on the Capitol specifically to expand and "to look nowhere else but to the stars." And then he adds, "To other people land may be given with a fixed limit. / But for the city of Rome its space is the same as that of the world." (*Gentibus est aliis tellus data limite certo / Romanae spatium est Urbis et orbis; Fasti* 2.667–84.) Ovid's description fits alongside the famous passage in Virgil's *Aeneid,* when it is Jupiter who assures Rome that it will have *imperium sine fine*—an empire with no limits (Dumézil 1966, 205; Piccaluga 1974, 198–200).

Augustus's posthumous policy of *coercendi intra terminos imperii* therefore was not, by demanding restraint, enunciating a new frontier principle. When Roman generals reached the Elbe, Augustus also restrained them from crossing, since beyond this tribes were living in peace and, he said, he had no wish to incite them (Strabo 7.1.4). He was certainly not indicating that Romans should never cross. It was a tactical, not a strategic decision. When reporting Augustus's posthumous *consilium*, Cassius Dio, who wrote a century after Tacitus, makes Augustus explain how the restraints he was advocating fit in with what he claimed was the policy he himself had exercised in his lifetime; that is "to be satisfied with present possessions and in no way to *seek* to increase the empire . . . He himself," he adds, "had always followed this principle in word and action, since, although it had been possible for him to take much barbarian land, he had not *sought to*" (Dio 56.33).

The repetition of "in no way to seek to" and "he had not sought to" shows the principle Augustus was articulating. He was not advising his successor never to move the *termini imperii*, since obviously he himself had done just that. But he was telling him that he should not seek aggression for aggression's sake. That was the absolutely traditional Roman republican policy of the *bellum iustum* for which Augustus was subsequently praised by his biographer, Suetonius. "He never made war on any nation without just and necessary cause and was so far from the desire of increasing the empire or his own warlike reputation in any way, that he forced barbarian leaders to swear . . . they would keep their word and the peace" (*Aug.* 21.2).[15]

In this as in so much else, Augustus, the first emperor, for all his innovation, was a traditionalist at heart.

Two

Frontiers and the
Growth of Empire

Before we look at Roman frontiers in a more theoretical way, it is important to remember that, in practice, countries that are expanding have little interest in the limits to their power. The aim of this chapter is to trace very broadly the story of how the Roman Empire grew and to see to what extent consciousness of frontiers impinged on that experience when the main phase of conquest slowed down or came to a halt in some parts of the world.

Maps and Imperialism

In Rome as in Greece, maps were a rarity. Yet where they are mentioned they were almost always associated with conquest. On the eve of the great Sicilian expedition in the fifth century we are told the Athenians were so dazzled by the glittering prospects that all over the city young and old alike began drawing maps of the countries they hoped to conquer (Plut. *Nic.* 12). The first map we know about in Rome, which was probably a kind of picture map of Sardinia—what Livy called a *simulacra picta* (41.28.10)—was to commemorate the victories of Tiberius Gracchus the Elder over the Carthaginians, and it was put up in a temple in Rome in 174 B.C.

The notion of taking the Roman *imperium* to "the ends of the earth" (*ultimos terrarum fines*) had gained currency in the second century B.C. as Rome's empire grew; but it reached its climax in the age of the dynasts of the first century. Pompey, we are told, "wanted to reach with his victories Oceanus which flows round the world" (Plut. *Pomp.* 38.2), and he set up an inscription recording his "deeds" with a full list of the *gentes* he had subdued, saying, "He has taken the boundaries of the empire to the limits of the earth" (Diodorus 40.4). No doubt this was the model for the later *Res Gestae* of Augustus. Pompey's propaganda was accompanied by trophies and statues bearing representations of the *oikoumene*, the globe of the whole world (Dio 37.21.2).[1]

Soon after this Julius Caesar commissioned the first known world map, probably as part of his great triumphal monument on the Capitol, portraying himself in a chariot with the globe of the world at his feet (Dio 43.14.6, 43.21.2). Latent in this imagery is the ideology that there were no limits to his conquests; and indeed, Ovid says Caesar was planning to "add the last part of the orbis" by a campaign against the Parthians when he died in 44 B.C. (*Ars am.* 1.177).[2]

To the idea of *ultimos fines* of the periphery, which are contained in these accounts, we must add the geographic notion of an imperial center. The historian and antiquarian Varro, who lived at the same time as Caesar and Pompey, describes in his treatise on agriculture (*RR* 1.2.1) how he met some friends at the temple of Tellus, where they were examining a map of Italy painted on the wall. That led to a discussion of the natural advantages Italy had over all other nations of the world because of its geographic position. It was only a short jump in imagination to start thinking that the geographic position of Italy was divinely ordained to ensure that Rome, which was in the center of Italy, could control the world. As the architect Vitruvius wrote at the time of Augustus, "The Roman people have the perfect territory [*veros fines*] in the middle of the heavens [*mundus*], with the whole world and its countries on each side." Therefore, Vitruvius concluded, "The divine spirit has allotted to the Roman state an excellent and temperate region *so that they may rule the whole world*" (De arch. 6.1.10–11).

Frontiers and Imperialism

With the emperor Augustus Roman concepts of space and geographic measurement took a momentous leap forward. It is not surprising that as a single, autocratic emperor took control of the administration we should wish to ask about a frontier "policy" as such. Strabo, who wrote the finest work we possess on the political geography of the Roman Empire, inspired by Augustus's organization of the empire, says, "It would be difficult to govern in any other way than by entrusting it to one person" (6.4.2). But there is a sense in which the Augustan empire marked a change in intellectual outlook too, much as was later to take place with the rise of the absolutist state. In both cases administrative efforts were made to coordinate scattered citizens, accompanied—as in Colbert's France of the seventeenth century—by an intense interest in geography and cartography with the aim of fiscal efficiency.[3] The center and the periphery were being drawn together.

As we saw in chapter 1, Augustus's personal interest in the organization of space was explicit. His attention to cadastration is referred to in the work of the *agrimensores*, who talk of "distances given by *limites* according to the law and decision of Augustus" (Hyg. Grom. *Cons. limit.*, p. 157 Thulin). The emperor himself is said to have been "the first to display the world by chorography" (*Div. orbis* 1), and at his death he left a *breviarium totius imperii*—a detailed account of the empire's resources (Tac. *Ann.* 1.11).

But Augustus was a child of the republican *conquistadores*. Never at any stage of his life is it easy to prove that he lost the dream of world conquest or that he recognized permanent limits to growth. In the list of his achievements, the *Res Gestae*, which he left to be inscribed on his mausoleum and in various centers of the empire, his proudest boast was *omnium provinciarum . . . fines auxi*—"I have extended the boundaries of all the provinces" (*RG* 26). The boast was echoed by poets, artists, and architects.[4] On the celebrated Vienna cameo, the Gemma Augustea, the emperor is flanked by figures personifying Tellus (Earth) and Oceanus, while

Fig. 6. The Gemma Augustea, made about 10 B.C. The cameo, now in Vienna, shows Augustus enthroned like Jupiter, next to the goddess Roma, holding the military staff of command and looking at Tiberius in his victory chariot. Below are Roman soldiers with barbarian captives. Behind Augustus are personifications of Oceanus and of Oikoumene, who is crowning Augustus. Photograph by permission of the Kunsthistorisches Museum, Vienna, inv. no. ix.A.79.

being crowned by a figure who is thought to represent Oikoumene. Above him are a globe and his personal astrological sign, Capricorn (fig. 6).[5]

It was Augustus, too, who was responsible for the display of Agrippa's map in 7 B.C., the first world map we know very much about, although it was obviously in the tradition of Caesar's earlier map. Since it was set up in the Porticus Vipsania alongside other great public buildings of Augustus and Agrippa in the Campus Martius, it was very much a public monument to Augustus's own conquest of space or, as Pliny the Elder put it, "The world for the city to see" (*orbis terrarum urbi spectandus; NH* 3. 17) (Dilke 1985, 41 ff.). Besides a detailed "chorographic" commentary which Pliny the Elder was able to consult, and which may be the same work that was later said to have been written by the emperor, the map itself would have depicted only the major landmarks, like the great rivers and mountains. This is perhaps why later authors, such as Josephus, Tacitus, and Herodian, so often described the Roman Empire with frontiers "hedged about by the sea of Oceanus and remote rivers" (Hdn. 2.11.5; cf. Tac. *Ann.* 1.9; Jos. *BJ* 2.371 ff.). But there is no reason to think Augustus or Agrippa thought in terms of such "natural" limits.

At Augustus's death he left three documents along with his will; two of them, the *Res Gestae* and the *breviarium totius imperii*, have just been mentioned. The third was a book of instructions, a kind of codicil to the *breviarium*. Contained in this, probably, was what Tacitus says was the famous *consilium* I discussed in chapter 1. Tiberius, we are told, took it as a command, "that the empire should be confined within limits."[6] The exact context and significance of this codicil are matters for debate, but it is generally agreed that it was written by Augustus at the end of his life as he contemplated the result of the rebellion of the Pannonian auxiliaries in A.D. 6 and the appalling military losses by Varus in the Teutoberg Forest of free Germany in A.D. 9. It constitutes the first evidence of an imperial frontier policy—if that is what it was.

But was it really a "policy"? At the most it was surely temporary advice to Tiberius that the provinces of the empire were not yet sufficiently Romanized to allow further expansion. Roman historiography contained a deeply pessimistic consciousness of the fragility of imperial rule if allowed to outgrow its own resources, and this may well have been reflected in Augustus's practical counsel to consolidate. It would have been truly astonishing if Augustus had really intended all his successors to forgo the Roman virtue of winning military glory. Strabo, who wrote during Tiberius's reign, gave no hint of any ideological restraint in what he wrote. Tacitus in the next century made no comment on the fact that

Gaius and Claudius apparently ignored the advice when planning the invasion of Britain. On the contrary, Tacitus lamented the long delay in conquering Germany.[7]

In fact, the ideology of *imperium sine fine*, an empire without limit, remained central to the Roman stereotype of a good emperor, proclaimed on coins or inscriptions and inserted in panegyrics. Pliny the Younger in A.D. 100, for instance, imagined Trajan on the banks of the Danube dealing with some insolent barbarian king, whom "nothing will protect from our very territory taking him over" (*Pan.* 16)—as indeed happened a few years later when Dacia was annexed. Cassius Dio's analysis of Trajan's motives for the conquest of Mesopotamia boiled down to "his desire for glory" (Dio [Xiph.] 68.17.1). Dio attributed the same motive to Septimius Severus a hundred years later (Dio [Xiph.] 75.1.1).

Trajan was not a pathological megalomaniac; in Roman upper-class mythology he was the most popular emperor after Augustus, with whom he was often associated. It was true praise thereafter to applaud an emperor as "braver than Augustus and better than Trajan" (*fortior Augusto melior Traiano*). Hadrian obviously realized this and anticipated, but was unable to prevent, the unpopularity of his withdrawal from Mesopotamia by claiming a republican precedent. Antoninus Pius, the most unwarlike of Roman emperors, also appreciated the force of the ideology and gave great publicity to the fairly ordinary military achievement of his reign when the frontier in Britain was advanced. Marcus Aurelius, we are told, was contemplating annexation of two new provinces north of the Danube when he died. His son Commodus was proposing to carry on the policy of going on "as far as Oceanus" until he discarded his father's senatorial advisers. With Septimius Severus the slogan *propagatio imperii* rose to new heights.[8]

So if there was a discordant note, it appears to have been confined to Greek authors, whose tradition reflected more strongly than that of Roman nobles the sense of moral "otherness" and the barrier between urban order and the disorder beyond the city walls. Appian and Aelius Aristides, both Greeks writing in the reign of Antoninus Pius—the first an imperial official and the second a professional orator—are often cited as examples of a new mentality of defensive imperialism and frontier fortifications that came to the fore in the mid-second century. This is what they said:

> Beyond the outermost ring of the civilized world you drew a second line, quite as one does in walling a town. . . . An encamped army, like a rampart, encloses the civilized world in a ring. (Ael. Arist. *Ad Rom.* 81–82)

> The Romans have aimed to preserve their empire by the exercise of prudence rather than to extend their sway indefinitely over poverty-stricken and profitless tribes of barbarians. (App., *pr.* 7)

But there are good reasons to reject these as typical views of the Roman Empire. Both may have been expedient ways by which those dependent on imperial favor interpreted the quiescent roles of Hadrian and his adopted heir, Pius. Even Aelius Aristides, however, went on to praise Rome because "you recognize no fixed boundaries, nor does another dictate to what point your control reaches" (*Ad Rom.* 10). That does not support the theory some have suggested, that Hadrian—who, it is true, was disliked by the Roman elites for his love of Hellenism—had adopted the Greek ideal of the cosmopolis. Although there was a kind of "moral" ideological barrier between Rome and barbarians, in practice Romans were far less rigid and had always accepted their civilizing mission.[9] Roman authors who lived under Hadrian still spoke in the Roman tradition. Tacitus, although rarely explicit, was undoubtedly sympathetic to imperial expansion. Suetonius, his contemporary, was circumspect in praising Augustus for not seeking imperial glory at any cost, but he admired the wars of Germanicus that Tiberius had halted. Florus openly regretted the folly of Varus that had halted Roman expansion into Germany, while recognizing that there were *gentes* who could be left beyond direct rule provided they respected the majesty of Rome.[10]

It remains to be seen how far the ideology of Roman frontiers corresponded to the reality. The account is arranged in chronological order, beginning with Augustus, but is divided between West and East. The object is to discover whether there were any fundamental strategic differences either between emperors or between regions of the empire.

The Western Frontiers

The places mentioned in the text can be found on the maps in figure 7 (Rhine), figure 8 (Danube), figure 9 (Africa), and figure 10 (Britain).

Not surprisingly, after the civil wars Augustus found himself immediately faced with a series of urgent military problems that had to be solved without reference to deep-seated policy studies. Spain, where he was involved in fighting until 19 B.C. as a result of the factions of the civil war, led on naturally to Gaul, where Caesar's conquests had not halted the progress of Germans crossing the Rhine. Not content with crossing the Rhine, Augustus's commanders had by 9 or 8 B.C. reduced the region between the Rhine and Elbe to "practically a tributary province," says Velleius Paterculus (2.97), who was a serving officer under Tiberius. What our sources do not ever say is what modern writers have tried to infer, that Augustus was looking for a strategic riverine frontier or a shorter line of communication. Indeed, the Elbe had been crossed in 9 B.C., and in about 2 B.C. the Roman army had set up an altar on the north bank.[11]

The significance of this religious act, as illustrated later in A.D. 16 by Germanicus's consecration of a trophy between the Rhine and the Elbe, was to bring the territory within the spatial *cosmos* of Roman discipline.[12] In fact, it seems plausible that Augustus genuinely intended to reach Oceanus. He boasts of sailing in Oceanus as far as the Cimbri of Jutland, and in about A.D. 4 the fleet made an attempt to sail around from Jutland to find the passage to Scythia, to the Caspian Sea, and to India but was deterred by bad weather. If Strabo is correct that the emperor forbade crossing the Elbe in order not to antagonize the tribes beyond, it was only for reasons of temporary prudence.[13]

In Dalmatia and the Balkans much the same situation existed as in Gaul and Germany. Even before the defeat of Antony the territory of what was vaguely called Illyricum had required military

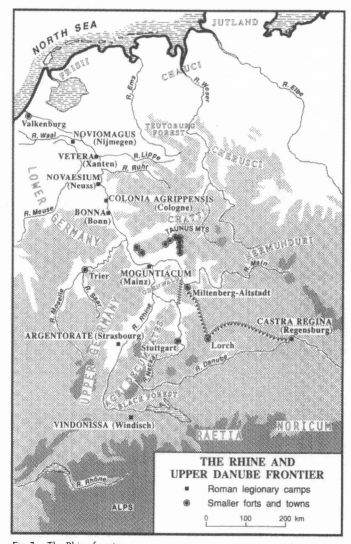

Fig. 7. The Rhine frontier

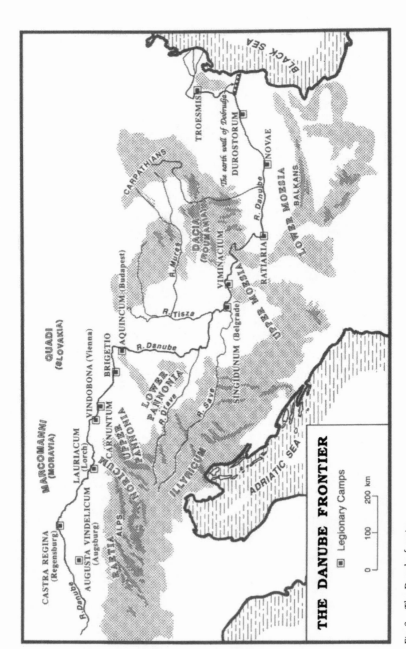

Fig. 8.   The Danube frontier

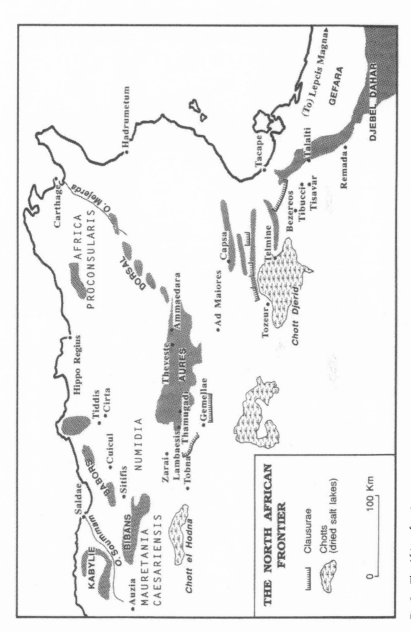

Fig. 9. The African frontier

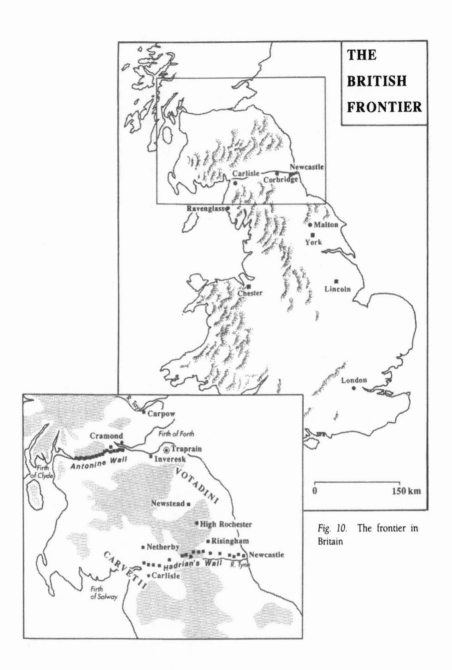

Fig. 10. The frontier in Britain

action, and a peace had been patched up with a diplomatic return of captured Roman standards. The urgency lay in the threat to the heart of Italy through the key passes of Raetia and Noricum (roughly Switzerland and Austria), which was rapidly resolved in 15 B.C. by the coordinated movement of two armies from the Rhine and northern Italy. The upper Rhine and the upper Danube were now connected. By 9 B.C. the middle Danube had been reached in tandem with the trans-Rhine campaigns launched from Gaul. Italy was henceforward firmly linked to the Balkans.[14]

In both these cases it is easy to see the value of the single commander-in-chief, Augustus, and the possibilities of a strategic policy. That in turn has led modern scholars to wonder whether further pincer movements between 7 B.C. and A.D. 6 were ultimately aimed at providing a shorter line of communication between Germany and the Balkans, specifically along the river Elbe and its tributaries. Plausible as the strategy may appear, it is unfortunate that almost all our sources are defective for the period. Reconstructions based on inscriptions to some extent clarify the movements, which certainly included penetration into southern Slovakia. It may well be, too, that the campaign to the north bank of the Elbe had begun from the Danube. But nothing is said about a frontier.

If ancient sources do not attribute this activity to the search for a frontier, we may well ask, what was the objective? Augustus himself said that he believed all lands from Illyricum "to the banks of the Danube" were part of the Roman Empire (*RG* 30), which sounds as if he really did think the Danube was a frontier. But he did not confine his activities to the west bank of the river. "My armies," he says, "crossed the Danube and compelled the Dacian *gentes* to submit to the Roman people". The campaign was designed, much like that against the Germans beyond the Rhine, to keep back the penetration of new peoples pushing southward and took the route along the river Mureş, crossing the Danube somewhere south of Budapest into the Carpathians.[15] But there is no question that Augustus believed he had the right to rule them. The Danube was clearly not the limit of Roman power but is a good illustration of the dividing line between internal and external control.

Nothing illustrates better the difference in Roman thinking between the limits of organized space and their claims to imperial control beyond these limits than the progress of the army in Africa. By A.D. 14 the main legion of the province had advanced its base camp as far as Ammaedara (modern Haidra) on the high Tunisian upland plain. A boundary road was constructed linking Tacape (modern Gabes) and the camp, followed soon after by a massive work of centuriation of the land in the southeast.[16] In a sense, therefore, we are right to regard this as a frontier line. But the Romans did not. The extraordinary southern expedition of Cornelius Balbus in 19 B.C. took Romans deep into the interior as far as the Fezzan. Despite the absence of any known posts or direct administration, Pliny the Elder—and no doubt Agrippa's map—signified this action as evidence that "we have subjugated the *gens* of the Fezzani" (*NH* 5.35).[17]

After Augustus it is often argued that, apart from Roman Britain, there was no substantial territorial addition to the Roman Empire in the West until Trajan's annexation of Dacia in the early second century. The rest is put down to retrenchment, adjustment, and administrative organization (for example, Nicolet 1983). This view gains its validity by stressing the point Suetonius made in his biography of Augustus, that allied native kings were from the start regarded as *membra partisque imperii* (*Aug.* 48)—an integral part of the metaphorical body of the Roman Empire. So when Claudius changed the government of Raetia and Noricum, Mauretania and Thrace from that of native alliance to provincial rule, he merely reclaimed what had originally been "the gift of the Roman people" and was not making any great new advance.[18]

On the other hand, it was on the appeals from native British kings, who had also shown their submission to Augustus, that Claudius invaded Britain. In a sense they too were allied kings and therefore parts of the empire. But it is surely stretching the imagination to see the invasion as merely an administrative adjustment, when Claudius was so obviously an emperor who desperately needed military glory, as the twenty-seven military salutations in his reign prove.[19] Nor was Britain, once invaded, left again to its kings, and although Suetonius claims that Nero considered abandoning Britain (*Nero* 18), since it was beyond *terra cognita*, there was also no sign in his reign of any search for a frontier.

It does not appear that Claudius felt any restraint in crossing the Rhine and Danube either, although the legionary camps now began to acquire stone buildings and an air of permanence along the river line. More and more archaeological evidence shows a Claudian and Neronian presence in the Taunus-Wetterau salient and in the Black Forest–Neckar region of Germany (Schönberger 1969; cf. Tac. *Ann.* 12.28, 13.56). Much propaganda was made about the return of the standards and some of the prisoners captured by the German Chatti from Varus in A.D. 9, which carried the same symbolic significance of submission as the return of the Parthian standards in Augustus's day. One reason for thinking that first-century emperors were involved in more than mere consolidation of Augustan *termini* is that, as some allied territories were annexed as provinces, further allied kings were brought into play as the "limbs" of empire: the Cherusci in northern Holland, the Vannian kings of the Suebi on the middle Danube, and the Quadi and Marcomanni in Bohemia and Slovakia. A famous inscription records how a Roman governor of Moesia under Nero fought the Sarmatians beyond the Danube and transported thousands of people, with their princes and kings, across the Danube into the province.[20] "The might and power of the kings," says Tacitus, "depends on the authority of Rome" (*Germ.* 42).

The Flavian emperors more or less carried on from where the Julio-Claudians had left off, despite the destabilizing effect of the civil wars that had set alight the Germans of the lower Rhine. It is not easy to detect any real change in policy or the establishment of a "scientific frontier" by radical new measures, as has been claimed.[21] In Britain Tacitus is explicit that in A.D. 81 Agricola ignored what might have been considered a scientific frontier at the Forth-Clyde, which was, after all, the shortest distance between two seas. It was not adopted, significantly, because the Roman commanders were driven on "by the courage of our armies and the glory of Rome" (*Agr.* 23). When a halt was finally called, it was not for reasons of local strategy but because the military manpower was needed in Germany.

In Germany the Taunus salient and the *Agri Decumates* territory around the headwaters of the Neckar, Rhine, and Danube now acquired permanent Roman posts, and there appeared along the Taunus Mountain heights a chain of fortlets and palisades, the first example of a visible, linear frontier. But we must beware of reading too much into the development. Frontinus, who took part in Domitian's German wars, regarded this line and the forest clearance that went with it as a tactical device to avoid surprise raids (*Strat.* 1.3.10). The fortifications were probably not continuous and are now considered protection for roads leading into the Wetterau as much as a lateral defense. It is in the context of this new Flavian organization that Tacitus says, "After the *limes* was made and the guard posts were moved forward, they [the *Agri Decumates*] were considered to be a projection of the empire and a part of the province" (*Germ.* 29). The word *limes* here obviously meant not a border for frontier defense but a road, perhaps with its original sense of a road as an administrative limit.[22]

In the Balkans and Africa it is even less easy to detect any sign of natural and scientific frontiers under the Flavians, despite the claim that this period marked a new strategic concept and the beginnings of a closed linear fortification system. What it amounted to, in fact, was the concentration of legionary and auxiliary forces along the Danube, which was the main route of supply and hardly constituted an effective barrier (Mócsy 1974b, 41 ff.; Gabler 1980, 637–40). Domitian's long Dacian wars between A.D. 85 and 92 show how the military balance of the empire was changing and requiring more and more troops. But there is no evidence that the Danube was now being consolidated as the limit of advance. It appears that the Dacians were expected to confine themselves to the river Tisza, over a hundred kilometers east of the Danube in the Hungarian plain, and that the Romans claimed to control the native princes in that region. Before Dacia was annexed under Trajan, we have a papyrus we call "Hunt's Pridianum," which is an annual review of the strength of an auxiliary unit on the lower Danube, and which records garrisons and the collection of military supplies far across the river.[23]

In Africa the military outposts moved farther west, along the lines of the Aures range in Numidia and Mauretania Caesariensis, while in the eastern Tripolitanian sector there were a number of recorded military and commercial expeditions. Like Balbus's expedition earlier, they provide evidence of Roman penetration into the Fezzan and the Libyan valleys, which has left its mark by imported archaeological artifacts.[24]

It is, of course, with the emperors Hadrian and Antoninus Pius that most people think of the Romans as arriving at a new policy of visible, defensive, and static frontiers in the West. It is true that between Trajan in the early second century A.D. and Marcus Aurelius at the end there were no western wars of conquest on the scale of those in the East—that is, if we count the Dacian wars and the lower Danube, as Romans did later, as part of the eastern front. It therefore looks as if Roman expansionist policy, in the West at any rate, had come to a halt.

On the other hand, the arrest had not begun with Hadrian. Domitian had begun the chain of forts in Germany. And Trajan, who was so obviously uninhibited by any defensive notions of the *termini imperii* in the East, is now believed to have laid the wooden palisades along the line of the Solway Firth and to have stabilized the road of the Stanegate between Carlisle and Newcastle in northern Britain before the building of the wall under Hadrian (G.D.B. Jones 1982; Higham 1986, 159). Quite probably it was Trajan, too, who completed the row of auxiliary forts on the line of the *limes* in Upper Germany, the so-called *Odenwaldlimes*, linking the Main with the Neckar (Schallmayer 1984, 19).

The great works of the visible frontiers in the West are Hadrian's Wall in Britain between the Tyne and the Solway; the so-called *fossatum* in Africa, running intermittently along the predesert between the Libyan valleys and the Hodna basin of Algeria; the Antonine Wall in Britain between the firths of Clyde and Forth; and what we often call the "outer *limes*" of Upper Germany, which runs between Miltenberg-Altstadt on the river Main and Lorch (just east of Stuttgart) before turning due east to the Danube at Regensburg. But how are we to understand the purpose of these massive constructions? And why, after the enormous efforts of constructing the first lines of forts and walls in Britain and in

Germany should they have been almost immediately abandoned or—as we are increasingly coming to believe—supplemented by a second line?

In Africa the walls, forts, and ditch of the *fossatum* in southern Algeria and Tunisia are—in origin at least—rightly attributed to Hadrian. But they are intermittent and quite unlike the continuous wall in Britain. In Tunisia the *clausurae* walls are also associated with a series of tribal allotments, marked by boundary stones, which were made by order of the emperor Trajan and which lay to the *south* of the wall system. In other words, here is a vivid and visible example of the care one must take not to think that walls were the outer *fines* of Roman territory (*CIL* 8.22782–88; Trousset 1978).

Whatever we may think about the debut of a new policy or strategy or defensive frontiers in the mid-second century A.D., it is obvious that on the middle Danube the Romans felt no restraint about crossing the river line. In southern Slovakia and Moravia a remarkable number of Roman-style buildings and legionary building tiles have been found on sites in the northern valleys of the Danube's tributaries (fig. 32).[25] Across the Hungarian plain Trajan's annexation of Dacia led to the construction of a west-east road from the Danube to the mouth of the river Mureş, where a Roman *vehiculatio* or posting station is recorded on an inscription. Marcus Aurelius's proposal, after defeating the Marcomanni and Quadi, to annex two great new provinces north of the Danube would have carried Roman administered territory as far as Bohemia and must surely indicate that there was no agreed new defensive frontier policy. Although he did not carry out the project, there is no reason to think Romans gave up believing their sovereignty extended that far. In the fourth century the emperor Valentinian died of apoplexy when the kings of the Quadi behaved as though they were independent.[26]

Likewise in Britain. After the curious advances and withdrawals between the occupation of Hadrian's Wall and the Antonine Wall, which are becoming clearer as more epigraphic evidence is unearthed, the Scottish line was finally abandoned in the reign of Marcus Aurelius. But then in 208 Septimius Severus launched a new campaign in the footsteps of Agricola and worked his way right up the east coast of Scotland, only to return to the line of Hadrian's Wall. Severus's aim was explicitly to win glory and victories in Britain, according to his contemporary Herodian, and he probably first thought of extending the provincial boundary. As we know from a fragmentary inscription, the large camp at Carpow on the Tay and the fort at Cramond on the Forth remained in commission well into the rule of Caracalla. Although the visible line of Hadrian's Wall therefore was consciously and expensively refurbished, Severus intended that the Roman writ should run in Scotland.[27]

The Eastern Frontiers

The names mentioned in the text can be found on the maps in figure 11 (Syria and Mesopotamia), figure 12 (Armenia and the northern Euphrates), and figure 13 (Palestine and Arabia).

The theory of a single grand strategy of the Roman Empire is a priori implausible, since geographic and political conditions were so different between various parts of the empire, particularly the eastern and western halves. Much of the western borderlands consisted of unformed states, loosely organized *gentes* and federations that were poor and little urbanized. In the East Greek culture and trade had penetrated most of the states Rome came into contact with, quite apart from the fact that over long periods the Persian, Greek, and Macedonian empires had imposed forms of centralized controls and urban organization.

In the West the driving force of Roman imperialism was primarily the glory of conquest, although tinged with some expectation of profit. In the East it was almost the reverse. The motive for an expedition under Augustus to Arabia Felix was "the report that they were very wealthy" (Strabo 16.4.22). The myths of El Dorado were fueled by the more immediate and sometimes tangible reality of the luxury trade and by tales from enterprising travelers, from the Caucasus Mountains, where it was said the rivers ran with gold, to the shores of the Yemen with their caravans from the East.[28]

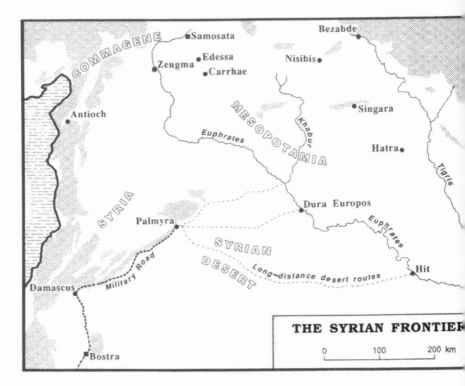

Fig. 11. The desert frontier of Syria and Mesopotamia

But above all other differences was the existence of the Parthian empire, which was taken over after the third century A.D. by the revived Persian empire. The Parthians had their own ambitions—or so the Romans persuaded themselves—of recovering the lands of their Persian predecessors with an imperial administration and army that, though not perhaps the equal of the Romans', was centralized, Hellenized, and familiar with the Roman legal concept of negotiated borders.[29] By the time of Augustus they had also demonstrated their ability to inflict severe damage upon incautious Roman generals, such as Crassus at Carrhae.

This was a different world from that of the West. The Parthian king Orodes, it was said, was watching a performance of Euripides'

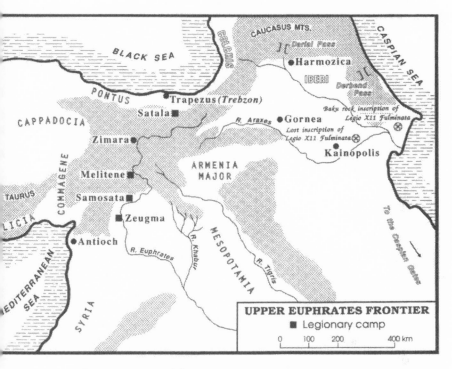

Fig. 12. Armenia and the northern Euphrates

Bacchae when the head of Crassus was brought to him. Ten thousand Roman prisoners were settled in Parthia and married local women after the battle. In A.D. 36 the Roman governor of Syria, L. Vitellius, negotiated with a Parthian noble who was also a Roman citizen. It comes as something of a shock to realize that C. Julius Antiochus Philopappus, Roman consul of A.D. 109, who has left his visible mark on the skyline of Athens, was the grandson of a Parthian king.

If the two worlds of East and West were so very different, then, the critical question must be asked, Did the Romans have a different policy and a different concept of frontier in the East from that in the West? In the East we would expect, perhaps, an administrative boundary, legally negotiated between equals and determined by

51

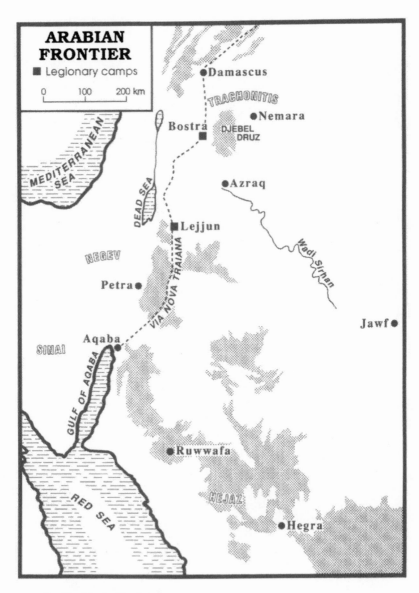

Fig. 13. The Arabian frontier

political rather than military conditions. For this idea of power sharing there is some evidence in the sources and in several historical examples of treaties negotiated around the assumption that the river Euphrates was the legal boundary, the most obvious being that of Augustus in 20 B.C., when the standards of Crassus were returned by Parthia.[30]

But we need to take some care in assuming that this is the whole story. When Pompey was asked to recognize the Euphrates as a treaty line, he gave the unsatisfactory reply, "Rome would adopt a boundary that was just" (Plut. *Pomp.* 33.6). And Augustus publicized on coins the return of the standards as submission to Roman rule.[31] The eastern front was, in any case, more than just Syria and the Euphrates. There were Palestine and Nabataean Arabia to the south, while to the north were Armenia and the shores of Pontus as far as the Caucasus. The Euphrates was perhaps a plausible dividing line to negotiate in northern Syria, but in the southern desert part it was the main route of east-west movement.[32] The contrast between deserts, steppes, and mountains was as great on the eastern front as between Hadrian's Wall and the African *fossatum* in the West.

There is another difficulty in answering the question: the relatively undeveloped state of archaeology in the East compared with the West, despite important new work in the past decade that has radically changed some old concepts and ideas about the eastern frontiers.[33] One simple fact that militates against the notion of a fixed, linear frontier in the East is that in the first and second centuries of the Empire more Roman military inscriptions have been found beyond the Euphrates on the Cappadocian front than on the immediate line of what was once called the eastern frontier (Crow 1986b). Whether this is an accident of research or a reflection of reality is impossible yet to judge.

The irony about our ignorance is that the eastern front was occupying proportionately greater and greater Roman attention and manpower than the West from the first century to the fourth. Whereas Pompey's settlement considered three to four legions in Syria sufficient as the sole garrison for the whole Middle East, by the second century there were eight legions and as many auxiliaries stretched out from the Black Sea to the Gulf of Aqaba, a force of some hundred thousand men, to which Septimius Severus added two more legions in Mesopotamia.[34]

Between Pompey's settlement in the late Republic and the emperor Nero there were no fundamental territorial changes in the area directly administered by the Romans, and even Corbulo's campaigns into Armenia under Nero in the 60s did not annex any new province. But this certainly did not mean there was an aversion to military action or advance. Pompey's answer to Parthian demands for a treaty recognizing the Euphrates as the common frontier was in effect a refusal. Romans knew that at his death Caesar was planning a campaign against the Parthians in which Octavian was to participate (Suet. *Aug.* 6). Augustan poets reflect the dreams of eastern victories taking Roman arms to India. According to the contemporary poet Propertius, "the ends of the earth are preparing triumphs for you, Tiber, and the Euphrates will flow subject to your jurisdiction" (*Carm.* 3.4).

Even after the diplomatic settlement of 20 B.C., we are informed that the emperor's grandson Gaius, when he died in 2 B.C., was planning campaigns "extending the *termini* beyond the Rhine, Euphrates, and Danube" (Sen. *Brev. vit.* 4.5). After Augustus had claimed that he could have made Armenia a province but had preferred to leave it a dependent kingdom, all future emperors regarded the country as a Roman "gift," revocable at any time. It was a Roman right to install and control the kings of Armenia, a right they were prepared to enforce with arms.[35]

Farther south, on the Syrian front, it is completely ambiguous whether Palmyra, the caravan city, was inside or outside the Roman Empire, and Appian calls the residents "border people" who skillfully played off Rome against Parthia (*BC* 5.1.9). But that was hardly the way the Romans would have seen it. They could claim to have some authority over the city by A.D. 18, when we find a Roman tax law published there. Theoretically, therefore, that extended Roman military rule, through Palmyrene militia, along the desert routes and watering points as far as the lower Euphrates and perhaps beyond. But it is a perfect example of control without rule or of ideology before reality. Parthia too had interests there, and it is a measure of the fluidity of the frontiers that Palmyrene militia were permitted to operate from Dura-Europos and Ana on the Euphrates even while they were still Parthian cities in the first century A.D. Palmyra remained an Arab city with considerable support among the tribes of the Hauran and northern Arabia, which allowed it to act as an intermediary between Parthia and Rome while marshaling the desert trade routes. Possibly Hegra in the Hejaz played a similar role in the second century A.D. in controlling the routes from Petra to Saudi Arabia.[36]

Claudius was probably the first to construct a fort on the line of the Euphrates; but he also seems to have reinforced the Armenian king beyond the Euphrates with a Roman garrison (Dobrawa 1986, 96–97; Mitford 1980, 1174). Indeed, the campaigns of Corbulo under Nero were conducted primarily to "hold on to Armenia"— that is the way Tacitus described it (*Ann.* 13.8)—and already in A.D. 62 the territory was being regarded by the governor of Syria as ready for direct provincial rule (Tac. *Ann.* 15.6). There were also Roman fortified sites in Mesopotamia at this date. Although in the settlement after Corbulo's wars the Parthians demanded Roman withdrawal to the Euphrates line "as before" and the Romans are said to have set up a line of forts "against the Armenians" (whatever that means), it is not said that Nero formally accepted the Euphrates as the Roman frontier.[37] Strabo, who wrote under Tiberius, probably captured the ambiguity of the situation when he said that, although the Parthians regarded the Euphrates as the "limit" (*horion*) of their territory, "Parts within are held by the Romans and the phylarchs of the Arabs as far as Babylonia; some of them adhere more to the Parthians and others more to the Romans" (16.1.28).

As in the West, the Flavian achievement in the East has to be judged almost exclusively by archaeology. Here too theories have been put forward of a new, scientific approach, the start of a new policy of fixed frontiers. But many are now inclined to revise earlier claims of a Flavian master strategy and to regard as a myth the idea of a fortified frontier along the Euphrates that supposedly anticipated and resembled that of the fourth century.[38]

The most striking change was in the disposition of the legions. Cappadocia was developed as a first-class military province, and the two legionary bases were built at Satala and Melitene, roughly along the lateral line of the upper Euphrates and its extension road to the Black Sea. In Syria-Commagene there was probably a parallel pair of legionary bases at Samosata and Zeugma, although the precise archaeological date for their foundation is lacking. Both were important crossing points of the Euphrates, certainly occupied earlier and probably customs posts on the provincial border.[39]

But these sites did not so much form a military front as provide a base for invasion routes into Armenia or Mesopotamia and control of caravan routes coming out of the East. Legionary bases were not normally placed on the leading edge of a military front. Rivers, as I will stress again and again in this book, generally were not natural frontiers but lines of communications and supply. The legionary camps on the rivers were therefore the rear base for attacks.[40]

In fact there is more evidence of the Flavian army beyond the upper Euphrates and Pontic road than on it. In Azerbaijan a rock inscription records a legionary detachment overlooking the Caspian Sea one thousand miles from its base at Melitene. Another detachment was placed in the Caucasian Gates (modern Darial Pass), where a wall also was built for the Iberian king at the southern end of the pass. A fort was rebuilt at Gornea near the Armenian capital of Artaxata, and another inscription (now lost) records a Roman detachment on the Araxes.[41]

The evidence gives substance to the poem of Statius (*Silv.* 4.1.41–43) suggesting that Domitian was planning an expedition to India and the Far East. Another possibility is that Colchis and the Caucasus were being brought under control to prevent piracy of grain supplies for the legions from the Black Sea, which was arriving at the port of Trapezus (modern Trebizond).[42] Colchis is another example of an ambiguous frontier state, which Procopius later described as "subject to the Romans without paying tribute" (*BPers.* 2.15.2–3).

What seems sure is that Romans did not think they had reached the limits of empire in the East when Trajan came to power in the early second century. His annexation of Armenia and Mesopotamia between A.D. 114 and 117 provides illustrations of the sort of frontier thinking that existed in the East. But it is worth noting that as Armenia was organized, so too were the military garrisons on the Euphrates, now far to the rear, strengthened. An obvious example is the new fort at Zimara, where the upper Euphrates makes a sharp bend southward as it flows out of Armenia.[43] There is no question, therefore, of concluding from the archaeological evidence that a fortified river front line was intended. Armenia itself came under the governor of Cappadocia, as far as we can see, but no attempt was made to define the eastern borders.

Although Hadrian reverted to an Augustan type of Roman control of Armenia through allied kings and abandoned Mesopotamia, there is no reason to think he renounced all claims to control east of the Euphrates. If we can trust the story that Hadrian's excuse for pulling back Roman troops was the example of Cato's withdrawal from Macedonia in the second century B.C. (HA *Hadr.* 5), the analogy was one of control by indirect rule. Both in the far north (Iberia, Armenia) and beyond the middle Euphrates (Edessa, Osrhoene, Bactria, Hyrcania) we are told of the submission of allied kings, not all of it empty propaganda.[44] There is no warrant to conclude from this evidence that Hadrian had adopted a purely defensive policy.

Whatever we may think of Hadrian's intentions, however, it is obvious that during the rule of Marcus Aurelius and Verus (A.D. 161–69) Trajan's policy of direct rule and administration of Mesopotamia as a province was thought both possible and desirable. Although the final coup de grace of annexation had to come from Septimius Severus, probably in A.D. 198, there were already Roman garrisons, forts, and some sort of imperial administration (at Nisibis) in the northern part of the interriverine territory before it became a province: "occupation without annexation," it has been termed (Kennedy 1979). It is a good example of how indeterminate the frontier remained and how little the Romans felt constrained by the differences between directly administered provinces and indirectly controlled territory beyond. In Armenia Marcus

Aurelius deliberately left the king in place but bolstered up by a Roman garrison in the new capital of Kainopolis (Dio 71.3.1[1][Suda]).

Severus did not then actually change the frontiers of Mesopotamia. He only converted the area of indirect control into one of direct provincial administration. The cities of Mesopotamia continued to be the keys to Roman power without there being in any real sense a new frontier. The city of Hatra, which Severus unsuccessfully assaulted, became a base for Roman troops soon after, but we look in vain for any sign of a frontier. On the middle Euphrates we know more about Severan forts below Dura-Europos as a result of recent discoveries, and Dura itself had become the base of a *dux ripae* under the Antonine emperors. That must mean the Romans controlled both banks of the river and the trade traffic that used the river, but it is difficult to see what territorial significance this had (Isaac 1990, 147–53).

Trajan's attempt to add Mesopotamia to the list of provinces was paralleled by his organization, to the south of Syria, of the new province of Arabia, where recent study has clarified his work. What emerges is that the Arabian frontier was in reality no more than a road—the *via nova Traiana*—studded with fortified posts, which ran from the Gulf of Aqaba to Bostra. The road followed the old King's Road that had been worked by the Nabataean Arabs to control the trade routes from the Red Sea and the Yemen to Petra; and in many ways it resembled the earlier construction.

The road was supplemented by long-distance outposts at Hegra in the Hejaz (Saudi Arabia) and along the route of the Wadi Sirhan, although the precise dates for these last developments are uncertain. The military evidence from the Azraq oasis in the Wadi Sirhan is Severan in date, and the organization of the Arab tribes in the Hejaz by the Roman governor is first attested by a famous inscription at Ruwwafa establishing an emperor cult in the time of Marcus Aurelius.[45] But these dates are only *post quem*, and it looks at least possible that from the start the Romans established patrols of native troops paying allegiance to Rome on the southern and eastern flanks of the Arabian road to serve in much the same way as Palmyra did at the northern end. They were meant not so much for defense in depth as for surveillance of nomadic movements and to provide caravan escorts.

In other words, the Arabian frontier was a true *limes*, a road for movement and not a blocking, defensive system. In the Palestine sector it has been suggested that the road forts were posted more for internal security against the bandits of Judaea than to protect the territory against external, nomadic raiders. But this perhaps underestimates the need to monitor even peaceful transhumants. The fort at Khan Kosseir, for instance, which lay on the inner steppe of Syria along the road from Damascus to Emesa, recorded its construction under the Severan emperors "for the sake of public security and against the terror of the Scaenitae Arabs" (*CIL* 3.128). But there is no way of deciding whether these raiders came from within or from outside the *limes*.[46]

The important point, however, is that we do not find in this sector anything that could be called a frontier "system." Here particularly we have confirmation that the eastern frontier, as it is traditionally described, from the Pontic shore to the Red Sea was in essence a line of communication and supply, the base from which the Romans extended their control without any sense of boundaries.

This does not mean that such lines were never defensive when external attacks came. We have already seen how the concept of a *praetentura* of forts "stretched out" like a battle line had been applied by Tacitus to the Armenian front. But it is not proved that *fines imperii* were perceived as having a permanently defensive role. Indeed, it has been calculated that recorded Parthian attacks on Roman provinces over three centuries were only half the number of those launched by Romans on Parthia; and it is never proved that the Parthians took the initiative.[47]

In short, although strategy obviously differed between East and West, the concept of frontiers was remarkably similar. That is the subject of the next chapter.

Three

Why Did the Frontiers Stop Where They Did?

lthough it is obviously true that we are as suscepti-
ble to the conceptualization of our contemporaries
as were our forebears, let me begin by making two
confident assertions about frontiers drawn from
modern experience and theory.

Scientific and Natural Frontiers in History

First, it is almost universally agreed, except perhaps among ancient
historians, that the ideal of the "scientific frontier" is an unattainable
objective. The term "scientific frontier" was coined by Lord Roberts,
British commander in the Second Afghan War of 1890, in his
attempt to push the North-West Frontier of India beyond what
was previously thought to be the "natural line" of the Sulaiman
Mountains, to a wholly artificial line between Kabul and Kandahar,
well beyond the outer boundary of India (Davies 1975, 6–7). Yet
despite Lord Curzon's praise of the scientific frontier that "unites
natural and strategic strength" (Curzon 1907, 48–49), Roberts's
line was abandoned because no military strategists could agree on
its precise location or on how to cover the logistics of its supply.
None of the several other proposed military frontiers ever coincided

with the eventual political frontier of the Durand Line in 1893, incorporating many tribes, said Curzon regretfully, "over which we exercise no jurisdiction and only the minimum control" (Kirk 1979, 43; Curzon 1907, 40; Davies 1975, 13–16).

"Natural" and "best" frontiers have proved as elusive historically as scientific frontiers. This does not mean there were never any rational debates about where territorial lines should be drawn, but there is always conflict between military, political, and administrative considerations (Nordman 1977, 436). Politicians find rivers or mountains convenient geographic markers around which to bargain or focus patriotic fervor. I cited earlier Lucien Febvre's wise statement that mountains, rivers, and deserts, far from being barriers, "are promoted to the dignity of being a natural frontier" by victorious nations in the process of expansion and in the desire to define space (1922, 325–31; Alliès 1980, 70).

Militarily, however, rivers were untenable, as was plainly stated by the duke of Wellington in 1808 when rejecting the mighty river Indus as India's northern frontier. "The art of crossing rivers is so well understood and has been so frequently practised . . . that we cannot hope to defend the Indus as a barrier" (Davies 1975, 4, 6). Jurisprudentially, the more powerful nation always demands rights over the far bank. Mountains, though militarily obvious, are administratively impossible to control, as the British experience of the Khyber Pass or the French experience of the Pyrenees has demonstrated, since they have a dynamic of their own and are not fixed lines (Febvre 1922, 330).

Broad geographic definitions of territory are neither natural nor even real. The frontiers of Europe in the seventeenth and eighteenth centuries were regularly cited as the gifts of nature, divinely ordained and defined by rivers, mountains, and seas. Danton's famous speech in 1793 built upon this myth in order to define the new French nation: "Ses limites sont marquées par la Nature; nous les atteindrons toutes des quatre points de l'horizon, du côté du Rhin, du côté l'Océan, du côté des Alpes." They are words that resemble in tone Tacitus's description of the Roman Empire when he says it is "hedged about by the sea of Oceanus and remote rivers" (Tac. *Ann.* 1.9).[1] But this ideological view did not stop

61

long and bitter negotiations over the status of Alsace, the Franche Comté, and Greater Hungary in the eighteenth century. Nor did it limit Roman expansion in the first century A.D.

Far from being natural lines, therefore, frontiers are, and always were, ethnically confused. The British found it impossible to separate the Pashtu speakers who were socially and culturally spread over the North West Province and Afghanistan (Davies 1975, 16, 42). When the Russian Kievan state of the tenth to the twelfth century fought the pagan Polovtsy beyond their southwestern borders, the Polovtians on their own side, though nominally Christians, were still thought of as "our pagans" because of their ethnic and cultural homogeneity with those beyond (Wieczynski 1976, 16). Historical geography is made up of confused borderlands, marches or marks, the root, we think, of the ancient name Marcomanni, the river March in Slovakia, and the English medieval Mercians, who lived on the borders of Wales.

On the medieval Welsh Marches one of the great engineering works of the eighth century is Offa's Dyke, constructed from Prestatyn to Chepstow—a work estimated to have cost four million man-hours. Yet the considered modern view of this enormous effort is that it was not so much a military frontier as a "control line" in Mercian territory; it did not mark the limit of Offa's kingdom, and it ran through the middle of existing communities that continued to function as before.[2] No cultural boundary existed: no-man's-lands have never worked. A frontier must always be considered in "its broad form as a zone."[3]

A Grand Strategy for the Roman Empire?

Given this background of modern experience, therefore, can we believe that the Romans ever achieved a "scientific frontier," or even thought they could, by virtue of a "grand strategy"? Edward Luttwak's book with that title has been received with favorable reviews and continues to be cited by reputable historians and archaeologists alike.[4] His theme is simple; the systematic development by Roman emperors of a comprehensive imperial strategy. The term "scientific" frontier appears in the central chapter heading describing the evolution under the Flavian emperors in the later first century A.D. of the optimal line of military defense combined with what was most cost effective—a conclusion surprisingly close to Lord Curzon's vain ideal quoted earlier. Above all, Luttwak argues, in both the pre- and post-Flavian phases, frontier policy evolved through what he calls a "rational administrative policy" based on a single strategic objective—a perimeter boundary manned by auxiliaries, faster communications between fronts, and (by implication) a good flow of information between the emperor at the center and his generals on the frontiers.

None of this seems unreasonable at first sight. It is not at all implausible that, with the arrival of the principate, there also arrived a coherent strategic policy. The emperor was like "a helmsman," said Fronto, "at the tiller of a warship" (2.251 Haines). The physical remains of Hadrian's Wall in Britain, the African *fossatum*, and the German *limes* lend credibility to the idea of a single strategic plan, if we compare them on photographs (figs. 14–16). Fronto's contemporaries Appian and Aelius Aristides, cited in the previous chapter, also gave the impression of emperors, like great landowners or camp commanders, carefully planning a world strategy, surrounding the empire "with a circle of great camps . . . like an estate" (App. *pr.* 7), separating off the uncivilized barbarians with "a rampart enclosing the civilized world" (Ael. Arist. *Ad Rom.* 81).

Let us leave aside the minor irony that all three authors were probably addressing their compliments to Antoninus Pius, one of the least active emperors in all Roman history in foreign affairs. For there is a sense, of course, in which the Augustan frontiers did mark a change in intellectual perceptions of frontiers, as we saw in the previous chapter. And Augustus was certainly at the hub of foreign affairs, not above giving advice, in this as in almost every other respect, about how to manage them and how the empire should be defined. Almost certainly his was the basis of Tacitus's holistic description of the empire bounded by great geographic features, just quoted, to which we find parallels in other writers such as Josephus (e.g., *BJ* 2.16).

But the fact is that Augustus was not successful in persuading

Fig. 14. Hadrian's Wall at Cuddy's Crags, Housesteads, in Britain. Photograph by C. R. Whittaker.

Fig. 15. The wall of the Djebel Tebaga in Tunisia. Photograph by permission of P. Trousset.

Fig. 16. An aerial view of the Roman *limes* at Hirnstetten, Germany. Photograph by O. Braasch (catalog no. GS 300/9119-82), reproduced by permission of H. Becker, Bayerische Landesamt für Denkmalpflege. In these pictures of the walls of the Roman Empire shown in figs. 14–16, is it possible to detect a grand strategy at work?

his successors to observe any sort of orderly *termini imperii*, even if that is what he meant to do, and the annexations that took place after his death cannot be dismissed as negligible until Trajan came along.[5] The pressure to expand was too great and was not controlled by strategy. The image of the empire as a *polis* or an estate, conjured up by the two Greek writers, was very much an idealized view of the sacred space of the Greek city, which perhaps owed something to Roman ideas of *limitatio* or land division. But arbitrary, artificial lines had little to do with reality, let alone imperial military strategy. As long as an imperial state has neighbors, the neighbors are necessarily inferior and the state has no frontiers in our sense. That is a conclusion that applies to all early empires (Claval 1978, 109).

The criticism of Luttwak's *Grand Strategy* has been twofold. The first objections were launched by John Mann, an archaeologist of considerable experience on the British frontier, who declared his belief that frontier lines were "little more than an accident" drawn at the point where the Roman war machine ran out of steam. Frontiers for him, therefore, were a "symbol of failure" of the Roman ideology of expansion, even if the ideology itself persisted. But more important, given Mann's background as an archaeologist, is his conclusion—made from an examination on the ground of the choice of frontier sites—that it is impossible to perceive strategic or tactical value, or even any single coherent response. His opinion is confirmed by those who have studied the Antonine Wall in Scotland.[6] And a recent study of the eastern frontier concludes that "it simply did not matter much to the Romans where the boundary ran," since they did not see borders in terms of military defense. In the East it is even more difficult to spot any kind of "system" or rational, scientific, cost-effective thinking behind what were basically ad hoc decisions.[7]

The second difficulty with Luttwak's thesis is that, although Roman authors—and therefore, we may assume, Roman emperors—thought about the strategy of frontiers, nevertheless rational decisions were fatally flawed owing to the absence of any sophisticated concept of strategy and to a chronic lack of information.[8] That refers, of course, to the poor state of cartography in the ancient world. Neither generals nor emperors can have had much of an idea about the geography of a territory before beginning campaigns or about what was really happening on and beyond the frontiers.

A striking example is that given us by the historian Cassius Dio, who says that when Septimius Severus was campaigning in Mesopotamia, he was "short of information" (Dio [Xiph.] 75.9.4). This was a hundred years after Trajan's similar campaign and two hundred years after the Romans started invading the land.[9] So there was not so much a "moral barrier" (a celebrated phrase coined by Andreas Alföldi, about which I have my doubts)[10] as an information barrier. We can get some idea of the information flow from Velleius Paterculus, who actually accompanied Tiberius in Germany in the campaign of A.D.4–6 toward the Elbe. Yet even so, he overestimated the distance from the Rhine to the Elbe, where it borders the Hermunduri, as 400 miles (2.106) instead of 200 to 250 miles—an error of nearly 100 percent. That shows what scientific data were available to help emperors in their decisions after the campaign, quite apart from how little they knew beforehand.

Even if one believes, as I do, in the rationality of imperial decisions, it is hard to find much evidence even of "scientific" thinking in the sense of cost-effective, economical decisions. In the celebrated case of Britain, which both Strabo (4.5.3) in the first century and Appian (*BC*, pr. 5) in the second tell us was not worth conquest economically, we are faced with the ironic fact that the Romans nevertheless occupied the country. The reason is given to us explicitly by Florus, who links Britain to Armenia: "It was fine and glorious to have acquired them, not for any value, but for the great reputation they brought to the magnificence of the empire" (*Ut non in usum, ita ad imperii speciem magna nomina adquisisse pulchrum ac decorum; Epit.* 1.47.4).

In practice, of course, this often meant bringing great reputation to a particular governor, as Tacitus's father-in-law, Agricola, knew (Tac. *Agr.* 27). So generals may not always have been scrupulous in giving information to the emperor. One is reminded of the French government's inability to control the ambitions of its own officers in the scramble for Africa because of poor communications, inadequate maps, and the confused machinery of administration. General Lyautey, we know, even altered the names of the towns of Morocco in his dispatches in order to deceive Paris.[11]

It is not so much that Romans, writers and emperors alike, were irrational about frontiers when they alternated between their expansionist desires for *laus imperii* or *propagatio imperii* and the ideological image of an empire that, in the words of the third-century historian Herodian, "was hedged about with major obstacles, rivers, ditches, and mountains or desert regions that were difficult to cross" (2.11.5). They were talking about different things. There was first, as in the seventeenth-and eighteenth-century examples quoted earlier in this chapter, a kind of global perception about space and power based on natural boundaries and a recognition of what it meant to be Roman, subject to Roman law. That was neatly summed up in the Roman law of *postliminium*, the rights a Roman citizen had when returning from exile or capture to Roman territory—that is, *intra fines*. There must have been some recognizable point when one crossed into Roman jurisdiction.[12]

But there was also an unwillingness to accept that Rome had any boundaries. That feeling derived perfectly rationally from certain ideological principles. It is an extraordinary fact that no Roman geographic description or map tells us where the boundaries of empire actually lay or whether there were ever any marker stones. It is true that two places are marked as *fines Romanorum* on a section of the Peutinger Table depicting Syria and Mesopotamia, a medieval copy of a fourth-century A.D. Roman road map. But apart from dating difficulties, these *fines* look as if they were the boundary between the provinces and a client state (possibly Palmyra), since underneath one is written *fines exercitus Syriaticae*, showing where the military responsibility of the Roman army ended. It could have been a trading post as well, since the words *commercium barbarorum* are also written, and we know that a customs officer was stationed at Zeugma on the Euphrates (Philos. *V. Apoll.* 1.20), appearing just above this point on the map.[13] But a provincial checkpoint need not have been the military frontier, since at the customs post of Zarai in Africa an inscription informs us that the army unit had moved away (*CIL* 8.4508). That, however, is all the evidence we possess about marked border lines.

What it means in effect is that ideology is no guide to the reality of frontiers. As we saw in the previous chapter, there is no hint of a scientific assessment of the strategic advantages and disadvantages of Trajan's great annexations of Dacia and Mesopotamia. On the contrary, it is the conventional cries of imperialism that are deafening. Cassius Dio says that Trajan, like Severus later, was motivated by "a desire for glory" ([Xiph.] 68.17.1, [Xiph.] 75.1.1). Tacitus's description of Oceanus and various rivers as the limit of empire is absurd as a summary of Roman strategic policy, given that his own father-in-law, Agricola, won fame for his expeditions in Britain beyond Oceanus and that in Germany Flavian forts lay some sixty to seventy kilometers beyond the Rhine. If leaving Germany free was part of some scientific policy devised by the Flavian emperors, as Luttwak would have us believe, then Tacitus was himself not aware of it. *Tam diu Germania vincitur* (*Germ.* 37), he laments: How long will it be before Germany is conquered? (Mann 1979a, 178–79). Nor does close study of the upper Euphrates under the Flavian emperors offer any justification for the conclusion that they constructed a rational system of river-line frontier there either (Crow 1986b; Wheeler 1991).

The personal character of imperial rule and a very limited flow of information produced eccentric, not scientific, decisions. Despite modern attempts to save the reputation of the emperor Commodus in A.D. 180, Herodian and Cassius Dio, who were contemporaries, both say that the decision to abandon Slovakia and the Sudeten was against the advice of experienced generals.[14] So in this case, at least, the emperor deliberately ignored the best advice available. Can we then really believe that Antoninus Pius had been informed about the northern tribes of the Votadini and the Brigantes, much less the mysteriously advancing Broch and Dun culture in northern Britain? Yet these are the factors *we* discuss when trying to comprehend his incomprehensible decision to advance to the Antonine Wall (Hanson and Maxwell 1983, 60–61). The important fact is that, even if we can justify some direct imperial decisions on economic, tactical, or strategic grounds—

Claudius's veto on Corbulo's campaign against the Chatti (Tac. *Ann.* 11.19), for instance, or Domitian's withdrawal of Agricola from Britain (Tac. *Agr.* 39)—Roman writers and contemporaries interpreted these as acts of political rationality, which no doubt they were. It would be wrong to assume that emperors reasoned any differently from their contemporaries (Millar 1982, 3, 22; Isaac 1990, 392).

Strategy, in fact, is the one thing that manuals of *strategemata* did not contain (Millar 1982, 21). They were stratagems, not strategy. The *exemplum*, for instance, which Frontinus cites as the precedent for Domitian "to advance the *limites* in Germany by 120 miles," whereby "he subdued the enemy by uncovering their refuges," is that of Julius Caesar who "always sought to fight in a battle line" (*acie semper decertare studuit*, Front. *Strat.* 1.3.2 and 10). This odd explanation seems to mean that Domitian cleared much of the forest land near the frontier posts because Roman armies, since the time of Caesar, liked to fight set pieces on open ground. If that is so, I fail to see evidence here of "das Prinzip der linearen Grenzsicherung"—a new strategic "principle"—as a recent guide to the German *limes* claims.[15]

A Scientific or a Natural Roman Frontier?

It used to be fashionable to believe that the strategic policy of Augustus north of the Rhine and Danube was a rational quest for defensive frontiers and a shorter line of communication via the Elbe. This view, however, is a modern invention without foundation in the sources, which concentrate on the glory of the conquest of Germany and the threat of Maroboduus's power in Bohemia. See, for instance, the opinion of a contemporary soldier like Velleius Paterculus (2.108–9).[16]

The only emperors, it appears, who articulated any sort of policy of retrenchment either were dead, like Augustus giving his posthumous *consilium* to Tiberius and telling him to keep the empire within limits (Tac. *Ann.* 1.11), or became dangerously unpopular like Hadrian, who desperately sought to justify his policy of withdrawal from Parthia after the death of Trajan. But

Augustus, as I argued in chapter 1, was not really giving strategic advice at all, and Hadrian, according to his biographer, did not evoke any strategic principles. Instead he quoted a curious archaic *political* precedent of how Cato gave freedom to the Macedonians instead of annexing them (HA *Hadr.* 5.3). The example seems to be articulating a Republican principle of hegemonial imperialism, which was often combined with the common Hellenistic propaganda claim to be restoring liberty to those one wished to control. Neither Augustus nor Hadrian was credited or heeded by his successors, who apparently did not see any strategic necessity in what the emperors had said.

Indeed, the very idea of the frontier as a line on a map is modern. The Roman Empire illustrates well Lucien Febvre's theme that *fins, confins, limites* and *frontières* were never regarded as identical until the nineteenth century. Before then, Febvre said, "the word 'boundary' [*confins*] evoked . . . above all the idea of a band of territory."[17] Ancient *limites* were never linear but were always zones. It is clear that when it came down to detailed descriptions, even Roman writers themselves did not regard the great riverine boundaries of Europe as military fronts. For instance, Appian (*pr.* 4) said that "The Romans . . . rule some of the Keltoi *beyond* the Rhine." Keeping Dacians and Sarmathians *at a distance* from the Danube is what Florus (2.28–29) says of Roman policy in the second century, despite the ideological recognition that the Danube was some sort of geopolitical dividing line from the time of Augustus (Strabo 6.4.2; Aug. *RG* 30.2).

But the notion, proposed by Luttwak, that after the Flavians Roman strategy began to dispense with client kings on their borders in favor of linear fronts is demonstrably wrong.[18] Claudius and Marcus Aurelius, who are separated by a hundred years, behaved identically in Armenia. In the biography of Hadrian—the emperor who above all is supposed to have pursued scientific, linear frontiers—there are no fewer than seven specific references to "friendly kings" as well as the general statement that "he showed many favors to many kings" (HA *Hadr.* 17.10); and the slogan, "A king has been given to the Quadi" (*rex Quadis datus*) is one of the few

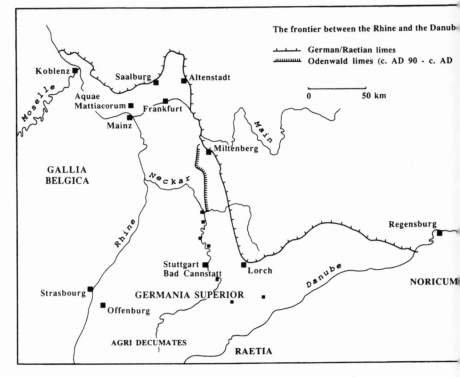

Fig. 17. The frontier of Upper Germany between the Rhine and the Danube

publicized acts of foreign policy on the coins of Antoninus Pius (*RIC* 3.620).

In short, by forgetting the difference between a border *line* and a frontier border *land*, we make the classic confusion between political, military, and administrative frontiers. Can anyone who looks at the map of the upper German frontier (fig. 17), which runs in a straight line from Miltenberg to Lorch, over eighty kilometers, believe it was built as a tactical or strategic frontier? The difference is, of course, profound. A frontier line separates and differentiates; it is a limit of bureaucratic order and administration. A frontier zone, what the French call a *frange pionnière*, by contrast, unites and integrates those who are culturally diverse.[19] This is an important point to which I shall be returning often.

As for a coordinated or uniform "grand strategy" in the whole of the Roman Empire, Mann was rightly contemptuous of such a modern notion when he compared Hadrian's Wall in Britain, where forts were manned by thousands of auxiliary soldiers, with Tripolitania, where no troops at all seem to have been stationed beyond the high Djebel Nefoussa until the time of Commodus or Severus— and even then most were detachments of the legion—or with Mauretania Tingitana, where no linear frontier seems to have emerged at all in the defenses of Volubilis and Sala.[20]

The scientific frontier therefore remains as elusive in the ancient world as it was in the nineteenth century. Even Lord Curzon regarded the scientific frontier as having "little place in the ancient world," since "no one expected and few desired that stability should be predicted of any political frontier" before the eighteenth century, when one first hears of international commissions to define frontiers (Curzon 1907, 48–50).

If, then, scientific frontiers formed no part of Roman thinking, what are we to make of the idea of natural frontiers as an item in Roman strategic policy? The "natural" frontiers of the West, like the Rhine and the Danube, used to be the subject of intense debate by ancient historians, and there is no need for me to reopen the historiographic problem of *Völker zwischen Germanen und Kelten*, which was the title of a book by Hachmann, Kossack, and Kuhn (1962). It was all based on the question of who lived on the Rhine before the Romans arrived; in other words, Was the Rhine a natural frontier between Celts and Germans?

I can see no way to resolve the differences between "Celtomaniacs" and ideologues of the "noble German" as to who was the dominating pre-Roman influence in the Rhineland, nor can I pronounce a verdict on who arrived first at the Rhine, the Germans or the Romans. Already in the late nineteenth century the inadequacy of Caesar's simplistic concept of the natural frontier had been demonstrated, and we can now go so far as to say that the Germans were "almost a political invention of Caesar's."[21] The debates, however, are largely irrelevant to my argument here, which is less about ideology than about actuality. But their very intractability reinforces the conclusion drawn by an excellent recent survey of the question: "The one sure fact is that the Rhine before the Romans came was not a boundary between cultures" (Wells 1972, 23; Cunliffe 1988, 116–17).

In fact, both Caesar and Tacitus contradict their own assertions that the Rhine was Rome's natural frontier in many examples. The Belgae, who lived south of the Rhine in northern Gaul, "were sprung from Germans," says Caesar (*BG* 2.4); the Menapii, another Belgic tribe, had their settlements—listed as *agros, aedificia vicosque*—on both sides of the Rhine (*BG* 4.3); the Volcae Tectosages were a Gallic people living, like those Caesar called Germans, beyond the Rhine (Caes. *BG* 6.24). Caesar's genocidal attacks on the Belgic tribes of the lower Rhine may have opened the way for some northern Batavi, Cananefates, and Frisavones to cross the Rhine (Roymans 1983, 57), but Velleius Paterculus (2.105) still found other Cananefates north of the Rhine in 12 B.C., and the Batavi were supposedly once part of the northern Chauci federation (Tac. *Hist.* 4.12).

After the Flavian advance beyond the Rhine into the Wetterau and up to the Main-Neckar line, there was a fortiori no natural ethnic or cultural separation. The inhabitants of the *Agri Decumates*, the land beyond the rivers between the sources of the Rhine and Danube, were joined by "vagabonds" from Gaul, according to Tacitus (*Germ.* 29), and the name of the territory is generally regarded as a Latinized form of a Gallic name, meaning "land of the ten cantons" (Hind 1984, 188, with references). The Mattiaci, despite their Celtic name, had once subsisted beside the German Chatti, and in A.D. 70 they joined the Chatti in attacks on Mainz (Tac. *Hist.* 4.37). Yet thereafter they remained at Wiesbaden (Aquae Mattiacorum), within Roman territory. One could multiply the examples. What they demonstrate is that even the ancient sources recognized the artificiality of the frontier zones in practice.

Archaeologically the evidence of cultural divisions at Roman frontiers is even less convincing. The date of the ending of the Late Iron Age Celtic La Tène culture in Greater Germany and abandonment of their large fortified settlements or *oppida* before the advancing Germanic and Balkan cultures remains unresolved. Although there is fairly consistent evidence that *oppida* beyond the rivers (fig. 18)—such as Manching in Bavaria, Steinberg bei Romhild in Hessen, the Staffelberg in Franken or Stradonice in Bohemia, and so on—were abandoned by the mid-Augustan period, this was not true of all, despite clear signs of the intrusive cultures from the north, which are called "Germanic" or Dacian (Collis 1984a, 204, etc., 1984b, 174).

What seems important, however, is not so much the arrival of new groups as the increasing evidence of a mixed La Tène culture after their arrival and the adaptation of new cultures to the existing substratum. The Celtic population was not simply displaced. A symposium held in 1977 by the Slovakian Academy of Science to review the whole of central Europe came to the conclusion that "one must subject to a radical revision the old views about antagonistic clashes between the native, that is, the Slovak Celts, the Dacians, and the newly arrived Germans, and one should reckon on parallel Celtic, Dacian, and German settlements for a considerable period."[22]

Neither the Euphrates nor the Rhine nor the Danube offers a natural barrier capable of creating great ethnic divisions except at certain points, such as the Euphrates gorge that runs through the Kurdish Taurus or the stretch between Passau and Vienna where high cliffs, plus the deep forests of the Bavarian and Bohemian woods beyond, tend to isolate approaches into Bohemia. But immediately east of Vienna, where the Romans stationed their legions at Carnuntum and Brigetio commanding the March and Vah valleys at the entry into Moravia and Western Slovakia, there we see an archaeological mixture of the "Dacian horizon" with the late La Tène and Germanic cultures—as also farther east along the Danube (Chropovský 1977, 8–9; Anderson 1938, 142; Mócsy 1974b, 57).

Ancient sources reinforce this conclusion. Tacitus believed that the "Germanic" Osii on the north bank of the Danube bend were a fraction of the Celticized Aravisci on the south bank around Budapest, just as the Cotini, who were tributaries of the Sarmatians in Moravia, spoke Celtic (*Germ.* 28 and 43). Certainly the Romans

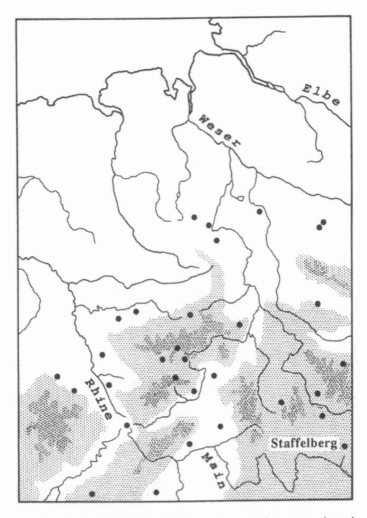

Fig. 18. *Oppida* and walled sites of the late La Tène period in Germany beyond the Rhine. After Hachmann, Kossack, and Kuhn 1962.

did not regard the Danube as a cultural or strategic frontier. An inscription from Budapest in the second century (*AE* 1914, 248) records a military officer *praepositus gentis Onsorum*—that is, a supervisor of the Osii on the northern bank. These people have been described as populations of transition (Mócsy 1974b, 57). In some regions like Bohemia it is true that there are signs of violent destruction and a "complete change of culture" (Collis 1984a, 50). But though there was an obvious weakening of Celtic *oppida* in central Germany (with all the economic implications that implies), there was no termination of the German Mittelgebirge culture or of the Dacian Carpathian culture at the Rhine and Danube. Caesar knew that not just Germans but Celts, like the Boii and Helvetii, could destroy *oppida* (*BG* 1.5, 2.29). Signs of violence are not in themselves evidence of cultural change.

The cultural continuum lies perhaps not so much in the *oppida* as in other features like the late Celtic *Viereckshanzen*, rather mysterious square cult enclosures that occur prolifically in southern Germany but are also found in many parts of Gaul (Planck 1985, map 340). They did not all fall out of use. One such group of *Viereckshanzen* lies near Kladno, not far from Prague—that is, in a region we think of as Germany after the Romans arrived. But it is in the middle of a large grave complex dating from the Roman period and, says the report, "testifies to the survival of a strong La Tène tradition . . . in the first century–second century A.D." (K. Motykova-Sneidrová, in Chropovský 1977, 239–48).

On the lower Rhine, where Roman forts never advanced beyond the river line, a recent summary of the confused pre-Roman archaeological evidence concludes, "There existed *to either side of the lower Rhine* [my italics] . . . a different type of social structure and culture" from the north or the south (Willems 1986, 209–10). This is the description of a typical march. But there is no archaeological evidence that the Rhine itself was a cultural frontier or that the Germanic *Einwanderung* had destroyed the La Tène tradition of the left bank in the Rhine-Meuse basin (Wightman 1985, 12). The power of Treveri too, based at Trier south of the Rhine, nevertheless had existed on both sides of the Rhine before the Romans arrived, as we can see by the distribution of their "Pegasus" coins (Wightman 1985, 31). Linguistically there is further evidence against the existence of a cultural frontier. There is a distinct fading away of Celtic place-names north of the Ardennes and Eifel, yet the language of Westphalia was not Germanic, says an authority on the subject. It was rather a "zone of transition or fringe area" (Kuhn, in Hachmann, Kossack, and Kuhn 1962; Petrikovits 1980b, 59). Among the German Ubii, whom Caesar describes as *Gallicis moribus adsuefacti* (*BG* 4.3), in the whole period of Roman history only 4.5 percent of names that have been found look Germanic (Weisgerber 1968, 165).

As for the river Euphrates, it has long been realized that it had nothing to do with ethnic divisions. Iranian culture had touched Cappadocians and Armenians alike on both sides of the upper Euphrates; Armenian was spoken by inhabitants of both Greater Armenia and Armenia Minor; and invaders over the centuries before Rome had found the river no obstacle to their expansion (Wheeler 1991, 505–6, with earlier references). I have quoted elsewhere Procopius's famous description of how the inhabitants of Chorzane, near Erzerum on each side of the northern Persian-Roman frontier, held common markets and even worked in each other's fields (*De aed.* 3.3.9–11). Strabo has a revealing passage about the Arabs farther south on the Euphrates in the time of Augustus. "The boundary [*horion*] of the Parthian power is the Euphrates with the country opposite [*peraia*]. But parts within [i.e., Parthian territory] are held by the Romans and the phylarchs of the Arabs as far as Babylonia; some of them adhere more to the Parthians and others more to the Romans who are their neighbors" (16.1.28). The precise meaning is not entirely clear, but the general sense is unmistakable, that the riverbanks were held by culturally identical Arab tribes, who were used by Romans and Parthians alike. The river was primarily a line of communication between north and south, not a cultural divide. But in the middle Euphrates region between Zeugma and Circesium (at the confluence with the river Khabur) was an area that invited entrance.

If we look still farther south, the place we and the Romans have called the "city" of Palmyra was thought of by Palmyrenes as a "port" (*mahuza*), a place where dues were paid for traffic passing east and west. That underlines the raison d'être of the site, which was essentially a nomad market serving both Parthia and Rome but forming no ethnic or strategic barrier.[23]

The Arabian frontier, after the annexation of the province by Trajan, was really nothing more than a road, the *via nova*, which was constructed from the Gulf of Aqaba northward to Bostra. It probably followed fairly closely the old Nabataean road intended to protect and control the trade routes from the East. There is a good deal of debate about exactly what purpose this "frontier" may have had, but one thing is clear: the road, which was built on the edge of the sedentary region, cut across the line that semi-nomads used to cross regularly for their seasonal pastures, and it was not intended to keep them out.[24]

Other frontiers demonstrate the same absence of clear-cut, natural lines. In Africa the revolt of Tacfarinas in A.D. 17, supported by the Gaetuli (a word as vague as Germani) and Garamantes, was provoked by the Roman military roads that ran from Ammaedara to Gabes in Tunisia and along the Tarhuna Eastern Djebel in Tripolitania. These roads were said to have "marked off" the land: *leimitavit* is the word inscribed on the boundary stones (*CIL* 8.22786), reminding us of the word *limes*, which we translate as "frontier."

But as later in 105, when the province under Trajan expanded south of the Aures, these roads acted as a control, not as a barrier, since they were constructed in territory customarily traversed by southern tribes with cultural and political affinities to the north, and they cut through federations like the Musulami, "who used to wander about far and wide" (*latius vagantes . . . artatis finibus coheruit*; Oros. 6.21.18). The roads were supplemented by *clausurae* walls, which were obviously not the front line of fortifications, as a glance at their location on the map (fig. 19) shows. Yet these are the walls that remind us most of Hadrian's Wall in Britain (figs. 14 and 15), and they were almost certainly initiated at about the same time.

The discovery of several new *clausurae* walls in the UNESCO Libyan Valleys Survey—now twelve separate sections, at least— confirms the judgment that they were never military barriers that

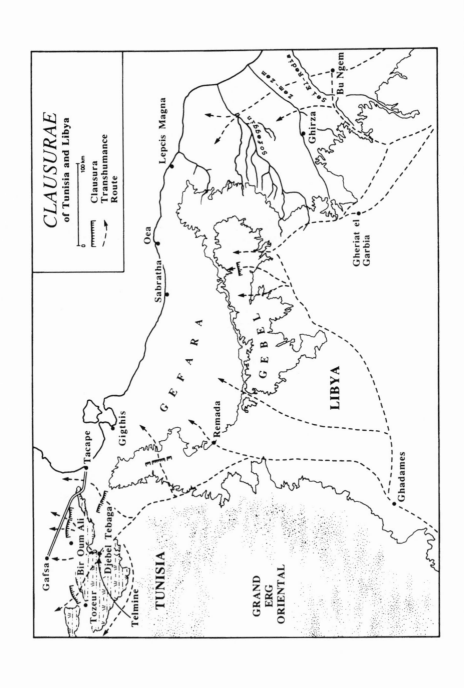

Fig. 20. The impressive remains of the *clausura* at Bir Oum Ali, Tunisia. Can it be called a frontier? Photograph by C. R. Whittaker.

divided the desert from the sown but were internal controls on shepherds and herdsmen who traditionally traversed them.[25] The spectacular walls at Bir Oum Ali (fig. 20), for instance, run along a ridge of hills some kilometers to the north of Telmine (the fort of Turris Tamalleni) on the Roman road that linked the desert oases in southern Tunisia. Similarly, an excellent study of the western Algerian fortifications demonstrates conclusively that the frontier system from Trajan to the Severi was predicated on two assumptions: that the main military fortified line (*praetentura*) lay well to the north of the forward survey posts, and that the dispositions were to control the movements of pastoral nomads (Salama 1977, esp. 586; cf. Whittaker 1978).

Increasing information about frontier geoethnography is also coming from northern British archaeology, where attention now

Fig. 19 (opposite). Some of the *clausurae* walls on the Tripolitanian *limes* in Tunisia and Libya, which lie well behind the Roman oasis forts of Tozeur and Telmine. After Mattingly and Jones 1986, 88.

focuses not so much on large federations like the Brigantes as on subgroups like the Carvetii, Lopocares, and Gabrantovices. The name Brigantes, in fact (meaning "highlander," perhaps?), is almost as vague as Gaetuli or Germani and is used of peoples to the north and to the south of Hadrian's Wall. But even the Carvetii in the West were not enclosed within the Roman frontier that ran from the Solway to the Tyne, since their center at *Car*-lisle, which reflects their name, is actually on the Roman wall and their territory must therefore have extended some distance to the north (cf. fig. 10). *Cor*-bridge (Roman *Cor*-iostopitum) on the Tyne may similarly reflect the name of the Lopo*cares* and may have had a similar function as the meeting center for a group who almost certainly extended northward and southward.[26]

Hadrian's Wall, therefore, was not the natural cultural boundary line that the late fourth-century *Vita Hadriani* says "was to divide Romans and barbarians" (HA *Hadr.* 11.2). If there was a cultural boundary anywhere, archaeologists say, it was some thirty kilometers to the north, where there were two Roman forward posts at High Rochester and Low Learchild (Jobey 1966, 6). The stakes that were set up by either Trajan or Hadrian along the Solway River in Carvetii territory were obviously not there to divide anyone, since an inscription tells us that the Carvetii were simultaneously being assessed for a tax census north of the Solway.[27] This raises an interesting question about Hadrian's activities in Germany at roughly the same time. If stakes were not the markers for a frontier in Britain, there is no reason we should believe Hadrian's biographer in the *Historia Augusta* when he says that this was the intention of the contemporary stakes set up on the Odenwald in Germany, even though he adds that "the barbarians are divided not by rivers but by boundaries"—if that is how we should translate *non fluminibus sed limitibus dividuntur* (HA *Hadr.* 12.6). Quite apart from the difficulty of imagining stakes (*stipites*) as a serious obstacle to other than petty thieves, I cannot help wondering whether this concept of "dividing off" the barbarians, which also appears in the quotation above about Hadrian's Wall, is not a piece of fourth-century ideology to add to those often found in the *Historia Augusta*.

These boundaries, like the *clausurae* in Africa, were surely for control of movements and were not military barriers. The contrary view has been stated forcefully, but it is difficult to believe if what I have just said is true.[28] To some extent the dispute is semantic. It is not a question of the wall's *never* serving *any* military purpose in time of emergency. The real question is what kind of military purpose and whether the wall was primarily defensive in intent. Even if we accept that Hadrian, with all his knowledge of Greek military science, established a wall (which some archaeologists believe was sited rather badly from a tactical point of view),[29] it is hard to explain why subsequent emperors continued to maintain the wall and even, as Septimius Severus did in the early third century, to give it a total facelift when the military threat was demonstrably not there.[30]

The same is probably true of Britain's second, briefly occupied frontier, the Antonine Wall in Scotland. We know that Rome had special relations with groups well to the north of the wall in the eastern Scottish Highlands (in South Strathmore and Fife) where the Maetae, Rome's allies, conserve their name in the hill fort of Dumyat, near Stirling, twenty kilometers north of the wall (Gillam 1958, 68). The phrase *summotis barbaris* in the *Historia Augusta* (HA *Pius* 5.4) cannot be used as proof that a no-man's-land was created beyond the wall, even if the writer of the Augustan history really believed "the barbarians were removed."

It is true there is some evidence that has made scholars believe it was standard policy for the Romans in forward zones along the walls or rivers to clear out the natives. Tacitus talks about land that was kept "free for military use" (*agri vacui et militum usui sepositi; Ann.* 13.54), which has been interpreted to mean that a no-man's-land was created to insulate the frontiers.[31] But history seems to contradict the idea that this was a regular practice. Otherwise it is difficult to see what the Mattiaci were doing in Wiesbaden, virtually on the north bank of the Rhine, or why the followers of Maroboduus and Cataulda were settled by the Romans on the north bank of the Danube as the core of the Vannian kingdom— a region that has now been plausibly identified between the river Morava and the Little Carpathians by its intense import of Roman goods (cf. fig. 32).[32] The device of a no-man's-land, as Curzon pointed out from his own colonial experience (1907, 29), was never durable and often was a diplomatic fiction. The Romans too found it virtually impossible to enforce, when they ejected first the Frisii and then the Ampsivarii in A.D. 58 from land the tribes claimed was "ancestral" (Tac. *Ann.* 13.54–55).

So, to sum up so far, we must not be beguiled by the myths that either scientific or natural frontiers surrounded the Roman Empire. There were no "frontiers" in the sense spelled out by Febvre, as the interface where Rome stood confronting the enemy. Nor was there any departure in the second century from a system of tributary, friendly kings. When Trajan, Hadrian, and Antoninus Pius carefully cultivated and controlled relations with Iasyges, Roxolani, Sarmatians, and Quadi beyond the Danube, they were still *membra partesque imperii*—integral parts of the body of the empire, beckoning Rome onward, as in Augustus's day (Suet. *Aug.* 48). They were not a defensive cordon sanitaire.

Spectacular monuments of empire can give a quite misleading impression of impregnable obstacles. Palisades, watchtowers, and walls were, in Curzon's judgment of the Great Wall of China, "more a line of trespass than a frontier," though they obviously served a military purpose against raiders.[33] This point has been made with great force in a recent study of Rome's eastern frontier, where the author stresses an important fact about archaeological remains. "It is easy," he says, "to confuse lines of communications provided with forts for the protection of military traffic with lines of forts intended to prevent enemy movement across them (Isaac 1990, 103). Just so.

Both the Chinese state and the Roman state made an enormous effort to post several hundred thousand men on the periphery of their empires. But each frontier remained "far more zonal than linear, despite the illusion of walls that emphasized it."[34] Rivers, says a recent study of ancient north Britain, "make poor boundaries and the distribution of late prehistoric settlements . . . is such as to suggest that river valleys acted as foci rather than boundaries for tribal groups" (Higham 1986, 147). That coincides closely with Febvre's judgment of the Niger as a frontier that "was not a dividing ditch, but a link" (1922, 328).

Why Did Roman Frontiers Stop Where They Did?

So why did Roman expansion stop where it did? That was the question Luttwak and Mann tried to answer. But despite Mann's valid criticism of Luttwak's scientific strategic frontier, I have to say I find the alternative of accidental boundaries equally unsatisfactory, since even unconscious decisions are determined by factors that can be explained rationally. Although we may be able to agree that Roman generals and emperors never sat down and worked out a grand military strategy, it is perfectly possible to make a structural and behavioral analysis of the choices they did make for their frontiers.

The weakness of Mann's attack lies, perhaps, in his assumption that military and political factors are the only ones worth considering. But Owen Lattimore's well-known contribution to frontier studies in his great study on the Chinese and Mongolian "inner Asian frontiers" lay essentially in his identification of the economic and ecological limits of imperial expansion. The Chinese frontiers, he believed, represented a compromise between the range of conquest and the economy of rule. Inevitably this compromise was not a clear geographic dividing line but a broad transitional region—an inner and an outer frontier, as he called it—where it was never obvious in the first instance whether the food supply or local production could sustain an army without its becoming an intolerable economic or logistical burden. The danger, he says, was that "centripetal gain was converted into centrifugal loss." In that sense, but profoundly different from any concept of an accident, frontiers represented "the limits of growth" and, says Lattimore, "that which was politically conceived as a sharp edge was persistently spread by the ebb and flow of history with a relatively broad and vague margin" (Lattimore 1940, 238–39, 243; 1962, 97–118).

These conclusions are confirmed on other frontiers where centrally organized states have encountered a dispersed, fragmented opposition as Rome did especially, though not only, in the West. Prince Gorchakov, faced with the same problem in Russia's imperial ambitions in Central Asia in the mid-nineteenth century, complained that the expenses were no longer worth the expansion

(Kirk 1979, 52). Lord Roberts's "scientific" frontier in Afghanistan failed because of problems of food supply and local production (Davies 1975, 13).

Yet even though some ancient historians have taken note of Lattimore's acute observations (and he himself, by the way, believed there were parallels between the Chinese and Roman frontiers), there has not been much systematic attempt to test his hypothesis against conditions in the Roman Empire. Does it work for the Roman empire? One of the studies that does take note of Lattimore criticizes him for misrepresenting the symbiotic exchange between nomads and farmers on frontiers.[35] The point is a good one, but it really misses Lattimore's main thesis, which concerned not so much the relations between this or that group as the marginality of the land. That was how frontiers were created, as he declared unambiguously: "When the combined economy, society and state, interacting with each other, had finally worked out the range of frontiers most profitable and satisfactory to them, *they thereby defined also* the geographical and environmental limits within which they could prosper" (1940, 241–43).

Decisions therefore were made both consciously and by what Lattimore called "unconscious trends." We can see something of the conscious decision making in Rome when Appian states that "the emperors have aimed to preserve their empire by the exercise of prudence rather than to extend their sway indefinitely over poverty-stricken and profitless barbarians" (*pr.* 7); or (in discussing Britain), "They have occupied the better and greater part of it but they do not care for the rest. For even the part they do occupy is not very profitable to them" (*pr.* 5). In other words, Roman emperors had some awareness, however crude, of what we would call the marginal costs of imperialism.

It is precisely this ecological and demographic marginality that is increasingly being documented in various archaeological studies of the Roman Empire. In Britain, for instance, air surveys of settlement patterns in the Solway and Tyne frontier regions show that on the Solway line, site density between north and south changes dramatically from 10.5 square kilometers to 3.6 square kilometers per habitation. Although much of this differentiation was probably the consequence, rather than the cause, of the wall, the surveys conclude that the wall "appears to incorporate in the decision-making process a desire to maximize the area of potential arable land within the frontier." This is of course only one specialized study of a region, from which it would be foolish to generalize. In the eastern sector, pollen analysis in the region beyond the Tyne frontier suggests "*extensive* clearance" before Roman occupation (Higham and Jones 1985, 78, 109; Jobey 1982, 13).

So the picturesque vision of northern Britain filled with nothing but "Celtic cowboys" before Rome's arrival is no longer tenable after the revelation of field systems by air photography and excavation. Nevertheless, and despite the problems of generalization, one can perceive a "noticeable thinning out" of the evidence of grain production and an increase in cattle grassland as one progresses northward toward the wall and beyond (illustrated in fig. 21). The frontier forts occupy what today is classed as grade 3 to 5 land—a classic zone of ecological marginality and demographic ambiguity.[36]

The same picture seems to be emerging on the German frontier. One study of pre-Roman Europe states unequivocally: "The limits of the [Roman] Empire . . . corresponded approximately to the limits of social development in prehistoric Europe towards early forms of the state and urban patterns of settlement and economy." It is the economic aspect that needs to be underlined here: the capacity to produce food. The Celtic *oppida* imply the existence of societies that could produce and organize food surpluses, in addition to whatever political implications they may have had (Champion et al. 1984, 323; Groenman–van Waateringe 1989; Cunliffe 1988, 174).

In the lower Rhine region of the northern frontier various studies confirm the existence of pre-Roman buildings (*aedificia*) in far greater numbers than were suspected in Picardy, and there was increasing clearance for agriculture in the Late Iron Age Rhine delta (Agache 1981, 48–49; Willems 1986, 204). But that development declined as the Romans advanced north into the territory of the Nervii, Menapii, and Eburones. Celtic field systems at Kempen on the Dutch border are smaller: the political and social systems appear archaeologically less stable (Roymans 1983, 52; Wightman

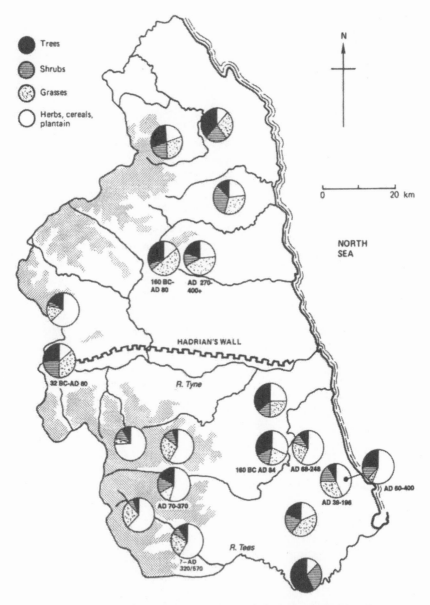

Fig. 21. The ecology of the region of northeastern England to the north and south of Hadrian's Wall. The proportion of grassland is higher to the north and that of cereal land greater to the south. From Greene 1986, 128. Reproduced by permission of B. T. Batsford Ltd., London.

1985, 24–30). In contrast to the relatively high population on the left bank of the Batavi and Cananefates, who served as Roman auxiliaries, it is evident from recent archaeological studies that the right-bank regions of Drenthe, Friesland, and Gröningen were sparse, isolated, and poor until the second century A.D. A study of the Dutch Eastern River area (Willems 1986, 223), for instance, speaks of the difficulties of finding enough food locally to feed the army as one reason the Roman advance was halted (Van Es 1967, 527, 531; Groenman–van Waateringe 1980, 1040).

Although, therefore, Tacitus says that the Frisii beyond the Rhine had their land "marked out" and that they provided tribute for the army, at one stage even being controlled by a fort (Tac. *Ann.* 11.19, 4.72), they were never annexed. Upstream, despite the difficult evidence, maps of early Germanic artifacts (fig. 22), graves, and botanical remains seem to indicate a striking lack of habitation in the German Mittelpfalz and Franken regions of northern Bavaria, and relatively empty zones in East Hessen and Lower Saxony.[37] Farther east there is again nothing in the Bavarian and Bohemian woods of the Oberpfalz. Tacitus's description of a land "bristling with forests and foul with swamps" (*aut silvis horrida aut paludibus foeda, Germ.* 5) remains valid despite some small areas of quite rich open cultivation, plus many relics of iron smelting and extensive cattle raising (Jankuhn 1961–63; Parker-Pierson 1984, 208). Only along the Lippe-Ruhr valley—the so-called Hellweg—and in the Main-Taunus salient is there any evidence of habitation in depth, where the Rheinwesergermanische-Gruppe were settled, who may not even have been German speakers (see above).

It cannot have been an accident that it was in just these regions of high population and food production along the Neckar, Main, and Taunus that the Romans did advance under the Flavian emperors. The Taunus-Wetterau salient and the Main-Neckar are the regions that have produced the greatest concentration of late La Tène cremation cemeteries and hill forts as well as of Roman pre-Flavian artifacts of any sector along the Rhine front.[38] Even if the *oppida* had been abandoned when the Romans arrived—which is by no means certain—the Roman advance in this sector supports the now generally accepted view that the German *Völkerwanderung*

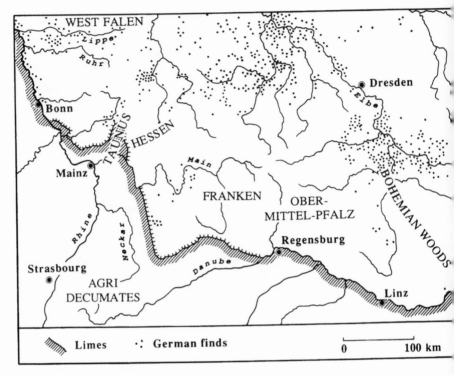

Fig. 22. German artifacts found beyond the Roman frontiers of the Rhinelands. Note the relatively empty quarter to the southwest. After R. Koch, T. Kolník, G. Mildenberger, and R. Uslar.

had not radically altered the ecological or demographic balance of the late Celtic period.

Indeed, there is some reason to believe that *oppida* survived later in the Wetterau than elsewhere, and there is evidence that hill forts like the Glauberg and Gelbeberg were still occupied after the Flavian period.[39] The only other concentration of late Celtic habitations bordering the Rhine was in the southern Schwartzwald region of the Swiss and Baden-Württemberg borders, the Gallicized territory of *Agri Decumates* that, says Tacitus, was never reckoned part of Germany but attracted many Gauls to "cultivate" the land (*Germ.* 29).

On the Danube, as we now see from the studies in the valleys of the Morava, Vah, and Vron, there were significant settlements north of Regensburg and farther east in Moravia, Slovakia, and Bohemia, which became important areas of importation of Roman goods and clearly represented regions that could support populations.[40] It was in just these territories where advances of the Roman frontier were made or contemplated. As we know, Marcus Aurelius in the later second century thought them suitable for annexation as provinces, according to his biographer (HA *Marc.* 27).

But what about Africa, which French scholars have often considered the *pons asinorum* of Anglo-Saxons who have tried to liken everything to Hadrian's Wall? Was it so very different, despite the totally different terrain and ecology? If we consider the African frontiers as zones of ecological ambiguity, then maybe the principle is not all that different. Marginal zones usually cause seasonal population movements. The African *limes*, we are assured, was, "a means of control and of regulation for movements of population and exchange of goods," never a barricade (Trousset 1980, 935; 1981, 62). That resembles closely a specialist's opinion about Hadrian's Wall saying that its function also was "to control movement not to prevent it" (Breeze and Dobson 1976, 77).

One has only to look at the north-south road running through the fort at Castle Nick on Hadrian's Wall and compare it with the *guichet* controlling the crossing of the Tebaga *clausura* in Tunisia to see the similarity (figs. 23 and 24). In fact one French archaeologist rightly draws our attention to the fact that the African frontier resembled the British not because they were frontiers of exclusion, but because they both controlled large zones beyond the visible frontiers. He concludes, "We must completely reject the idea that a barrier was erected . . . beyond which existed only a strange and hostile world" (Rebuffat 1982, 508). The myth of frontiers as iron curtains must be abandoned.

If one excludes, therefore, local tactical and strategic problems, which differed as much between the lower and upper Rhine within the German frontier as they did between Britain and Tripolitania, there is a closer parallel in ecological and demographic determinants than one might guess. The British evidence of marginal

Fig. 23. An aerial view from the north looking at Castle Nick on Hadrian's Wall. The two gates opposite each other controlled traffic across the frontier zone. Photograph by permission of N. Higham.

production and farming turns out to be surprisingly similar in principle to the evidence from Africa. The southern Tunisian and eastern Algerian dispositions lay in regions that have been described as those of "ecological ambivalence," "in the zone of bioclimatic transition between the steppes and the desert" (Trousset 1985, 65; see fig. 25). Farther west on the Mauretanian frontier of Algeria, it is striking how the forts of the Severan *limes* correspond almost exactly with what is called "the natural limit of profitable cultivation for dry farming of cereals," although the actual controls and forward posts extended over the high steppes well to the south, which were far from being barren deserts (Salama 1977, 578). In Morocco the difficult terrain of forest and marsh effectively made the Sebou the limit of military occupation, despite control of Sala and Volubilis to the south (Euzennat 1984, 377) and despite the long-distance patrols up to a hundred miles beyond (Rebuffat 1982, 485–90).

But perhaps the most dramatic new evidence about frontier lands has come out of the UNESCO Libyan Valleys Survey. It

Fig. 24. The *guichet* on the wall of Djebel Tebaga, Tunisia. It is the only fort on the wall and is designed to allow transit of traffic. The wall can be seen stretching toward the hills in the distance. Photograph by C. R. Whittaker.

shows that the Romans south of the Gebel in the third century A.D. advanced not to a fixed line of cultivation but into a zone of mixed farming, precisely as Lattimore described the Chinese frontiers. As is clear from the statistics, there was a transition from agriculture to pastoralism. On the Tarhuna-Fergian Gebel, for instance, 262 olive presses have been recorded, compared with fewer than 100 in the Wadis Sofeggin and Zem-Zem. In the valleys themselves the larger olive presses lay in the north, whereas in the south there were more stock enclosures (Mattingly 1985, 38–39; Barker and Jones 1982, 19).

Although we know less about the eastern frontier, it is fairly clear that the road of Trajan in the Jordanian sector was rather like the Africa desert frontier. It was not a line between desert and sown. "There was no clear line of demarcation," says a study of Roman Arabia, "nor should we expect to find one" (Bowersock 1983, 103). It was shown long ago by Père Poidebard, in his great study of the Syrian desert, how the line of road corresponded closely to the climatic map of the region between the 100- and

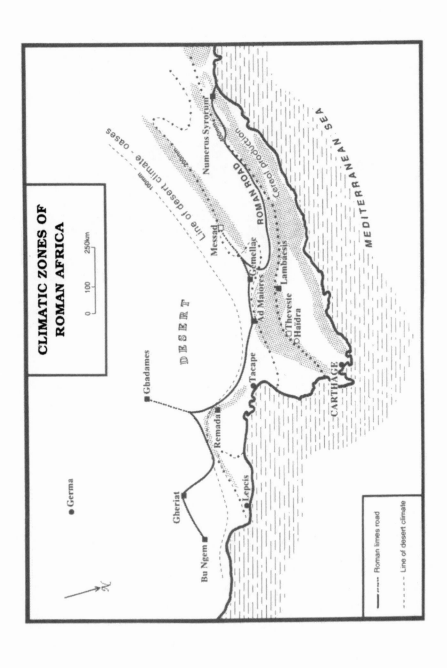

CLIMATIC ZONES OF ROMAN AFRICA

0   100   250km

DESERT

MEDITERRANEAN SEA

Line of desert climate - oases

100mm

250mm

Numerus Syrorum

ROMAN ROAD

Cereal production

Messad

Gemellae

Lambaesis

Ad Maiores

Theveste

Haïdra

CARTHAGE

Tacape

Ghadames

Remada

Lepcis

Gheriat

Bu Ngem

Germa

N

--------- Roman limes road

--------- Line of desert climate

250-millimeter isohyet lines—on the edge of the zone, that is, where there was sufficient water to attract sedentary farming (fig. 26). In this steppe region there can be abundant growth after rainfall, but it is incapable of supporting flocks once the summer heat begins, thereby causing transhumant movement up onto the high steppes of Palestine, Lebanon, and the Armenian massif. The Roman frontier road did not run along a "natural frontier" on the edge of the desert, as is sometimes claimed. It cut through a region where life was sustainable, but only seasonally, and that was usually pastoral.[41]

It was just because lands beyond the frontier were marginal that the decision where to stop was equivocal, though not accidental. Nor did history stand still. This was why Lattimore believed that though every frontier sometimes operates a "closed border policy" to control and to supervise, it is usually not to exclude. But every regime also operates a "forward policy" that negates the concept of a linear boundary and creates two frontiers (Lattimore 1940, 244). In that sense, as has been claimed of the African frontier,[42] all frontiers were "unfinished."

The administrative line of a frontier therefore did not inhibit the Romans from advancing beyond. Roman Africa was not unique. The trans-Rhine Frisii were subject to *obsequium*, says Tacitus (*Ann.* 4.72); that is, they were controlled despite never being annexed. A Roman soldier is marked on an army list in Tripolitania as working *cum Garamantibus*, but the Garamantes were never part of the formal province (Marichal 1979, 451). The Anavonienses of North Solway were given a census in the Trajanic period at a time when frontier stakes were planted to the south.[43] The two official Antonine itineraries of Britain that claim to run from the line of the wall (*a limite, id est a vallo praetorio*), in reality started at High Rochester and Birrens some thirty to forty kilometers north

Fig. 25 (opposite). An unusual perspective of Roman Africa, showing the isohyet lines of rainfall. The frontier road and forts were more or less between the 200- and 100-millimeter isohyet lines, where pastoral life was possible but difficult. The limit of dry cereal farming is at about 400 millimeters of rain. From Trousset 1987; reproduced by the author's permission.

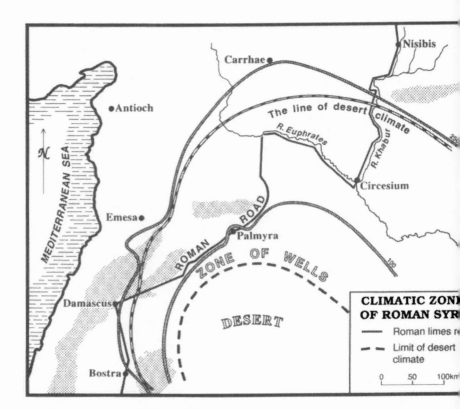

Fig. 26. On the Syrian and northern Arabian frontier the climatic zones show how the road to Mesopotamia ran between the 100- and 250-millimeter isohyet lines, a region of pastoralism and transhumance. After Poidebard 1934.

of the wall. It was perhaps this element of marginality that led Marcus Aurelius to contemplate annexing Moravia and Bohemia, only to have his decision reversed by Commodus in return for supplies and safeguards (HA *Marc.* 27; Hdn. 1.6.8; cf. Whittaker 1983, 119–20).

This illustrates the problems of supply posed by marginal lands. If one plausible reason for advancing the boundary of Britain to the Forth-Clyde line was to take advantage of the economic prosperity of the Votadini and their food supply, as has been proposed (Hanson and Maxwell 1983, 68), it is equally plausible that the

Romans retired to Hadrian's Wall so soon after, just as Commodus had done in Marcomannia, because annexation brought no advantage in supplies. The society in lowland Scotland was not socially structured to produce enough for Roman armies.[44] Nevertheless, the Romans faced a dilemma. The very existence of stability created by a frontier, and the prosperity that frontiers brought in terms of goods and markets changed and developed the social and ecological conditions that, as I have argued in this chapter, halted the progress of the imperial armies. Either frontiers expanded to incorporate these new regions, or the frontiers themselves came under attack and pressure. That was the dilemma. So supplies and frontiers are an important subject, which I shall discuss in the next chapter.

Four

Economy and Society
of the Frontiers

n A.D. 4, after Tiberius, the future emperor, had advanced deep
into Germany and eventually arrived at the river Elbe, the thing
that impressed his staff officer Velleius Paterculus most was his
"wonderful fortune and care" because he arranged for the fleet
to meet him at the Elbe, "bringing with it a great abundance
of all kinds of supplies" (Vell. Pat. 2.106). A century later Hadrian, who was famous as a military planner and traveler and by
whose "divine order" (RIB 1051) the line of Hadrian's Wall was
chosen, "worked hard," according to his biographer, "to learn
about military stores, carefully examining also what came in from
the provinces, so as to supplement whatever was difficult" (HA
Hadr. 11.1).

These two examples are enough to prove to me that frontier
supply, on which I shall concentrate in this chapter, was a factor
no Roman general or emperor could afford to ignore and that the
provisions they made in locating suitable sites for their camps
were certainly not accidental. That is the main objection to the
"accidental theory" of frontiers, discussed in the previous chapter.
It is similar to the objections put forward against the well-known
thesis that a Roman emperor never acted but only reacted, because
it ignores the initiative that emperors took in warfare.[1]

Frontiers and Supplies

In the previous chapter I insisted that rivers formed a prominent part of Roman frontier ideology not because they presented barriers to barbarians but because, as Curzon saw, "they connect rather than separate," creating essential routes of access. Delbrück, in his great *Geschichte der Kriegskunst im Rahmen der politischen Geschichte*, pointed out that the Roman legionary fort at Xanten on the Rhine was located at that point not to maintain hegemony in the region but to serve as a supply depot at the confluence of the Rhine and Lippe "for a march into the interior" (Delbrück 1990, 2:59–60). Being a pupil of Clausewitz, he had learned that "the defensive is the stronger form of making war"—a sharp contrast with the disciples of Ratzel, noted in the introduction, who regarded the establishment of fixed frontiers as evidence of weakness.

The point Delbrück makes is so obvious that it sometimes escapes consideration; namely, that the Euphrates, the Danube, and the Rhine existed primarily not as *points d'arrêt* but as a "logistic frontier" (A.H.M. Jones 1964, 844). If, as has been recently estimated, it was impossible for the Cananefates (marked on fig. 33)—a community of about 14,000 persons—in southern Holland to sustain some 16,000 to 22,000 military personnel (including dependent *vici*) in that region, even after the region developed in the second century A.D., clearly river supplies were not merely desirable but an essential lifeline when the Romans arrived.[2] That was the theme of Eric Gren's study of imports from the Asian provinces to the Balkan armies along the Danube. The imposition of about 120,000 soldiers on the Danube lands between Vienna and the Dobrudja would have fallen as an almost impossibly heavy burden on the relatively sparsely populated Danubian provinces if they had to raise their food production to meet the demand.[3]

Ian Richmond, one of the great frontier archaeologists, noted in his study of Trajan's army that all the frontier legionary forts were on rivers.[4] But they were for supply, not defense. Trajan's forts on the right bank of the Danube in the Dobrudja, for example, were built at a time when the Roman army was at one of its most aggressive and expansive phases beyond the river (Barnea and

Ştefan 1974). The same is true of the Euphrates; its "defenses" were improved by Trajan just as he advanced far to the east of the river line (Mitford 1980, 1198–99).

That was no accident. Nor was it because the rivers were considered frontiers. We have many examples, some cited in later chapters, of how the rivers were used for transport of essential supplies. An interesting idea put forward about the upper Euphrates—which as far as I know still lacks precise confirmation—is that the Black Sea and the road from Trebizond to the headwaters of the river were a grain route to the eastern armies from Nero's time onward.[5] That would certainly explain why the military installations in a barren region like Armenia stuck close to the river. One simple reason, in addition to the ecological problems discussed earlier, why the Elbe was never a serious possibility as Rome's northern boundary is that, though the Rhine could be reached easily by the inland Rhône-Moselle river system, the Elbe could be reached only by the long journey through the North Sea, which Germanicus found to his cost was treacherous and, says Tacitus, "stormier than other seas" (*Ann.* 2.24).

It is for this reason—to digress for a moment—that I am unconvinced by a recent interesting study of military supplies—the *annona militaris*—that Spanish Baetican oil usually came to the Rhine by the Atlantic, through the dangerous Bay of Biscay, rather than by the longer but safer Mediterranean and Rhône route.[6] Even had the army calculated the cost on the sort of economic scales we use (about which I am skeptical: When did an army ever think in these cost-effective terms?), it would still have been 30 to 40 percent more expensive to reach the upper Rhine camps by the Atlantic sea route. True, it would have been about 50 percent cheaper to reach Britain, if one measures the cost strictly by distance and mode of travel (cf. fig. 29).[7] But such a calculation takes no account of the high capital cost of deep-sea ships against river barges (Hopkins 1983, 101).

In any case, a lot of the goods were carried by extraeconomic use of either civilian corvée or military shipping, as inscriptions and ancient authors record on the Danube and the Rhine.[8] Requisition of transport and the compulsory burden of accompanying it (called *prosecutio* or, in Greek, *parapompe*) is well documented because it provoked quite a number of complaints.[9] The reliefs on the tombstones at Nijmagen showing ships carrying wine barrels depict military, not civilian, transports. Wrecks from Zwammerdam and Guernsey show that cheap native barges could carry grain across the English Channel.[10] From the unusual distribution of stamped military bricks and tiles of the *classis Britannica*, which are found moving from England to France, and from the tiles of the legion at Xanten, which traveled two hundred kilometers upstream, we can plausibly conclude that both were being carried as ballast in empty ships returning from carrying military supplies (Peacock 1982, 145–46).

Of course some Spanish oil did come by the Atlantic route, as we can see from the increasing evidence of the famous onion-shaped Spanish oil amphorae (Dressel 20) on and off the coasts of Brittany and Normandy. But most of the evidence of distribution en route makes it impossible to doubt that exotic supplies usually reached the German and British armies by the Rhône-Rhine axis. We have only to see the distribution maps of the Mediterranean wine amphorae, typed as Pelichet 47 (Dressel 30-Gauloise 4; fig. 27) (Peacock and Williams 1986, fig. 21), or the evidence of barrels and barrel-making involved in transshipment of wine, which follow a similar pattern, to confirm this (Boon 1975, fig. 3).

It follows from the theory of economic marginality, which I presented in chapter 3, that it was impossible for the army, even in the period of greatest provincial development, to rely totally on the vagaries of the local market for its supplies. This was all the more so, therefore, in the early phases of occupation. Vegetius, the military theorist of the later empire, said that hunger is fiercer than the sword (*ferro saevior fames est*; 3.3)—as every general knows.

The high variability of wheat yields in the ancient world made imports inevitable, even if we believe the theory that each camp possessed a *territorium, (militarisches Nutzland)* sufficient for its needs.[11] Such a theory—based on distribution of military tile and brick stamps—has been seriously challenged, however, and does

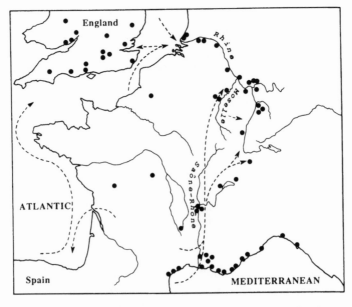

Fig. 27. Military supply routes to the western Roman armies and the distribution of "Gauloise 4" amphorae, showing that they were exported principally for military use. After Peacock and Williams 1986, 65, and Middleton 1979.

not find support in regional studies. A recent study of Batavia, for instance, concludes that the lands "were never able to provide the necessary food for all the soldiers stationed there" (Willems 1986, 189–92, 264, etc.; Vittinghoff 1976). Even when the land was theoretically able to feed the extra soldiers, as a recent study of the Roman frontier in Wales calculates from Iron Age agricultural sites, botanical studies of wheat grains at Caerleon fort in the early second century have revealed the presence of Mediterranean weeds (M. L. Jones 1984, 43–45; Helback 1964). Theoretical calculations about the land area required to feed an army unit almost always ignore two important factors: the capriciousness of the climate and the difficulty of raising productivity among a subsistence community. A military commander, however, could not ignore them.

The problem of quantities was compounded because wheat was

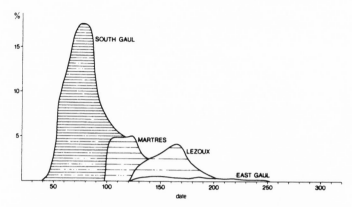

Fig. 28. British imports of *terra sigillata* pottery from Gaul and Germany. This pottery was of low value and therefore generally accompanied other perishable or more valuable imports, especially grain. From Fulford 1984.

the staple for Roman soldiers but more rarely produced by local farmers. Deposits from the latrines at Bearsden fort in Scotland support the view that the soldiers' diet was mainly vegetarian and that the wheat was almost certainly not local (Breeze 1984, 269, and 1989, 228; Knights et al. 1983). That evidence can be supplemented from a number of other sites on the northern frontier, where wheat grains have been discovered in earlier periods when local culture almost certainly was producing only barley (Groenman-van Waateringe 1989, 99–100). Imported *terra sigillata* pottery in London is now recognized as usually the visible sign of other cargoes, mainly of foods and cloth, which supplied the British army until at least the late second century (Fulford 1984, fig. 1) (fig. 28). The same is true of both Belgica and Bulgaria, where local ceramics did not replace imported ware until the later second century. This does not, of course, exclude the well-known fact, which has been illustrated in Britain, that as soon as the army arrived at a new camp it set about either making pottery through its own craftsmen or stimulating native potters to increase production where a local tradition existed.[12]

That we find imported amphorae on every Roman campsite proves by itself that no military unit was ever completely self-sufficient. But a study of the military fort at Bearsden, on the

Antonine Wall in Scotland, has shown dramatically just how much extra the army of northern Britain needed in addition to oil, wine, and wheat. The author calculates that 10,000 horses and 4,000 mules were needed for the British army, plus 12,000 calves per annum for replacement of leather tents as well as 2,000 animals a year for sacrifice (using the Roman military calendar, the *Feriale Duranum*, found on the Euphrates frontier [Breeze 1984]). This meant that enormous quantities of barley and fodder were required, far more than any hypothetical *prata legionis* (the term used for grazing lands attached to the camp) or military *territorium* could have provided.

Without imports the army could not have functioned at all in the early days of occupation, since no local community could suddenly have started to produce the surpluses required to feed the troops. We would expect imports to have gradually declined over time as domestic production increased, always excepting the fact that certain products, such as olive oil and wine in Britain, could never have been obtained on the spot. That seems to be confirmed by the imports of *terra sigillata* into London, which can be seen on the chart of imports (fig. 28). Assuming, as we did before, that cheap pottery was a marker for food imports, the early quantities in the mid-first century were reduced to virtually nil by the early third century. That makes sense, since we know that Britain became an important net exporter of grain in the later Empire.[13]

Supplies and Suppliers

But while it is relatively banal to prove that the frontier armies attracted long-distance supplies, a more interesting question is how such supplies reached them. There is no convincing proof that the entire provincial *annona militaris* was coordinated by the *praefectus annonae* in Rome, as Theodore Mommsen originally argued in 1887 to prove the existence of a state bureau a *copiis*. The theme was taken up later by Denis van Berchem (1937) when he put forward the theory that supplies were the responsibility of the imperial office "*a rationibus*" through local governors and procurators. The most that can be demonstrated with certainty from a study of Spanish oil distribution (which is nevertheless an important contribution) is that there were specific links between various Rhine forts, like Saalberg, Mainz, and Nijmegen, with individual oil shippers or estates in Spain—enough to deduce "a directed commerce" or at least "preferred commercial relationships."[14] We can confirm that fact from the papyrus called "Hunt's *Pridianum*," the annual personnel return submitted by a military unit in Moesia, which shows rather surprisingly that agents were sent out by the unit to Gaul to get supplies.[15]

There is a good deal of support for this conclusion from evidence of other supplies. Ironically, the evidence comes not from the economic distribution of commodities, as some archaeologists believe, but from their *noneconomic* distribution. So, for instance, color-coated fine pottery found in the fort at Usk in South Wales was imported from a number of different production centers—from Italy, Spain, Gaul, and the Rhineland. But though the pottery is all of similar quality, the least amount comes from the closest source on the Rhine (Greene 1979, 139). The same is true of *terra sigillata* coming into London from southern, central, and eastern Gaul; the least came from the nearest centers.[16]

Similarly, Campanian (Dressel 2–4) wine amphorae are found almost exclusively on the northern frontiers, rarely in the Gallic interior, despite the availability of Spanish and Gallic wine in amphorae of the same type.[17] Obviously this could mean that there was simply a preference for Italian wine. But that would not account for the highly specialized distribution of two particular fabrics of Rhodian amphorae, found almost exclusively on pre-Flavian sites in Britain that coincide with Claudius's military invasion and not found in Germany. It has been suggested that this distribution could be associated with the tribute newly imposed by Claudius on Rhodes, which seems a most attractive idea (Peacock and Williams 1986, 62). It is evident the wine did not reach Britain by normal commercial transactions.

Others have drawn attention to the particular forms of amphorae carrying garum (Pelichet 46, Dressel 7–11, forms C, D, E), found only at Vindonissa and elsewhere in Switzerland, despite the widespread existence of other forms of garum amphorae in western Europe (Ettlinger 1977, 10). Distribution of that sort must be caused either by special monopolies or by state subsidies. It is not the distribution created by free market competition and a market open to all sellers.

The most interesting evidence that military traffic to the Rhine and Britain went principally by the Rhône-Rhine axis comes from the uneven distribution of inscriptions commemorating trading by the *negotiatores* and the freedmen frequently involved in trade, the *seviri augustales* (fig. 29). Their monuments show that these men probably represented the richer members of their professions. Again, by far the most have been found along the military routes— "the privileged directions" leading to the northern frontiers— though the existence of amphorae on the Narbonne-Bordeaux axis or along the Loire-Seine shows that traders of a lesser scale certainly used these other routes (Middleton 1979; Goudineau 1980, 376).

It is difficult to resist the conclusion, then, that these men were contractors of either shipping or supplies with the army, even if perhaps not quite "agents of the imperial government" (as Rostovtzeff believed, 1957, 166). They were no doubt like Secundus, the man recorded on a Greek inscription in Lydia with what looks almost like a formal title of *pragmateuomenos . . . parakheimastikois legionōn* in the second century (*AE* 1939, 132), which seems to mean he was "a businessman for winter supplies of the legions." There is nothing to show whether he was a civilian or a soldier, but in the opinion of some experts "this refers to a man who was concerned with supplying the legions in their quarters during the winter."[18]

I am a loss to know why the notion that military supplies were obtained through the open market seems to be gaining currency. The influential study of the fort at Bearsden, to which I referred earlier, has persuaded a number of scholars that because of the variety of pottery types on the Antonine Wall, military supplies were almost exclusively brought by "traveling salesmen" to the *vici* and sold at market prices (Breeze 1977). But if we look at the distribution of cheap kitchen pottery in Britain, such as the so-called Black Burnished ware in the second century and later, it

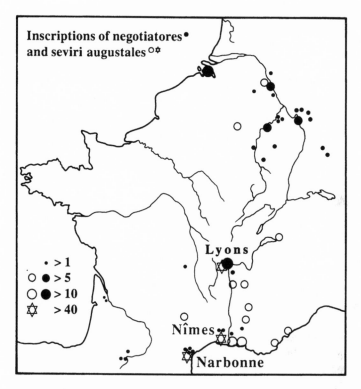

Fig. 29. The distribution in Gaul of inscriptions of *negotiatores* (traders) and freedmen *augustales*, who often took part in trade. Lyons in the center and Narbonne in the south were important distribution points for military supplies. Note the near absence of inscriptions on the rivers other than those used for frontier supply. After Middleton 1979 and Goudineau 1980.

does not look like a true market distribution at all. One fabric arrived on the western part of the northern frontier from Dorset and the other fabric came to the eastern part from the Thames estuary and East Anglia.

It is true that the Dorset ware was sent to many long-distance civilian sites in western Britain too; nevertheless, a large proportion was produced for the military market. More significantly, the eastern ware hardly went to any civilian sites, apart from purely local ones. But it was supplied in quantities to the army of the north, at first almost exclusively to the soldiers on the Antonine Wall and subsequently, when they moved, to other army sites. The same general pattern of distribution is also true of the distribution of *mortaria* (grinding bowls) in Britain, which missed out the civilian regions between local production sites and the northern army (fig. 30).

The authors of the studies of these two ceramics conclude—in my view rightly—that "military contracts played a part."[19] My guess is that the ceramics came with grain, which ceased to arrive from the Continent just at this period (cf. fig. 28) and was probably now being produced in southern Britain in sufficient quantity to feed the army. The abrupt end of imports of Dorset Black Burnished ware to Hadrian's Wall after 367 may in part be due, as has been suggested, to the insecurity of sea routes. But the western coast of Britain was not much under attack and more probably we ought to look to changes in military procurement to explain the change.

It is certainly possible to find examples where the state placed direct contracts for food and military equipment, many of them preserved in papyrus records from Egypt, such as that for uniforms and blankets (e.g., *P. Berl.* 1564). Army officers and soldiers are also recorded collecting the food and clothing, although it must have been rather unusual to go as far afield as the example quoted earlier from Hunt's *Pridianum* (Fink 1971, no. 63). On the same papyrus some men of the unit were recorded nearer home in the Haemus Mountains in the Balkans fetching cattle.[20] Compulsory requisitions were frequently made for a variety of goods from grain to camels to shield covers, often for payment, but sometimes as an extra tax indiction. All this is too well known to need further comment from me.[21]

None of these examples, however, are incompatible with the existence of middlemen, called variously traders (*negotiatores*) or contractors (*conductores*), who bid for public contracts, not to produce but to provide supplies. The history of Roman civil and military procurement and supply was based on a system of civil contract, *locatio-conductio*, whose existence in the second century A.D. disproves the view that the system had been taken over by the state. An example is the *conductores faenarii* recorded on a

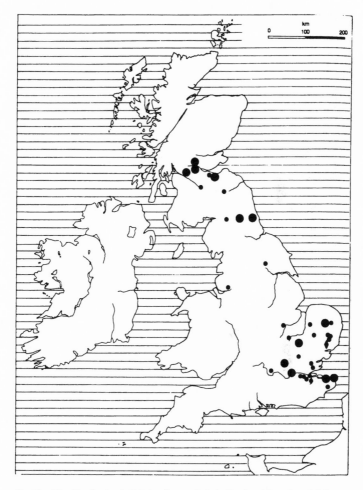

Fig. 30.   The distribution in Britain of *mortaria* (grinding bowls) made at Colchester in the second century A.D. They were obviously exported largely to the army in the north. From Peacock 1982, 102, after Hartley 1973. Reproduced by permission of Longman Higher Education, Harlow.

papyrus dated to 130, the hay contractors, who were given a receipt by the *procurator* attached to a cavalry unit (Fink 1971, no. 80).

But in one record of A.D. 90 we find a *conductor* actually on the strength of the third Cyrenaican legion in Egypt (Fink 1971, no. 58), and in 192 someone's job was listed in a military unit as *in quaesturam pro contuctione (sic*, meaning "looking for contracts"?). That perhaps means it was quite common for civilian contractors to be attached to army units. We know, for instance, of Julius Caesar's agent C. Fufius Cita, who accompanied him "for the sake of business" (*negotiandi causa*) on his Gallic campaign and who, writes Caesar, "was in charge of the supply of grain on Caesar's orders" (*qui rei frumentariae iussu Caesaris praeerat ; BG* 7.3.1). A similar man, M. Solarius Sabinus, appears on an inscription in Hadrian's day, apparently attached to the army *eis tas annonas* ("in charge of supplies"; *AE* 1921, 1).

This quasi-official position of military traders receives some support archaeologically. In Belgium the organization of the early villages or *vici* at Bavay, Tongres and so on suggests they may have been centers for "*negotiatores* working for the army" (Mertens 1983, 163). But were these free market traders? We have quite a lot of evidence from military camps and their nearby *vici* of courtyards that have been called marketplaces for "licensed merchants" (Greene 1984, 411–12; cf. G.D.B. Jones 1984, 78). But there is one piece of evidence that has emerged from Corbridge on Hadrian's Wall that, if correctly reported, must be against these being free markets. There the so-called pottery shop burned down at a time when it was stocked with *terra sigillata*, color-coated pottery, and *mortaria*. But although the date of the fire is proved by coins to have been in the fourth century, some of the pottery is dated in the report from the third and even the second century.[22] If true, that must surely be decisive. How could any *negotiator* have run a commercial enterprise with such a slow turnover?

If, as I began by saying, no prudent emperor could leave the supplies for the army to chance, and certainly not to the hazards of whether traders and the market thought it worthwhile taking up such contracts, we ought to find—as we do in the supply of food, the *annona*, to Rome—some evidence of state encouragement to traders. Vegetius is explicit about the way the emperors (and, I assume, their generals) "are especially concerned that whatever seems needed by the army should not be short in the camp" (2. 11). The legal evidence concerning military supplies and *negotiatores* makes it fairly clear that this happened by manipulation of the system of contracts. In the *Digest*, for instance, we read:

> Concerning goods that governors order to be transported for themselves, the deified Hadrian wrote that whenever a person sends someone to purchase them for the use of commanders of provinces or for armies . . . he shall sign a note [*libellus*] with his own hand and send it to the customs man [*publicanus*] so that if he transfers more than is ordered it shall be liable to tax. (*Dig.* [Paulus] 39.4.4.1)

The implication is that goods for military and government personnel came in tax free and to order: "It is deemed that goods prepared for the army shall not be liable to tax levies," said the law (*res exercitui paratas praestitioni vectigalium subici non placet; Dig.* [Paulus] 39.4.9.7). In another law we hear of concessions to traders in grain, *frumentariis negotiatoribus* (*Dig.* [Paulus] 50.5.9.1), although not explicitly referring to military supplies. Governors could also control *negotiatores* by having the right to exclude persons from *negotia publica* (*Dig.* [Ulpian] 48.19.9.8), which I assume to be public contracts of all types.

Although the laws quoted here were not formulated before the mid-second century A.D., it would be wrong to suppose the principle of tax concessions for essential supplies began only then. An inscription concerning requisitioning of transport in Pisidia dates from the reign of Tiberius and makes it clear that "those who carry grain or anything similar" (*qui frumentum aut aliquid tale . . . portant*) were not permitted to demand free transport if the goods were for private use or for sale.[23] The contrast between official contracts and private supplies is evident, so there is no doubt that state supplies were subsidized.

But we can go further. All these laws show that they were often honored in the breach. The very need to issue such an instruction indicates that the same men who contracted for official supplies used state transport for their private profit if they could get away with it. It must have often been quite impossible for the customs officers to separate a public from a private cargo. But even if tax was paid on the supplementary cargo, as the decree insists, the transport for both public and private supplies was the same and would have effectively given a subsidy to the goods that came to the market. Military contracts made men rich, not for the last time in history.

The civilian market, of course, contributed greatly to the profitability of the military contract, particularly since, as most now agree, transporters almost always carried mixed cargoes. If it is correct that the lead tags (*anabolici*) marked *R.C.* found at Lyons stand for *ratio castrensis*—that is, the "military account"—they were perhaps to identify such military supplies for tax concessions in mixed cargoes. The same would explain the barrels at Budapest marked *immune in r(ationem) val(etudinarii)*, tax free because they were destined for the military hospital (Laet 1949, 430; Davies 1981, 219). From outside the province remission of the provincial *portoria* tax brought an immense advantage to the lucky contractor, since *portoria* taxes existed on entry to every province, Roman city, and military camp. In most provinces they were between 2 and 2.5 percent, still leaving good profits for the suppliers.[24] The value of the military contract explains why we find such a concentration of inscriptions set up by wealthy *negotiatores* along the military supply routes.

The distribution of goods and the private contractual character of the arrangements for procurement and transport look almost as if units arranged their own supplies. That is the lesson of the study of Spanish amphorae, and it helps explain the noneconomical distribution of commodities.[25] The grant of tax concessions must have meant that, quite apart from the attraction of the military market for traders, along with the goods destined for the military market commodities were drawn to the civilian sector of the frontier regions and places en route that would not otherwise have been supplied commercially. A study of British imports seems to show no difference in the character of the supplies of the Dressel 20 oil amphorae going to towns in Britain from those going to military sites. Does this mean that the army purchased its oil "from the system operating to supply the civil market," as the authors of the study suggest (Williams and Peacock 1983, 270)? Or was it not rather the other way around? In short, frontier regions of a province benefited from a subsidized market and the trickle-down effect of a military economy.

Supplies from across the Frontiers

This brings me to the second part of my theme for this chapter, which is the other side of the coin: the source of frontier supplies from local resources and the general social and political effect this had on the frontiers as zones of interaction.

There are plenty of examples of how Roman traders and military personnel on the frontiers collected supplies both locally and from beyond the frontier. On the lower Rhine Tacitus tells us that in A.D. 69, when Brinno the Cananefates leader called upon the Frisians to attack the Romans, the area was swarming with *lixae* and *negotiatores* (*Hist.* 4.15). Almost certainly, therefore, this occurred both north and south of the Rhine, and the inclusion of the term *lixae* (often translated loosely as "camp follower")[26] implies that both groups had a military connection. This is confirmed by the famous wax tablet containing a contract found at Tolsum in Friesland (*FIRA* 3.37). It is written in crude Latin and concerns the purchase of cattle by a certain Gargilius Secundus, who looks like a military purchaser, since he was assisted by two centurions as witnesses. The native seller, whose name is difficult to reconstruct, lived in what the tablet calls a *vila* (note the misspelling). It was probably a large estate, since *villa* happens to be the word Tacitus also used to describe the domain of the Frisian chieftain Cruptorix, once a Roman auxiliary, which housed four hundred Roman soldiers. It was no small cottage (*Ann.* 4.73).

Apart from purchases, the Romans imposed a tribute of oxhides on the Frisii (Tac. *Ann.* 4.72). On Hunt's *Pridianum*, to which I have referred a number of times, some of the men of the Danube unit are recorded as going "across the Danube on an expedition" in A.D. 105 and also "to defend the *annona.*" Though we cannot tell whether this was tributary grain, it could have been coming from the rich plains of Wallachia across the Danube, where two outposts of Buridava and Piroboridava are mentioned in the papyrus text.[27] On the Tripolitanian frontier ostraca record Libyan Garamantes "bringing four mules" and perhaps camel loads of grain (Rebuffat 1977, 408, and 1982, 505, with further references).

All these supplies came from beyond what is conventionally called the frontier. Yet in the case of the Danube unit's *pridianum* the soldiers' duty is specifically listed under the heading *intra provinciam*. The long arm of a Roman procurator stretched also past the German frontier. At Cannstatt east of the Neckar a Greek inscription refers to a procurator of the *chora hyperlimitane* (*ILS* 8855), which ought to mean "land beyond the *limes*." In Algeria the unusually low *portorium* customs tax of under 0.5 percent on cattle at Zarai was set "with the aim of favoring commerce between neighboring peoples" (Cagnat 1882, 74). Two inscriptions of auxiliary units found near Jedburgh about fifty kilometers north of Hadrian's Wall show that patrols controlled such *Vorlimes* regions (Frere 1967, 181).

Archaeological evidence supports these records of symbiosis and exploitation beyond the frontiers. North of Hadrian's Wall in Northumberland and East Lothian, signs of both grain and cattle culture increase significantly after Roman occupation—carbonized grain, pollen evidence of land clearance, stock pens, and sheep shears. The Roman style of rotary quern is "ubiquitous" (Macinnes 1984, 194; Jobey 1982, 15). There is a zone some thirty kilometers deep beyond the wall where the settlements look almost as though ordered by imperial control (Jobey 1966, 6). The crop marks around the native *oppidum* of the Votadini at Traprain Law give archaeologists the impression of "its agricultural potential with a view to provisioning the garrisons," while in the other direction Roman fine pottery reached Traprain "in quantity."[28] Perhaps the bundle of cowhides found in the Roman fort at Cramond in Scotland was tribute, like that given by the Frisians (Jobey 1982, 14). Among the Frisians "villa" was obviously the name Romans gave to the long German *Hallenhaus* type of wooden house that became so prominent by the late second century A.D. on the sandy *geest*

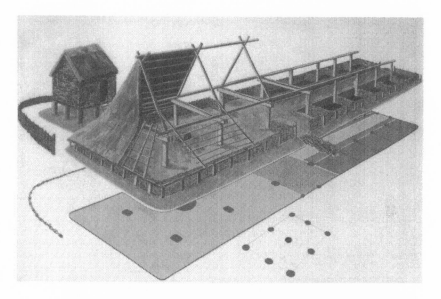

Fig. 31. An artist's reconstruction of a farm building at Feddersen Wierde, Germany, typical of many "longhouse" farms north of the Rhine, with cattle stalls and a detached grain store. Photograph by permission of W. Haio Zimmermann.

and clay *terpen* of Holland and northern Saxony, like the example found at Feddersen Wierde (fig. 31). They were often grouped around a larger central *Herrenhof* and devoted mainly to raising cattle (fig. 36; cf. the map in fig. 33).

"Villa" has also been used to describe a series of Roman-looking buildings among the Suebian peoples across the whole length of the middle Danube between Vienna and the Danube bend, in the valleys of the Morava (March), Váh, and Hron rivers of Moravia and Slovakia, often far beyond the northern borders of Pannonia (fig. 32).[29] The precise purpose and inhabitants of these buildings are still not resolved; it is not clear whether they were Roman military and trade stations or were inhabited by German princes— as most or all certainly were by the later empire. Some clearly were connected with Marcus Aurelius's Marcomannian wars, but some were built earlier and others later. At Cifer-Pác, for instance, the "villa" contained German (and Roman) pottery and was

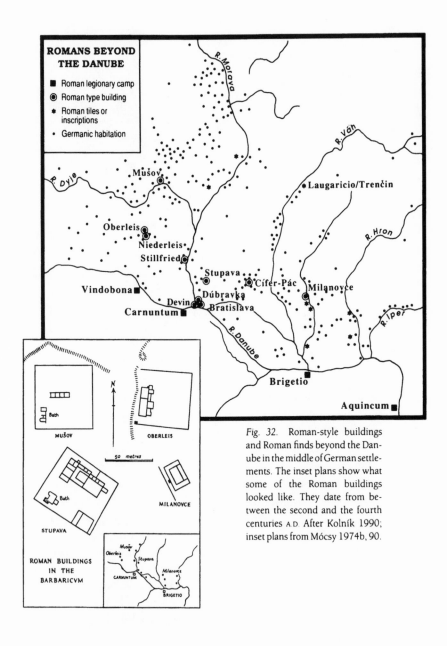

ROMANS BEYOND
THE DANUBE

■ Roman legionary camp
◉ Roman type building
✳ Roman tiles or inscriptions
• Germanic habitation

R. Morava

R. Váh

R. Dyle

Mušov

Laugaricio/Trenčin

R. Hron

Oberleis

Niederleis

Stillfried

Stupava

Cífer-Pác

Milanovce

Vindobona

Devin

Dúbravka

Bratislava

Carnuntum

R. Danube

R. Iper

Brigetio

Aquincum

MUŠOV

Bath

N

OBERLEIS

50 metres

MILANOVCE

Bath

STUPAVA

ROMAN BUILDINGS
IN THE
BARBARICVM

Mušov
Oberleis
Stupava
CARNVNTVM
Milanovce
BRIGETIO

Fig. 32. Roman-style buildings
and Roman finds beyond the Danube in the middle of German settlements. The inset plans show what
some of the Roman buildings
looked like. They date from between the second and the fourth
centuries A.D. After Kolník 1990;
inset plans from Mócsy 1974b, 90.

surrounded by a wooden enclosure and Germanic huts with sunken floors (*Grubenhäuser*), which make it look like a chieftain's house (Kolník 1990, 783; Pitts 1989, 53–54). But at the site of Mušov, on a tributary of the Morava, the discovery of Roman armor and weapons, plus legionary tiles of the late second century, suggests it was a Roman outpost, although even here the presence of a fine princely tomb nearby shows that their relations with Germans were close.[30]

The important thing to note about these Romanized buildings is the quantity of Roman artifacts inside, which must have been traded against local goods. One such early trader in that part of the world, Q. Atilius Primus, known from an inscription in Slovakia, announces himself as a former soldier and interpreter turned *negotiator* (*AE* 1978, 635). Another early example of traders comes from the land of the Marcomannian king Marobodus. Tacitus describes how when a rival, Cataulda, broke into the "palace" fortress of the king "he found the long-accumulated plunder of the Suebi, as well as camp followers and traders who had been attracted to an enemy's land" (*Ann.* 2.62). I regard this "palace" as a good description of the other Suebian examples found by archaeologists, where princes and Roman traders lived side by side.

When we come to ask what was traded, the answers are not easy. There was always the attraction of the amber route, which brought Roman traders north of the Danube. But these valleys were also rich in agricultural produce, and it would have been surprising had the army not availed itself of the facility. Most of the "villas" have roof tiles marked with legionary stamps. One, at Stupava in the Morava valley, had a *horreum* (grain store), thought to have been built by the army for the Marcomannian war but presumably used thereafter for export of grain.[31] Roman pottery in some of the "Ringwall" *oppida* twenty to thirty kilometers beyond the middle Rhine *limes* of the Wetterau and Main are perhaps parallel signs of control and symbiosis beyond the frontiers (Todd 1987, 15–16).

These "villas" make me think of the *opus Africanum* buildings now recognized as farms, not forts, in the Tebaga corridor of Tunisia and in the Libyan valleys, and of the mausolea of Garamantes chiefs well beyond the line of military advance in Tripolitania (Mattingly 1987, 84–85). They too are full of Roman pottery and are described as "symbols of a symbiosis." So stable were they that after the military withdrawal from the forward forts of Castellum Dimmidi, Bu Ngem, Gheria, and other forts in the third century these local elites continued to maintain Roman rule and sovereignty in those regions (Rebuffat 1982, 502, 509).

The desert frontiers of both Africa and Arabia were similar in that transhumant seminomads regularly crossed into Roman territory. In the case of Africa we can begin to guess at what sort of exchange and symbiotic relations existed from the customs list at Zarai and the ostraca discovered at Bu Ngem—the latter, of course, establishing a direct link with the army. In Arabia, as far as I can tell, similar information is not available. A somewhat fruitless debate has been conducted about "mutualism" between the desert and the sown and to what extent relations between them were peaceful or controlled by Roman force (Banning 1986, 1987; Parker 1987b, 1991). Neither side denies the sort of symbiotic benefits that usually accrue when shepherds bring their labor and their flocks to harvest, and later to fertilize, the farmers' lands. But it remains unclear whether any of the transfrontier produce of pastoralists (meat, wool, etc.) supplied the army. The Romans certainly needed camels and horses and used Saracen cavalry extensively in the later empire. The transformation of the Roman infantry into a cavalry-based army almost certainly owed something to the availability of horses and cavalry techniques acquired from the nomadic border folk.[32] But that is about as far as we can go.

There is no way of determining what proportion of the military requirements were raised locally and how much came from beyond the frontiers. In both the Rhineland and Pannonia, bone evidence proves the increase in size of cattle as a result of Roman breeding, which in Pannonia, at least, spread beyond the Danube frontier (Petrikovits 1980b, 127; Bökönyi 1988). But there is no obvious conclusion to be drawn from this concerning supplies to the army. Certainly the impression one gets from Holland, Africa, and Britain is that the main items imported from beyond the frontier were cattle, horses, and sheep, for which, as we saw, the army created a huge demand. That no doubt provided an incentive to improve the quality of the stock. In exchange, where this was not simply tribute, the attraction must have been grain.

This impression is supported by the ancient sources, since both Caesar (*BG* 6.10.22) and Tacitus (*Germ.* 14.26) comment on the shortage of grain or unwillingness to exploit agriculture fully among the free Germans. But obviously the relationship would have grown over time, particularly as populations beyond the frontiers increased in the second century A.D. We have several dramatic examples provided by Tacitus in first century A.D. of the northern Rhine people desperately seeking food and land in periods of famine (Tac. *Ann.* 13.54 –55; *Hist.* 4.64–65), and in the third century we know that grain, salt, iron, and whetstones were items that the Romans banned for export to declared *hostes* (*Dig* . 39.4.11 pr.). But probably the most interesting, though inevitably circumstantial, evidence that such symbiotic interchanges took place across frontiers is what emerges from an ecological map of the Rhine-Meuse basin (fig. 33). There we can see vividly how there were two regions side by side, that of cattle producers to the north of the frontier in Holland and Lower Saxony and that of grain producers in the south, where such an astonishing number of Roman-style farms and villas have been discovered by aerial photography in Belgium, Picardy, and the Ardennes (Bloemers 1983, 181–82).

Whether the northern Germans also exported iron is less easy to decide, although the technique and production of German ironwork was much greater than Tacitus knew.[33] An apparent decline of metalwork in Roman Belgica by the later empire might have been the result of such trade.[34] What cannot be doubted is that overall, and on every frontier, there developed increasing social and economic ties between trans- and cis-frontier populations. Tacitus talks of the Hermunduri Germans, who, he says, were the only tribe permitted to trade deep within Roman territory (*Germ.* 41). His words have often been carelessly interpreted to suggest that the Hermunduri were the only Germans permitted to engage in trade with Romans, whereas Tacitus explictly records that others traded on the frontiers.[35] In A.D. 175 the Marcomanni,

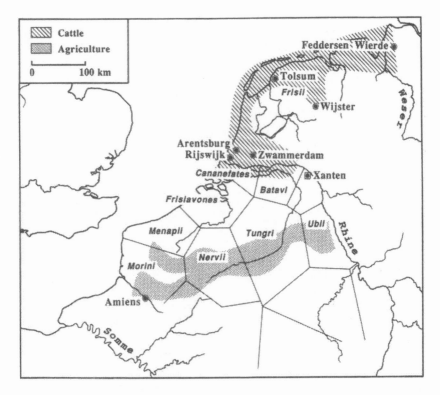

Fig. 33. The lower Rhine-Meuse basin, showing the area of cattle raising to the north and the rich agricultural land of villas in Picardy and the Ardennes to the south. After Bloemers 1983.

Quadi, and Iazyges in the Hungarian plain were permitted access to the markets on the Danube (Dio [Ex. U^G] 71.15–16 and 18–19), and of course we know that in this area the Romans were quite prepared both at the time of the Marcomannian war and in the later empire to use trade sanctions and famine as weapons.[36]

This is the relevance and the effect of the absence of natural, ethnic, or linguistic frontiers, which I discussed in the previous chapter. History demonstrates that not even mountain ranges are obstacles to the continuation of exchanges that preceded political frontiers. The Treaty of the Pyrenees in the seventeenth century, for instance, could not alter the rhythm of the transactions or the conventions of *lies et passeries* between local communities (Febvre 1922, 330; Nordman 1977, 434, with references). Transfrontier commerce was deliberately encouraged by the British in India by market fairs among Pashtu-speaking groups, in which the imperial power controlled and profited by trade permits, tolls, and sale of medical supplies and luxuries (Davies 1975, 237). The policy of the Han dynasty in China in the second century B.C. was specifically to "bait" the Mongol nomads with luxuries and food to control them (Raschke 1978, 765), in much the same way that Spanish invaders in North America made the Chichimeca Indians of their frontiers addicted to the commodities and foods they could provide (Lamar and Thompson 1981, 176–77). The most recent opinion of the function of Offa's Dyke on the Welsh border concludes that it was primarily designed to compel travelers to cross at certain places under control (Noble 1983, 165).

That was precisely the conclusion Lattimore reached to explain the purpose of ancient palisades erected between China and Manchuria or Korea, or of the Great Wall itself; that is, to maximize the profits of natural exchange, not to exclude them (1940, 244, etc.). On Roman frontiers such controls are still visible in the single gate or *guichet* entrance constructed in the wall of southern Tunisia, which runs between the Djebel Tebaga and the Matmata Mountains (fig. 24) (Mattingly and Jones 1986, 89). The location corresponds with the opinion, quoted earlier, about the design of Hadrian's Wall "to control movement, not to prevent it" (Breeze and Dobson 1976, 37). So often the small forts or *burgi* constructed on frontiers have been interpreted as instruments of defense and exclusion, whereas one inscription explicitly tells us that on the Danube "the *burgus* had the name *commercium* [i.e., trading post] because it was constructed for that purpose" (*CIL* 3.3653).[37]

The Push and Pull of Frontiers

The consequences of all these movements of Roman and foreign trade were twofold, what has been called the "pull" and "push" of frontiers. China's endemic problem was that its northern frontier was always "pulled" toward its northern neighbors away from the center of government. The "push" was the tendency for border regions on both sides of the frontiers to evolve differently from their hinterlands. The very stability of frontiers, which stimulated the social economy, also created pressures to break them down. The success of the border policies in China and India created a "sword of two edges" (Lattimore 1940, 245, and 1962, 107, etc.).

I do not wish to underestimate the national solidarity actually created by a frontier and its myths, a fact noted in a modern study of the Franco-Belgian frontier (Lentacker 1974; cf. the important review by Nordman 1977). The parallel in the world of antiquity is the study by Andreas Alföldi (1952) of the "moral barrier of Rhine and Danube," in which he stresses the collective sense of Romanness within the boundaries of the empire, beyond which lay wild and woolly barbarians (see p. 8 above). I discussed the imperialist and nationalist aspects of this kind of stereotype in chapter 3. But socially and economically it is manifest that none of the factors identified in modern nationalism as the essential preconditions for national solidarity—the circulation of capital, human migration, and internal circulation of commerce—can be sensibly applied to ancient preindustrial society. Circulation of capital, or any other kind of capital accumulation for that matter, simply did not exist to any significant extent. Human migration, which I shall discuss in chapter 6, took place across frontiers, especially in the later empire. But ethnic distinctions, far from increasing, became blurred as contacts grew more frequent. The circulation of commerce, with which I am chiefly concerned here, was not purely internal and had quite different and unexpected effects.

The first effect was the increasing definition of an invisible frontier beyond the formal provincial boundaries and the military *limes*, a *Vorlimes* region consisting of those who received the more mundane commodities of regular exchange—ceramics, wine, and probably wheat—in contrast to those beyond, to whom there went mainly rare, prestige articles of bronze, glass, and silver associated with gift exchange. This effect has been amply demonstrated by the graphic analysis of exports to free Germany (fig. 34).[38] The zone

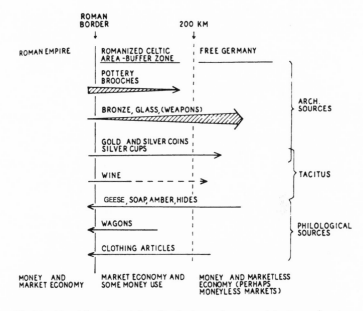

Fig. 34. Material goods and their distribution as they crossed the Roman frontier. The goods going to the frontier zone differed from those traveling beyond. After Hedeager 1987, 127.

adjoining the frontier at the interface with the Roman province corresponds to the area where Roman coins have been studied and mapped beyond the Rhine and Danube, although this should not be taken to mean that its economy was monetized (fig. 35).[39] It has perhaps misleadingly been called the zone of "market economy," although I prefer the notion of a "corridor" through which goods passed by exchange or entrepreneurial activity. Both studies illustrate the earlier conclusions, that frontiers were drawn across zones of transition where there was no clear ecological, cultural, or economic division.

The second effect, however, was the social distribution of goods within the *Vorlimes*. This is illustrated very well by the excavation of settlements in northern Holland and northwestern Germany, where the main concentration of imported commodities has been found in the central *Herrenhof* sites, like that of Feddersen Wierde (fig. 31; map, fig. 36) (Schmid 1978, 137; Jankuhn 1976,

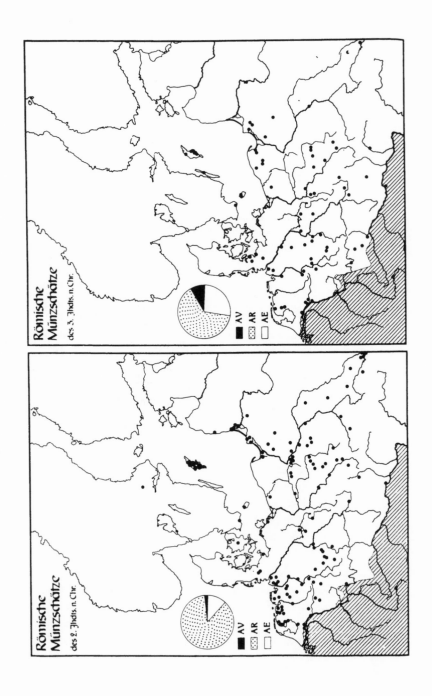

Römische
Münzschätze
des 3. Jhdts. n.Chr.

AV
AR
AE

Römische
Münzschätze
des 2. Jhdts. n.Chr.

AV
AR
AE

94–95). Social and economic life, including metalwork and grain stores, revolved around this center. In Britain there is a similar concentration of Roman imports north of Hadrian's Wall at the Scottish hill fort site of Traprain Law (map, fig. 10). Unlike the Dutch and German sites, Traprain was already a substantial site when the Romans arrived, and it declined in about the fourth century. But it does illustrate how Roman occupation reinforced local aristocracies beyond the frontier. Few Roman goods have been found in the ordinary farm dwellings, but Traprain virtually monopolized exotic imports, and it possessed a stock of querns, almost as though to control their distribution, as well as manufacturing metal tools and weapons.[40] It was at Traprain, too, that Latin graffiti were found (Macinnes 1984, 195)—evidence of the cultural package that came with trade, not unlike the Latin contract found at Tolsum in Holland or the Greek inscription at Zinchechra in the Fezzan (Daniels 1968, 182–83).

In other words, frontier trade and the cultural contacts that went with it had an important impact on the societies of the *Vorlimes*. But we must be careful not to exaggerate or to assume that Roman artifacts turned transborder folk into Romans. We must always remember that the number of such material contacts was small in comparison with the goods that were circulating inside the Roman province itself. The impact is probably best summarized in the words of an anthropological study of these types of external trade contacts, which concludes: "Often the rest of society, aside from the chiefs or the king's agents, have little to do with the interactions of outsiders . . . and gain little or nothing as a result of exchanges unless the chief redistributes some of the imported materials" (Wells 1980, 8).

Trade in these circumstances reinforced the control of the elite, of men like Cruptorix, the former Roman auxiliary who retired to his Frisian "villa," or the local Tripolitanian *principes gentis* living

---

Fig. 35 (opposite). The distribution of Roman coins of the second and third centuries A.D. discovered in free Germany. They are concentrated mainly in the zone between the Rhine and the Elbe. From Lüders 1955.

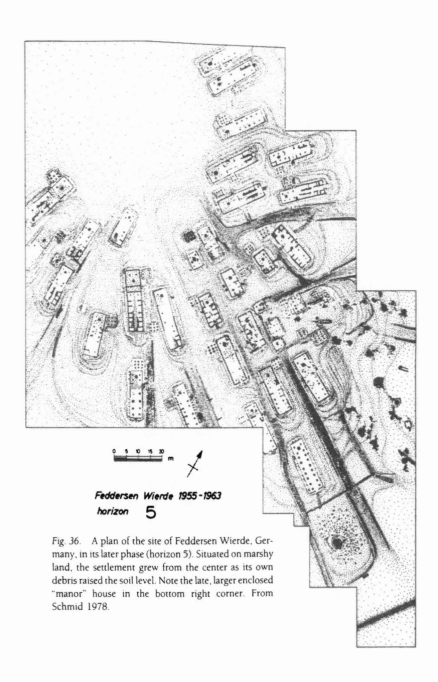

0 5 10 15 20
m

Feddersen Wierde 1955-1963
horizon **5**

Fig. 36. A plan of the site of Feddersen Wierde, Germany, in its later phase (horizon 5). Situated on marshy land, the settlement grew from the center as its own debris raised the soil level. Note the late, larger enclosed "manor" house in the bottom right corner. From Schmid 1978.

in the farms and fortified *gsur* of the Libyan valleys. It is difficult to believe that the rising political importance of Arab groups in the second century A.D. did not have something to do with the Roman Arabian frontier set up by Trajan at the beginning of that century. The most famous example is that of the Thamudaeans, who built a local shrine at Ruwwafa in the Hejaz, between Petra and Leuke Kome on the Red Sea, far beyond the frontier (map, fig. 13), where they set up an inscription in Greek honoring Marcus Aurelius. These were the first of the "Saracens," a term almost certainly meaning a political federation (Graf and O'Connor 1977).

But we can go further. Frontier zones extended to both sides of the *limes*, and frontier trade affected both. After studying the analysis of goods going beyond the frontiers, one archaeologist has suggested that there is a reasonable possibility that the absence of prestige goods in the *Vorlimes* zones could be the consequence of the regular reuse and melting down of the metal (Fulford 1985 passim, esp. 100, 105). The important fact, he thinks, is not that high-value imports were absent from such zones but that the more mundane products of Roman culture were *not* generally going beyond that zone. It is an interesting idea, though it does not really change the basic conclusions I have already drawn. But it is two other observations by the same author along the way that interest me most. The first is that the range of Roman goods found at Traprain is greater than on any other site in northern Britain—with the exception of the military forts and their attached *vici*—until one reaches the *colonia* at York. Second, he notes: "Altogether the range of finds in the 'buffer zone' is comparable to that from rural settlements *within* the *limes*, although quantities may vary considerably" (my italics).

What these two crucial assertions mean is that not only must we include within our economic theory of Roman frontiers the pattern of distribution to the *Vorlimes* zone, which differed from the region beyond it, but we must also build into the model a parallel between the rural populations on both sides of the frontiers, who were relatively starved of the goods that went to the elites. In terms of material goods the countryfolk, not surprisingly, lived at a lower standard than their own elites, who occupied the villas, towns, and camps on one side of the frontier or the native forts or Romanized "villas" on the other. And in the range of goods they used, they resembled each other more than they did their own upper classes.

Support for this conclusion comes from archaeological studies in Britain and Germany. In Britain it is a notorious fact that the civilian urban-villa economy of the south virtually failed to develop in Brigantia, almost certainly because of intense rural exploitation by the military. Coinage is almost never found beyond the military sites, and only low proportions of *terra sigillata* and glass reached the isolated farm settlements (Higham 1986, 175, 199–201, 225). The story is repeated on the frontier in Wales (M.L. Jones 1984, 55). What stands out is the contrast between these nonmonetized, isolated farms and the *vici*—settlements like Vindolanda, attached to military camps, that resembled towns, with shops, inns, and a wide range of Roman imports, Latin documents, and coinage.[41] The segregation of military *vici* from the civilian is proved by the fact they did not outlast the military camps.[42] Locally recruited regular legionary and auxiliary troops appear only rarely to have served on the home frontier, which completed the isolation of the army (Saller and Shaw 1984, 142–43).

The same segregation of military recruits from civilian communities is also proved by inscriptions in the Germanies, which contrast sharply with those from Africa and have implications for the later empire. In Lower Germany a comparison between Roman and native pottery from various settlements on both sides of the frontier illustrates the separation. There is a high correlation between what is found in the Roman fort at Zwammerdam, the military *vicus* at Valkenburg, and the Romanized *municipium* of the Cananefates at Arentsburg. It contrasts, however, with the pottery found in the provincial, civilian village at Rijswijk, which correlates with the assemblages of the translimes native Frisii settlement of Wijster (map, fig. 33).[43]

This is not a precise parallel to the evidence from Traprain Law, since in Holland the record is only of quantities, whereas in Britain it is the range of goods. But if we were to add to the artifacts found at Wijster the fabulous accumulation of wealth in the princely hoard at Beilen nearby, on the assumption that they belonged to the same local chieftain, then the range of goods is extended. And if we also remember that within the native settlements of Holland, Roman material was concentrated in the *Herrenhof*, as it was at Traprain, then the situation in Holland appears more like that in Britain, where the rural population on either side of the frontier zones was apparently little affected by Roman culture, while the native leaders were as tied to the Roman economy as were the Roman urban and military classes.

We can add some precision to the cultural differences between the urban and rural population within a Roman frontier province from a study of Gallia Belgica. There we can compare the distribution of Latin inscriptions and monuments over the region to discover more and less Romanized communities; similarly with the use of the Roman *tria* or *duo nomina* as against the use of single names by less Romanized natives. The contrast will appear less stark than it really was because only the better-off part of the population put up monuments; but it is still striking, if not unexpected. *Civitates* communities involved in frontier supply, like Trier and Metz, differed profoundly from the rural *civitates* of the Remi and Leuci in the way they used Roman-style names, not to mention the northwestern *civitates* of the Nervii, Tungri, and Menapii, who hardly began to adopt the Roman habit of putting up inscriptions and monuments at all. The author of the study goes so far as to talk of "internal frontiers" within the province between Romanized and non-Romanized (Wightman 1985, 162–77, and 1978).

These zones or cultural "frontiers," which existed not only beyond the *limites* but also behind them, have also been remarked upon in studies of other frontier zones. On the Upper Moesian frontier in northeast Serbia, for instance, a team of American and Yugoslavian archaeologists and anthropologists were able to identify a Romanized cultural region. The Danube, however, was not the border line of this cultural zone but the midway line. To the south of this region they noted a band inside the Moesian province "devoid of Roman presence," which, they said, "was as much a frontier zone for the Romans as the northern area above the Danube" (Bartel 1980–81). One of the most experienced of the archaeologists working on the Arabian frontier claims that the frontier region itself is the most densely occupied region in the later Empire; but, he adds significantly, "occupation terminated abruptly just west of the *via nova Traiana*—i.e. at the rear of the defensive zone" (Parker 1987b, 39).

I could not ask for better descriptions of what I have been trying to suggest, illustrating perfectly Lattimore's concept of the frontier "pull" as zones on each side of the formal frontiers came to resemble each other more than their own hinterlands. And what is so important for the history of the later Empire is that it was in these Romanizing borderlands on both sides of the frontiers that Roman emperors regularly settled Dacians, Germans, and Arabs in large numbers: *infinitos ex gentibus* (HA *Marc.* 24.3).[44]

Toward a Model for the Roman Frontiers

The time has come to draw together the strands of this chapter and to summarize my hypothesis. Military markets and consumers attracted local but also exotic supplies that followed no rational market forces, because the state offered tax immunities to suppliers. Such subsidized cargoes of mixed commodities spilled over into civilian markets along the military supply routes and in frontier regions, for the greater profit of the *negotiatores*. Frontier supplies reached not only the towns and military *vici* of the province, but also a zone of interaction beyond the frontiers, which thus reinforced and encouraged the political power of the native elites, since they controlled the distribution of the goods. As for the rural poor on both sides of the frontier, the cultural influence of Romanized goods that reached them did not differ greatly, although the cis-frontier population naturally received more. The consequence, therefore, *ought* to have been that, although the culture of the transfrontier elites corresponded in some degree to that of the provincial, urban, and military elites of the Roman province, their rural followers could have been absorbed imperceptibly into the provincial countryside.

I have been speaking, of course, only of observable material culture, not of social and political organizations, about which it is difficult to find sensible information. Ancient writers were obsessed, as are many modern historians, with the stereotypes of the moral divide between the way of life of Romans against that of *immanitas barbariae*. As long as authors like Galen could say, "I am no more in favor of Germans than of wolves and bears," they were unlikely to provide sensitive descriptions of the process of acculturation created beyond the frontiers by trade and exchange. One of the few exceptions was Cassius Dio. His well-known description of what he claimed was the result of the Augustan invasions beyond the Rhine was in fact written with the benefit of his experience as governor on the Danube in the early third century A.D. "The barbarians," he says, "were adapting themselves to the Roman world. They were setting up markets and peaceful meetings, although they had not forgotten their ancestral habits, their tribal customs, their independent life, and the freedom that came from weapons. However, as long as they learned these different habits gradually and under some sort of supervision, they did not find it difficult to change their life, and they were becoming different without realizing it" (56.18.2).

"Becoming different" through unconscious processes and my model of acculturation on the frontiers are the subjects I wish to examine more closely in relation to the later Empire.

Five

The Frontiers under Pressure

This chapter is a digression from the main theme. It aims to give a factual survey of the events on the frontiers of the later Roman Empire, since I have found—and perhaps others will also—that they are sometimes extremely difficult to follow. The Roman Empire is divided up into regions, and the history of each is traced from the advent of Diocletian in the late third century. The narrative of this chapter ends in the early fifth century but is resumed at the beginning of chapter 7. At that date the eastern empire continued, and the frontiers remained intact. But in the West there was a strange twilight period when it is often impossible to tell whether Roman frontiers existed.

It is just this ambiguity that explains the transformation of the empire into the successor "barbarian" kingdoms. We use the term *barbarian* too loosely, for want of a better word, to describe non-Roman peoples who entered the Roman Empire. It is unsatisfactory because it gives the impression that the battles and struggles of the fourth and fifth centuries were between the civilized Roman citizens of the provinces and uncivilized intruders from outside the empire. The reality is more complicated and more interesting: it was a process of the gradual assimilation of border folk into a culture that was itself changing by adapting to the pressures. So in the end it was unclear who were the barbarians and who were the Romans.

To start with, frontiers did not all have identical problems and responses. The territories of the Roman Empire stretched over six thousand kilometers from the deserts of the Negev and Jordan to the passes of the Caucasus, from the open plain of Wallachia at the foot of the Carpathians to the marshy delta of the Rhine, and from the rolling hills of Northumberland to the high tell of Algeria. The theory of a grand military strategy to cover such a variety of peoples and places (Luttwak 1976) becomes less and less attractive the more closely one looks at the details (Whittaker 1989, 28–29; Isaac 1990, 50–52). The surprise is perhaps that within so much diversity it is still possible to make any generalization at all about Romans' political attitudes toward their neighbors and about assimilation into the Roman Empire.

In retrospect it is clear from the events of the two centuries between Diocletian and the first Germanic kingdoms in Italy that there were two major points of pressure on the empire. The first came from the Saxons and Franks on the lower and middle Rhine, the second and more dramatic from the Goths on the lower Danube and its delta, who were in turn pressed by the Huns and Alans moving off the Russian steppes.

On the Rhine the German Franks not only attacked but were also among the first barbarians to be absorbed into Roman armies, often in high office, and they were perhaps the first to win de facto rights to settle in a semi-independent enclave, Toxandria, though it was certainly not legally recognized as such. It was Clovis, a Frankish king, who delivered the formal, though only symbolic, coup de grace at Soissons in A.D. 486 to the last remnant of Roman armies in the western provinces, and it was the Franks who became the final heirs to the Roman western empire.

On the lower Danube the Goths, forced by the Huns to cross into the Roman provinces, inflicted on the Roman army one of its most unforgettable defeats, at Adrianople in 378. Goths, Huns, and Alans then spread across central Germany to threaten the

Rhine as well as the Danube. As the first certainly attested settlers of federate (that is, autonomous alliance) status within the empire under Theodosius, the Goths served massively in Roman armies in the late fourth century. It was one of these groups of federate Goths, the Visigoths led by Alaric and Athaulf, that sacked Rome in 410 and went on to form the first barbarian kingdom within the empire in Aquitania. Another group, the Ostrogoths under their king Theodoric, became the first recognized German rulers of Italy.

This does not mean there were no threats on other frontiers. Diocletian in the late third century might have thought the main problem lay on the middle Danube from Sarmatians and Quadi, vaguely pressured by Vandals beyond. In the mid-350s Julian probably believed the threat of the Alamans and Burgundians on the upper Rhine and Danube was the most urgent. Under Valentinian the Tripolitanian cities looked as if they might fall to Austurian tribes raiding north from the desert. Saracen federations on the Palestinian and Syrian borders were a constantly increasing menace to the desert routes. And then there was Persia, the only centrally organized power to compare with Rome and therefore in Roman eyes always to be feared. But despite some punishing disasters inflicted by Persian armies, it is difficult now to be sure Rome did not greatly exaggerate the long-term Persian threat (Isaac 1990, 28–31). And though Alamans and Africans continued to harry the Roman borders, they lacked the organized force necessary to take over from Roman rule.

The Eastern Frontier

The East makes a good starting point for a frontier survey, since here, despite—or perhaps because of —the Persian presence, was established the most stable frontier of the period. The foundations of the military dispositions were laid by Diocletian after his campaign in Arabia in A.D. 290 and probably were subsequently adjusted during his long stay at Nicomedia in the eastern half of the empire. Because the frontier changed relatively little, the information contained in the *Notitia Dignitatum*, which for this part of the empire appears to have been composed about 395, gives us a fair idea of what Diocletian intended.

From the Sinai peninsula to the Black Sea fourteen to sixteen extra legions were added to the existing twelve, with probably a similar increase in auxiliaries, including a notable use of barbarian units such as Franks and Alamans. In theory the total number of soldiers on the frontiers was approximately 248,000 (as opposed to about 72,000 in the army of the second century A.D.), to which we must add the field army (*comitatenses*) established under Constantine of some 104,000 (A.H.M. Jones 1964, 56–60, table 15). Even if these huge forces were largely paper figures (Kennedy and Riley 1990, 44–45), we can already see in Diocletian's settlement two major principles of the late imperial policy: a greatly strengthened military presence and a liberal use of the very tribal groups who were pressing to enter other parts of the empire.

PALESTINE–ARABIA–SOUTHERN SYRIA

See Map, Figure 13.

The most monumental feature of Diocletian's work was the desert road called the *strata Diocletiana*. "On the *limites*," we are told, "he built *castra* from Egypt [the Gulf of Aqaba] to the Persian borders" (Malal. *Chron.* 12.308 [Dindorf]). The most urgent need in this area of the Palestinian-Jordanian frontier was to fill the vacuum created after the rebellion and destruction of Palmyra by Aurelian in the third century. In addition to the need for patrols for the long-distance caravan routes coming up the Euphrates, which Palmyra had previously provided, the change had perhaps unleashed groups of transhumant border Arabs who wished to cross seasonally into Roman provincial territory (Gichon 1986).

There was also growing political union within these seminomadic tribal peoples, who stretched from the Negev to the Syrian border. It was already evident in the second century among the Thamudean groups in the Hejaz and among the Safaitic groups in southern Syria. But it became most pronounced among the Tanukhids and Lakhmids, who migrated westward from Mesopotamia across the Euphrates in the third century.[1] The term "Saracen,"

135

used in the later Empire, was undoubtedly a generic word to describe these kinds of federations and unions. Just how dangerous these tribal groups became is a matter of much dispute.[2]

The increased long-range movements and raids by such groups in the later Empire have often been ascribed to their "bedouinization" through the greater use of the camel and the introduction of a new type of saddle (Bulliet 1975, 87–105). But the nomadic threat was not a new problem, and it was more plausibly the introduction of the Arab cavalry horse and its use in conjunction with camel transport that changed the balance of power (Kuhnen 1991). Some of the impetus toward federation, however, also clearly came from the Romans and the Persians themselves, who saw advantages in alliances and in building up the power of friendly tribal chiefs (phylarchs). For Rome the continued use of the caravan routes from the Euphrates—from Hit to Palmyra, for instance—depended on such Saracen chiefs after the fall of Palmyra (Kennedy and Riley 1990, 38). One such prominent example is that of Imru'l-qais, an early member of the Lakhmids (later a powerful dynasty that emerged out of the Tanukh federation), who was described in an inscription of 328 as "*malek* [king] of the Arabs" and as lord of a number of tribal chiefs attached to Rome.[3]

Diocletian's strategy for dealing with the problem was not new but a continuation of that used both by Trajan and Severus; that is, control of watering points and the construction of strong road links, along which were placed watchtowers, forts, and cavalry patrols, more or less along the edge of the predesert on the 200-millimeter isohyet rainfall line (fig. 26).[4] Ammianus Marcellinus gives a description of the region as already "filled with strong camps and forts erected in suitable and readily defendable ravines to repel the raids of the neighboring tribes"(14. 8.13), to which Diocletian and his successors simply added. In addition, some of the legionary camps were brought forward (Lejjun and Aqaba) and a road (*praetensio*) was fortified running like an extended antenna from Bostra southeast to the oases on the Wadi Sirhan. But neither was this a new idea, since the Romans had long manned military posts along the routes leading to the caravan center of Jawf in Saudi Arabia. By the end of the fourth century the Wadi

Sirhan seems to have been abandoned by Roman units, and control apparently was exercised through local Arab leaders, something like the *principes gentium* of Africa.[5]

Ammianus has a puzzling reference to *limites interiores* (23.5.1–2) in this area, which may perhaps refer to the *strata Diocletiana* in contrast to these long-distance "outer" posts, although there was also an inner road between Damascus and Palmyra parallel to the *strata Diocletiana*. There is also a confusing probability that the term *strata* came to mean grazing lands. Whatever the explanation, it is clear that no attempt was made in this region to establish a single fortified barrier. Many of the so-called forts appear to be no more than road stations, at most points to control those moving across the borders and to guard the water reservoirs against raiders (fig. 37). There is little evidence of a systematic defense in depth, as some have alleged. In a case like that of the "fort" at Qasr Bshir in Jordan, not far east of the legionary camp at Lejjun, it is not even certain that it was a military building (fig. 38).[6] Raids by Saracens are regularly described throughout the fourth to the sixth century, stretching from the Sinai peninsula to southern Syria but without causing any serious alteration to the military or political arrangements made by Diocletian.

Just how dangerous the Saracen raiders were on this frontier is a matter of dispute. There are those who think the main problem was one of internal brigandage or unrest and that the frontiers were therefore designed to assist quick police action. Others believe there were regular movements of seminomads across the frontier that were mainly peaceful but needed constant surveillance. And there are those who argue that the various Saracen confederations could turn what were normally raids of low intensity into major confrontations (Parker 1991 sums up the debate).

The alternatives are not incompatible. Ammianus has many descriptions of border raiders who "swooped down like scavenger kites" (14.4.1; cf. 24.2.4, etc.), and inscriptions back up his picture of the disruption even small attacks caused. For example, a fort was built northeast of Damascus for security against the *terrorem* of the Arabs (*CIL* 3.128); a new reservoir had to be constructed near a fort on the road from Bostra to Asraq "because very many

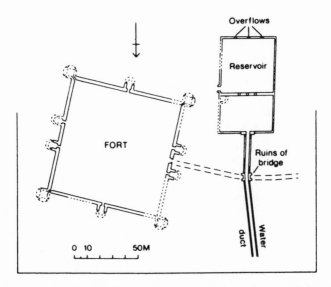

Fig. 37. A plan of the fort at Khan el-Manqoura, Syria, on the *strata Diocletiana* between Damascus and Palmyra, listed in the *Notitia Dignitatum* as the fort for a military cohort. It appears that its main purpose was not defense but control of the water supply. After Poidebard 1934; Kennedy and Riley 1990, 183.

of the countryfolk were ambushed and killed by Saracens while fetching water" (*AE* 1948, 136). Transhumant pastoralists can be extremely destructive if not checked by border controls (Gichon 1986). And there can be no doubt of the potential dangers of a powerful leader if we remember that when the Saracen queen Mavia rebelled in 378 she reached the borders of Egypt (Shahid 1984, 142–52). With the rise of the Lakhmid dynasty and its support of Persia in the sixth century, we are told that Rome met its "most difficult and dangerous enemy" (Procop. *BPers.* 1.17.45), to which it opposed its own sponsored dynasty of the Ghassanids.

We can therefore try too hard to separate low-intensity threats from great invasions. In the later Empire it was more often by the infiltration of small groups, often classed as bandits, that the frontiers were penetrated. It is a mistake, certainly, to regard all Saracens as a united force. It was perhaps the very fact that both Rome and Persia exploited this disunity, by supporting various

Fig. 38. An aerial view of the "fort" at Qasr Bshir in Jordan, near the camp at Lejjun. It looks like a building for frontier defense, but an inscription tells us that it was built by Diocletian and called *castra praetorii Mobeni*, suggesting a civil purpose as a governor's *praetorium*. Are we too quick to think all frontier buildings were for defense? Photograph by J. Sauer.

tribal phylarchs against each other, and because they made regular use of the fine Saracen cavalry units in their own armies, that ultimately they created a force they could not control.

NORTHERN SYRIA–MESOPOTAMIA

See map, figure 11.

Mesopotamia was won and lost a number of times after its first conquest by Trajan in the early second century. It was here between the Euphrates and the Tigris that Rome stood face to face with Sassanian Persia on its southern border, even though Armenia to the north of Mesopotamia also remained a pivotal point for Roman-Persian relations. The victories of the tetrarchy in 298 over a weak king brought Roman territory well beyond the Tigris. But the rule of Shapur II for sixty years (309–69) reestablished Persian power west of the Tigris and culminated in disastrous defeats for both Constantius II and Julian. Julian himself died on campaign after his retreat from his ill-advised attack on Ctesiphon in 363. Jovian, Julian's successor, was forced to make large concessions, including the loss of Armenia and the Transtigritan states, plus the abandonment of territory east of the Khabur Pass, along with the key city of Nisibis on the southern frontier.

And so the situation remained for over a hundred years until the sixth century, with brief clashes in 421–22 and 439. Even in the seventh century, on the eve of the Arab invasions, little territorial change had taken place. It is uncertain that the Persians ever wanted to drive Rome out of the eastern provinces as a whole, or even out of northern Mesopotamia, despite Roman claims to the contrary (Julian *Or.* 1.27A Lib. *Or.* 59.71; Amm. Marc. 18.6.3). More probably they reacted to the fact that Rome was destabilizing their western provinces by its aggressive occupation of the Tigris forts and the positions of Nisibis and Singara. Political control of Armenia, too, was always a point of conflict (see below). But compromises were acceptable. Both sides seem to have realized that the true dangers lay not in confrontation but in the threat from the north.

One might suppose from this history of almost ritualized clashes and negotiated treaties between the two superpowers in the East that it would be easy enough to define the territorial frontiers. The reverse is the case, partly because the wars were largely conducted through the sieges of key cities (such as Ammida, Bezabde, and Nisibis), which Ammianus (20.11.24) calls *claustra*, meaning barriers against enemy attacks (Isaac 1990, 252–60). Between the cities there ran "lines of observation posts and country guard posts" (*praetenturis et stationibus* . . . *agrariis*; Amm. Marc. 14.3.2), designed to keep off petty raiders but certainly not intended as a frontier "system."

Broadly speaking, the frontier here too was a line of roads established by Severus in the third century, running northward from the Euphrates along the river Khabur and Jebel Sinjar from Circensium toward Mosul on the Tigris. But it is impossible to specify a precise border. After 364 the cities east of the Khabur (Nisibis and Singara) were ceded to Persia, and it may be that the river Jaghjagh was thought of as some sort of boundary. But this too is far from clear. As farther south, we know that the military defenses were largely laid out under Diocletian. He fortified Circensium on the Euphrates and made Singara and (possibly) Bezabde on the Tigris into legionary bases, although after 364 these two bases were displaced to Constantina, over one hundred kilometers to the west of Nisibis, and to Cepha higher up the Tigris.

At no time, however, does all this look like a defensive frontier, or a frontier in depth, or an agreed limit of Roman power. Even if it is true that the Tigris was recognized in 298 as a formal boundary (Pet. Patr., fr. 14), it is quite obvious that the function of the fort at Bezabde was to control politically the *regiones Transtigritanae* beyond the "frontier" (Warmington 1976; Lightfoot 1983). Julian praised Constantius because, he says, "You often crossed the Tigris with your army and spent a long time in the enemy's country" (Julian *Or.* 1.22B). It is noticeable that even after the loss of Bezabde and the control of the Transtigritan states, Rome still kept a legion at Cepha higher up the Tigris.

Similarly, the Euphrates south of Circesium formed some sort of notional boundary. When Julian crossed the Khabur where it meets the Euphrates at Circesium, he treated the event as though he was traversing the boundary of empire. But he is also said to have regarded the recovery of the cities and deserted camps along the left bank of the Euphrates as "reinforcing the Roman state by making this side safe" (Amm. Marc. 23.5.18). And the *Notitia Dignitatum* (*Or.* 33.20) records a Roman camp at Ana, about 150 kilometers downstream. Although this may have been only a short-lived occupation (Kennedy and Riley 1990, 114), control of the Euphrates was a Roman objective.

ARMENIA–UPPER EUPHRATES–BLACK SEA

See map, figure 12.

Armenia and the upper Euphrates valley had been a thorny problem ever since the Romans had come to the East. With new research it is becoming clearer that the Euphrates had never, even in the earlier Empire, been the political or military border. It is only in the *Notitia Dignitatum* that the Euphrates appears as the line of garrisons, from Zeugma and Melitene across the mountains from Zimara to Satala and then to Trapezus on the Black Sea. But even this may record the temporary situation between the treaty forced on Jovian in 363 and the recovery by Theodosius II in the early fifth century (Crow 1986b; Wheeler 1991). Certainly there is little to indicate that the river was ever considered a defensive line, much less a limit to Roman political activity.

It was the political control of Armenia that preoccupied both Rome and Persia, since its loss by either side presented the other with a large territorial reentrant into its own empire. There is an enigmatic Armenian reference to Romans and Persians agreeing in the late third century to a division of the kingdom, which "renewed the frontiers by setting stones in the ground" (Moses of Chorene 2.77). But there is no sign this was ever a military fortification, and it was not until the treaty of 363 that Rome renounced the right to appoint a puppet king. After 363 there were only fluid spheres of interest determined by alliances with feudal families (*narkharars*).

Valens's aggressive policy and victory advanced the Romans into Armenia again, but as a result of pressure by Goths on the Danube he was happy to settle for an agreement to a division of spheres of influence in 375. This was based on alliances with the *narkharars* and left large areas of territory undefined, so that in the early fifth century we find the Roman port of trade was Artaxata, far within the Persian sphere of control (*CJ* 4.63.4[408–9]; Blockley 1987). Perhaps the best description of the nature of the upper Armenian frontier is that given by Procopius (*De aedif.* 3.3.9–10) in the sixth century: "The land [of Chorazane] is not marked off from Persian land by the water of any lake or by the stream of any river or by mountains that force the road into a narrow pass; but the two boundaries lie mixed up together. So the inhabitants of this region . . . even intermarry and hold a market for their produce and cooperate in farming." On the Black Sea, the defenses that had been destroyed by Goths in the third century were partially repaired by Diocletian and Constantine, to which Valens later added. The organization of the region was based on a series of forts, such as Aspasus, Sebastopolis, and Pithyus. But the new threat in this area was from the Huns coming through the Caucasus, which was a danger to both Roman and Persian territories. Broadly speaking, the regions between the Black Sea and the Caspian were divided, with Rome in control of Colchis, Lazica, and Pontus while Persia ruled over Albania (Azerbaijan) and the Caspian routes. Dispute arose over Iberia (South Georgia) and the forts of the Darial Pass, which by 369 were partly occupied by Persia. Theodosius withdrew Roman troops from Iberia in 394 for his wars in the West, and the Huns came through the Caucasus. In the end the Romans were prepared to pay Persia to maintain the garrisons of the Caucasus (Isaac 1990, 229–34).

Egypt and North Africa

The general picture in Africa in the later Empire is not so very different from that in the East; that is, a recovery and retrenchment after the disorder of the third century, but growing pressure and increasing numbers of raids from desert tribes. Despite the serious damage done by the incursions of the Austuriani into Tripolitania and Cyrenaica between the later fourth and early fifth centuries, behind whom loomed the federations of Laguatan tribes, and although there were two serious internal rebellions in Algerian Mauretania toward the end of the fourth century, this was not a region of the empire where Rome was seriously pressed and to which it diverted many resources. The main problem was always small, sudden attacks, causing fear and disorder but with little danger of invasion. Rome's prime concern was that Egypt and Africa were the granaries of Constantinople and Rome, and so even small disruptions to farmers had serious repercussions.

EGYPT AND CYRENAICA

In Egypt and Cyrenaica (Libya) Diocletian probably laid the basis for the military organization that is found in the *Notitia Dignitatum,* where both territories are listed under the same command. The

Panoplis papyri, which date from the last years of the third century, show what Diocletian achieved in his visit to the Panoplite nome after the repression of the revolt of Domitius Domitianus in A.D. 296–97 (Berchem 1971). The evidence of papyri also indicates that in essence there was little strategic change throughout the fourth century from that established by the tetrarchy, especially in the garrisons of Lower Egypt, and that therefore the *Notitia* list is not an anachronism (Price 1976). The same was almost certainly true of Cyrenaica, although the ducate list is missing, and little appears to have changed from the earlier Empire (Goodchild 1976).

As in the East, the paper figure for numbers of troops of both the *limitanei* and the *comitatenses* was vastly increased, with over sixty thousand men for the eighty-eight or so units in Egypt in the frontier posts, where previously there had been only one legion. But there must be doubts whether anything like this number really existed, since in Cyrenaica the evidence of Synesius in the fifth century shows there were few units, and even those were far below strength (A.H.M. Jones 1964, table 15; Roques 1987, 252, contra A.H.M. Jones 1968).

According to Procopius (*BPers.* 1.19.29), Diocletian abandoned the poor territory of Lower Egypt south of Elephantine, thinking he could use allied native tribes to protect the region against intruders, though without much success. In Egypt the main military problem areas were the Fayum and the northwest coast. Almost certainly this reflected the same threat that faced Cyrenaica, since we know of raids by the Macetai (possibly the same as the African Mazices) and Austuriani in the early fifth century, which spilled over in Egypt out of the western Libyan desert and continued most of the century. We also have references to Blemmyes attacking villages and monasteries in the southern Egyptian oases, where there are still the remains of some impressive forts.

The real question in Egypt is what was the main function of these troops, and whether one can even begin to talk of frontiers in any realistic sense. There is much to recommend the view that the major task of the soldiers was to protect the grain supply, since this was one of the two key producer regions of the empire (Berchem, in Bell et al. 1962, esp. 17–18). The celebrated Abbinnaeus Archive, a series of papyri dating from the 340s, gives a vivid picture of a garrison in the Fayum that appears to have had little military employment apart from collecting and handling the *annona militaris* (Bell et al. 1962).

This is not, of course, incompatible with the location of the garrisons at key points to protect the territory against desert raiders. But many of the splendid oasis forts on the west bank of the Nile give the impression of serving as protection for farmers and controlling water collection or—like the large temple fort at Douch—as depots for the *annona* service (Reddé 1991). In the eastern desert the frontier was nothing more than a series of roads linking the Nile to the Red Sea, along which fortified outposts and signal stations were scattered, and in this sector it is not even possible to decide where Roman administration ended (Sidebotham 1991).

In Cyrenaica it is no less difficult to talk of frontiers in any clear sense. Despite the hyperbole of Synesius in the fifth century, the military threat was largely that of the desert raiders. Some of them, the Maketai, whom Synesius called *mixobarbari,* were permitted to reside within the border zones of the high steppes (Roques 1987, 269). The main forts and fortified farms indicate the direction of the pressure from the west; but they are scattered all over the cultivated areas of the interior as well, along the wadi approaches, so that it is virtually impossible to detect any coherent line of frontier in a country where— to quote a modern authority— "the whole province had become a *limes*" (Goodchild 1976, 204). The surprise attack of Maketai and Austuriani in 405 showed that years of inactivity had reduced the troops to perilously low levels, but recovery was rapid and there was no real danger, despite repeated raids by "robbers" through the next centuries (Roques 1987, 286).

TRIPOLITANIA

See map, figure 9.

The frontier *limes* between Tripolitania and Algeria is unique in the later Empire in that it is listed by sectors in the *Notitia Dignita-*

tum, with twelve commanders (*praepositi*) under the *dux* of Tripolitania and sixteen under the *comes* of Africa (Cagnat 1913, 748–50). Why this was so is unclear. One reason may have been that by the date of the *Notitia* in the early fifth century most of the regular legions and vexillations had been transferred to the field army, leaving only local "tribal" troops of *gentiles* in place under Roman officers.

Exactly when this happened is equally obscure, but it was not necessarily general before the reign of Honorius, perhaps when the former field army of *comitatenses* had been recalled to Europe (A.H.M. Jones 1964, 197, 652). No doubt the use of native *gentes* on the frontiers evolved over time. We have a record, for instance, of a Roman *praefectus limitis* who was stationed in a small fort or *centenarium* as early as about 244–46 in the Libyan valleys (*IRT* 880), soon after the African legion had been withdrawn, when the region was apparently peaceful. But elsewhere, at the fort of Remada in eastern Tunisia, for instance, we find the same regular army cohort in the fifth century as in the third century (*ND* Oc. 25.33). An alternative subsidiary force came into its own because Africa was not a crisis spot.

Between Tripolitania, eastern Tunisia, and the Aures Mountains it is difficult to see any radical physical change from the roads, forts, and walls (*clausurae*) that had been established in the earlier Empire by at least the second century. On the Antonine Itinerary of the third century, the inland Djebel road between Lepcis Magna and Gabes (Tacape) is explicitly identified as the *limes* (*iter quod limitem Tripolitanum ducit*). East of Lepcis, also, the *limes* was reduced to the coastal road, since the earlier forts of the Augustan legion in the Libyan valleys were not manned after about the middle of the third century, apart from Gadames, which seems to have had a military presence in the fourth century. But the region was peaceful and prosperous, and there is no reason to think Roman control was lost (Rebuffat 1977, 410–16).

It is in this area that we know of early fortified posts (*centenaria*), which operated in conjunction with smaller outposts and large fortified farms (*gsur*), which are found all over the Tripolitanian frontier region (Barker and Jones 1982; Trousset 1974, 37–38,

136). The necropolis at Bir ed-Dreder in the Wadi Soffegin shows that in the mid-fourth century local, neo-Punic-speaking men were holding Roman military titles, such as *tribunus,* and it cannot always have been easy to tell the difference between a civilian landlord who put up a private *centenarium* "to guard and protect the zone," as an inscription says (*IRT* 889), and an official commander of an outpost (Elmayer 1985).

This is no reason, however, to believe that the frontiers had been turned over to unpaid farmer-soldiers, as has often been argued. The occupation of forts and land by *gentiles* and other troops near forts on the African frontier is well documented by legislation in the early fifth century, which forbids others to usurp this property (*CTh* 7.15.1 [409] and *NTh* 24.4). But though *gentiles* or *limitanei milites,* as they were called, were allowed to cultivate land, they were still *milites* under army officers. Neither were *gentiles* the same as federates who settled under treaty from beyond the frontiers, as became common after Theodosius, since federates served under their own leaders. We do in fact have a record in the fifth century of such a treaty tribe in the service of Rome— the Arzuges, who lived on both sides of the provincial boundaries in southeastern Tunisia, to whom the frontier officers had to administer an oath of loyalty.[7] But they did not man the *limes.*

The *limites* were maintained by *praepositi* who occupied head-quarter forts, which often gave their names to the sectors (e.g., *limes Bizerentanus* at Bezereos). All lay along the predesert road of the second century, which bore little relation to the short stretches of walls and ditches that have come to light increasingly in recent years, since some of them run behind the road, others in front (Mattingly and Jones 1986). These fortifications were referred to in the edict of 409 (above) as the *fossatum,* explicitly linked to the *limes.* But from their position it is certain that they were not defensive. The *centenarium* fort at Tibubuci, for instance, which was put up about the time of Diocletian (*CIL* 8.22763), containing stalls for cavalry horses, is about thirty kilometers in advance of the ditch-and-wall system of the Matmata Mountains (map in Trousset 1974, fig. 37).

We must conclude that the function of the *fossatum* with its *clausurae* walls was to control and direct transhumant tribes who then, as more recently, moved seasonally from the predesert to the Tunisian and Algerian high plains. It was not meant to keep the barbarians out or to defend Romans against barbarians. The story of Stachao the Austurian, who was allowed free access to Roman territory even though the Austuriani had been raiding across the frontier for some years, gives some idea of how open the frontier was (Amm. Marc. 26.4.5, 28.6.2–3).

It may be that the citizens of Lepcis Magna paid for the light manning and open frontier in the Tripolitanian sector. A series of raids are commemorated on inscriptions from Sabratha and Lepcis about 355–60 (e.g., *IRT* 569), and about the same date we know of two governors of Tripolitania who restored some of the frontier buildings after damage: two inscriptions record *propugnacula* at the fort of Talalati (*CIL* 8.22766–67); another speaks generally of *limitis defensionem* (*IRT* 565). In 363, several devastating raids on the cities of the coast caused a scandal because of the inactivity and corruption of the *comes* of Africa, to whom the command had been entrusted (Amm. Marc. 28.6). But there is more politics to the story than meets the eye, and it is far from clear that the frontiers had really been neglected or badly damaged.

It was, however, a warning to the Romans of what could happen when they ignored political control of the tribes beyond the frontiers. The Laguatan confederacy that swept north in the sixth century was not an unknown force of camel nomads riding out of the desert but included people like the Arzuges, who had once been managed by Rome (Mattingly 1983).

NUMIDIA AND MAURETANIA CAESARIENSIS

Between the Tripolitanian *limes* and that of Numidia the road simply continued westward, south of the Aures Mountains. It too was divided into sectors that from time to time, like the *limes Gemellensis*, included a wall-and-ditch *clausura*. As in Tripolitania, we must assume that the purpose was to control but not exclude seminomads, using more or less the same line of forts as those established in the earlier Empire. This impression is confirmed by inscriptions recording restoration of a fort south of the Aures under

Diocletian (*CIL* 8.2480 at *Ad Maiores*) and the construction of a new *centenarium* near Tobna (Tobunae) in the Hodna depression under Constantine (*AE* 1942/43, 81 at Aqua Viva). Under Valentinian's rule a fort was constructed at Cellae on the route leading north from the Hodna to Setif (*CIL* 8.10937).

The only real difference from the earlier Empire, therefore, is that some forward antennae in the desert were abandoned. But Mauretania remained "an open country" (Salama 1966). We have record of some people called the Ba(r)bari Transtagnenses raiding in 296/97 (*CIL* 8.9324), which probably refers to transhumant tribes coming up on to the central Algerian plain from beyond the salt *chotts* (marshes) of the Hodna and the Chergui in the predesert (Courtois 1964, 96).

The real difficulties in this part of Africa, all of which came under the command of the *comes Africae,* are shown by the *Notitia Dignitatum* to have come not so much from the desert as from the mountains. It records a series of *limites* in the interior of the country between the desert frontier and the sea. They were, in effect, roads that ran through the wild mountain ranges of the Babors (the *limes Tubusubditanus*), the Grand Kabylie (the *limes Bidensis*), the Bibans and the Soummam valley (the *limes Auziensis*), and the Ouarsenis and the Chelif valley (the *limes Caputcillensis*).[8] Two points stand out: the term *limes* manifestly does not refer to the limits of southern control; and this was not a problem new to the later Empire. The function of the *limes* was to keep the roads of the interior open, not to form "a strategic line," as once was thought (for instance, by Cagnat 1913, 270). Under the Severi already there were established so-called *novae praetenturae* (*CIL* 8.22602/4), which like the Syrian *praetensio* were guarded military roads.

These armed lines of communication in Mauretania correspond with what our military literary and epigraphic sources tell us about the disturbances of the territory in the later Empire. For instance, under the tetrarchy there was a large-scale alliance of tribes, the Quinquegentanei (meaning "five peoples"), fierce people who "relied on inaccessible mountain ridges and natural protection" (*Pan. Lat.* 7[6] 8.6). The inscriptions commemorating their defeat show that they were in the Babors. At the end of the fourth century the rebellions of Firmus and Gildo used strongholds along the axis of the Kabylie Mountains and the Soummam valley, through to Castellum Tingitanum and Castra Tigava in the Chelif valley (Amm. Marc. 29.5.25). At Auzia, the pivot of this line, we find a *praepositus limitis* stationed already in 301 (*CIL* 8.9025).

The mountains of Mauretania were also the land of small *centenaria* and *castella,* some of which were regular military bases (as can be seen in the names above). Some, however, appear to have been names for private fortified farms and estates, such as the *centenarium* in the Kabylie Mountains that names a certain M. Aurelius Masaisilen who put up the building at his own expense (*CIL* 8.9010) or the *castellum Tulei* nearby (*CIL* 8.9005–6).[9] They are very like the Tripolitanian forts, where the difficulty is to know whether such buildings, variously called *turres* (towers), *burgi* (fortlets), *castella,* and such, were put up on the instructions of the military commander, were stations put up by civilian liturgy to service the *cursus publicus,* or were simply private estates. The ambiguity is not something new to the later Empire.[10]

There are some remarkable remains of fortified estates, like those at Kaoua or Nador, but one of the most interesting is that identified as the *castellum* of a Mauri chief, Flavius Nubel, near Rusguniae (where he also dedicated a church; *CIL* 8.9255), since it was Nubel's sons Firmus and Gildo who rebelled one after the other against the emperor in the second half of the fourth century (Gsell 1903). Nubel was also father to other sons who had estates in the Algerian mountains, like that at Petra in the Soummam valley, which an inscription describes as "a fortress of eternal peace" (*praesidium aeternae . . . pacis; ILS* 9351). Nubel himself had served as commander of a unit in the *comitatenses,* and his father may have held the rank of retired companion (*ex-comitibus*) and *praepositus* of the *limes* (Salama 1954).

Firmus and Gildo were both Roman court officers who, when they rebelled, drew upon local forces, some private and tribal, but some from the Roman *comitatenses.* Gildo directed some of the Roman forces that put down Firmus, and Mascezel, another of Nubel's sons, led the Roman force that in turn defeated Gildo.[11]

All this goes to show just how complex the interrelations were between regular and irregular forces of the *limites* and how impossible it is for us now to disentangle the precise role each played in frontier defense, or even to tell whether these "kings" were inside or outside the frontiers (Camps 1985; Decret 1985; cf. below). But we are not talking about "barbarians." As the central power of the Roman state disintegrated, it was these kings who carried forward the baton of Roman culture.

MAURETANIA TINGITANA

As with western Caesariensis, it used to be thought that Tingitana was abandoned by Diocletian, apart from a small area around Tingis (Tangiers) itself, which was administered from the Spanish diocese. Now we know that the information in the *Notitia Dignitatum* giving Sala (Rabat) as a military position is correct, since a dedication to Constantine has been found in the town (*IAM(L)* 304 b.); but it was an island of Roman occupation with a solid fortification between the sea and the Bou Regreg, whereas the rest of southern Tingitana was abandoned (Euzennat 1989, 173). Clearly there was a much reduced administration of the province, and the troops recorded in the *Notitia* are significantly listed not as *limitanei* but as belonging to the *comes* of Tingitana.

Where identifiable, most of the camps seem to be in the north, along the coastal road from Lixus to Tingis and the Rif Mountains. It is unclear if Volubilis was still under provincial administration, and there is a small four-towered fort that may belong to the later Empire (Euzennat 1989, 263). But the population was very Romanized and the story here may therefore be one of Romanized, independent rulers. To the east of Djebel Zerhoun there is little sign of Roman occupation. But then there never had been much, and a good deal of diplomatic effort in the earlier Empire had gone into building up alliances with native tribes like the Baquates. The proof of the success of this policy toward both eastern montagnards and southern nomadic peoples is that there were no military incidents of importance in this part of the later empire. Tingitana remained, as it always had been, a "marginal province" (Frézouls 1980a).

Britain

See map, figure 10.

On the British frontier of Hadrian's Wall we are faced with a paradox and a lesson in the use of sources. For the literary record, historians like Ammianus note a large number of violent incidents and attacks on Britain, especially on Hadrian's Wall. Yet the archaeological records and the army lists in the *Notitia Dignitatum* suggest generally peaceful and static conditions there. Recent careful work now shows that Hadrian's Wall was not abandoned either in the late third century at the time of the usurpation of Allectus or in the later fourth century, as once thought. The "barbarian conspiracy" recorded by Ammianus in 367 (Amm. Marc. 27.8.1), when the Picts and Scots overran northern Britain while the Saxons and Franks diverted attention on the Gallic coast, has been described as "probably the biggest non-event, archaeologically, in the 360 years of Roman rule in Britain" (Welsby 1982, 104). Ammianus's account of the recovery by Count Theodosius, which was wrongly thought to include withdrawing the northern frontier to the south, is also generally regarded as exaggerated (Tomlin 1974; admitted by Johnson 1980, 95, but not on 98).

The fact is that we do not possess a single closely dated inscription on the wall after the reign of Diocletian (*RIB* 1912), and there are none for the forts of the Saxon Shore (Welsby 1982; 91; Wilkes 1977). This has led to the incorrect attribution and interpretation of all kinds of fortifications, to square with events recounted by historians. But above all it shows how vulnerable we are to the limitations of our written sources, which may omit important events or be biased ideologically—or may simply be wrong.

Plenty of problems remain. Although we now know that the forts of the wall were not abandoned, the settlements near the camps (the *vici*) certainly were, in about 370—not just in Britain but in Germany too (Snape 1991; Sommer 1991). Various reasons have been proposed: possibly soldiers' families were moving into the camps, as skeletal remains suggest; possibly *laeti* or federate soldiers took over the camps with their families, even though the military lists do not record them (Cunliffe 1977, 5; Daniels 1980,

189). There may be other contributory factors: civilian traders, who had used the *vici*, became absorbed into the military supply service in the later Empire; legal recognition of marriage in the third century meant soldiers (and veterans) increasingly lived away from the camp *vici* and caused problems of absenteeism, noted in the late Roman codes. The implication of all this for the British northern frontier is that there were no protracted crises, which may have led to sometimes dangerously low levels of manning.

THE SAXON SHORE

See map, figure 39.

In reality it was clear already in the late third century, from the numerous episodes of plundering sea raiders (e.g., Eutrop. 9.21; Oros. 7.25.3), that the center of pressure in Britain was shifting from the north to the southeast coast, which the Romans called the Saxon Shore. Out of the navy of the old *classis Britanniae* and its bases developed a new command under a *dux,* responsible for the coasts of both England and France. Carausius, the later usurper, had held a special command in 285 and was responsible for building the large new fort at Portchester. But his was not the earliest of a series of new forts, some of which appear to date stylistically from the early third century (Cunliffe 1977).

The dangers increased. By the early fourth century the *dux* had become a permanent command. Sometime in the second half of the fourth century a more senior *comes* of the Saxon Shore in Britain was appointed, perhaps to coordinate naval and military units along the British coast and on the wall itself. The appointment, which was senior to the *comes* of Britain, who commanded only a small field army, shows the rising dangers about the time of Valentinian. The *comes* had a subordinate in Gaul in the *dux tractus Armoricani* (Hassall 1977). By the time the *Notitia Dignitatum* was written in the early fifth century, there were ten or eleven forts on the *litus Saxonicum* running from Norfolk to the Isle of Wight (though only nine are recorded in the *Notitia*), built in different periods. Most were large new-style forts used particularly, though not only, for mobile cavalry units.

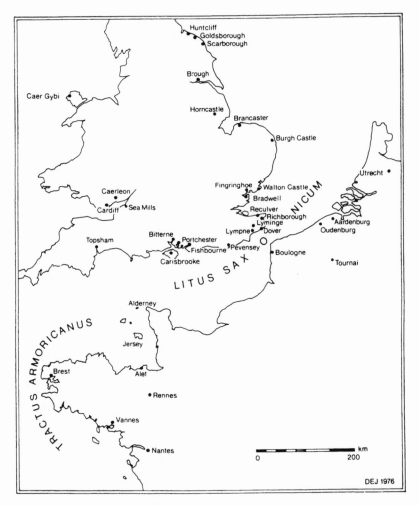

Fig. 39. The forts of the Saxon Shore. Reproduced by permission of D. E. Johnston.

HADRIAN'S WALL AND THE NORTHERN FRONTIER

It is uncertain what Diocletian and Constantine did to change the defenses of Britain, apart from formalizing the command structure with a *dux* for the frontier troops and the Saxon Shore, while a *comes* commanded the mobile field units. Very few of the latter are known in Britain, and possibly none permanently before Stilicho since the Gallic field army could serve in Britain when needed (Mann 1977, 14). The main function of new inland forts seems to have been to protect the roads, and all of them probably came under the *dux* (Breeze and Dobson 1976, 214; Johnson 1980, 91).

The real change on the northern frontier at this time concerns the forts to the north of Hadrian's Wall, where no coins have been found after Diocletian, suggesting that they were abandoned (Casey 1978). But there are certainly signs of occupation and reconstruction in some of the forts (Risingham, High Rochester, Bewcastle), and Netherby was occupied through the fourth century. Ammianus tells us also about irregular troops called *areani* or *arcani*, whose job was to spy on neighboring people "over a great distance" (Amm. Marc. 28.3.8). That presumably means they operated beyond the provincial boundaries, and their *stationes* may have been these advanced posts (Johnson 1980, 94; Welsby 1982, 103). If so, the posts would have been operational until 367, when the *areani* were abolished for entering into the "barbarian conspiracy."

The general picture in the north seems to be one of petty raids, which occasionally blew up into serious trouble, as in 342 and 360. On the last occasion "places near the frontiers" (*loca limitibus vicina*; Amm. Marc. 20.1.1) were attacked, which might refer to the points where the friendly allies assembled north of the province, as they did on the Danube (Mann 1979b, 145). But there is nothing to suggest that these events caused any radical changes or damage on the wall.

Even the great "barbarian conspiracy" of 367—when obviously there was a serious crisis, since both a *comes* and a *dux* were killed—does not sound like an attack on the wall. Although Count Theodosius is said to have repaired the camps and *limites* with "watchtowers and fortified lines" (*vigiliis et praetenturis*, Amm. Marc. 28.3.7), the archaeological evidence gives little reason to suppose that the repairs on Hadrian's Wall were general, much less that there was any thought of abandoning it. It is entirely possible that the Picts attacked by sea and that this accounts for damage and repairs at Ravenglass on the Lancashire coast and for the construction of new signal stations on the north Yorkshire coast between Malton and York (Breeze and Dobson 1976, 221). But the date is difficult to prove, and the raids on Yorkshire may as easily have come from Saxons.

It is now believed that much of the later fourth-century reconstruction of Britain came with the appointment of Magnus Maximus as special *comes* in 382, and that it was he who built the Yorkshire coastal forts, along with a more general reordering of the defenses of England and Wales. From Britain he launched his claim to the western empire in 383, and for five years he controlled the Gallic diocese, possibly removing some troops from Britain to the Continent. The same is said of Stilicho in the early fifth century, when he made some changes in Britain and required troops against Alaric. Both are possible; neither is certain (Casey 1979b).

It has often been thought that the *Notitia Dignitatum* section for Britain, supposedly dating from the early fifth century, must be out of date, since many of the troops recorded "along the line of Hadrian's Wall" (*per lineam valli*) appear in the same old-fashioned auxiliary units of cohorts and *alae* that were there in the third century. But there is no good reason to support this, now that we know Hadrian's Wall was not abandoned. What the *Notitia* evidence means is that the wall had not been reinforced and restructured like other fronts. The main danger was now from the sea, and the soldiers on the northern frontier had become like a "state frontier police" (Hodgson 1991).

The Rhine Front

See map, figure 40.

It is impossible to give a systematic account of two hundred years on the Rhine frontier, a frontier that stretched nine hundred kilometers, from Lake Constance to Katwick on the North Sea—and more if we add in the borders of the two provinces of Raetia, a distance of three hundred kilometers, incorporating Switzerland and southern Bavaria as far as the river Inn. Raetia, which linked the Rhine to the upper Danube, included the Brenner Pass, through which the Goths of the early fifth century poured into Italy. Along this whole length there was no single enemy during the two centu-

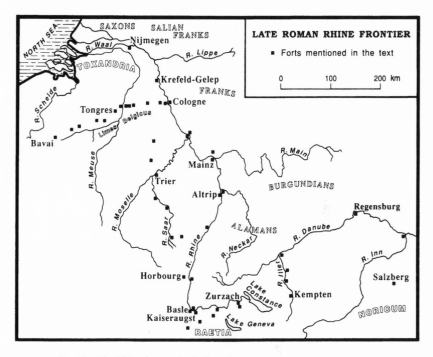

Fig. 40. The Rhine frontier in the later Empire

ries of the later Empire—no single problem, and therefore no single solution. For the Romans the difficulty of dealing with heterogeneous peoples, not united under single tribal command- ers, constantly splitting up into new alliances, serving under Roman generals one day and against them the next, must have been as great as it is for us today to fully understand them.

But there can be no doubt of the importance of this frontier in the history of the later Empire—first, because of the sheer continu- ity of the pressure. From the mid-third century until the beginning of the fifth there is a stream of information about attacks by Saxons, Franks, and Alamans, who are the three broad groups most prominent in our sources. They were responsible for the crisis of the third century in the great invasions of 275, when the Romans gave up their formal occupation of the *Agri Decumates* and the Taunus salient, both regions on the right bank of the

Rhine. It tells us something about the different conditions of the western and eastern Empire that many Goths, Huns, and Alans moved from the eastern marches of the empire toward the West along the line of the upper Danube, across Bohemia to the Rhine, or into Italy through the Brenner Pass.

The second importance of the western frontier is demonstrated by the evidence of the *Notitia Dignitatum*. The list of military units recorded in this sector about 425 shows that the western frontier was virtually stripped of all its regular *limitanei* troops by the time the invasions of the fifth century took place. That can only mean a massive reliance on federate soldiers and the replacement of Roman authority on a grand scale. The Romans had encouraged immigration as a political tactic over a long period of history; settlement, that is, of groups of border peoples within the empire, who were variously termed *laeti, gentiles, dediticii,* or *tributarii.* Again we find a difference from the eastern empire in that such migrants are more frequently and earlier attested in the western provinces, at first under direct Roman jurisdiction and control, often serving in the army as native units.

But by the end of the fourth century border tribes were increasingly settled as autonomous enclaves within the boundaries of the provinces by "treaty" (*foedus*; and hence the term "federate") to serve Rome. Although the first federate settlements took place on the Danube, most seem to have been within the western provinces. It is perhaps not surprising, therefore, that it was in the West that the most successful successor kingdoms grew out of the federate settlements in the fifth century: the Visigoths in Aquitania and Spain and the Franks in northern and central Gaul.

The Romans treated the line of the Rhine and Danube less as a frontier behind which to set up their defenses than as a line of communication and supply along which it was important to keep control by fortifications. In principle it was not very different from the other fortified roads and river valleys that were used for supply and communication in the western provinces; the so-called *limes Belgicus* between Bavai and Cologne, for instance, or the Mosel-Saar-Saône line, or the Aare line running from Lake Constance to Lake Geneva to link the Rhine and the Rhône. They resembled what in other parts of the empire were sometimes called *praeten-turae*. The reason for the added importance of these surveyed routes in the later Empire was varied; partly because an elaborate taxation system of *annona* for military supplies was developed that required depots and transport, partly because the very principle of mobile field armies of the *comitatenses* required posting stations and good communications.

But some of the reason for these watchtowers and forts was without doubt the character of what we call "the barbarian invasions." It is an unsatisfactory term, because it projects an image of large invading armies, whereas the threat from northern peoples came not so much from mass movements, although there were some, as from chronic petty raiders and infiltrators. "Wild beasts, accustomed to live by plunder when the guardians are negligent" is the way a conservative Roman soldier like Ammianus described them (16.5.17). On the great lateral rivers, therefore, which in a symbolic sense were the frontiers of Roman administration, in reality the Roman army did not cower behind fortifications but was constantly controlling the crossing points to the far bank, making counterraids to check rising powers, and organizing alliances of tribes far beyond the provincial boundaries.

THE SAXON SHORE

See map, figure 39.

In the *Notitia Dignitatum* a command is listed under the *dux* of the *Tractus Armoricanus et Nervicanus limes,* extending over five provinces and based on nine forts along the Normandy and Brittany coast between the mouth of the Seine and the Loire. A second set of units is listed under the command of the *dux* of Belgica II between the Somme and the northern mouth of the Rhine delta. In both lists there is a reference to the "Saxon Shore," although it looks very much as if the responsibility of the duke of the Tractus Armoricanus was for the whole length of the west coast of France south of Rouen (Brulet 1989 identifies the known sites).

How to interpret this evidence is by no means clear, since the administration of the units and forts that are listed in the *Notitia* under two regional *duces* does not rule out the possibility that the operational control of the Saxon Shore fell to the British *comes* (Mann 1977, 14). But the more usual interpretation is that what had once been a single command in the late third century was divided into regional ducates under the Gallic *magister* by the time of Valentinian, perhaps after the occasion in 370 when it was evident that the Saxon naval raids down the Gallic coast required coordination between the fleet and the Gallic *comitatenses* (Amm. Marc. 28.5).

Most of the sites in these commands have been identified. Some of them, as in Britain, were, like Boulogne or Oudenburg, old forts of the *classis Britanniae* fleet. Others, like Alet or Aardenburg, were really civil sites with fortifications. But all show signs of importance in the later fourth and early fifth centuries and therefore reflect the growing menace of sea raiders and land infiltrators (Brulet 1991). This is confirmed by the large number of "Germanic" burials in the area of Boulogne-Etaples and even far inland north of the Somme, though whether they were invaders or defenders is impossible to say.

THE LIMES BELGICUS

The *limes Belgicus* is a modern term and is included here for the sake of completeness, although it is debatable whether it really served as a frontier in any other sense than as a *praetentura* that ran south from the Rhine at Cologne to Bavai in the direction of Boulogne. Much of the road was fortified in the second half of the third century, a time of much disturbance in northern Gaul, to keep supplies going to Cologne. The tetrarchs kept the forts in repair, and Constantine built a new fort at Liberchies. But by the late fourth century there seems to have been very little occupation, and some of the forts—Morlanwelz, Givry, and Cortil-Noirmont, for example—were in disuse (Brulet 1977).

The interesting question is whether the *limes Belgicus* did perhaps represent a dividing line between the Roman administration of Belgica II—Germania II to the east and lands ceded to federate Franks to the west. If so, this was the first example in Roman history of such a formal concession. Close political relations between Romans and some Frankish groups went back to Constantius Chlorus and Constantine. Ammianus also says that Julian was approached by the Salian Franks in 358 to grant them the land of "Toxandria," where they had already settled. Toxandria must be near the medieval *pagus Toxandria* in southern Batavia and related to the area of northern Brabant that was referred to in the fourth century as the *regio Francorum* (Willems 1986, 438). So it fits well with the military evidence. Some historians have also seen evidence of a Frankish protofederate state in the fact that the record of Lower Germany (Secunda) in the *Notitia Dignitatum* is missing; but that was almost certainly only an error of transmission (Mazzarino 1990, 336). In the end, however, Ammianus makes the formal fact clear: Julian agreed to the Franks' request only on their unconditional submission (*deditio*; Amm. Marc. 17.8.1–4)— perhaps as *laeti* or *dediticii*—not by treaty. So all thoughts of a protofederate state must be put aside.

But that does not rule out the possibility that there was a large influx of Salian Franks and perhaps Saxons into this area, since in 350 the usurpation by Magnentius in Gaul had caused enormous disruption. The emperor Constantius apparently countered Magnentius's threat by inviting large numbers of Saxons and Franks beyond the Rhine to settle in the northern Gallic and German province, with terribly destructive consequences (Lib. *Or.* 18.33– 35). Many of the Gallic garrisons were then stripped for Julian's subsequent campaign (Julian *Or.* 1.34–35). Recent archaeological research confirms the scale of the damage done in the mid-fourth century in the northern provinces. Northwestern Gaul and Lower Germany beyond the river Meuse were in any case only very sparsely populated after the third-century invasions. This gives special interest to the work done recently on rural sites in Belgium, particularly around Tongres and Maastricht, where there is increasing evidence that Germanic populations were installed in abandoned Roman villas and hill fort sites, most notably from the mid-fourth century until the fifth century.[12] Not only do these squatters make their appearance, but long wooden houses that included stables (*Wohnstallhaüser*) were sometimes built on the villa sites, as well as Germanic dugout huts (*Grubenhaüser*). Both are like those found at Wijster and elsewhere in free Germany. The settlements and dwellings can often be associated with the German-style burials in necropoles nearby.[13]

Even if substantial numbers of Franks were settled in Toxandria, however, it does not really tell us whether the *limes Belgicus* was in any sense a military or even an administrative frontier, although archaeologists claim there is a stronger Gallo-Roman cultural tradition perceptible to the east of the road. Perhaps the most important observation is that there was really little difference between the immigrants and the local population, and that the real discontinuity in this region came in the upheavals of the early fifth century (Mertens 1986, 196).

THE LOWER RHINE

Dividing the frontiers of Upper and Lower Germany was a Roman administrative convenience that does not neatly correspond to the reality of the external pressures. The occasional post of *comes per utram Germaniam* shows that in terms of the military threat there was often no clear tactical line between the two; and in the later fourth century the *dux Mogontiacensis* (Mainz) in Upper Germany seems to have been responsible for the lower Rhine under the *comes* at Strasbourg in Upper Germany (Mazzarino 1990, 336–37).

On the lower Rhine the absence of any clear line of river in the delta and the marshy area to the north makes it unclear how much of this area was abandoned in the crisis of the third century and how much of the earlier imperial frontier was restored by the tetrarchs and Constantius Chlorus in the late third century. The key town of Nijmegen on the Waal-Rhine was apparently abandoned in the late third century. But Constantine built a smaller military camp at Valkhof nearby on the Waal and a coastal camp at Valkenburg on the northern delta near the Hook, as well as giving a good deal of attention to the Waal and Meuse fortifications in general (Groenman–van Waateringe 1986; Willems 1986, 444).

These precautions are consistent with reports of repeated raids by Franks between 306 and 312 (*Pan. Lat.* 6[7], 10.1–2, 7[6].4.2, etc.) and with the construction of Constantine's prestigious fort at Deutz on the Rhine opposite Cologne (fig. 41). We could not have a better demonstration of the total absence of a defensive mentality in Roman frontier ideology. The situation of the fort on the right bank, with its massive walls that later became a medieval castle, together with its inscription make an ideological statement about Roman frontiers: "Following the subjection and control of the Franks through the virtue of Constantine, the *castrum* of the Divitienses was constructed in their territory in the presence of the emperor himself" (*CIL* 13.8502). The fort is also a marvelous testament to the ambiguity of the frontier relationship, since the Saxons and Franks on the lower Rhine frontier were simultaneously furnishing Rome with large numbers of troops of "brilliant reputation," according to Julian (*Or.* 1.34c–d).

Heavy damage was done during the period of the usurpation of Magnentius against Constantius, followed by "long neglect" (Amm. Marc. 15.5.2, 8.1) in the 350s, when Franks profited by coming into Lower Germany in large numbers, to judge by the coin hoards (Willems 1986, 450). As we saw earlier on the *limes Belgicus,* there are considerable signs of new settlements at just about this time. But it is impossible to confirm Julian's own claim that by 355 forty-five major towns in Gaul had lost their walls or that Germans controlled the whole length of the left bank of the Rhine to a depth of nearly forty miles and were making the countryside unsafe to a distance of over a hundred miles (*Ep. ad Ath.* 279A).[14] The catastrophic fall of Cologne in 355 must be linked to the assassination just before this of Silvanus, one of the many Roman Franks at court, who had been sent there as Roman commander and then—according to Ammianus, who played an odd personal part in the affair—tried to declare himself emperor (Amm. Marc. 15.5).

Julian's restoration of order in Gaul and Germany made his reputation, and there is plenty of evidence of the repairs he carried out on the frontier. Cologne was recovered in 356. Several major campaigns were waged against the Frankish tribes, which carried him far up the Lippe (Amm. Marc. 20.10.2). But it was the constant petty raids into even the territory of the northern capital of Trier that caused most trouble, a fact illustrated by the colorful history of Charietto, a Frankish "robber" who profited from smaller "rob-

Des romains. Nouvelle Ponte sur 300 m Chu

bers" by relieving them of their booty as they returned home. So successful was he that Julian employed him and ultimately gave him a formidable military command in 365 as *comes* over both Germanies (for details, see *PLRE*, vol. 1, s.v. "Charietto 1").

The main concern seems to have been the restoration of the Rhine as a supply line for the army, since all our sources comment on the transport of grain from Britain to the Rhine (Amm. Marc. 18.2.3–6, etc.). No doubt this was to compensate for the territory ravaged by raids, but the new granaries at Valkenburg show it was to be a more permanent arrangement (Groenman–van Waateringe 1986). Valentinian carried on the work. The importance of the middle Rhine can be deduced from the fact that the emperor now made Trier his capital. The northern frontier had again been weakened by the Persian campaign in 369 when the Gallic army was taken east, and Ammianus was much impressed by the energy of Valentinian's restoration on its return of "camps, forts, and towers" the whole length of the Rhine "right to the channel of the North Sea" (*ad usque fretalem Oceanum;* 28.2.1). But what impressed him even more was the number of forts on the right bank, although most are known in Upper Germany.

In general on the lower Rhine the policy of Julian and Valentinian seems to have been similar to that of Constantine and indeed that of the earlier Empire (Bogaers 1971). Certainly there is little evidence of a difference in military strategy between Diocletian and his successors toward a supposed system of defense in depth.[15] The danger is that we attribute too much undated material to individual emperors like Diocletian or Valentinian (Petrikovits 1971, 184). Throughout the fourth century the Romans aimed to control, though not to occupy, the trans-Rhine area by a series of bridgeheads; the main legionary camps were maintained, even if with reduced garrisons (Schönberger 1969, 180); the number of

Fig. 41 (opposite). An artist's engraving of what the great fort at Deutz, opposite Cologne, was believed to look like, based on its medieval successor. Although recent research has thrown some doubt on whether it did look like this, it was a formidable building and far from defensive. Photograph by permission of Rheinisches Bildarchiv, Cologne.

smaller military sites along the river was increased and the army spread out, although this was already a tendency in the third century (Oelmann 1952); and supplies to the Rhine stations were maintained by a fleet and roads protected by small forts, though the proliferation of *burgi* along supply routes was also common enough in the earlier Empire (Labrousse 1938, cf. at note 10 above).

Both Arbogast and Stilicho conducted campaigns against the Franks across the Rhine, though we do not know where, in the last years of the fourth century. A Roman provincial now could freely cross the Rhine in safety and take his flock to the Elbe, the poet Claudian writes with more enthusiasm than accuracy (*De cons. Stil.* 1.218–31). But we note the ideology. Trier was still an important administrative center in 396 when Stilicho fought, but already the emperor had moved to Vienne in southern Gaul, and Stilicho was probably responsible after his campaigns for moving the Gallic prefecture to Arles (Mazzarino 1990, 94). With the move went a political decision to leave Lower Germany to Frankish federates, and in 401 Stilicho apparently removed the regular Roman units to Italy to deal with the invasions of the Goths (cf. Claud. *De cons. Stil.* 2.186–89; *De cons. Honor* 4.455–59).

It was a policy of desperation and boldness, but the Franks (probably mainly Salians) responded with loyalty. In 407, however, they were unable or unwilling to resist the new pressure of Vandals, Alans, Suebi, and others (Oros. 7.38), and the Rhine frontier was breached. All the signs are that it was Upper Germany, near Mainz, that took the brunt of the attack (Mazzarino 1990, 100), although the archaeology of the Frankish settlements around Tongres shows disruption there too in the early fifth century (Ossel 1983, 168).

This was not the end of the Rhine army or of a Roman presence, as we shall see; but a distinct shift was taking place in the population. The mid-fifth century is archaeologically the time when many of the Germanic habitations of Toxandria, such as Neerharen on the Meuse or Liège, show signs of discontinuity (Brulet 1990; Mertens 1986, 195). A study of the *Vorland* of the southern part of the lower Rhine shows a much reduced number of civil settlements in the later fourth and fifth centuries, something less than a third of those in the previous century, almost all concentrated in the Lippe valley (Kunow 1987). The trans-Rhine north had moved southward on a grand scale deep into the Roman provinces.

THE UPPER RHINE AND RAETIA

The frontier of Upper Germany and Raetia was always peculiarly mobile, even in the early Empire, when the Romans found themselves progressively drawn up the valleys of the Neckar and the Main. The result was annexation of the *Agri Decumates* (roughly Baden-Württemberg and Bavaria) and the Taunus Salient (beyond Wiesbaden and Frankfurt almost as far as Giessen) into the province of Upper Germany and the effective demilitarization of Switzerland and Austria. The evacuation of the *Agri Decumates,* probably by Aurelian in the third century,[16] naturally required a radical readjustment of an area that was always difficult for communications with the Danube. It was a sensitive area in that the river Inn, which divided Raetia II from Noricum, gave easy access to Italy through the Brenner Pass.

The main pressure in this area since the third century came from the Alamanni or, as they were often termed, Suevi or Suebi (hence modern Swabia), whose massive eruption into Italy and Gaul in the latter part of the century led to the building of the very walls of Rome. They were unusual in that they occupied territory that had almost all been Roman (Demougeot 1979, 280; Matthews 1989, 306). The name Alamanni, like "Franks," is a portmanteau term ("All-men") for a number of subgroups under their respective *reges, regales,* and so on, who settled in the *Agri Decumates,* occasionally uniting into alliances, constantly raiding the Roman provinces, and sometimes joining with other groups like the Franks.[17] They in turn were under pressure from the Burgundians, who lay on their outer border (Amm. Marc. 18.2.15, 28.5.11). The sources make much of the way they harassed Roman cities, although they avoided besieging the urban centers. (Zos. 3.1; Amm. Marc. 16.4.2). But they were difficult to control just because of their very lack of political coherence (cf. Amm. Marc. 18.2.18).

What is important for our understanding of the Alaman frontier is that the peaceful traffic across the borders of the Roman provinces was intense, quite apart from any incursions. Crocus, an

Alaman chief, had played a key role in Constantine's proclamation in 306 (*Epit. de Caes.* 41.3). Alaman nobles often rose to high office in the Roman command structure, Alaman units served regularly in the Roman army, many Alamans settled within the borders of Roman territory, and there is an exceptional density of Roman imports and trading coin in Alaman territory.[18] In these respects their relations with Rome were as ambiguous as those of the Franks or the Goths, and there is no real justification for the view that Alamans were somehow more obdurate than other border tribes. The real question to ask is why they should have been so aggressive in the later fourth and early fifth centuries. The answer must surely be pressure from Burgundians and other groups moving westward.

Roman policy toward the Alamans does not vary substantially during the fourth century. It is stated most clearly in the late fourth-century compilation of the *Augustan History,* which often tells us more about contemporary attitudes than about the lives of the earlier emperors it claims to recount. The third-century emperor Probus is said to have driven the Alamans back beyond the Neckar and the Swabian Alb. Then "he placed camps opposite Roman cities on barbarian soil, and there he stationed soldiers. He also provided land and granaries and homes and grain for all across the Rhine—that is, for those he had stationed there *in excubiis*" (HA *Prob.* 13.7–14.1). The last part is difficult to understand, since it seems to mean that Alamans were set up in civil settlements, on the right bank with Roman subsidies to provide "guard posts" (*excubia*). But the interesting point is how closely this resembles Ammianus's account of the controls of the trans-Rhine territory by Valentinian: "He fortified both banks of the Rhine with high camps and fortlets [*castellis*] to prevent the enemy from ever being able to attack our territory unobserved" (Amm. Marc. 30.7.6; cf. 28.2.1). Once again it is clear that Roman political frontiers were not limited to the formal, provincial boundaries.

Most of the changes in the later Empire followed from the fact that the *Agri Decumates* were no longer under direct Roman administration. The tetrarchs established camps along the Swiss Rhine as far as Lake Constance, with their main base at Kaiseraugst.

The so-called Iller *limes* protected a road running north from Lake Constance to Ulm on the Danube, while a second road ran from Lake Constance via Kempten, the Inn valley, and Salzburg to Linz. In the opposite direction another line of fortlets ran south along the Aare to link up with the Rhône at Geneva. In effect it was an elaborate system of communications and signal stations, some of which can be dated to Diocletian and some to Valentinian, but that evolved over the century (Laur-Belart 1952).

The tetrarchs made no attempt to restore the Roman province of Upper Germany beyond the Rhine as it had been before Aurelian, but they did conduct a campaign in 287 down the Neckar and right across the *Agri Decumates* to the Danube, followed by a savage repulse of the Alamanni near Windisch in Switzerland, as though they intended to keep control over the region (*Pan. Lat.* 8[5]2.1; 6[7].6.3; 10[2].5.1). Perhaps as a result Constantine established firm treaty relations with the Alamans, and they appear not to have joined with the Franks in the invasions of 306–21 (Demougeot 1979, 285). Constantius II apparently even hoped to turn Alaman enemies into allies by incorporating them into the Roman army, much to the disapproval of Ammianus (14.10.14; Frézouls 1983; Stroheker 1975, 34).

Ammianus's distrust may have been acquired in retrospect after a massive breakdown of control took place, when Franks and Alamans entered Roman Germany and Gaul in 355 and captured a number of important cities, including the military bases of Strasbourg and Mainz, reaching as far as Autun (Amm. Marc. 16.2). Two years later the Juthungi Alamans raided Raetia. But Julian's famous victory at Strasbourg in 357 was followed by campaigns that again appeared to aim at linking the Rhine and the Danube. Ammianus says that Julian restored some old Roman fortifications in the German interior and established bridgeheads on the right bank (Amm. Marc. 17.1.11, 18.2.15). In other words, Julian's military policy was very much that of forward control, as it had been under his predecessors.

Valentinian's devotion to strengthening the Rhine fortifications is well documented, as we have seen, by Ammianus and confirmed by inscriptions. But there is a tendency to lay too much stress on

Valentinian's activity, which archaeology does not prove to have been substantially different in aim or achievement from that of his predecessors (Petrikovits 1971, 184). Like Julian and the tetrarchs, he aimed to control the Alamanni by *ultra flumen* fortifications, illustrated by his attempt to fortify the Alaman hilltop *oppidum* of Mons Pirus (possibly Heidelberg; Amm. Marc. 28.2.5). We know of a number of pairs of forts on the left and the right banks such as Zurzach-Reinheim, Kaiseraugst-Whylen, Basel-Robur, Altrip-Neckerau and Horbourg-Breisach,[19] which in kind follow the model of Constantine's bridgehead at Cologne-Deutz.

After Valentinian, history again becomes difficult to follow. An Alaman attack into Alsace in 378 was sharply checked, and the Alaman Lentienses (note the name of modern Linzgau) on the upper Danube were forced into an alliance (Amm. Marc. 31.10). After Alamans and Franks supported the rebellion of Eugenius, Stilicho was praised as *Rheni pacator,* and Honorius "drew up laws for the yellow-haired Suevi" while imposing kings on them and the Chauci in 398 (Claud. *In Eutrop.* 1.379–82). But the Alamans were considered the greater threat, since Stilicho is said to have refused to recruit them into the Roman army (*De cons. Stil.* 1.233–36). In 401 Stilicho was forced to hurry to Raetia and Noricum to check the first attack of Radagaisus, which threatened to destabilize the whole region (Claud. *BGoth.* 363 ff.). The removal of units (Claud. *BGoth.* 414 ff.) probably accounts for why a number of forts around Lake Constance were evacuated, though the Iller line was strengthened. As on the lower Rhine, much of the frontier was turned over to federates, since the *Notitia* shows that the soldiers of the *dux* of Mainz were upgraded to the field army.[20] Not all Roman troops, however, were withdrawn from Noricum, since some were still in garrisons in the 470s when Saint Severinus came to live there.

The Danube Frontier

See map, figure 42.

As on the Rhine, we are confronted with a huge frontier. It stretched from the upper Danube in Switzerland to the Danube delta in

Romania, a distance of some two thousand kilometers, which, after Constantius II, was split between the eastern and western empires. In the order of battle of the *Notitia Dignitatum* there is a western command under the *magister militum per Illyricum* and an eastern command under a *magister militum per Thracias*. So it would have been surprising if both sectors had been organized in the same way.

Like the Rhine, the Danube was rarely if ever the political or military frontier. Its principal role was transport and communication. Themistius, the fourth-century orator, talks of ships loaded with trade goods moving along the river (*Or.* 10.135). The military counterpart to this was the fleet patrolling the river to stop infiltrators (Amm. Marc. 31.5.3) or Julian carrying his troops by ship from Raetia to Lower Pannonia (Zos. 3.10.2), or military bricks being moved down from Upper Pannonia to the lower Danube.[21]

The main pressure of populations beyond the frontiers was shifting eastward during the second and third centuries, from the middle Danube, where tribes like the Marcomanni and Quadi occupied Slovakia and the Hungarian plain, to the lower Danube— Bulgaria, the eastern Balkans, and the Dobrudja. In particular, the rich lowland plain of Wallachia, which Bucharest now dominates, was always attractive to tribal groups moving off the Russian steppes via Ukraine and Moldavia. Goths, Vandals, Huns, and Alans followed this route in the fourth and fifth centuries, they in turn being pressed by Bulgars, Slavs, and Avars in the sixth century. The Scythian *limes,* the most eastern sector, was the most vulnerable. Constantinople, the new capital of the eastern empire, unlike Rome, was a strategic center and a regular residence for emperors.

The main change from the high Empire on the Danube frontier was the loss of Dacia, roughly the area of modern Romania. The decision to give up the territory was made by Aurelian about 282 and parallels the abandonment of the *Agri Decumates* in the West. Strategically it was never viable, and it had become outflanked by the Goths, who moved into the Dniester region in the early third century, when the province was already under pressure in Transylvania and the Carpathians from other groups like the Carpi, the

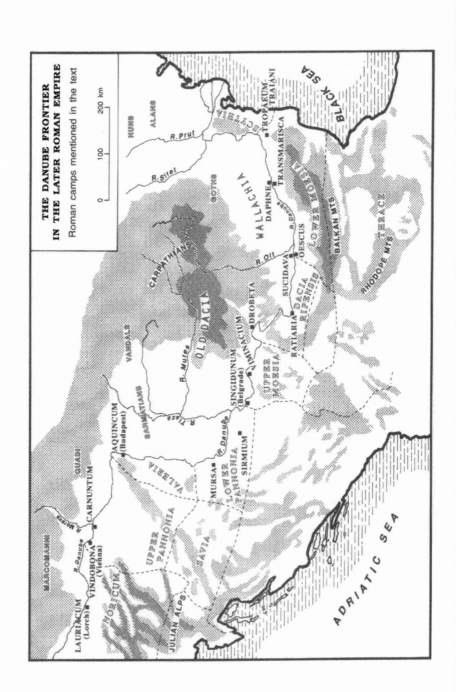

THE DANUBE FRONTIER
IN THE LATER ROMAN EMPIRE

Roman camps mentioned in the text

0   100   200 km

Roxolani, and the Sarmatians. Some, but not all, of the population of Dacia was moved south of the Danube to two new provinces of Dacia Ripensis and Dacia Mediterranea. But like the *Agri Decumates,* it is clear that old Dacia was not regarded by Roman emperors of the fourth century as out of their control.

For most of the fourth century it was the Goths who occupied the center stage of the Danube. We know more about them than any other "barbarian" people, and in many ways they paved the way for the transformation of the Roman Empire. The Goths were the only intrusive people who were literate when they arrived. They were the first to be recorded by our sources as "organizing into a federation" (Amm. Marc. 26.6.11 *conspirans in unum*) for attack. They were responsible for what Ammianus regarded as the most catastrophic of defeats upon the Romans at Adrianople in 378. After the battle Theodosius I gave them the first formal, federate enclaves within the Roman Empire, which was a step toward the first kingdom within the Roman Empire, when they settled in Aquitania. And it was the Goth Alaric who sacked Rome in 410. By any standard the lower Danube was a key frontier.

On the other hand, in recent years there has been a strong tendency to revise the *Katastrophentheorie* of Balkan history and to lay more emphasis on the continuity of occupation. The Roman *limes* system remained intact on the lower Danube into the seventh century. High levels of epigraphic evidence are signs of restored confidence. Despite damage by raids and loss of wealth, not a single major city of Thrace fell to Goths or Huns in the fifth century, and only one fell to the Slavs in the sixth (Velkov 1977, 59). A persuasive case can be made for saying that Adrianople was not the great turning point or crisis that Ammianus wishes to make it (Wolfram 1988, 128–30).

The political and military organization of the Goths can also be exaggerated; their main activity was petty raids and infiltration. In 362 Julian refused to waste time dealing with such attacks, since he was "looking for a better enemy" (Amm. Marc. 22.7.8).

Fig. 42 *(opposite).* The Danube frontier in the later Empire

Themistius, a contemporary, described the river and marshy region of the Dobrudja where raiders come in small groups "not as soldiers but as robbers," against whom the only solution was to construct many small fortlets (*Or.* 10.136–38; Velkov 1977, 209).

One other revealing feature about the Danube frontier is that the units listed in the *Notitia Dignitatum* are relatively complete, since they were not stripped in the early fifth century as they were on the Rhine. That allows us to make some analysis of what earlier dispositions of the units, going back to Diocletian, might have been. It is here, if anywhere, that we can make some judgments about the military strategy and tactics of warfare on a riverine frontier, even though we know very little about the way the field army operated in relation to the frontier troops.[22]

Broadly speaking, it appears that the frontier *limitanei* contained units for both defense (*auxilia, equites, cohortes*) and for attack (*cunei, auxiliares*), the latter being given a higher status as *ripenses* than units of the line in their position on the army list, the *laterculum minus*. If that is so, Roman policy on the Danube was never purely defensive. This conclusion is reinforced by the evidence of double camps at river bridgeheads, much as on the Rhine, where artillery units were often situated in *barbarico* (Brennan 1980; Mócsy 1974b, 267). Examples are at Transmarisca/Daphne or Oescus/Sucidava on the lower Danube or the two left-bank forts opposite Aquincum (Budapest) and Bonnonia on the middle Danube (Soproni 1977).

NORICUM

The frontier of Noricum met the Raetian frontier at the river Inn and continued eastward almost as far as Vienna, where Pannonia began. Restored by Diocletian's defeat of the Alamans in 287, its units were brigaded together with Pannonia Prima in a single ducate as far as Brigetio (under the *magister militum* of Illyricum), probably from Constantine onward (Alföldy 1974, 201). That shows that the main pressure was expected from the eastern approaches, even though there was some trouble from the Alamanni in the northwest. The main population centers north of the river were in the Wienerwald-Tullnerfeld region, and hence

Lauriacum (modern Lorch) was the Roman military center, though the scatter of small forts along the river line shows that infiltration was the main problem. As in the earlier empire, the Romans did not hesitate to establish posts north of the Danube in the Tullnerfeld (Alföldy 1974, 205).

Alaman pressure in the region has already been described, but it was not until the fifth century when Goths entered the territory that it became critical. In the fourth century Pannonia Prima contrasts strikingly, in the lightness of its defenses, with Valeria, the adjacent province of Pannonia running southward from the Danube bend (Gabler 1977).

THE MIDDLE DANUBE

The eastern and western empires in the *Notitia Dignitatum* divided between the frontiers of Lower Pannonia (Secunda) and Upper Moesia (Prima); the division fell at Belgrade, the ancient city of Singidunum, which lay at the end of the southernmost trans-Illyrian route from Italy to the Danube, a route that ran along the Save valley and passed through Sirmium, an imperial capital city under the tetrarchy.

During the high Empire a line of stone-built camps and forts stretched from Vindobona (Vienna) to Singidunum along the right bank of the Danube, with some left-bank forts to enforce order among the treaty states to the north. The important thing to note is that this river line of frontier and small fortifications was mainly administrative, not political or military, and certainly not defensive. Marcus Aurelius was prepared to annex the trans-Danubian territories of the Quadi and Marcomanni (roughly speaking Slovakia), had the conditions been right, and his successor, Commodus, constructed an elaborate system of *burgi* and *praesidia* watchposts on the Danube against raiders into the Roman province (Mócsy 1974a, 196). Archaeology is also making it increasingly clear that there were extensive Roman settlements dating from this period in the free German lands to the north, some apparently military but others more obviously for trade, whose control was part of the function of a *burgus* (e.g., *CIL* 3.3653).[23]

In short, the main elements of the fourth-century Danubian

frontier—small fortlets, dispersed military units, and controls beyond the river—were already in place by the third century. It is important to note, when one remembers that it was from this region of Illyricum that so many of the late third- and fourth-century "Illyrian" emperors came, that this was the form of frontier organization they were most familiar with (Mócsy 1974b, 268, gives a list of the emperors).

The immediate action required from Diocletian at the end of the third century from his base at Sirmium was to continue the work of Probus, Carus, and Carinus against the Sarmatians, who appear to have been pressed southeast of Budapest by the Vandals in the north. In 294 we have the first reference to forts on the left bank of the Danube (*Chron. Min.* 1.230), some deep within the Hungarian plain between the rivers Danube and Tisza (e.g., *CIL* 3.10605; Mócsy and Gabler 1986). Probably about this time, too, a number of crossing points and landing stages on the middle Danube were constructed (Mócsy 1974a).

The most spectacular but mysterious of the trans-Danubian constructions are the massive "Devil's Dykes," seven hundred kilometers of earth ditches, some in triple lines, that formed a kind of outer enclosure of the Sarmatian lowlands from Aquincum (Budapest) to Viminacium in Moesia (fig. 43). Opinion is divided about the exact date of this *limes Sarmaticus,* as it has been called, and it may have had a first century A.D. origin, although the lines were certainly reinforced in the late third or early fourth century (Horedt 1977; Soproni 1977). There is no reason, however, to suppose that the Romans ever manned them as a military frontier, even though there are one or two later Roman forts that appear associated with the ditches (Nagy 1974). In essence they were not fortifications but a visible political boundary, perhaps a mark of

Fig. 43 *(opposite).* The so-called *limes Sarmaticus* earthworks, or Devil's Dykes, beyond the middle Danube and the "Giant's Furrow" (Brazda lui Novac) beyond the lower Danube. They had no military value but were visible signs of power and probably were associated with the appearance of the Sîntana de Mureş culture (the Goths), whose main settlements are marked. After Mócsy 1974b; Vulpe 1974; and Heather and Matthews 1991.

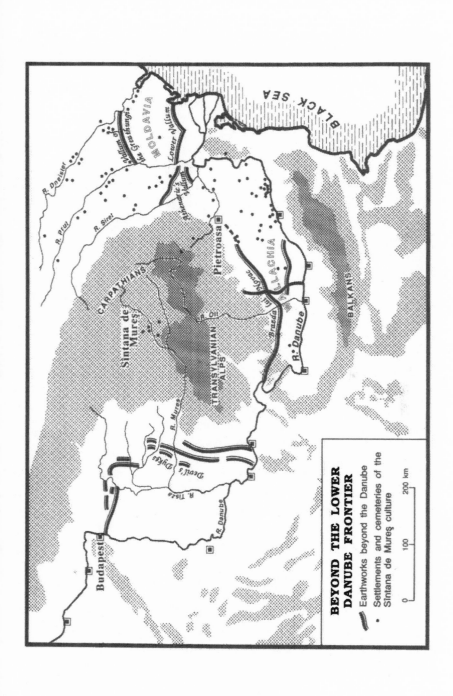

BLACK SEA

MOLDAVIA

Vallum of the Greuthungi

R. Dneister

R. Prut

R. Siret

Athanaric's Vallum

Lower Vallum

CARPATHIANS

Sintana de Mures

Pietroasa

WALLACHIA

R. Olt

TRANSYLVANIAN ALPS

Brazda lui Novac

R. Danube

BALKANS

R. Mures

Devil's Dykes

R. Tisza

R. Danube

Budapest

BEYOND THE LOWER DANUBE FRONTIER

⌇ Earthworks beyond the Danube

• Settlements and cemeteries of the Sintana de Mures culture

0   100   200 km

Roman control, to distinguish Sarmatians, who were regarded as "permanent *clientes* of the Romans" (Amm. Marc. 17.12.15), from the Vandals, Gepids, Taifals, and Goths to the north and east (Mócsy 1974b, 271).

That fits quite well into the context of Constantine's wars against the Sarmatians in 322 and with the fact that he accorded a *receptio,* or formal surrender, to some Sarmatians moving into Roman territory as they were pressured by Goths and Gepids from the Banat and Transylvania. It was followed by trouble between two groups of Sarmatians, the Agaragantes and their subject Limigantes (presumably a Roman nickname acquired after their settlement on the Danube "*limes*"), which led to a second invasion by Constantine in 334 and ultimately (in the next reign) to radical resettlement of both groups. The action went together with a considerable number of forts and roads on the Sarmatian side of the Danube and the strengthening of the whole sector with watchtowers and forts southward from Aquincum, which itself seems to have been upgraded as a camp. It is difficult, however, to see why all this should be thought a defensive strategy, or why Constantine should be said to have abandoned the perimeter established by Diocletian—both alleged by historians.[24]

Constantius II followed the same policy. We must assume that the wars of succession, which lasted until 352, gave, as so often, encouragement to raiders on the borders, and it was necessary to take radical action against the troublesome Sarmatian Limigantes and Agaragantes. Both were finally settled in the Tisza valley along the Sarmatian *ripa* of Lower Pannonia and Upper Moesia after deep Roman invasions of the Banat, as far as the Transylvanian mountains, in 358–59. Exiled Sarmatians had spread the disturbance also to the Quadi in southern Slovakia, who attacked the province of Valeria, although it is not easy to see what action was taken in retaliation by Constantius, apart from demands for their allegiance.

Valentinian, however, was enormously active on the Pannonian front and particularly around the Danube bend where the Quadi bordered on the Roman provinces. Perhaps this is unsurprising, given Valentinian's origins as a Pannonian landowner. But it is also a sign of the growing political coherence of the Quadi in the fourth century (Pitts 1989, 52), as well as an indication that they in turn were almost certainly being put under pressure from the East. Valentinian's response was energetic but unoriginal. Inscriptions of 371–72 record the construction of large numbers of *burgi* on the Danube bend, where Sarmatian and Quadi territories met. The Roman presence was reinforced by military deployment deep inside Quadi territory—so much so, says Ammianus, that it was "as if the country of the Quadi were already under Roman rule" (29.6.1–2). Examples of Valentinian's forts are at Hatvan-Gombospuszta, sixty kilometers northeast of Aquincum (Budapest) and the large camp at Felsögöd, a short distance beyond the Danube, both probably associated with the Devil's Dykes noted earlier.[25] Their location looks as if part of the Roman intention was to keep the Sarmatians and Quadi apart.

It is in this context that we should note the remarkable series of so-called villas that have been found scattered over a wide area of present-day southern Moravia and Slovakia, some of them near the left bank, some up to a hundred kilometers beyond the Danube (fig. 32). Although long known, they are being increasingly studied and excavated (Kolník 1986, 1990, 1991; Pitts 1989). Most are in the river valleys that run into the Danube in the sector between Carnuntum and Brigetio, a region that broadly corresponds to the territory of the Marcomanni and Quadi. The buildings are constructed very obviously in Roman style, some with bath houses, some using Roman military tiles, and all full of Roman artifacts.

The interesting questions, of course, are who lived in these houses and what do they tell us about Roman frontiers? Some probably housed Roman traders, since they lay along the famous amber routes that came down from the north to Carnuntum. Others may have been forts or houses of Roman military agents, like the one at Mušov that contained Roman weapons and armor. Some were surely the residences of native princes. The buildings were not a novelty of the later empire, since some date from the period of the Marcomannian wars of Marcus Aurelius in the later second century. But all seem to have been reused in the third and fourth centuries, though not all by Germanic peoples. At Cífer-

Pác, for instance, the Roman-style house looks very much like that of a German prince and his followers, since it is surrounded by wooden enclosures, within which are typically German *Gruben-häuser* huts inhabited by people using Germanic pottery. At Iza opposite Brigetio, however, it is fairly clear that Romans reoccupied the fort.

The natural conclusion is that here we have an illustration of the remarkably close and generally peaceful relations that existed between the Quadi and the Romans. The small military presence is less revealing than the large amount of trade goods and Roman traders in the territories. The Roman "villa" at Bratislava, whether occupied by a Roman or by a Quadi leader, shows the conditions of peace that prevailed, especially when set alongside the rich princely grave nearby at Krakovany-Strázë.

It could be that Valentinian's hyperactive frontier policy provoked the Quadi to attack in 373, as Ammianus says (19.6.2), but archaeologists warn us not to exaggerate the danger and damage of wars in the middle Danube region (Kolník 1991). Quadi, Sarmatians, and Iazyges served regularly in ethnic units of the Roman army, and most of the disturbances can be put down to petty raids and intertribal rivalries in which pro- and anti-Roman sentiment was exploited. The judgment of Ammianus at the end of the fourth century was that the Quadi were "a people [*natio*] not to be feared very much" (29.6.1); and the Sarmatians were "better fitted for robbery than for open war" (17.12.2). By and large, Roman policy of control of the *Limesvorfeld* was a success, even if in the end it could not contain the pressures of inland Suebi, Vandals, and Goths beyond.

After Adrianople the temporary collapse of the lower Danube front was bound to have repercussions on the middle Danube as rumors of hostile tribes beyond the frontiers increased (Amm. Marc. 31.4.2), echoed by Ambrose a few years later in Milan (Ambr. *PL* 15.1806). The instability was encouraged by the east-west rivalries between Theodosius and the usurpers Magnus Maximus and Eugenius, who were not above making pacts with "barbarians" (e.g., Zos. 4.45.3). The middle Danube provinces of Valeria and Upper Moesia were selected by Theodosius for his early federate settlements of Goths, Huns, and Alans in 382, though it is difficult to trace exactly where—possibly in the Drave valley.[26] All we can really say is that Alaric, the Visigothic federate leader by the end of the century, had been appointed *magister militum per Illyricum,* and that he moved to Pannonia from Dacia about 402. But we do not know how he and his Goths integrated, if at all, into the Roman forces.[27]

Nor is it at all certain what relation such federate enclaves bore to the frontiers, which they were presumably contracted to defend. We do not even know when federates were part of the regular army or when, as seems to be more frequent, they were recruited as irregulars for specific campaigns. There is evidence of new types of military forts at about the turn of the century that were built into the corners of previous military camps, such as Carnuntum, along the whole length of the Danube from Noricum to Scythia (fig. 44). They could have been built as the result of a massive transfer of regular *limitanei* troops to the *comitatenses* and their replacement by federates.[28] The widespread use of a new type of glazed pottery and the decline of circulating coin after about 375 may be further consequences of the changes, but it is impossible to be sure.

Indeed, it is sometimes difficult to know how much of the frontier was actually maintained. The Romans invaded Sarmatia again in the 380s (Sym. *Rel.* 47), and though we hear of attacks from beyond the Danube, the problem is that some sources greatly exaggerate the damage done. Jerome, for instance, speaks of "half-wrecked dwellings" and "devastation in Illyricum" (*semirutae villulae . . . Illyrica vastitas*) after 380, but he was still able to sell his father's estate at Stridon at the end of the century (Mócsy 1974b, 344, provides many references). Pannonia was besieged in 399, but Stilicho's campaign on the Danube was a success according to Claudian (*De cons. Stil.* 2.191–92), and the Danube was still considered Roman.

It must have been about now, too, that the Marcomanni under their queen, Fritigil, were forced to cross the Danube to seek

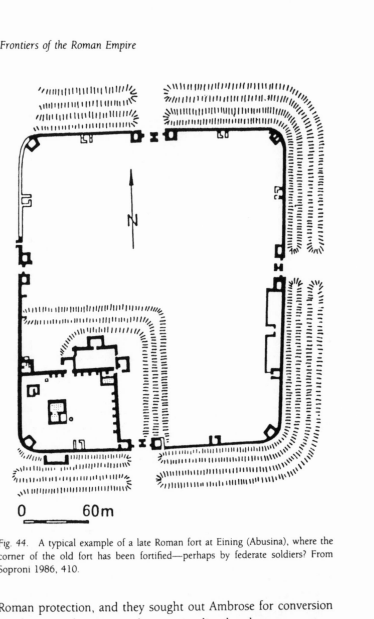

Fig. 44. A typical example of a late Roman fort at Eining (Abusina), where the corner of the old fort has been fortified—perhaps by federate soldiers? From Soproni 1986, 410.

Roman protection, and they sought out Ambrose for conversion (Paulin. *V. Ambr.* 36). But the story implies that there was protection to be had, and it is confirmed by the *Notitia Dignitatum,* listing a Roman officer placed as tribune in charge of the Marcomannian *gens* (*ND* Oc. 34.24). It was not until the fifth century that Upper Pannonia, like Noricum, was badly disrupted.

THE LOWER DANUBE

We come at last to the lower Danube, which probably occupied more of the attention of Roman emperors of the fourth and fifth centuries than did any other single sector, since it was through the corridor between the Carpathians and the Balkans that Goths, Huns, and Alans poured into the empire. Yet the interesting fact is that, unlike the upper Danube or the Rhine, this frontier did not dissolve in the fifth century but continued intact until the seventh century. The lesson we should draw is that frontiers collapsed not just because of the severity of external military pressures but because of the instability of the internal political state. Upper Moesia, Dacia, Lower Moesia, and Scythia—the provinces along the Danube stretching from Belgrade to the Black Sea—were part of the eastern empire, which continued long after the West. Even though the battle of Adrianople was remembered as one of the great defeats of the Roman army, and despite the plethora of foreign, federate settlements in this part of the empire, neither was necessarily as destructive as is sometimes thought.

We start with the loss of the old Dacian province and the strategic decision of Aurelian to abandon Transylvania and the Carpathians after his victories over the Goths. The event coincided with the archaeological appearance of a new culture in Muntenia and Moldavia in the late third century, the so-called Sîntana de Mureş–Cerniachov culture, which tracks a population moving westward from Ukraine and the Don, then spreading down the Dniester and Prut valleys into Wallachia, although very rarely across the river Olt (fig. 43). Without much doubt these were the Goths.[29]

It is clear, however, that the Romans had no intention either in the third century or later of relinquishing control over the rich plains of Wallachia and the Banat that lay between the Carpathians and the Danube (Wachtel 1977; Toropu 1974). The fort of Sucidava, for instance, which lay on the northern bank, was occupied throughout; though overrun in the fifth century, it was reoccupied until the seventh century. This means that the Danube was considered an administrative boundary and a fortified supply line—

part of the *limes* but not *the* frontier, which was a far broader concept.

Two facts will illustrate the point. In 316, when repairs were carried out at Tropaeum Traiani (Adamklissi), they were commemorated by an inscription claiming they were "to strengthen the safety of the frontier" (*ad confirmandam limitis tutelam; CIL* 3.13734); yet the site is well to the rear of the Danube in the Dobrudja. On the other hand, the forts in the Dobrudja on the southern bank of the Danube, which looks like an impressive defensive line, were established by Trajan in the early second century at precisely the time when Roman arms were at their most offensive and expansive across the Danube (Barnea and Ştefan 1974).

Diocletian and the tetrarchy have left many records of their presence on the lower Danube and of their battles against the Sarmatians and the Goths. Inscriptions show the attention they gave, particularly to Lower Moesia and to the *limes Scythicus* in the Dobrudja. The sector of the Iron Gates around Drobeta also records their activity, where an inscription from the camp at Zanes, which was probably accompanied by a fortlet on the island opposite, records the building of a "bulwark of the state for the future and for ever" (*pro futurum in aeternum rei publicae praesidium;* Petrović 1977) It has a formulaic quality similar to that of a number of other inscriptions in Lower Moesia (*CIL* 3.6151, 7487, etc.), showing that a systematic reconstruction was taking place (Sarnowski 1990). Diocletian was probably responsible for the basic dispositions of the units we find recorded in the *Notitia Dignitatum,* and already by 297 it sounds as if a treaty was established between him and the Goths (Jord. *Get.* 110–12).

Constantine, and before him Licinius (between 315 and 319), carried on Diocletian's work. But the wars of succession between Constantine and Licinius resulted in *neglectos limites* (Exc. Val. 1.21) and encouragement to the Goths to join in the wars when Licinius used them in his army. Their breakthrough into Moesia and Thrace in 323 obviously prompted Constantine's decision to deal more comprehensively with the problems of the lower Danube. This led to a strategic shift of resources to the East and a decision to transfer the eastern capital to Constantinople.[30]

The shift was accompanied by a determination to extend control beyond the Danube. The propaganda Constantine gave through coins to his new bridge across the Danube at Transmarisca-Daphne in Lower Moesia is evidence of the importance he attached to such control (Demougeot 1983). Another bridge, in stone, was constructed in Dacia at Oescus-Sucidava to control the Taifals in Lower Wallachia, and a road was built running from Sucidava up the river Olt through Oltenia to Romula, the former capital of Dacia Malvensis. Some have supposed that this road formed an east-west frontier, the *limes Alutanus,* dividing off the Goths of Wallachia from the Romanized inhabitants of Oltenia. But the first road was constructed in the early third century, before the Goths had arrived, and was probably no more than a typical *praetentura,* of the sort we have encountered in other parts of the empire, designed to keep open communications in the *Vorlimes* region.

Another element in the frontier may have been a second set of ditches, like those in Sarmatia, the so-called Brazda lui Novac ("the furrow of Novac the giant"), the northern branch of which ran for three hundred kilometers from the Iron Gates along the foot of the Carpathians (Vulpe 1974, 272) (fig. 43). It is difficult to be sure of either the date or the purpose of these massive earthworks, but like the Olt road, the "Giant's Furrow" was a relic of earlier Roman occupation that continued in use in the fourth century.

It was probably the effectiveness of Constantine's grip that drove some of the Goths westward, where they began to put pressure on the Sarmatians of the middle Danube, a movement that coincides with the approximate appearance of the Sîntana de Mureş culture in Transylvania and the Mureş valley. But harassed by Roman forces and under starving, freezing conditions, the main group, whom our sources now identify as Tervingi, were forced into a treaty agreement with Constantine in 332 by which they had access to Roman trade and received subsidies of cash and food in return for hostages and service in the Roman army (Anon. Val. 1.31; Jord. *Get.* 112). The event, which was celebrated as a Roman victory on inscriptions, marks the beginning of the integration of Goths into Roman life (Wolfram 1988, 62). The close relations between Gothic chiefs, such as Aoric, father of Athanaric, whose statue was set up in Constantinople, and Roman emperors was to dominate much of Roman history for the next century.

The *foedus* of 332 held during the rule of Constantius II and Julian, though under some strain. In 348 some *Gothi minores* (as they were called) were forced to seek refuge in Lower Moesia as settlers, since they were Christians who, with their bishop Ulfilas, were feared as Roman collaborators (Jord. *Get.* 267, Wolfram 1988, 63). Soon after this, in 358, Constantius, using Gothic Taifals as allies, finally settled the Sarmatian Agaragantes in the Banat, after great slaughter of the Limigantes who had been occupying the territory. In both cases we can see a similar interventionist tendency at work. Christianity was regarded by Romans and Goths alike as subversive of Gothic culture, destroying "the faith of our fathers" in the eyes of the Goths (Soz. 6.37.12).[31] Settlement of the Banat was part of Constantine's determined effort to hold political control beyond the provincial boundaries (Mócsy 1974b, 288).

No doubt the personal reputation of Constantine and his policy of integrating Goths were the glue that held the treaty together. Certainly the Goths claimed that after the death of Julian they had legitimately supported the last survivor of the House of Constantine, the ursurper Procopius, when he had ordered their help in his bid for the empire against the upstart brothers Valens and Valentinian (Amm. Marc. 27.5.1). The justice of their claim was not easy to discount (Eunap. fr. 37, p. 53–5 Blockley).

It raises the question who was responsible for the Gothic war of 367, which in turn reflects on frontier attitudes. Valens was seeking a military reputation and was perhaps only too happy to believe reports that a barbarian coalition was forming (Amm. Marc. 26.6.11; Wolfram 1988, 66–67). The Goths likewise had been chafing at the terms of the *foedus* and may have decided to take advantage of Julian's defeat in Persia (Heather and Matthews 1991, 20–25). Preparations for the war by Valens began before news of Procopius's rebellion (e.g., *CTh* 15.1.13 [probably dated 364]). But that supports either argument. Ammianus himself, however, believed Valens was the aggressor in wanting to punish the Goths for their support of Procopius (31.3.4).

More relevant to the question of frontiers is that the war and the subsequent treaty of 369 marked an important change in Romano-Gothic relations and perhaps a new attitude toward the lower Danube frontier. First, there was an aggressive trade restriction on the Goths, limiting them to the two sites on the Danube, at Daphne and Noviodunum. This was done, says Themistius, a contemporary orator, as a demonstration of power and to keep the barbarians under surveillance (*Or.* 10.135). Second, there was strengthening of the Danube forts, especially in the marshy Dobrudja (Them. *Or.* 10.136–37), which was so general that it makes one wonder whether the Romans were worried about a more potent threat of Huns than the Goths on their doorstep (Petolescu 1977).

The dramatic negotiation of the new treaty on a boat in the Danube might look like Roman recognition of the Danube as the Gothic boundary and a retreat from Constantine's earlier policy of *Vorlimes* control (Amm. Marc. 27.5.9, 31.4.13). But Ammianus tells us that Valens agreed to such a meeting only under pressure because of the religious taboos of Athanaric, whose position as a Tervingian "judge" forbade him to leave Gothic territory. Themistius described the purpose of the new river forts as a deterrent against infiltrators, not as a retreat into defensive positions—precisely what we would expect if the Goths were being forced by Huns to migrate from the northeast. It is true that archaeologists report a distinct drop in Roman coins in Oltenia, which might indicate the withdrawal of Roman control (Toropu 1974). But it could just as easily be the result of the severe new trade restrictions and the wars, particularly since the coinage picked up again after 383. Valens changed none of the forward military posts on the frontier, as far as one can see.

But we must also take into account the development of Gothic political institutions and the sense of territoriality implied in the story of the Danube as the religious boundary of "Guttiuda." This is the term used originally by Goths to mean "Gothic people" but now beginning to refer to their territory (Wolfram 1988, 91). It coincides with Ammianus's reference to the "rampart" (*vallum*) of the Greuthungi Goths near the Dniester and to Athanaric's "walls" (*muros*) constructed against the Huns in the region of the Prut-Dniester valleys (31.3.5, 7). If these were the earthworks discovered in Bessarabia between the Prut and the Dniester and in Lower Moldavia between the Prut and the Siret (fig. 43), they were more like territorial boundaries than defenses (Vulpe 1974).

This is not the place to discuss Gothic state formation, but there is little doubt that Athanaric's position as "judge" (*kindins*) represented an evolved form of political confederation among the Tervingi Goths that went beyond the traditional "divisions" (*kunja*) and war leaders (*reiks*) (Wolfram 1988, 93–98). The Romans and the Huns between them successfully stifled this evolution.

Under pressure from the north, Rome permitted large numbers of Tervingi to settle legally across the Danube in 376, but without any proper *foedus* agreement (Oros. 7.33). Nor did the army control the crossings, and they failed to stop numbers of Taifals and Greuthungi Ostrogoths from coming over too. Official incompetence, greed, and lack of planning were responsible for brutal mistreatment of the starving refugees (Eunap. fr. 42, p. 61 Blockley). Many sold themselves into slavery in return for food (Amm. Marc. 31.4), and many were left to wander about.

The dominant attitude of the Roman upper class, found in writers like Eunapius and Ammianus, is that this was when the Goths began "to take over the Roman empire" (Eunap. fr. 42, p. 63 Blockley) and brought about "the ruin of the Roman world" (Amm. Marc. 31.4.6).[32] Again and again we are told of the contempt the Romans had for Goths, who were often regarded as savage beasts (e.g., Them. *Or.* 10.139). But the rural poor in Roman provinces were less ideologically motivated and perhaps far closer to Goths than we realize. When the Goths rebelled against Roman maltreatment, they received help from "traitors and fugitives" (e.g., Amm. Marc. 31.6.5–6, 31.15.2, 31.16.2; Velkov 1977, 254). Though many were Goths who had been sold into slavery or subjected to servile rural status, we also hear of poor miners who could not pay their taxes, and it is evident that tensions between the army and the farmers who had to support it were sometimes severe (Them. *Or.* 10.138).

The events leading up to the defeat at Adrianople in 378 demonstrate less the weakness of the frontiers than Roman incompetence through contempt for the Goths and unwillingness to grant them treaty status. This demand Valens, like Ammianus (31.12.8–9), thought to be a trick, but it could have been perfectly genuine, since just this kind of internal federate state was created in the end. The defeat shocked the Roman world, and Ammianus gave it enormous dramatic prominence. Two-thirds of the army was destroyed, and the body of the Roman emperor Valens was never found. The Greuthungi Goths (Ostrogoths) made their first appearance in the Roman Empire in the battle, and soon after Huns and Alans were marching with them on Constantinople.

But for all that, it was not the military disaster that is often claimed, since it brought no general collapse of the lower Danube frontier. There are plenty of signs of violent destruction at some forts—at the Iron Gates, for example, or in the Dobrudja (Vasić 1991; Scorpan 1980, 122). But some forts, like Halmyris in the Dobrudja, were untouched (Zahariade 1991); others were quickly repaired, and within a year Theodosius, the new emperor, had restored order in the provinces.

But the political effect was profound and radical for the organization of the whole length of the frontiers. It led to a massive use of Goths in the army; and the Goths themselves were granted what they had requested before—autonomous federate status within the Roman Empire. The great *foedus* of 382, celebrated in Roman annals as the "surrender" of the Goths (*Anon. cons. Constantin.* a.382), was the work of Theodosius, whose liberal policy has earned him praise and blame. The terms broadly speaking were grants of tax-free Roman land in return for service in the Roman army.[33] But the novelty was that now for the first time official recognition was given to communities of independent peoples, "barbarians," living within the Roman Empire.[34]

It is fairly clear that the settlements were intended to be more than a crisis measure and became an instrument of frontier policy, since there were similar settlements almost at once on the Danube and in Phrygia that included Greuthungi Ostrogoths as well as Huns (Claud. *In Eutrop.* 2.153). It must be this that Ambrose, bishop of Milan, referred to when he wrote at just about this time in tones of disapproval: "Have we not heard that the whole length of the *limes*, which starts from the Thracian boundaries and goes through Dacia Ripensis and Moesia to all of Pannonia Valeria, is in uproar caused by wicked voices and barbarian movements? What disasters will these dire neighbors bring to us? How can the Roman state be defended by such forces?" (*De fide* 3.16.140). In 400 Synesius, future bishop of Cyrene, delivered a similar scathing speech, *On Kingship*, in Constantinople concerning the folly of using wolves as watchdogs and urging that Goths should be returned to beyond the Danube where they had come from (*De regno* 5 ff.).

Unfortunately it is difficult to know precisely how these federate settlements related to the frontiers, although we saw above some of the evidence in Lower Pannonia. As on the middle Danube, various signs of these federate forces have been detected in the military forts along the Danube. The living conditions of the camps in the later fourth century appear simpler and cruder than before, though still regimented, while telltale ceramics and combs of the Sîntana de Mureş culture begin to appear inside the camps.[35] On the other hand, we must not forget that, according to the *Notitia Dignitatum*, the forts were still manned by regular units, some of them "barbarian" to be sure, but not the same as federates, who were not usually recorded on the lists.

There is no reason to doubt, however, that Rome still maintained some control beyond the Danube, since all the main crossing points were manned. After the great treaty we have numerous references to attacks. A second wave of Greuthungi was checked at the Danube in 386 (Zos. 4.35, 38 ff.); in 391 Theodosius had to deal with infiltrators into the Macedonian marshes (Zos. 4.48); in 394–95 the Huns took advantage of Theodosius's absence with his Goths in the West to cause severe damage to the federate settlements in Moesia and Dacia; and so on. But the frontier still held.

The death of Theodosius in 395 ended the special relationship with the Visigoth federates, who had virtually given him victory at the Frigidus over the western usurpers and who, under their leader Alaric were angered at the failure to pay them. When their demands for a new *foedus* were not met, the issue was forced by Alaric's joining the Huns and ended with his appointment as *magister militum per Illyricum*. What had before been implicit became explicit. Federate kings were now demanding by right of arms what Rome had long granted to foreign military officers after their submission: access to high office at court. Some contemporary Romans believed (as do some modern commentators) that Alaric was encouraged through the political maneuvers of the regent Stilicho, who was aiming to reunite the empire under his direction.[36] It perhaps also marks the emergence of a new style of political superkingship among the Visigoths as the prelude to their move westward, where they set up in Aquitania the first federate kingdom unrelated to frontier defense (Wolfram 1988, 143–46).

Six

The Collapse of the Frontiers

Astory was told about the emperor Theodosius the Great, who was returning to the East in A.D. 391, after defeating the western usurper Magnus Maximus. At Salonica in Macedonia he found the land in turmoil because barbarians were attacking the inhabitants by night, but during the day they hid in the marshes. They were, says the story, "like ghosts instead of men." Theodosius's remedy was to select a band of five horsemen with spare mounts and to ride continuously around the countryside incognito, eating at country inns. At one such inn, where he was received by an old woman, he noticed another traveler who kept to himself and said nothing. Surprised by this, Theodosius asked his hostess who the stranger was. She replied that she did not know but that he had been with her for some time, going out all day and returning home at night exhausted. Theodosius thereupon seized the man, tortured him, and discovered he was a spy for the barbarians hidden in the marshes, giving them information about the movements of the Roman army and where they could attack. So the man lost his head and Theodosius found the barbarians.

I do not ask you to believe this tale of Zosimus (4.48), which has all the marks of folklore, not history. But it contains authentic characteristics of life in the later Roman Empire, when the frontiers were coming under pressure from populations beyond. These particular barbarians were probably deserters from the Roman army, concerning whom Theodosius had just issued an edict.[1] But they could just as easily have been invaders. The extraordinary history of Charietto, the German barbarian raider, bears this out. Crossing the frontier in about 350, he lived at Trier with a band of robbers, but he also made profits by killing Germans who raided across the Rhine as they slept in the woods at night in a drunken stupor. So successful was he that the future emperor Julian employed him and his men as an irregular military unit, mixed with some Salian Franks Julian had just defeated, against invading Chauci and Chamavi—peoples who were themselves often counted among the Franks.[2]

Charietto went on to hold a high command as a Roman general on the Rhine, which is extraordinary enough. But the important point here is that dealing with the invasion was, as Ammianus the soldier knew, often better done "through undercover piecemeal action and through banditry" (*particulatim perque furta magis et latrocinia*; Amm. Marc. 31.7.2). The word "banditry" (*latrocinium*) crops up again and again in our sources, as we shall see. It often refers to irregular, as opposed to formal, military operations. The disruption these raiders caused was selective but continuous. And yet the rural community coexisted with them and, in our story, could not necessarily identify them by dress or language. They were absorbed into the countryside "like ghosts." After the Goths had won their shattering victory at Adrianople in 378, they disappeared, says Themistius, "like a shadow" (*Or.* 16.206d). Many of them had been living in the Thracian countryside round about for several years (Amm. Marc. 31.6.5–6). Charietto apparently had no difficulty living with his bandits even in the territory of the imperial capital of Trier. The frontiers of the barbarians, whatever the Romans may have imagined, were in fact extending deeper into the Roman Empire.

It is this aspect of the social and economic reality of the frontiers in the later Roman Empire that I shall examine in this chapter. Indeed, the question we should ask is whether the concept of the collapse of the frontiers is not a by-product of stereotyped preconceptions about linear frontiers that I discussed in my first chapter. Conservative Romans, like Ammianus, may have viewed the invasions "like a river that has burst its banks" (31.8.5). But it would be interesting to know how the inhabitants of the frontiers viewed the process. Or for that matter, what German Franks and Goths, Arab Saracens, or African Austuriani, who were coming and going across the frontiers all the time, thought about it. One of the problems of our sources is that from the fourth century to the sixth they all come from the Roman side. Not a single text is written by a Vandal or a Burgundian or a Frank.[3] The Saracens (or rather, various language groups of those Arabs we call Saracens) have left hundreds of inscriptions but little to tell us about their history. The Goths, some parts of whose Bible have survived, wrote nothing about their history until Jordanes in the mid-sixth century. And his history was in Latin, often following stereotypes of Roman tradition—as when, for instance, he describes invaders as only just human (*quasi hominum genus; Get.* 122).

Roman Ideology

Even if we will never know how most of the inhabitants of the later Roman Empire perceived events on their frontiers, it is worth looking more closely at two pronouncements from the latter half of the fourth century A.D. made by two more or less contemporary writers who were close to the court and the center of power. The first is Ammianus Marcellinus, who is often quoted because he wrote by far the best history we possess of his own day up to the Battle of Adrianople in 378: "At that time [he says], as if the trumpets were sounding the war note throughout the Roman world, the most savage people roused themselves and poured across the nearest frontiers" (26.4.5). The second is the writer of an anonymous tract called "Concerning Matters of War" (*De rebus bellicis*), who writes: "We must recognize that the madness of tribes baying all about are hemming in the Roman Empire and treacherous barbarians . . . menace every stretch of our frontiers"

(6.1). The impression these two writers give is one of chaos and pessimism, while Rome cowered behind its defenses.

Before we accept such gloomy descriptions, however, we must remember what was said earlier—that the classical Roman ideology of frontiers was based on the idea of expansion and of control of the barbarians beyond the provinces, which created an unwillingness to accept any other power as an equal. Ammianus, a soldier and minor imperial functionary, was classically conservative in his opinions and could only regard any change in the balance of power as a disaster (Ladner 1976; Dauge 1981, 346). The nameless pamphleteer, probably a minor civil servant, has produced a strange document containing advice about the ills of the empire, but in military matters he is no more than a "genial dilettante."[4] Both men were writing soon after the shock of Adrianople; both were entirely negative about the character of the "barbarian" pressures.

Nor does either author help us much to understand what was happening to the complex network of Roman *limites* in the later empire, with all the historical differences that existed between the de facto frontiers of provincial administration, the military frontiers of control, and the political frontiers of influence (cf. Trousset 1993). Although the empire had evolved over three centuries, it is uncanny how from the Roman upper-class point of view, which most of our fourth-and fifth-century sources reflect, nothing had changed. The main themes of Roman upper-class ideology persisted from the earlier empire with an even greater intensity (Dauge 1981, 308). The Goths took on the traits that Scythians, Getae, and Sarmatians had formerly possessed. It may have been a kind of defiance, suggests one recent writer, who says: "The menacing shadow of the barbarian Goth allowed writers to reaffirm the grandeur of Rome in the face of the barbarian world" (Teillet 1984, 47).

Perhaps so. An anthropologist in Africa has noted that ideology tends to be at its purest on the frontier, where it is most under pressure (Kopytoff 1987, 13). But my own impression is that many Roman attitudes from the days of imperial expansion were simply frozen into stereotypes, as so often happens when people are afraid to face change. It can be seen every day in the racist myths of our own world, and the charges are similar. Prudentius in the fifth century, like Velleius Paterculus in the first, still portrayed Germans as animals (Prud. *C. Symm.* 2.816–19; Vell. Pat. 2.117). The story of Charietto illustrates that in Roman minds Germans were still perpetual drunkards, as they had been in the first and second centuries when Seneca and Tacitus wrote (Tac. *Germ.* 23.2; Sen. *Ep.* 83.22).

The barbarians' lack of construction skills was standard diet for Roman readers. Cassius Dio, for instance, told them that Domitian and Trajan had had to teach Dacians the civilized arts, and the same was still apparently believed by the imperial chancellery of Germans and Goths, since in 419 Honorius and Theodosius II threatened to execute those who betrayed the arts of shipbuilding to the barbarians (*CTh* 9.40.24). This was declared even though the Scythian Borani had subjected the empire to devastating sea attacks in the mid-third century (Zos. 1.32–34) and though Saxon raiders had long experience of seafaring. Anyone who thinks the Huns were primitive nomadic raiders should read the personal account by Priscus of Pannium about the elaborate machines they built to capture Roman forts and cities (pp. 230–32 Blockley).[5]

The classical ideology of the Roman Empire from the Republic onward was quite simply that Rome ruled the world, either directly in the provinces or indirectly by political influence. One does not have to look far to see the persistence of this claim in the later Empire. A Gallic panegyricist praised Constantine's campaigns against the Frankish tribes for having "rooted them out from the very homes of their origins and from a farthest shores of barbary" (*Pan. Lat.* 6 [7].6.2). Even more sober inscriptions, like that commemorating the building of Constantine's fort at Deutz, on the right bank of the Rhine opposite Cologne, announced "the subjection and control of the Franks" (*CIL* 13.8502); and his imperial coinage showed Francia prostrate and weeping.

The evocation of early Empire and even Republican ideology is often explicit. Another Gallic orator, in a deliberate reference to Augustus, praised Theodosius because the terror of his name had reached India, Arabia, and the icy north and his rule had gone beyond the "terminal points of nature" (*ultra terminos rerum metasque naturae; Pan. Lat.* 2[12]. 22–23, 33). Alexander the Great's dream of conquering Persia, apparent in earlier emperors like Trajan and Severus, was alive in Constantine (Joh. Lyd. *De Mag.* 3.34). Julian's claim to be invading Persia only for revenge was no more than the kind of rationalization for conducting a *bellum iustum* used by Republican heroes, whom Julian actually recalled in the speech reported by Ammianus (23.5.16 ff.).

The ideological tension between the Greek concept of an empire surrounded by fortified frontiers to separate provincials from the irredeemable savagery of the barbarian exterior and the more Roman vision of universal rule also continued in the later Empire. A tetrarchic inscription on the Danube in Lower Moesia claims that the emperors had "established an eternal guardpost" (*praesidium*), suggesting the notion of a protective screen.[6] But despite the increasing pressure, it does not appear that the Romans ever seriously contemplated walls as a means of frontier defense.

It is true that in the later Empire a large number of examples of walls are known, especially in mountain passes, such as those in the Balkans and Caucasus (Napoli 1989; Crow 1986a). With the possible exception of the Caucasus passes, which were used to block the Huns, these walls were all behind the frontiers and served as internal tactical controls. In this respect they resembled city walls. Indeed, the *makron teichos* that ran for forty-five kilometers between the Black Sea and the Sea of Marmora was probably built in the later fifth century, just like city walls, to protect the aqueducts of Constantinople (Harrison 1974). In the Julian Alps a complex system of fortifications and wall sections across valleys, known as the *claustra Alpium Juliarum,* was constructed in the later Empire, possibly begun under Diocletian or Constantine, to control traffic between Italy and Illyricum (Christie 1991). But not a single example is known when this system was used to keep out barbarian invaders, not even the Gothic incursions of the early fifth century. The walls, in fact, appear to have been intended as tactical battle defenses against rival political pretenders, not as frontiers of empire.

Frontier ideology, therefore, far from adapting to assimilation, became more extreme in its praise of traditional Roman values and superiority. African inscriptions from Maximian to Theodosius reveal all the themes of mastery of barbarians (*dominatio gentium barbarum*) and expansion of the empire (*propagatio Romani imperii*) that were typical from Augustus to Septimius Severus (Kotula 1985). The Gallic panegyrics echo them precisely. The tetrarchic emperors were exalted because "they had carried forward the boundaries of Roman power by their courage" (*Romanae potentiae terminos virtute protulerant; Pan. Lat.* 8[5].3). The final unreality arrived when the Goth Theodoric the Great was proclaimed in Italy as *propagator Romani nominis, domitor gentium* (*CIL* 10.6850).

We might say that the ideology of an empire without limits almost prevented Romans from admitting that a frontier ever existed. This does not mean that all Romans were completely blind to the problems of populations beyond the frontiers or that they refused to make accommodations. But the compromises included the dreams. For example, Themistius, a consular at Constantinople in the fourth century and a firsthand observer of the formidable reality of peoples moving from central Europe and off the Russian steppes into the lower Danube and Balkans, recommended that Rome should peacefully absorb the Goths and in this way, he adds, would expand its frontiers. Libanius, a contemporary teacher of rhetoric in Antioch, had the same idea of the providential role of a universal monarchy under Rome.[7]

The unpopularity among conservative Romans of a more realistic policy of accommodation with barbarians was manifest against emperors and military leaders such as Constantius II, Jovian, and Stilicho. When Jovian conceded the city of Nisibis in Mesopotamia to the Persians after the disastrous campaign and death of Julian, Ammianus Marcellinus indignantly claimed (quite incorrectly) that this was the first occasion since the foundation of Rome when any territory had been lost to the enemy (Amm. Marc. 25.9.9). Even in the fifth century, with invasions threatening the gates of Rome, Stilicho lost support among Roman upper classes because he recruited barbarians to preserve the unity of the empire rather than crushing them (Frézouls 1983, 186; Mazzarino 1990, 215; Matthews 1975, 290). What could he do in face of the sheer absurdity of intelligent men like Synesius, later bishop of Cyrene, when the latter demanded that Rome employ no Goths or Huns but instead send all philosophers, craftsmen, merchants, and idle circus spectators to serve in the army (*De regno* 14)?

There were de facto boundaries, of course, both administrative and political, but modern historians find them difficult to define and contemporaries were never inclined to do so. Justinian's edict ordering the recovery of Africa from the Vandals in the sixth century commanded his generals to go "to that point where the Roman state had its boundaries [*fines*] before the invasion of the Vandals and the Moors" (*CJ* 1.27.4). The order was followed by detailed instructions concerning the maintenance of the frontiers (*limites*). They gave the illusion of certainty. But Justinian was in reality making a propaganda statement for public consumption to announce the restoration of the empire, and whether he really believed that boundaries and frontiers could be so easily discovered, we cannot know.

It is difficult, also, to agree with those who argue that Christianity enriched Roman opportunities for assimilating barbarians "by opening up new ways to them" (Dauge 1981, 375). Ambrose, bishop of Milan, followed the traditional view of drunken enemies when he encouraged the sale of wine to barbarians, in order, he said, "that they may dissolve in drunkenness and thus be weakened" (*De Elia et ieiunio* 54). To him barbarians, Christian or not, were the enemy. For instance, he considered that usury, forbidden to Christians, was quite proper in deals with barbarians, since "where there is a right of war, there is also a right of usury" (*De Tobia* 15.51). Both examples, incidentally, assumed that trade and the capacity to enforce contracts existed beyond the frontiers, despite whatever bans the state may have wished to impose.

The conservatism of such perceptions was hardly likely to produce a frontier policy that recognized the reality of a new kind of coexistence with the population pressing in upon the Roman Empire. The treachery of barbarians who served in the army is taken for granted by almost every contemporary source. Yet it was not, by any modern, objective assessment, particularly frequent or striking (A.H.M. Jones 1964, 1037–38; Thompson 1982, 182). The savagery and deceit of Franks or Alamans, which our sources recount, was easily matched by Romans (Frézouls 1983, 182). It was not that the Romans were simply responding in like manner to "barbarians" because they lay beyond the moral frontiers of behavior. Even within the Roman world judicial and administrative savagery, such as mutilation and pouring molten lead down the throats of deserters, robbers, and criminals, was now a regular feature of Roman law (MacMullen 1986). As Romans and barbarians became more alike, the dominant upper-class ideology of Rome became more shrill in its chauvinistic refusal to recognize the fact.

The Concept of Limes

The reality of frontiers and their historical development is complicated: first, by the Roman ideology of power that always claimed to reach beyond the formal lines of administered territory; second, by the strategic design of control that varied according to conditions from frontier to frontier; but third, by our own interpretation of the vocabulary Romans themselves used to describe various forms of military and civil limits, which perhaps took on different meanings in the later Empire. Since many of the terms had become fixed in Roman perceptions by the later Empire, this may be the right time to digress for a moment about the meaning of *limes*. It has been the subject of much study recently, and I shall only give a summary of the argument.[8]

As we saw in chapter 1, the word *limes* itself was originally a surveyor's term, adopted for military purposes to mean a road, and this technical sense was preserved throughout the later Empire in Roman surveyors' manuals.[9] In practice, too, we can see how in Algeria, for example, many of the sectors of the *limes* in the fourth century A.D. were simply lines or roads through the difficult mountains, such as the Grand Kabylie, which lay well to north of the line of military control. The road could even go forward at right angles to the front. In Jordania a recent inscription found in the Wadi Sirhan oasis records a road, although in this case it is called a *praetensio,* built by Diocletian's soldiers from the camp at Bostra southeastward down the Wadi Sirhan toward Saudi Arabia and far beyond the trunk road of the earlier *limes*. The term *praetentura*, linked to *praetensio*, was often used to indicate a line of points for observation rather than protection (e.g., Amm. Marc. 31.8.5; see Speidel 1987).

Not surprisingly, a military road linking camps on the fringes of empire, often lined with watchtowers and staging posts, was bound to invest the term *limes* with a sense of boundary or border in both earlier and later Empire (Isaac 1988). And not only roads, since rivers were just as often used as means of transport to camps that, for that reason, were often situated along their banks. The term *ripa*, riverbank, therefore also took on some of the notions of frontier, even though it signified a border region rather than a precise river line.[10] This does not mean, as I have tried to stress, that the river thereby became considered a defensive barrier. On the contrary, it could hardly have served as a line of communication if that were so. In the later Empire the Danube, which was regularly considered a *limes*, was used in 361 by the emperor Julian for the transport of three thousand troops from Raetia to Singidunum (Zos. 3.10.2), just as the Rhine was used by the same emperor for the supply of grain (Amm. Marc. 18.2.3; Lib. *Or.* 18.83, etc.). But because soldiers occupied the forts on the *ripae* of the *limites*, the name *ripenses* probably became an alternative for the term *limitanei* to mean troops on the frontiers.[11]

Use of the rivers for transport, however, obviously meant control of both banks, so it is not surprising to find that the emplacement of forts *in solo barbarico* ("on barbarian soil") remained a tactical necessity throughout the period.[12] But the need for political control beyond the administrative boundary, either through direct military occupation or through alliances, explains why *limes* came to mean a frontier zone as well as some sort of boundary.[13] In fact, it is unclear whether the word *limes* was ever official terminology except on the African frontier, where special conditions came into force by the early fifth century. Otherwise the term seems to have been used informally to describe a region within which military buildings were constructed both in advance of and behind the line of administered frontiers.[14]

Possibly this idea of a deep zone of forward control explains the description given by a sixth-century writer, John Malalas, about the flight of a Saracen phylarch from a Roman frontier officer of the Syrian frontier, first through an "outer" and then an "inner" *limes* toward the Indias."[15] The notion of control without administration also corresponds closely to the curious topographic lists, which I discussed in chapter 1, contained in such works as the *Sphaera* or *Cosmographia* of Julius Honoratus. These cosmographies, which named territories such as India or Gaetulia (in Africa) as "provinces" of the Roman Empire, were compiled in the form in which we have them today and put in circulation during the later Empire. As we saw, the term *limes* never occurs in those lists.[16] The ambiguity of the word *limes* in the later Empire, therefore, and its sporadic use show that the idea of a fixed military or political frontier was never strong and that Roman strategic aims had not radically altered from those of the earlier Empire. What changed was the extent to which the aims were achieved and how far the claims to control corresponded to reality.

The Strategy of Late Imperial Frontiers

Parallel with the propaganda, frontier strategy remained simplistic and unchanged. Just as in the earlier empire, conquest of the enemy and control beyond the *limites* were all that emperors desired, if the sources are an accurate guide. Although Constantine claimed to have recovered the empire of Trajan (Jul. *Caes.* 329c), he made his proselytizing zeal for Christianity into a vehicle to claim power beyond the frontiers, insisting on religious clauses in treaties with Sarmatians and Goths and proposing himself as protector of Christians within the Persian Empire (Barnes 1981, 258–59). His actual control of southern Dacia west of the Olt and his impressive bridge over the Danube, publicized on coins, show that the Danube was in no sense recognized as a military barrier or a strategic limit (Demougeot 1983).

There is one other revealing feature about the Danube frontier that has received little attention. The military units listed on the *Notitia Dignitatum* are relatively complete, since they were not stripped away in the early fifth century as they were on the Rhine.

That allows us to make some judgments about the military strategy and tactics of warfare on the riverine frontier, even if we know very little about the way the field army of the interior operated in relation to the frontier troops.[17] Broadly speaking, it appears that the frontier *limitanei* contained units both for defense (*auxilia, equites, cohortes*) and for attack (*cunei, auxiliares*), the latter having a higher status and perhaps the special name of *ripenses* to distinguish them from the units of the line.

This shows that Roman strategy on the Danube—and quite probably on the Rhine—was never intended to be defensive. The conclusion is reinforced, furthermore, by the evidence of double camps at major river bridgeheads, where artillery units were often situated on the far bank (Brennan 1980; Mócsy 1974b, 267). Examples of these doublets were noted earlier at Transmarisca/Daphne and Oescus/Sucidava on the lower Danube and at the two left-bank forts opposite Aquincum (Budapest) and Bonnonia on the middle Danube.[18] On the Rhine we have the evidence of double forts at a number of sites, such as at Zurzach/Reinheim, Kaiseraugst/Wyblen, Basel/Robur, Altrip/Neckerau, and Horburg/Breisach.[19] They are thought to be Valentinian, but we must not forget that the most famous doublet of left- and right-bank forts at Cologne/Deutz was Constantine's work. The system on the Danube, according to those who have studied it, was not the work of a single emperor but developed from Diocletian over the fourth century.

Constantine's successors could not appear weaker or more defensive than the founder of the dynasty. Ammianus admired Julian for his "completely republican outlook" that criticized even Trajan and Severus for seeking personal glory before defense of the *res publica* (Amm. Marc. 23.5.17–18).[20] In practice, however, Julian behaved like the great *propagatores imperii*: Ammianus stresses that it was *Trajan's* fort in Alaman territory that Julian rebuilt; much stress is laid on the fact that food was requisitioned from Alamans beyond the Rhine as from other "contractors" (*susceptores*). Julian advanced beyond the lower Rhine and attacked Franks by moving up the river Lippe (Amm. Marc. 17.1.11, 17.10.4, 20.10.2). His war with Persia, although defended by Ammianus as not of his seeking, was on Julian's own admission (*Caes.* 33a) conceived long before with Alexander and Trajan in mind. The strategy was almost aimless, beyond the desire for glory and titles, but it was probably not unaffected by the fact that Roman interests beyond the Tigris were challenged (Matthews 1989, chap. 8, esp. 136–38). On the Danube, where any decent information service would have forecast trouble, Julian contemptuously dismissed the Goths, since he was "looking for a better enemy" (Amm. Marc. 22.7.8). That gives us some idea of the prevailing mentality.

Valentinian was no less traditional in his "Augustan efforts" (Ternes 1972, 263). That means he advanced Roman claims *etiam ultra flumen* (Amm. Marc. 28.2.1) deep into transliminal territory of the Rhine and Danube. The Roman outpost at Hatvan-Gombopuszta, sixty kilometers beyond the Danube, gives substance to Ammianus's claim that he built forts in the middle of Quadi territory "as if already annexed to Roman rule" (29.6.2).[21] On the lower Danube there seems little doubt that, whoever was responsible for the war that broke out between Rome and the Goths in 367, Valens was seeking not a strategic first strike to stem the pressures from the Russian steppes, but simply to win a military reputation.[22] The sloppy inattention to the infiltration of Goths between this date and Adrianople shows how little military matters counted.

Even after the damaging usurpation of Gaul by Eugenius and Arbogast in 395, Honorius and Stilicho were praised by Claudian for imposing laws on the Chauci and Suebi across the Rhine, as though nothing serious was amiss. (*In Eutrop.* 1.378–84; *De cons. Stil.* 1.218–31). The momentous strategic decision by Stilicho, and before him by Theodosius in the East, to use federate troops to man the frontiers goes virtually unnoticed and could be argued to have been a policy adopted faute de mieux (Mazzarino 1990, 95–100). Yet the frontier had been effectively stripped of its regular troops, leaving the Rhine exposed for the great invasions of New Year's Eve 406.

There is no need to pile on examples. If there was a "more realistic vision," a strategy of accommodation and peaceful coexistence, that found form in the policy of Constantius II or Stilicho, that vision remained as unpopular and as unacceptable to most Romans as it had been in Hadrian's day.[23] Stilicho lost support disastrously when he was prepared to treat with Alaric's Goths in order to protect Italy, since the Roman upper class still believed the only way to treat barbarians was to crush them into unequal subjection.[24]

I draw two conclusions. The first is that at no stage and in no source after the recovery under Diocletian was it ever publicly admitted that the frontiers of the high Empire were diminished. Even in the obvious cases of Dacia, north of the Danube, and of the *Agri Decumates,* east of the Rhine, which had been lost in the troubles of the third century (see map, fig. 17), it is extraordinary how difficult it is to find any mention of them. Not only was the withdrawal from Dacia not total, in that many provincials were left behind, but *Dacia restituta* was already proclaimed by the panegyricists before the end of the third century (*Pan. Lat.* 8[5]3.3; cf. 10.4), and the name Dacia was given to a new province south of the Danube. Furthermore, the Roman emperors of the fourth century seem to have regarded much of the lowland region of old Dacia as still their fief, even if there was no longer a trans-Danubian province.

As far as the loss of the *Agri Decumates* is concerned, the strange silence of our sources is significant. An interesting suggestion has been made recently that much of the population was transferred across the Rhine to a region known as *Decem Pagi* near Metz (Hind 1984), creating perhaps the illusion, as with Dacia, that the Romans continued to control the region. Certainly "Alamannia," the territory that covered the old *Agri Decumates,* was claimed by the same panegyricist cited above to be *totiens proculcata:* "often crushed." The Augustan history, written in the late fourth century, probably reflects what Romans would have liked to believe, when it says that the emperor Probus recovered and settled the land up to the river Neckar and the Schwabian Alb (HA *Prob.* 13.7). We saw earlier something of the same mentality when the emperor Justinian in the sixth century proclaimed with élan that the *fines antiquae* of Africa would be recovered in their entirety (Trousset 1985). No emperor could afford to admit that Roman territory had been lost, since that would have contradicted the ideology of the sacred *termini,* discussed in chapter 1.

It is wrong to think this was all bluff. Emperors believed their own propaganda. Valentinian died of apoplexy because the Quadi dared to claim it was provocation when he built fortifications in their territory (Amm. Marc. 30.6.2–3).

My second conclusion is more tentative. In chapter 3 I doubted the sophistication of strategic planning by Roman emperors. I am equally skeptical, therefore, about the development in the fourth century of some new rational system—what has been called "defense in depth" or "elastic defense"—and the abandonment of the old system of what is called "perimeter defense."[25] If it was right to reject the existence of a linear strategy for earlier frontiers, we cannot now assume that there was a conscious modification of a nonexistent concept. Zosimus's attack on Constantine for ruining the security of Diocletian's frontiers by withdrawing most of the army to the cities in the hinterland (2.34) is, as far as I can see, the only direct ancient evidence that can be used to defend such a supposed change in strategy.

But it is also demonstrably rubbish. There are as many, or more, military buildings on the perimeter *limites* of the Rhine and the Danube dated to Constantine's reign as to that of Diocletian (Johnson 1983, 166; Petrikovits 1971, 182–87, 207–18). The disposition of forts on the Arabian *limes* has been misunderstood as providing strategic defense in depth rather than protective centers for the local population. Furthermore, there is positive evidence that Constantine did not withdraw Diocletian's advanced posts in the Wadi Sirhan (Isaac 1990, 187, 205; Lewin 1990, 161–65). The history of the later frontiers, which is recounted in chapter 5, does not reveal any new grand strategy on the Danube. Africa, Arabia, and Mesopotamia in the fourth century remained more or less as Diocletian left them.

Indirect evidence of new strategic thinking has been claimed from the changes in military organization that took place during the fourth century. What is meant, of course, is the new provincial field armies of the *comitatenses*. This is not the place to discuss the birth of these mobile armies and the quality of the remaining frontier troops (variously called *ripenses* or *limitanei*), which have not lacked commentators. Calculations from the army lists contained in the *Notitia Dignitatum*, which are necessarily approximate, suggest that between 50 and 60 percent of all troops remained on the frontiers until the end of the fourth century. If the army at least doubled in size in the later Empire, as most historians believe, that must mean there was no absolute decline of numbers on the frontier. As to the quality of the *limitanei*, there is one irrefutable argument to show they had not declined; that is, regular upgrading of units from frontiers to *pseudo-comitatenses* must prove that they had not degenerated into a peasant militia.[26] The growth of regional field armies (as opposed to Constantine's central, mobile force) could just as well have been the consequence of the divisions of the empire under the sons of Constantine. The army, that is, was divided regionally for political, not strategic, reasons.[27]

It is sometimes suggested that the building of city walls and new types of urban defenses in the later empire is proof of a new frontier strategy of defense in depth, which was linked to the weakening of the frontier troops and the creation of the mobile field army of *comitatenses*. In other words the cities, as in the medieval period, were part of a calculated policy of nodal defenses, which allowed the enemy to enter Roman territory but delayed them while Roman forces grouped for counterattack. This is the interpretation given to the passage of Zosimus (2.34.1–2) already referred to, which says, "Constantine allowed the barbarians to penetrate land ruled by the Romans without hindrance . . . by withdrawing the majority of the soldiers from the frontiers and installing them in the cities, which had no need of protection."[28]

Quite apart from the accuracy of Zosimus's statement about the frontiers, which I doubted earlier, there are serious objections to such an interpretation of the role of cities as part of a supposed new strategy in the fourth century. In the East it is clear that city fortresses had always served as the basis for the frontier system, particularly in Mesopotamia and on the desert fronts, where any other form of frontier alignment is difficult to detect. But this was as true of Diocletian's strategy—or for that matter of Trajan's—as of that of Diocletian's successors. (Isaac 1990, 254–55). In the West, while it is true enough that in Gaul and Britain many cities in the later empire were equipped with new walls, including projecting or external towers and other defensive features, the great majority date from just after the crisis of the mid-third century, when the frontiers had been badly breached and the cities of the interior exposed. Current research tends to regard the emperor Probus, who ruled from 276 to 282, as the author of this activity in Gaul, Britain, and perhaps the Danube provinces, too (Johnson 1983, 114–15, 189, 251, etc.).

By contrast, there is no evidence of a systematic or coherent plan of city fortifications in the fourth century, such as one would expect had there been a new defensive strategy. A modern comprehensive study of fortifications in the later empire barely discusses the policy attributed to Constantine by Zosimus and makes no reference at all to cities as an element of some new strategy (Johnson 1983, 255). Another study of Gaul and Germany concludes from the great variety of defenses that even if one can see some regional similarities, "there can have been no central directive covering fortifications in the north-western empire."[29]

In Britain, where most cities had already acquired walls between the late second century and the third century, some of them to form part of the Saxon Shore system of defenses in the later third century, there may have been something more like a systematic restructuring of urban and small-town walls in the later fourth century by the addition of external bastions. The development has often been attributed to Count Theodosius, although without any archaeological evidence, because Ammianus (28.3.2) says, "He restored the cities and forts." But it can have had nothing to do with a strategy linked to Hadrian's Wall, which remained intact after Theodosius, since many of the northern forts did not receive any of the new external towers. Again, those who have studied these defenses in detail talk of "a studied lack of standardization" and "an indifferent understanding of the tactics involved (Johnson 1980, 92–98; Wacher 1974, 77–78). The pressures had shifted from Hadrian's Wall to the sea raiders of the Saxon Shore.

In fact, we know very little about the garrisons of the *comitatenses* in the provinces, nor can we tell whether the special units of *laeti* and *gentiles*, which are recorded as being stationed in *civitates* in documents like the *Notitia Galliarum*, were inside the town walls or encamped in the countryside. The spectacular *Langmauer* just north of Trier probably marked out a huge imperial estate within which were stationed troops, including units of the *comitatenses*, who are recorded as helping to build the wall. But Trier was an imperial capital in the later fourth century, and the emperor normally had a "praesental" army (as it was called) attached to the court. Otherwise the only explicit reason I can trace in the sources for stationing military units to the rear of the frontiers in the cities is that given by Ammianus, himself a soldier, who speaks of their "being distributed throughout the cities in order to be better supplied" (*ut commodius vescerentur;* 16.4.1; cf. 31.16.8). Obviously such dispositions were closely linked to the greater insecurity in the countryside, which made it necessary to store food in the cities (Amm. Marc. 31. 8.1). Troops were required, therefore, in *castella* and *burgi* or along the major routes to protect the collection and transport of supplies. It may be, too, that extensive settlement of foreign communities within the frontiers had increased the danger of sudden raids on cities, as we hear of on more than one occasion. Ammianus (16.11.4) tells of one such incident when a group of *laeti* made a sudden attack on Lyons, which just managed to keep them off by closing the city gates.[30]

But this was hardly a new principle of defensive strategy in depth. It was merely prudence and tactical common sense. It supports the thesis I have been proposing, that the main problem on both the western and eastern fronts was dealing with small-scale raiders and infiltrators, not large invading armies. A good example of the sort of conditions that prevailed in Gaul in the later fourth century is described in the *Life of Saint Martin of Tours* (Sulp. Sev. *V. Mart.* 18), when a sudden rumor of an attack by raiders put the city of Trier in a panic until Martin identified the devils who were spreading the false news. It was this, if anything, that produced new strategic thinking, which had begun even in the later second century A.D. But that is a very different matter from a defensive frontier policy.

The Nature of the Barbarian Invasions

It is easier for us to see with hindsight that the reality of frontier pressure in the long term was very different from the ideology. But I find it also quite difficult to believe that the emperors (and those who wrote about them), who boasted of their exploits, were totally self-deluded as to the nature and size of the happenings in front of their eyes, which we have subsequently termed the "great invasions." That is the problem. On the one hand, the language of panegyric, inscriptions, and doomsday predictions necessarily demanded bombastic phrases like those Ammianus uses when he proclaims that "the barricades of our frontier were unlocked" (*nostri limitis reseratis obicibus*) or that "barbarian columns" were flowing like lava from Etna (31.4.9). Others used the image of storms that raged and tore the empire (Claud. Cons. *Stil.* 1.282–83). But on the other hand, that is no good reason for us to be seduced into using the same hyperbole of "floods and waves" of barbarians just because they do.[31]

The fact is that, when we come to look in detail at the ancient sources, they seem to contradict themselves. On the eastern frontier, says Ammianus, the Persians made a strategic decision that large-scale campaigns were profitless and that the best procedure was *per furta et latrocinia* (16.9.1). That was the phrase I picked out at the beginning of this chapter in discussing the small-scale raids and infiltration that were taking place on the western front. It also corresponds closely to Ammianus's opinion of the mode of warfare conducted by the Saracens, a people who were "like rapacious kites" and "fitted for clandestine acts of war" (*ad furta bellorum appositi;* 14.4.1, 23.3.8). Ammianus's perception was shared by other contemporaries with direct experience of the East, such as Jerome, who told of kidnapping and raids on monasteries by small bands of marauders. And even the emperor Julian said that he regarded the Saracens as no more than "bandits" (*lestai; Or.* 1.21b).[32]

All this finds interesting parallels with other frontiers, although obviously no one would want to say the threats were exactly the same. On the Danube the fleet patrolled the river to stop infiltrators

(Amm. Marc. 31.5.3). Themistius, a contemporary orator, described the marshy regions of the Dobrudja where raiders came in small groups "not as soldiers but as robbers" (*Or.* 10.136–38). Julian thought the Goths no more than a petty nuisance (Amm. Marc. 22.7.8). In Valentinian's day the Quadi were judged to be "a people [*natio*] not to be feared very much" (Amm. Marc. 29.6.1). The Sarmatians were considered "better suited for robbery than open war" (Amm. Marc. 17.12.2). Charietto's value to Julian on the Rhine was that he knew how to cope with the small raiding bands of Franks. And so on.

We can get some idea of what this meant from the archaeology of rural establishments in northern France, Belgium, and the left bank of the German Rhineland. There some settlements were being abandoned even before the destructive invasions of the later third century, perhaps for economic reasons. But there was a considerable revival in the early fourth century, more marked in some places than others, that subsequently suffered a serious setback after the usurpation of Magnentius in the mid-fourth century. Thereafter the settlements underwent progressive change and impoverishment of buildings until the end of the fourth century and the early fifth century (Ossel 1992, esp. 104–5, 182–83). The rebellion of Magnentius, we must remember, was a civil war, not an invasion, in which both sides invited Franks and Saxons to enter Roman territory.

Indeed, we might ask, on how many occasions were the "barbarian invasions" really invasions as we would think of them? This is not, of course, to disregard the seriousness of the great set piece, field battles like Strasbourg or Adrianople, or the devasting effect of the irruptions into Gaul and Italy in the early fifth century for those inhabitants who lay in the path of the invaders. The real problem is to assess the importance of these dramatic but isolated events in comparison with the more banal but continual pressure of the small bands of infiltrators.

I have not seen anyone challenge the arguments put forward by Delbrück in his famous *Geschichte der Kriegskunst in Rahmen der politischen Geschichte,* published in the earlier part of this century, concerning the strength of Roman and barbarian armies. After careful analysis of the figures given by our sources for the battles of the fourth century and the *Völkerwanderung* of the fifth century, Delbrück—who was a pupil of Clausewitz and no fool on military matters—came to the conclusion that most of the tribal movements never consisted of more than 5,000 to 15,000 fighting men, and in some cases, like that of the Burgundians in the mid-fifth century, the numbers were as low as 3,000 men (Delbrück 1990, 2:285–99).

Even the figure of 80,000 Vandals (including old men, women, and children), which has been considered more authentic than others because they had been subject to a census before taking ship to Africa in 429—even that figure has been challenged on the grounds that it was "black" propaganda put out by Geiseric himself to deceive the Romans as to his strength.[33] Ammianus's figure of 243 Roman dead at Strasbourg (16.12.63), Delbrück thought, was a more accurate guide to the size of the forces engaged in battle than the thousands upon thousands of Alamanni reported by Libanius and Ammianus. So much for the rivers of lava. We have to break away from the stereotypes of "tribal" history and mass movements of tribal migrations, which, when we can trace them archaeologically (as we can in the case of the Goths), seem to be slow movements of infiltration by small groups of warriors. Aetius's glorious victory over the Salian Franks at *vicus Helena,* enthusiastically hailed by Sidonius (*Carm.* 5.219–29) as a great victory, turns out to be no more than a "minor skirmish" when the Romans broke up a wedding party.[34]

Of course, from time to time there were larger but also more ephemeral federations that, typically in our reports, lacked cohesion and organization. News of the great Gothic coalition in 365 was not apparently serious enough to divert Valens from his expedition against Persia (Amm. Marc. 26.6.11);[35] and the Gothic migration in 376 was in Ammianus's simplistic account divided under the leadership of at least seven or eight chieftains with their followers. There were reports of a "mob" (*multitudo*) of unknown *nationes* "wandering around the Danube," says Ammianus, "scattered with their families" (31.4.2). The terms "Goths"—similar to "Franks" and "Alamans"—is a generic term meaning "men" and gives a false impression of unity to what was basically a society fragmented into subdivisions that rapidly disintegrated after rare shows of unity.

The same applies to other invaders. Among the Alamans, it was their hydra-headed, multitribal organization—or lack of it—that made them so tricky to contain, according to Ammianus's narrative (e.g., 27.10.5; *reparabilis gentis motus timebantur infidi*). As for the organization of the Franks, Gregory of Tours was baffled by the constant references to petty chieftains (*reguli* and *duces*) in Sulpicius Alexander's history of the fourth-century Frankish invasions (*HF* 2.9). The "barbarian conspiracy" against Roman Britain in 367 turns out be difficult to document and almost certainly exaggerated by Ammianus for ulterior motives.[36] Even Attila's much feared Huns included the Akatziri, subjects described by Priscus, who "had many rulers by clans [*phyle*] and families [*gene*]" (fr. 11, p. 259 Blockley). And after Attila's death his whole kingdom collapsed like a pack of cards into rival groups.

On the eastern frontier, Persia, the only really unified force that might have launched a coherent attack on the Romans, was content to keep a relatively low profile. An important recent study has concluded that it is impossible to prove that the Persians had any general aggressive intent to occupy Roman territory.[37]

But the same was not true of the Arabs. It is also the "multiple structure" of the Arab federates that makes it impossible to identify the many phylarchs who lived on the eastern borders of Roman rule (Shahid 1984, 544). Indeed, one recent study goes so far as to argue that the whole Saracen menace was a myth invented by Ammianus and his contemporaries because of their obsessive paranoia about brigands on the borders of Roman civilization. Since most Safaitic and Thaumadic inscriptions have been found within the borders of Roman territory, we should, says the author, regard Saracen attacks as "cases of internal strife," not as "intrusions of distant tribes."[38]

I have to say I find such an extreme view difficult to accept. It is hard to talk away all the references to attacks from beyond the frontiers. Mavia, queen of one Saracen group, withdrew *extra limitem* (Rufin. *HE* 2.6) when she fell out with the emperor Valens before making a devastating attack on the provinces. The transhumance movements of the Jordanian border make it almost inevitable that there were symbiotic relations between folk on either side of the frontier that, unless controlled, could become destructive (but see Parker 1991). I am not concerned here whether Ammianus did justice to the Saracens or understood the differences between the relatively stable federations, such as the Lakhmids and Tanukhids, and nomadic bands of pastoralists.[39] The important thing to realize is that—just as in Africa—the border was open and the differences between external raiders and internal dissidents were difficult to disentangle.[40] The same might be said of the lower Rhine border between Frankish Holland and Toxandria.

In other words, we must be careful about what we are told. Take, for example, the description of the tough lives of the "Scythian" Huns and their terrifying cavalry, by which Ammianus does his best to stir up panic in Roman hearts. Not only is this a stereotype of "permanent nomads" that Herodotus would have recognized, but our suspicions are roused still further when we are told by a study of the ecology that it was impossible for any land west of the Carpathians to sustain a truly nomadic force of more than fifteen thousand warriors (Lidner 1981). In fact the eyewitness, Priscus of Pannium, found Attila living not on horseback but in a large "village" where the aristocracy had enclosures adorned with wooden walls, towers, and even a Roman bath (fr. 11, p. 264, Blockley). Archaeologists also report that on the Hungarian *pusztas* where the Hun's empire flourished "not a single usable horse bone has been found" (Bökönyi 1974, 267).

The Demography of Invasions

If the impression we get from the ancient sources, therefore, is that there were no sudden intrusions of great new populations, that impression is reinforced by archaeology, insofar as it is possible to generalize from the uneven spread of evidence. The most detailed information available comes as a result of the program of the Deutschen Forschungs-Gemeinschaft in Lower Saxony over the past four decades, and through a number of studies of the

Low Countries by various Dutch archaeological institutes. Enough settlements on the coastal clay *terpen/wurten* (like Feddersen Wierde) and on the sandy *geest* (like Flögeln), as well as at inland sites (like Wijster), have now been investigated for us to be reasonably certain that these areas were the heartlands of Saxons and Salian Franks in the fourth century A.D. Since these results are well known, I need do no more than repeat the conclusions that are relevant to my theme of frontiers.

First, the growth of population. On virtually every site there is evidence of a dramatic increase in the size of settlements between the first and the fifth centuries A.D., rising to a peak in the later fourth century. At Feddersen Wierde on the coast near Bremerhaven, the number of cattle stalls and farmhouses allows us to calculate an augmentation of population and herds of between 250 and 300 percent by the end of the third century (fig. 36).[41] Inland at Wijster, in the Dutch Drenthe province, the population "reached its greatest expansion," say archaeologists, in the period between 360 and 395 (Van Es 1967, 376).

I do not wish to overdramatize the impact of this evidence. We cannot produce census statistics to prove an overall increase in the population, although it seems probable. But expansion was not continuous, and site settlements plus pollen analysis suggest an actual decline of agricultural activity on both sides of the Rhine in the third century. At Wijster—though not in Lower Saxony—there was a hiatus about 225, but it was followed by a settlement that was culturally identical (Willems 1986, 314; Van Es 1967, 374; Zimmermann 1974, 60). It also seems certain that the climatic change of the Late Roman Transgression caused a rise of sea levels and salinity of lowlands that forced abandonment of pastures and greater nucleation at the period of greatest prosperity (Schmid 1978, 137; Willems 1986, 321). That probably accounts for the fewer but larger settlements that have been noted, despite a lack of reliable dating on many sites in the later empire (Willems 1986, 303, 314).

What has to be stressed, however, is the continuity of the material culture. When the site at Feddersen Wierde was finally abandoned because of the rising sea level in the early fifth century,

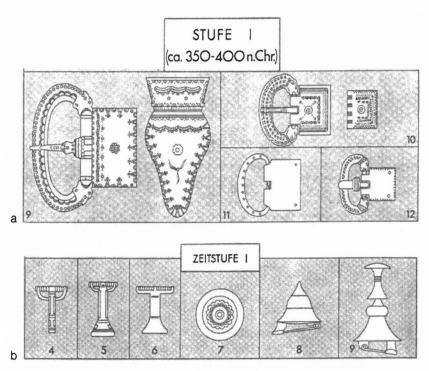

Fig. 45. Some of the earlier grave goods found in "Germanic" burials as they were classified by Böhme 1978, figs. 6 and 7, for the earliest period (Zeitstufe 1), though the dates are not always certain: (*a*) "dolphin" belt buckles and fittings; (*b*) fibulae of *Stutzarm* (crossbow) (4–6) and *tutulus* (trumpet) design (8–9). Reproduced by permission of Champion-Slatkine, Paris.

the silt covered early types of distinctively "Saxon" handmade pottery, which means almost certainly that they evolved locally out of the preexisting culture. *Stützarmfibeln,* too, were found. These are a type of brooch looking like a crossbow (*en arbalète*) common to all frontier societies along both sides of the Rhine, and for that matter along the Danube too in the same period. Although they are often associated with Germanic intruders and are illustrated as such in the chronological typologies of German grave goods that the archaeologist H.W. Böhme drew up (fig. 45), these same brooches are found in the Sîntana de Mureş culture, which we usually associate with Goths, along the Danube.[42] In other words, they look like a frontier cultural development that took place over a long period of time.

How far this picture of apparent population expansion and nucleation is repeated over the rest of the lands beyond the Rhine is difficult to judge from limited evidence. It has been suggested, in the absence of positive indications, that the Alamanni were a relatively unimportant force in comparison to the Franks, despite their ferocious attacks in the early fourth century, and that generally they had had little contact with Roman territory before the occupation of Schwabia in the third century (Demougeot 1979, 291; Petrikovits 1980b, 235). Perhaps so. But Roman cultural influence on the Alamans looks strong in the fourth century. There is quite a lot of archaeological evidence to support Ammianus's statement (17.1.7) that the Alamans built their houses in Roman style and that rather more "villas" of a Roman style were still occupied than might be thought. One such example studied at Bondorf has produced distinct, though limited, signs of continuity in graveyards.[43]

"The overriding impression conveyed by the excavated sites," says one archaeologist, therefore is "of stable and enduring communities" over "decades or even centuries" (Todd 1987, 99). That means that we must reject the myth of a late German migration. The unimportance of the Alamanni in the fourth-century invasions, even though they were described as a *gens populosa,* was surely because their population was not under pressure until finally pushed by the Burgundians in the late fourth century. They lived in a part of the world that was described in chapter 3 as the empty quarter of Europe.[44] But it was otherwise with the Franks. Theirs was the country of the "Germans" that Procopius describes as *polyanthropos*—full of people—in contrast to the Visigoths or the Thuringii (B*Goth.* 5.12.20–21). Whether he was talking of the lower or the middle Rhine Franks is impossible to know. Possibly both. The Meuse-Rhine basin has already been discussed, but we may note that the only real concentration of sites in the fourth to fifth century north of the middle Rhine was in the land of the Chatti Franks just north of the Lippe (Kunow 1987, 70).

Apart from the Germans, changes were also taking place on

other western frontiers. I have already noted that on the British frontier there is the well-known puzzle of what had happened to Hadrian's Wall. It is generally agreed that there had been a reduction in numbers of troops, especially in the western British province, perhaps by as much as 40 to 50 percent (Breeze 1984, 267–68). Regular occupation of posts beyond the wall declined after 310, and military demands and exchanges probably ceased. This is thought to be one reason British grain was now available for the Rhine army (Amm. Marc. 18.2.3, etc.), which in turn might explain why the farms of Picardy seem to decline (Wightman 1985, 244–45).

Quite simply, the threat by land from the north had disappeared and could be contained by native scouts (*arcani*), until they disgraced themselves (Amm. Marc. 28.3.8), together with the old auxiliaries on the wall.[45] The main preoccupation was raiders from the sea. Like the Alamanni, therefore, the British population in this region was neither under pressure to migrate nor stimulated by frontier exchange to expand, which seems to be confirmed by the lack of any increase of native sites north of the wall (Higham 1986, 197–98). Unlike the Alamanni, British troops and officers were also a negligible part of the later Roman army. The absence of disruption in pollen diagrams, despite the apparent abandonment of wall sites by 420, makes one think the region remained relatively static (Higham 1986, 250).

The African frontier, I said in chapter 5, was not one of the hot spots of the later empire—not, at least, in the fourth or fifth century. But it is a useful case to cite alongside the case of the Rhine, because of the rise in pressure on the Tripolitanian frontier, which began in the fourth century and came to a climax in the Byzantine period. During the period we can see something of the same developments that occurred on the Rhine, although on a lesser scale. The attacks began with the Austuriani in 363. They probably accounted for the reinforcement of the forts system attached to the *clausurae* in the mid-fourth century (Trousset 1984, 395; cf. map, fig. 19).

But a recent hypothesis argues that the attacks by the southern Laguatan of the sixth century were not the result of a single migrating population, as has often been thought, but the conclusion of a long period of raids, in the course of which long-standing border populations, such as the Arzuges and the southern Tripolitanian farms discussed earlier, were absorbed by the invaders. The attacks, it is further argued, were originally stimulated by overpopulation of the oases and loss of productivity owing to soil salinity, reverting back to an earlier hypothesis of "a desert momentarily overpopulated."[46]

In other words, we have here all the ingredients of frontier dynamics: surplus population, cultural homogeneity, and a long period of symbiotic exchange. The marginal lands of Tripolitania were by definition a poor region where there was competition for scarce resources. This bred endemic rivalry and factions that increased as the frontiers became more stable and the population increased (Buck 1985). Recent evidence suggests that there was a quite distinct, though small, temperature rise in the mid-third century, which put the ecosystem of the marginal territories under additional strain. If that is true, then we can understand how the stability might have become disturbed. For the moment, however, we must await further research to determine whether the climatic variation was the major determinant or whether, as seems more probable, it only contributed along with other factors like soil exhaustion and overgrazing (Burns and Denness 1985).

The Arabian frontier was perhaps not dissimilar, although there is a major dispute here about whether there was an external or an internal enemy. The debate at least highlights the fact that the seminomadic or sedentary inhabitants within the Roman provinces—the Safaitic language group of the Hauran in southern Syria and the Thamudic language group on the Jordanian plateau—were extraordinarily closely linked politically and culturally to Arabs beyond the frontiers, irrespective of which direction the seasonal migrations took place.[47] Clearly, where there was such an open frontier, the inhabitants on both sides always tended to be a law unto themselves, and it was impossible for the Romans to control them other than by political pacts and payments—an extreme example of frontier "pull."

Of particular interest, however, is what effect the Roman occupation of the key transhumance borderlands had upon the populations. And in this we can see some comparison with Africa. Information is limited, but those who work in the area speak of the prosperity of the frontier strip, possibly increased sedentarism, and increasing population and therefore increased clashes with pastoralists (Parker 1987b, 39; Isaac 1990, 218). There is some evidence of scarce resources that drove pastoral Saracens into Roman territory and of clashes caused by climatic change, although it is difficult to judge how serious it was in the long term (Isaac 1990; 244; Parker 1986a, 462). And it may be, if we are to judge by the increasing references to Saracen kings, that there was a rise in social and political organization, although whether this had anything to do with the "bedouinization" of the Arabs is a thorny and unresolved problem.[48] The Arabian frontier, like the African, was slow to develop, but the sixth century Procopius believed that the Lakhmid Saracen king Mundir was Rome's "most difficult and dangerous enemy" (*BPers.* 1.17.45).

At the extreme opposite end of the spectrum of stable and unstable frontiers lay the Gothic lower Danube. It is no accident that we know most about new intruders in this part of the frontiers and that it most closely resembles the Rhine frontier. Once again we can see the same ingredients as before that rendered the mass critical—an increase in population, scarcity of resources, and rapid assimilation through transfrontier contacts. The rise in population hardly needs comment, given the intrusive population into the Danube plain of Goths, succeeded by Huns, Alans, Slavs, Bulgars, and Avars. But it is right that we should be reminded that individual groups were small, and that the main problem was lack of resources, which together with population pressure produced chronic food shortages (Wolfram 1988, 7–9). On this frontier we have more recorded cases than on any other of voluntary "surrender" and *receptio* into Roman territory of groups, such as Sarmatians, Marcomanni, Taifals, Carpi, and of course Goths. The specific figures are large, always in the thousands, and probably exaggerated, but they illustrate the growth of pressures in the struggle for resources.

The social and cultural dimensions of the demographic changes of these frontier societies are the key to understanding the barbarian invasions in the West. The German and Dutch *Herrenhöfe* and the Tripolitanian *gsur* each illustrate growing social hierarchies on the frontiers, which, as I showed in chapter 4, controlled the scarce resources of imports and production as the various nuclei of population grew. At Feddersen Wierde the southeastern sector of the village was dominated by a single large longhouse surrounded by an oak pallisade and ditch, to which were attached storehouses, stables, and a kind of assembly hall (fig. 36). Not surprisingly, this complex has been termed the "manor" of a chief (Schutz 1983, 319). But it might almost be a description of the Tripolitanian *gsur*, the fortified farms around which large settlements of dependents developed. The export of Roman commodities, as I have tried to stress, whether they were acquired by trade, raids, or foreign troops, accentuated the social divisions.

The effect of the Roman frontier policy in encouraging alliances with local border chiefs and their employment in ethnic units must have reinforced their political power. Hence the significance of the Saracen Thaumadic federation, whose temple dedication to the Antonine emperors was found at Ruwwafa, far beyond the frontiers in the Hejaz.[49] And hence the plethora of phylarchs and "kings" we find cropping up in the confused history of the region, serving either Rome with their Saracen cavalry, or Persia, or neither. When Julian was retreating up the Tigris after his ill-fated expedition against Ctesiphon in 363, he found the Saracens hostile because "he had forbidden payments and many presents to be given, as in the past" (Amm. Marc. 25.6.10).

This growth of political control of economic resources by local elites was repeated on the Danube. Although the social grouping of retainers around *reiks* in Gothic society was a basic clan unit, the word *reiks* was an adaptation from *rex*, which may indicate the increased political power of chiefs after contact with Rome, no doubt often through service with the Roman army. There was also a growth of the importance of the Gothic *baúrg*—the fortified residence of a Gothic lord and his retainers, at the expense of the free peasant villages. The *Passion of Saint Saba* tells the story of how Saba in one such village was killed in 372 by the retainer of a *reiks*.[50] We saw earlier the considerable evidence on the middle Danube of chieftains' "villas" with their enclosures for retainers and their rich graves. They were quite clearly a development in relation to Roman trade goods from the second century onward and show by their contents the control such elites had of resources.[51] One wonders how much the *oikemata* of Attila—the royal residence visited by Priscus—resembled such buildings.

To conclude, we cannot doubt the pressures of growing populations and the demand for food on some of the frontiers, although not on all or at the same time. The sources are explicit, and I have studied them elsewhere in detail (Whittaker 1983). Fifty years before Adrianople Visigoths were dying of hunger, which drove them into treaty with the Romans (*Exc. Val.* 1.6.31; Jord. *Get.* 112). Vandals and Alans were forced by hunger to move westward to Frankish Germany, increasing the pressure on already scarce resources (Procop. *BVand.* 3.3.1). The warfare this generated only made the conditions more acute. Julian's invasion of Alamannia or Valentinian's attack on the Quadi devastated crops and must have created "the scarcity of food" that Ammianus notes (17.1.7, 30.6.2). Emperors were prepared to capitalize on hunger and disease by using economic warfare to control rebellious "barbarians" (Thompson 1982, 3–19). Ambrose, as a Christian, thought this quite proper (*Expos. in Luc.* 10.10 [*PL* 15.1806]), and it had some effect. But the normal permeability of frontiers by their very design, plus the long habitude of three centuries of symbiotic exchange of goods and manpower, ensured that in the end these vain expedients were unenforceable. It is that aspect I turn to now.

The Symbiosis of Frontier Societies

In earlier chapters I have tried to underline the differences between juridical or ideological frontiers, and the absence of such barriers in commercial, political, or cultural terms during the first two centuries of the Roman Empire. Interaction was not perfectly even but was limited to certain social groups, whose power and identity were defined by the exchanges. The result, according to my hypothesis, was a commercial and perhaps a cultural affinity between barbarian elites beyond the frontiers and the Roman inhabitants of the cities or camps on the frontiers, while the ordinary rural settlements on either side remained relatively untouched by Roman influences and, in terms of their artifacts, seem to have resembled each other more than their own elites. As we all know, the Roman urban and military system was almost designed to increase this sort of stratification in the provinces. While the economic gap between urban aristocracies and peasants grew wider (Garnsey 1978) care was taken—particularly on the British and Rhine frontiers—to separate native recruits from their native leaders by ending the employment of ethnic units locally or by mixing local recruits with recruits from other provinces (Saller and Shaw 1984; Speidel 1975, 203).

In the later Empire of the fourth century A.D. this separation was forgotten. It became increasingly common to employ native inhabitants from both sides of the frontiers as ethnic units in the army, frequently under their own chieftains, while at the same time more and more barbarians were admitted and settled within the frontier provinces, often on the borders. Social, economic, and cultural exchanges inevitably continued across the frontiers, despite—or perhaps because of—the use of trading privileges as a political weapon. Within the Roman province, therefore, the "pull" of exchanges increasingly created a frontier society that was fast becoming indistinguishable from that beyond.

Every frontier has had to face the difficulty of recruiting native irregulars. Holdich tells the story of how Sir Mortimer Durand, creator of the Durand Line on India's North-West Frontier, visited a hospital for soldiers and was astonished to find there two "wazirs" of the Mahsud Afghans enjoying the good life of the hospital at a time when Britain was waging a frontier war against their tribe. When he mentioned this to the two men, they roared with laughter and "expressed the pious hope that their own people were putting up a good fight" (Holdich 1916, 279). The story illustrates the ambiguity of frontier societies, repeated again and again in history. The Muscovite principality of the sixteenth century used border troops of "Cossacks"—a word as vague as Gaetuli or Goths—who were often peasants drawn from the enemy Mongols (Wieczynski 1976, 62–63).

In theory, of course, the Romans had recognized the dangers of employing recruits locally ever since the rebellion of Civilis in A.D. 69, and I can find no evidence of change in official policy in the fourth century concerning stationing native *ripenses* troops in frontier forts.[52] The law permitted a Roman *dux* to enlist recruits locally. But such recruits did not make up the whole of the local units, and the experience in 324 of the Christian monk Pachomius, who was locked up to stop him from running away while awaiting posting, suggests that even individuals were often sent abroad (*V. Pach.* 4). As so often, the *Historia Augusta* reflects fourth-century ideals when it recounts that the emperor Probus scattered sixteen thousand recruits in units (*numeri*) and frontier troops (*limitanei*) in different provinces, saying "that when the Roman was helped by barbarians it must be felt but not seen" (HA *Prob.* 14.7). That, I think, was meant to be official policy, and the only exception was in the occasional use of scouts and spies, like the Batavian *exploratores* at Roomburg near Leiden (*CIL* 13.8825) or the British *arcani* beyond the wall (Amm. Marc. 28.3.8).[53]

So in principle the policy of foreign postings for ethnic units was continued. Despite the problems we have in discovering precise frontier dispositions from the *Notitia Dignitatum,* particularly about those on the Rhine, it is remarkable that Alamanni units are never recorded in the West and that in Britain there is not a single identifiable ethnic British unit, although clearly some soldiers in the various mixed units came from Britain. Even in Africa, where the third Augustan legion had been recruited extensively from within the province in the high Empire, not a single legion, or vexillation, of those units that appear on our army list as being upgraded from frontier to field army can really be identified as an ethnic unit recruited in Africa. We can, of course, assume that many individual soldiers in the *Tertioaugustani* (*ND* Oc. 5.254)— the former frontier legion listed in the field army—were still Africans but were from the most Romanized part of the community.[54]

What changed this frontier policy in practice were two accidents that are linked. The first was local usurpations and wars of succession. On the Rhine frontier this perhaps started with Postumus in 259, but the most publicized example, which probably introduced the greatest number of transborder soldiers into the frontier forces, was that of Magnentius's challenge to Constantius II in 350. Born of barbarian parents settled in Gaul, he rose high in imperial service and recruited Keltoi and Galatai. But his most enthusiastic followers, according to the emperor Julian himself, "were by virtue of their ties of kinship Franks or Saxons, the most warlike of whom live beyond the Rhine and along the shore of the Western Sea" (*Or.* 1.34c–d).[55] At the same time, just to add to the complications, the orator Libanius tells us that Constantius had invited "barbarians" (almost certainly other Saxons and Franks) to cross the borders to make life difficult for Magnentius. One cannot miss the implications of an army—or armies—drawn from both sides of the frontier. It was suggested many years ago that the unusual number of gold coins in Westphalia dating 365–70 could be linked to this event (Christ 1957, esp. 24; fig. 46).

The Keltoi, who were probably "Celtic" Germans, and Galatai (Gauls of unknown origin) had served in brigades together in the Roman army since Constantine (Jul. *Ep.* 4.579; Hoffmann 1969–70, 134). But here we come to the second accident—the formation of the *comitatenses* by Constantine, as a huge field army that fought the wars of succession from 306–24. To do so he stripped the Rhine frontier, which was his power base, of many of its frontier units, to which were added any local recruits that could be mustered. The local manpower included barbarian units under their ethnic leaders, such as Bonitus the Frank and Crocus the Alaman. This is all well known and is proved by the privileged position subsequently occupied by the Franks, especially their "kings," at court (Amm. Marc. 15.5.11) and by the unusual grant of *ius matrimonii*, the right of legal marriage with Roman citizens, to them alone of foreign troops (Frank 1969, 64–67).

From this central field army evolved—probably under the sons of Constantine—the regional *comitatenses;* that is, different field armies stationed in various dioceses of the empire. This was the origin of a Gallic field army, which incorporated, of course, many of Constantine's Rhine frontier recruits. Their units could now be

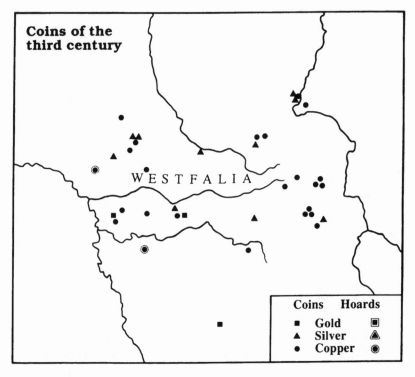

Fig. 46. The distribution of Roman coins from the third and fourth (opposite) centuries A D in Westphalia, Germany. The increase in gold pieces reflects growing service in the Roman army. After Christ 1957.

stationed at strategic garrisons, like Cologne, on the frontiers and controlling beyond (e.g., Amm. Marc. 15.5.15–16, 28.5.11), or in the provincial hinterland fortifying *burgi* and supply routes.[56]

In practice, therefore, by the time of Julian we are left in no doubt that many of his units, including those that took a leading part in his usurpation in Paris, were locally recruited with families living nearby, among whom some were explicitly *voluntarii* from beyond the Rhine (Amm. Marc. 20.4.4; Lib. *Or.* 18.95). The regular brigading together of German and Gallic units[57] strongly suggests to me that these were soldiers drawn from assimilated populations on both sides of the frontiers, whom Zosimus describes as "a vast

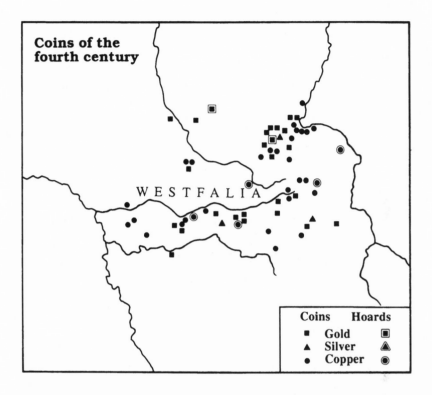

army of young men, both barbarians living near the Rhine and
farmers from the Roman provinces" (Zos. 4. 12). Many in the
army knew the territory across the river and passed on information
to both sides about tribal politics or Roman dispositions. Of this
we have plenty of examples (e.g., Amm. Marc. 14.10.7, 16.4.1,
16.12.2, 27.2.9, 29.4.7, 31.10.3).

It does not matter here whether the soldiers serving in these
armies were those who were called *gentiles* and *laeti*—that is,
peoples settled within the frontiers—or whether they were soldiers
from outside serving by terms of a treaty—those who, after 380,
were also increasingly settled within the frontiers under their own
kings. It is not always easy to tell the difference between them,
and they all derived broadly from the culture of the frontier zones.
Nor is it easy to imagine exactly how Goth, Saracen, or Mauretanian

chieftains fitted into the imperial court as high officers and officials. But the fact that they did so illustrates how far Romanization had progressed among the elites on both sides of the frontiers. Vadomar, the Alaman king near Augst, is a good example. We are told that he had often seen the Roman army in his youth because he lived near the frontier (*utpote vicinus limite*), and he ended up in the Roman service as *dux Phoenices*.[58]

The extraordinary history of the Saracen queen Mavia and her family in the later fourth century shows the same easy interchange. One moment she is ravaging the provinces, the next appointing an Arab hermit, Moses, as bishop of Alexandria, marrying her daughter to a Roman commander, Victor the Sarmatian, and sending her Saracen troops to defend Constantinople.[59] But the lesson of Silvanus, the Frankish *magister militum,* who was told he would be either killed or surrendered if he fled to his barbarian compatriots in 355 (Amm. Marc. 15.5.15–16), is that Frankish nationalism as such did not exist. It underlines the point I began with, that invasions were launched from a society made up of petty *regules,* temporarily united in confederations that were riddled with factions (cf. Amm. Marc. 18.2.16 discussing a treaty with the Alamanni).

What is striking at this stage in history is how far the economic and cultural interchange, partially created by the frontier, continued and even increased. To the barbarian soldiers and princes who passed from one side to the other we must add the Roman deserters or "collaborators" who voluntarily crossed into *barbaricum,* about whom we have many references (Thompson 1980). There is a significant proviso in a law of 366, which granted returning prisoners of war postliminal rights of recovering their property, *as long as they could prove they had not gone to the barbarians of their own free will (CTh* 5.7.1). The huge figures given for prisoners of war who were resettled either in Persia or in Roman lands show that many stayed. In one case we hear of a captured Persian soldier who had begun in the Roman army, was taken prisoner, married a local girl, and then served Persia.[60]

The stability, even stalemate, on the Persian frontier must, I think, be explained by the fact that, after the experiences of Constantius and Julian, there was no real possibility of Rome's regaining the initiative in Mesopotamia or Armenia. From the point of view of frontier assimilation, however, we have a lot of information about the interchanges that took place—hardly surprising in view of the way territories of the eastern Mesopotamian and Transtigritan states changed hands. The virtual absence of any defined geographic frontier line is underlined by the fact that the so-called Transtigritan states actually seemed to extend to both sides of the river Tigris (Warmington 1976, 510). This permitted a flow of traffic between Persian and Roman lands that is most interestingly illustrated by the hagiographic sources. They portray holy men or their clients crossing between the two without undue difficulty, though sometimes in disguise as merchants (Lieu 1986, 492–94).

Collaborators, fugitives, and prisoners constituted merely one class of transfrontier traffic, which also included traders, smugglers, slaves and technicians, and those who are simply called spies, sometimes posing as traders. Stachao, who came from one of the Mauri *gentes contermini* of the Tripolitanian *limes*, is described by Ammianus in 363 as quite normally "wandering freely in our land during the peace" until he was "proved"—unjustly, as the Libyans believed—to have been a spy (Amm. Marc. 28.6.3). Legislation in 323 envisaged the possibility that some provincials might give information to barbarians in order to share the plunder (*CTh* 7.1.1). So while we may agree with the view that "the course of the major invasions . . . was [not] seriously affected by dissident Romans" (Thompson 1980, 85), what we really need to ask is, What about the effect of ordinary Romans and barbarians moving freely across the frontiers? The impression given by contemporary sources is that the traffic had increased considerably and had a major effect on the character of the so-called invasions.

The archaeological evidence of such transfrontier movements is unambiguous. The excavator of Wijster in Holland, north of the Roman frontier, talks of this century as the "golden age" for Roman goods moving through the native center, many of them the buckles, belts, and fibulae typical of the frontier society (Van Es 1967, 553; fig. 45). In the German Westphalian village of Essen-Hinsel a third of the pottery is Roman, and at Westick in Westphalia the fourth to the fifth century was the most flourishing period for

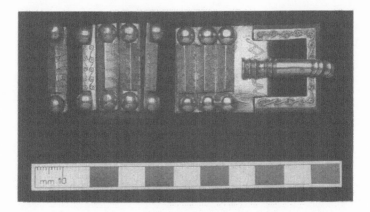

Fig. 47. Silver belt buckle and fittings from the treasure found at Traprain Law in Britain, typical of those worn in late Roman frontier societies. This was part of a treasure of silver objects that were badly crushed when found. Photograph by permission of the Trustees of the National Museums of Scotland, 1994, inv. no. GVA 147.

Roman imports (Petrikovits 1980b, 230). In Alamannia there has been found "an exceptional density" of Roman provincial *terra nigra* and Argonne pottery, reaching as far as the middle Main and Tauber (Demougeot 1979, 283). The profusion of bronze coins in this region up to 365 shows that it was the consequence not just of raids but of trade too. In old Dacia, now Gothic and Hunnic Dacia, the coin finds show a break just at the point when Valens imposed trade sanctions.[61] Themistius (*Or.* 10.135–36) assures us about the free trading before Valens.

The third to fourth century was also a kind of golden age for the Tripolitanian *gsur*, the fortified farms of the chiefs, which are found filled with African Red Polished Ware and monuments of wealth. Beyond the frontier it is not always evident whether the treasures that reached such men came through trading or raiding. At Traprain in Scotland the spectacular hoard of late Roman silver (fig. 47) might have been the result of raids, since it was discovered crushed into a heap, as though intended as bullion. But Traprain was the home of the Votadini, long-standing allies of the Romans, and it is more probable that these valuable goods reached them originally in the form of gifts. The buckles in the hoard could have been worn by either Romans or barbarians.[62]

But those who believe that Roman legislation could impose trade blockades as a political weapon for any length of time underestimate the age-old tradition of such exchanges, including smuggling. Herodian's reference to secret imports by merchants over the Persian borders (4.10.4) recalls the parallel I noted earlier about how impossible it was to alter the rhythm of economic exchange in the *lies et passeries* of the Pyrenees by international treaties. If the Italians in the nineteenth century were unable to stop the huge smuggling of tobacco, sugar, and salt from Switzerland by putting up a fence of wire netting, I doubt if their forebears could have done better. The significant part of the story of Antoninus, the Roman officer who defected to Persia in 359, is that he bought a farm on the very frontier in order, says Ammianus (18.5.3), to avoid suspicion. The implication is inescapable: frontier farmers were expected to cross borders.

One obvious reason for such interchange, which is well documented, is that huge numbers were moving across and settling in the Roman Empire under negotiated terms in the fourth century along the Rhine, the Danube and—though apparently to a much lesser extent—the eastern frontier.[63] It is difficult to estimate the scale of these movements from the vague statements of our sources; phrases often simply talk about "a lot" (*tot translati . . . in rura Romana cultores; Pan. Lat.* 8[5]1.4). Ancient figures, where given, are inherently untrustworthy, such as when three hundred thousand Sarmatians are said to have been resettled by Constantine (*Exc. Val* 1.6.32). But over twenty-five such reports along the Rhine-Danube in the century from Diocletian to Theodosius[64] must indicate a very large number indeed, at a guess well over one million foreigners along a frontier of some ten thousand kilometers. This figure does not include the federate settlements—the enclaves of foreigners under their own leaders—which became common practice after Adrianople. Nor does it take account of the sixteen distinct military units of *laeti* and *gentiles* recorded in the lists of the *Notitia Galliarum,* which though reconstructed is imperfect (Rivet 1976).

We know, of course, that not all such barbarians were settled precisely on the frontier, and that many were exploited on estates in the interior as *laeti* and *dediticii* under near slavelike conditions (*CTh* 10.10.25[408], etc.).[65] But judging by what we are told of the Goths in the period before Adrianople and of the way they were distributed, we can be reasonably certain that many *were* settled in the frontier zone or in the vicinity of the frontier. Information was given to invaders in 378 by Goths who had earlier been sold as slaves in the Roman province (Amm. Marc. 31.6.5–7).

The truly remarkable fact about these huge, peaceful shifts of population is how difficult it is to see any real sign of them in the archaeological remains. They disappear "like ghosts" into the countryside. That is to say, from the point of view of artifacts, they became rural provincials. Naturally we can talk about the end of Roman villas and of new styles of weapon-burials. Many villas certainly ended violently. But the picture of wholesale abandonment of villas in Belgium and northwestern France has recently been considerably modified, since it is clear from archaeology that many were occupied in the fourth century, even if only by squatters when the owners had apparently left. In some cases desertion of rural sites in Picardy and even those near Trier had apparently begun in the late second century, long before the invasions.[66]

And who can honestly detect the presence of *laeti* or *gentiles* among the peasants who remained in many of the *vici* adjoining the estates after the villa had collapsed? The nearest we can come is to identify wooden huts on the villa sites and Germanic handmade pottery or buckles and fibulae, which look like evidence of foreign settlers. In just a few cases in northern Gaul, such as the villa site of Donk (Limburg) in Belgium, we find unmistakable signs of Germans in the dugout huts or houses, the *Grubenhaüser*, and in long wooden houses with stables, the *Wohnstallhaüser*—the kind of houses found in free Germany. Just occasionally, as at Haarf or Froitzheim in the Rhineland, these huts date to the third century, although most begin after the mid-fourth century. In truth it is usually impossible to tell whether the artifacts are evidence of intrusive invaders, peaceful settlers, or even Gallo-Romans who had adopted the new frontier culture.[67]

North and south of the lower Rhine and Waal in the late fourth century much of the pottery is identical, even if Roman fabrics were fewer to the north (Willems 1986, 451). The Goths, as we believe from the appearance of the Sîntana de Mureş culture in the Transylvanian Alps and Wallachia in the late third century, had lived side by side with Romano-Dacian settlements, absorbing their culture, for over a hundred years before they crossed the Danube frontier in the later fourth century (Whittaker 1983, 117–18; Demougeot 1983, 97–99). They did not appear on the frontiers as raw barbarians, and once inside they cannot be traced archaeologically.

A good example of this kind of assimilation has been found by two Hungarian archaeologists working on a graveyard at Mözs, north of Szeksgárd. They discovered a group of graves they believe belonged to three generations of four families. The earlier bricklined graves were clearly Roman in tradition, some of them containing bird-head buckles. But at the same time the skulls were deformed in a manner associated with the appearance of Goths, Huns, and Alans. The later generations abandoned their Romanizing habits and adopted the artifacts associated with the period when Attila controlled the Roman province of Valeria on the Danube. Perhaps, the authors suggest, we can see here some evidence of how federated settlers from beyond the frontiers kept their religious customs but easily adopted Roman ways (Salamon and Lengyel 1980). In the Visigothic kingdom of Aquitania and Septimania even their distinctive art in the fifth century is judged to be exclusively the development of local Gallic artists. The settlements of Visigoths, Franks, and Burgundians in the fifth century, which are marked on maps, are really not distinguishable in terms of new cultures coming into Gaul from beyond the frontiers (James 1977, 61; see also his maps on 244).

This is the conclusion to be drawn from the massive literature on inhumation graves containing weapons, throwing axes, belt buckles, and fibulae that appear in the later Empire of the West (fig. 45 and map, fig. 48). A good deal of revision of long-held views about the character of the barbarian "invasions" has now taken place as a result of recent studies of these grave goods.[68]

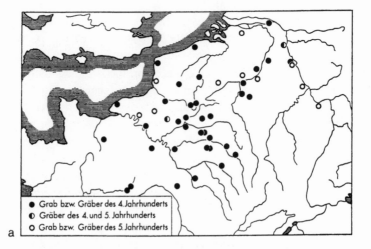

a

Grab bzw. Gräber des 4. Jahrhunderts
Gräber des 4. und 5. Jahrhunderts
Grab bzw. Gräber des 5. Jahrhunderts

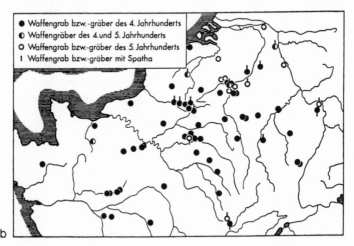

b

Waffengrab bzw.-gräber des 4. Jahrhunderts
Waffengräber des 4. und 5. Jahrhunderts
Waffengrab bzw.-gräber des 5. Jahrhunderts
Waffengrab bzw.-gräber mit Spatha

Fig. 48. Böhme's maps of the distribution of "Germanic" graves of the fourth and fifth centuries A D in Gaul: (a) graves of women with fibulae and jewelry; (b) graves of men with weapons (lines through the circles mark where long swords were found). From Böhme 1978, figs. 13 and 14. Reproduced by permission of Champion-Slatkine, Paris.

We can no longer maintain, for instance, that these are all the relics of barbarian soldiers or paramilitary *laeti* and *gentiles,* since there are children's graves among them also containing swords and throwing axes. They have a strong military idiom but often appear to belong only to families of high status (Wightman 1985, 250). Nor can we be sure they are all graves of Germans, since in Gaul many of these burials appear to be perfectly integrated in provincial communities, using the same graveyards without signs of disruption. Only occasionally do the burials indicate a discontinuity in the inhabitants of the villa.[69]

On the other hand, it is impossible to deny their close Germanic connections with similar artifacts in Saxon, Frankish and Alamanic burials found beyond the frontiers, particularly in the case of women's graves. This applies to various types of dress brooches (the *tutulus* trumpet-shaped brooch, or the crossbow-shaped brooch), whose prototypes appear to have evolved in an area between the Elbe and the Weser.[70] But so too was there a close Roman link, since belts, buckles, and military insignia were typical of both military and civilian officials of the late imperial army and court. And it is an interesting fact that weapon burials appear to be confined to people inside the Roman Empire and not to have been practiced by free Germans (Salway 1981, 386–87; Périn and Feffer 1987, 65).

In other words, we witness here the development of a frontier culture among peoples who were closely associated with Romans, possibly through military service. Fibulae, like the crossbow type, seem to be used by the Gothic Sîntana de Mureş settlements. And it is certain that some of the goods like the dolphin buckle or the swords were products of Roman manufacture.[71] The best illustration of this assimilation comes from a typical buckle of this type, found in a "Germanic" burial at Landifay (Aisne) in the north of France. But engraved on the dolphin buckle is the portrait of the man dressed like a Roman cavalry officer and his wife, dressed in Roman style without the fibulae normal for a German woman (Erison 1978, 39–48, with illustrations; fig. 49). That shows just how difficult it is to make any cultural separation between Germans and Romans in this period.

Quite a number of the graves and artifacts do, however, appear

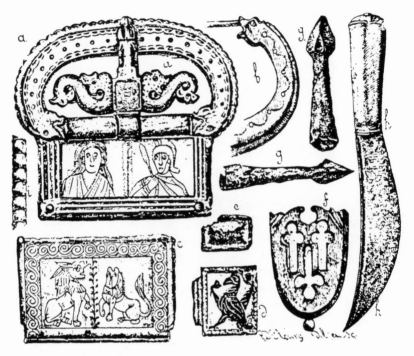

Fig. 49. The objects found in a "Germanic" weapons burial at Landifay near Guise (Aisne), France. On the "dolphin" buckle are depicted a Roman officer and his wife in Roman dress. From Erison 1978, fig. 1. Reproduced by permission of Champion-Slatkine, Paris.

to be linked with Roman military settlements. Just north of Valentinian's imperial capital of Trier is the famous *Langmauer*, a huge construction enclosing about 220 square kilometers of land that was almost certainly an imperial estate. Within the estate are two settlement sites where belt buckles, fibulae, weapons, and Germanic types of nonwheel pottery have been found. Plausibly these were the billets of German units serving in the imperial army of the emperor's garrison at Trier.[72]

Easily the most remarkable military evidence comes from the huge necropolis at Krefeld-Gellep at the Roman fort of Gelduba north of Cologne, where about five thousand graves have been excavated. The majority and the richest date from the mid-fifth century onward, some of them clearly princely, suggesting that it became a center of Frankish power.[73] But the most relevant fact here is that the necropolis demonstrates a continuity from Roman to Frankish periods, with a period from the mid-fourth century when the new style of "German" burial appeared and a new orientation of graves took place. There seems little reason to doubt that this is evidence of federate troops' taking up their station, although we must note that before the mid-fifth century there are few graves with weapons and many containing Roman pots. The change was not sudden.

Less dramatic signs of possible military units, whether of federates or of laetic and *gentiles* units, have been found at other sites like that at Vermand (Aisne) or Oudenburg (Belgium). Let me stress again, however, the point made by archaeologists. The new practices of burying weapons, clothing, and jewelry went hand in hand with the old Gallo-Roman grave goods of pots, food, and coins (for Charon). Cemeteries arranged in rows, the so-called *Reihengräberfeld,* which were sometimes (but not always) a distinctive Germanic feature, occurred sometimes also in the later Roman period (Périn 1980, 79, 100). In short, all these graves are evidence of what Böhme (1978, 38) called a *Mischzivilisation,* although perhaps not as he adds "specifically Gallo-Roman." They are the specific product, rather, of the frontiers where cultures met.

But it is not only in the military sphere that this change was taking place. There is extensive evidence of graves and of settlements in a more rural or civil context. In northern Gaul and in the Lower German province the local population clearly lived side by side with new settlers without constant violence. At the villa of Famechon (Somme) in Picardy the *villa urbana* section, where the rich landowner used to live, was abandoned, but the *rustica* section continued to be occupied. At some of the large Rhineland villas, like that at Konz or Leiwen, the *urbana* sector was transformed into baths in the later fourth century; in others the baths were used as kitchens and bakeries or as pottery kilns, and metalworks were built in the old cellars. But often alongside these peasant "squatters" there appear sunken-floor wooden buildings and wood longhouses, as in the villa at Donk in Belgium. So, as poor farmers and peasants were abandoning their Roman heritage, Germanic settlers were moving in alongside them, particularly in the later fourth century (Ossel 1992, 125–27, 176–77, 183).

In Britain, where the frontier of penetration had effectively become the Saxon Shore, there has been a lot of controversy about whether Saxon settlers overlapped with Romano-British villa owners in the fourth century. As along the Rhine, foreign troops were stationed in and died in the country, and evidence of their graves can be seen in Roman cemeteries, such as that at Lankhills near Winchester or in the late cemetery at Mucking in Essex in southeastern Britain. But it is impossible to identify them as Saxons rather than as soldiers wearing the typical late-frontier style of dress and practicing inhumation burial rites for themselves and their wives, which makes them indistinguishable in archaeological terms from other German groups like the Franks. Their cemeteries at Dorchester-on-Thames, Milton Regis, and other late Roman sites along the upper Thames valley suggests they may have been employed as federates by the British *civitates*. If so, they would conveniently date from the first decade of the fifth century when the last Roman troops had been removed in the wake of an attempted usurpation from Britain by the pretender Constantine (Zosimus 5.27, 6.10; Hawkes 1989, 86–87).

At some sites, such as Kelvedon near Colchester, Roman and Saxon artifacts are found side by side in fifth-century graves. At the rural site of Orton Hall Farm in Oxfordshire the Anglo-Saxon houses and artifacts seem to respect the earlier Roman buildings. Some early Saxon settlement sites, such as those at Mucking in Essex or at Catholme in Staffordshire, also seem to occupy the edges of Roman villas, which might mean that for a time Saxons lived symbiotically with the British owners.[74]

But it is all very inconclusive, and in general most Saxon evidence, when it can be dated, is now thought to date from after the end of the Roman province and often after a gap in occupation. Most important, these later settlers practiced cremation; they did not bury their weapons, and they possessed a completely un-Roman material culture that can be compared with that from northern Germany, Jutland, and southern Scandinavia. Almost certainly they were Saxons, Angles, and Jutes who had had very little contact with Roman frontiers and came in a second phase of settlement (Hawkes 1989, 88; Higham 1992, 174–76). Perhaps the most significant frontier lessons to be learned from Britain are counterfactual. The first is that, *unlike the Rhine or Danube provinces,* the seacoast of the Saxon Shore did not permit steady infiltration and assimilation, so that the break, when it came in the mid-fifth century, was far more radical and the continuity with Roman culture far more superficial than elsewhere. The second lesson, as one recent writer points out, is that "the collapse of Romano-British culture . . . cannot be attributed to a violent Anglo-Saxon settlement." There was continuity. But by the time the Saxons settled, the post-Roman British had already thrown off the veneer of Roman life and reverted to a subculture of rural subsistence and petty chieftainships that adapted quickly to Anglo-Saxon society. That is something we are only just beginning to understand.[75]

In the rest of the western empire the cemeteries add particularly to our general knowledge of the social changes that were taking place on both sides of the frontiers. Almost all the studies of such burials describe them as being clustered in groups. The rural cemetery at Abbeville-Homblières (near Saint-Quentin), for instance, began in the mid-fourth century near the site of an abandoned Roman villa and contains a number of weapons burials. But there are three groups of particularly rich graves, separated from the others, and it has been argued that this is evidence of a German-owned villa worked by Gallo-Roman labor. In the cemetery adjacent to the Roman villa at Frénouville, near Caen in Normandy, it is impossible to detect a break in continuity of the population from the late third to the late seventh century, except in the mode of burial and in the orientation of the graves in the mid-fifth century.[76]

The pattern is repeated all over the north—Vert la Gravelle in Champagne, Pry in Naumur, Mézerny in the Ardennes—small groups of graves belonging to twenty or thirty persons, including three to six rich graves containing weapons or women's fibulae. Sometimes they give the impression of being "familial concessions" or signs of noble Germanic families' taking over villas with their

Gefolgsmänner while surrounded by "the local, rural, Gallo-Roman population who remained where they were" (Böhme 1978, 32–35; Dasnoy 1978, 69–70). Small groups of graves arranged like this are also found in cemeteries beyond the frontier. At Kirchheim bei München in Bavaria a cluster of seventeen graves is thought to be those of the inhabitants of a rural villa (Christlein and Braash 1982, 254). At Rhenen near Utrecht a very large necropolis of mixed cremation and inhumation beginning in the fourth century contains graves arranged in three groups that are thought to represent social "clans" (Ypey 1978, 51–58).

The evidence of cemeteries and settlements, therefore, is broadly the same in its conclusions. Just as the northern German settlements were nucleated and became increasingly differentiated socially, so now too a similar kind of community started to develop south of the frontier. But it was not just because Gallo-Romans were being displaced by German populations, although it looks as if that had happened in the mid-fourth century in Toxandria.[77] But even among the later Roman communities smaller farms were disappearing while a few larger villas—Rheinbach-Flerzheim in the Rhineland, Saint-Ulrich near Metz, or Echternach in Luxembourg—survived and were fortified, often with protected grain stores. Many *vici* were abandoned or reverted to Iron Age hilltop sites and ramparts, but peasants at some sites appear to have taken refuge on the estates of the rich. Overall in Belgica, concluded a study a few years ago, "an increasing militarization of rural communities is clearly visible in the second half of the fourth century" (Wightman 1985, 246–50).

That statement must be qualified somewhat in the light of new information. The overriding impression of later fourth century developments in the north is that most villa owners departed, with a few notable exceptions like those cited above. But the peasant labor—or more probably tenants—moved in to share the villa buildings, obviously for protection. The same process has been observed on British villas, where one family among the peasants seems to be the richer.[78] The increasing nucleation meant greater social control by the powerful. That is a theme I shall take up in the last chapter.

A "Barbarian" View of Frontiers

I have one last thought that may help put the frontiers of the later Empire in a different perspective and that anticipates some of what I will discuss in the next chapter. The trouble with all our frontier studies is that they are made from the inside outward. At the beginning of this chapter I wondered how those whom Romans called "barbarians"—those beyond the frontiers—would have viewed the Roman frontiers from outside.

In the fourth and fifth centuries we witness the reverse process of the conquests that had begun with Julius Caesar and Augustus. The frontiers of the Roman Empire in the early Empire were administrative boundaries in an "area inviting entrance" (to use a phrase of Walter Prescott Webb's), even though often portrayed like a rampart ringing the Roman world (Ael. Arist. *Ad Rom.* 82). Now they seemed to take on the same quasi-juridical character from the barbarian point of view. Valentinian was forced to negotiate peace with the Alaman king on a ship in the middle of the Rhine, a symbolic but artificial compromise between two powers with conflicting territorial claims. Valens did the same on the Danube with the Goths (Amm. Marc. 30.3.3–6, 31.4.13). These are two of many examples of formal treaties recognizing the rights of outer *gentes,* in exactly the same way that the Romans had earlier recognized the Parthians by meeting them on the Euphrates (Vell. Pat. 2.101; Tac. *Ann.* 2.58; cf. Amm. Marc. 27.5.6; Lib. *Or.* 18.88; Greg. Tur. *HE* 2.9, etc.).

But just as Roman ideology—as opposed to practice—had claimed and never ceased to claim control beyond the formal *termini,* the reverse began to happen in the fourth and fifth centuries in respect to the barbarians. It was now the barbarian kings who permitted crossing of the rivers as a privilege of favored allies. The king of the Rugi permitted Roman traders to visit markets beyond the Danube from Noricum (Eugip. *V. Sev.* 9.1, 22.2), and it was the Huns and their boatmen who controlled the crossing of the lower Danube at Ratiaria (Priscus, fr. 11, p. 248 Blockley).

Meanwhile, barbarian political power extended deep into Roman territory. The Alamans in 352 devastated a band of territory

180 kilometers beyond the Rhine and claimed the right to settle a zone 60 kilometers broad on the left bank (Jul. *Ep. ad Ath.* 279a; Amm. Marc. 16.12.3). The "core" of Frankish power, judging by gold hoards and princely burials, seems to have been the Rhine itself, not farther north (Willems 1986, 458–60), which means that they too extended well to the south. A Roman embassy wishing to visit Attila, whose kingdom theoretically lay well beyond the Danube, was met by a band of Huns long before reaching the river, in "Roman territory," says Priscus, who was himself present. But then he adds that the region was used by Attila for hunting, just as part of Roman Pannonia too was said to be subject to him (fr. 11 pp. 248, 276 Blockley).

So though the Romans still claimed to exercise political power over Germans beyond the great rivers, we must try to imagine what the Roman world looked like from the German point of view. Roman ideology still regarded access to barbarian territory as open and unlimited by formal frontier lines. But barbarian kings were coming to adopt the same view in reverse. The Germanic Rugi and Alamans still recognized the Danube as a Roman frontier but levied tribute and disposed of villages and *castella* south of the river, as Eugippus's *Life of Saint Severinus* in the fifth century so vividly describes (8.2, 22.4, 31.1, 31.6, 42.1). Attila had forced the Romans to pay tribute (*phoros*), but, so we are told, it was concealed by the Roman court in the traditional manner as if it were payment of subsidies and supplies, in recognition of which they gave Attila the title *magister utriusque militiae* in the Roman army (Priscus, fr. 11, pp. 276–78 Blockley). Nothing could illustrate better differences in perspective of those who lived on each side of the frontiers. We see in this example the perfect contrast between ideology and reality.

Seven

Warlords and Landlords in the Later Empire

As more information is revealed about the war against Iraq in 1991, everyone now knows Iraq's strength was to a large extent the creation of the cold war between the world powers. So it should not surprise us to find that this was no new phenomenon in that part of the Middle East. First came the Romans and Parthians, then from the third century A.D. the Persians and the Romans, and finally the Mamluk governors of the sixteenth and seventeenth centuries; they all thought fit to manipulate the border folk of Mesopotamia and Syria, scattered peoples who emerged under the vague but ominous name Saracens, whom they tried to use as instruments of their own frontier policies. But they ended by having to grapple with the monster they had nourished. In 503, when the Byzantine emperor Anastasius mustered the largest army ever against the Persians (or so Procopius says, *BPers.* 1.8.4), Joshua the Stylite, who was witness to the war, wryly remarked, "To the Arabs of both sides this war was a source of much profit, and they wrought their will on both kingdoms" (79, Wright).[1]

The prosperity the Saracens enjoyed coincided, according to Ammianus, with a decision by the Persian army that large-scale attacks by field armies were profitless and that the best procedure on the eastern front was *per furta et latrocinia* (Amm. Marc.16.9.1). That is the phrase I referred to in chapter 6 as probably as good as any to characterize the barbarian invasions, and it finds interesting parallels on the western frontiers. It is this theme that also provides some understanding of how the Roman frontiers were transformed in the fifth century A.D. and beyond and that I want to examine in this chapter. But first let me take up the narrative from where events were left in chapter 5—that is, in the confused and difficult period of the fifth century onward.

A Narrative of the Last Days of the Frontiers

In the fifth century and beyond, the frontiers of the East and of the West had very different fortunes. In the East the later Roman territories survived more or less intact, and the frontiers passed without moment into the story of the Byzantine Empire. The organization of the frontiers of Justinian in the sixth century shows little change from the time of Diocletian (Grey 1973, 35), whereas in the West the frontiers melted—if not imperceptibly, at least sometimes unremarkably—into the kingdoms of successor federate chiefs and warlords as Roman troops withdrew.

THE EASTERN FRONTIER

In the East, oddly enough, it was the extreme ends of the frontiers that registered the greatest activity. The conflict with Persia in the traditional borderlands in Armenia, Mesopotamia, and southern Syria had reached a stalemate by the end of the fourth century, and despite some fierce clashes in the sixth century followed by an almost total collapse of the frontiers in the early seventh century, the only result was that each side exhausted the other's strength and made the victory of the Moslem Arabs relatively easy (Kennedy and Riley 1990, 35).

In the northeast sporadic clashes took place between the fifth and sixth centuries over control of the Caucasus. There the invasion of the Huns and other tribes moving off the Russian steppes in the late fourth century, which reached as far as Ctesiphon, was repeated in the fifth century and presented both Persia and Constantinople with serious problems of instability. With obvious reluctance the old antagonists were forced into some kind of agreement after "half a millennium of mutual destruction" (Grey 1973, 31; Isaac 1990, 265). The Romans sensibly left the military control of the eastern passes between Georgia and the Caspian to the Persians, whom they even subsidized in the sixth century. But they maintained their hold on Colchis (or Lazica) on the Black Sea by alliances and forts, although this was disputed by Persia (Isaac 1990, 230-35).

On the Arab and Palestinian frontier both sides continued to sponsor Saracen groups under their phylarchs, in an effort to maintain trade routes and the *status quo*. The best known is the Lakhmid dynasty, which switched alliance from Rome to Persia in the fifth century but was balanced by the Salih and Ghassanids, who supported Rome. These were only two of a plethora of names that seemed to gain prominence in the sixth century and that fought for supremacy with or without Roman or Persian encouragement (e.g., Procop. *BPers*. 2.28.12–14). But what is perhaps most interesting when one comes to look at the Roman West is how many such Arab federate groups within the Roman Empire converted to Christianity, their phylarchs rising to high office within the Byzantine army and even on occasion becoming bishops.[2]

In the far south, in the Sinai and Negev, the "problem of the Saracens" is highlighted again by the frequent attacks and sometimes deep invasions to which our sources refer. Does this illustrate the growing organization and menace of the Saracen confederations, or were these merely isolated raids of little military significance? Jerome in particular, from his contemporary residence in Palestine in the early fifth century, tells of a massive attack that "ran through the *limes* of Egypt, Palestine, Phoenicia, and Syria" (*Ep*. 126).

Doubters of the Saracen threat argue that these marauders were not Arabs but displaced North African nomads, although there is nothing to prove it.[3] Saracens were certainly responsible for many of the disturbances reported by worried Christian monks in their isolated monasteries. The scale and seriousness may have been exaggerated, but it is difficult to deny that they represented a growing force.[4] It was, after all, one such group on the borders of southern Palestine—led by Muhammad, who turned against Rome when it failed to pay his Muslim forces—that changed the face of a history that is still being written (Mayerson 1986, 43-44).

THE WEST

Because of the collapse of coherent central government in the West during the fifth century, we have to follow the history of each region separately. The interest lies in how often similarities are apparent.

Africa

The end of Roman administration in North Africa came about not because of the collapse of the southern *limes* but through invasion from across the Mediterranean Sea. The wheat of Africa was a magnet that attracted starving northern tribes who had already entered the empire as federates. The Visigoths, under Alaric in Italy in 410 or under his successor Wallia in Spain about 415, were on the point of making the crossing when their fleets were destroyed. What the Visigoths contemplated, the Vandals and Alans achieved in early 428. But it is worth stressing that none of these attempts were quite the straightforward "barbarian invasions" they might seem. Alaric wished to recover Africa for the Roman emperor Attalus against the *comes Africae* Heraclian, who was in theory loyal to the emperor Honorius but declared his independence soon after Alaric's death. The Vandal king Geiseric was invited to cross from Spain to Africa by the dissident Roman *comes Africae* Boniface, in his factional struggle with the Ravenna court (Procop. *BVand.* 3.3.22–25; Romanelli 1959, 630).

By 435 Carthage was in Geiseric's hands, although the fiction was created that he was an ally and a tributary subject of Rome (Procop. *BVand.* 3.4.13; Prosp. *A.* 435). The Vandals held the African provinces for a hundred years before Justinian recovered them through his generals Belisarius, Solomon, and John Troglita. With more optimism than realism, Justinian proclaimed in 534 that all former African *limites* were to be restored "as before the Vandal invasion" (*CJ* 1.27.1–2).[5]

But none of these events seems to have involved the marches of the former frontiers, where we have great difficulty knowing what was taking place. We hear of action against the Mauri conducted by Boniface, whom Augustine visited in 420 on the *limes* at Tobna in the Hodna region (Aug. *Ep.* 220.3 and 12) and who may have been responsible for the prisoners and slaves of the *gentes barbarae* to which Augustine refers a few years later (Aug. *Ep.* 199).[6] There is a further reference to a Mauri war under the Vandals (*CIL* 8.9286, dated 495), but in general the frontiers were strangely quiet.

The clue may lie in the intriguing list of Berber kings and kingdoms that emerged in the fifth and sixth centuries along the frontier regions from Altava in western Caesariensis to the Aures Mountains in Numidia. Many of these kings seem to have held Roman offices, like the *praefectus* Iugmena, known from the church he built at Berrouaghia on the edge of the Ouarsenis Mountains sixty kilometers south of Algiers in 474 (*AE* 1926, 60), or like Masties, whose inscription from the Hodna (*AE* 1945, 97) says that he had held the title of *dux* before becoming *imperator*—emperor![7] A dedication in the early sixth century at Altava, the old Roman fort in western Caesariensis, refers to Masuna as "king of the Moorish *gentes* and of the Romans" (*CIL* 8.9835), and the Christian tombs known as the Djedars in the region of Frenda in western Algeria are plausibly those of this dynasty (Camps 1985).

The House of Nubel in the late fourth century and its extraordinary role as both defender of and rebel against the empire provides us with an exemplar from which to understand the process of change taking place on the fringes of the African provinces. Altava lay in a region often thought to have been abandoned by Diocletian. But it has produced a series of inscriptions, including a dedication to Constans and Constantius II (*AE* 1935, 86) and a reference to a man killed by *barbari* in 429 (*AE* 1935, 85). A late empire list of bishops, too, extends as far as the farthest Roman fort at Numerus Castrorum (Courtois 1964, 89).

Perhaps, therefore, this part of the country and other parts of the frontier marches were maintained in the name of Rome by Mauri chiefs, many of whom once held Roman military offices as prefects and tribunes, many of whom were Christian. It was to the region of the Hodna that refractory Catholics were exiled by the Arian Vandals (Vict. Vit., *HPersecut.* 2.26–37). The frontiers did not collapse under barbarian attacks but dissolved into enclaves of rulers who were the heirs of Roman culture.

Britain

The last days of Roman Britain are as difficult to describe as those of other provinces. Rome stopped paying the soldiers in the early fifth century, as we can see by the absence of any gold coins after this and the end of bronze coin minting after about 395–402. Major pottery centers collapsed fairly abruptly in the first decade of the fifth century, implying the absence of a military market.[8] That fits with the traditional date of 410 given by Zosimus (6.10.2), when the emperor Honorius sent a letter to the cities of Britain instructing them to manage for themselves. But the soldiers did not simply disappear overnight. There had already been a series of rebellions between 406 and 407, ending with the usurpation of the West by Constantine III, who certainly removed many units from Britain to Gaul. There was a devastating attack by the Saxons in 410 in cooperation with yet another local rebellion. The events look very much like those in the third century, when provincial pretenders were in reality simply local commanders taking charge of their own defense. Zosimus tells us that the British, followed by the people of Armorica in Gaul, "ran many risks to ensure their own safety and to liberate their cities from the attacking barbarians; . . they threw out Roman officials and set up their own order, as they wanted it" (6.5.3). He also adds (6.5.2) the interesting information that the British "reverted to their native customs." Although the value of Zosimus's evidence is often questioned, archaeologists are now suggesting that by the time of the main Saxon invasions in the mid-fifth century, most of the British population had indeed already abandoned the Romanized urban and social order, creating "massive discontinuity" (Cleary 1989, 162, 173).

How long Rome exercised any control north of the wall is debatable. The famous hoard of Roman silver found at Traprain

Law might be the result of raiders from the Scottish Lowlands; but it could also be evidence of close treaty relations (Welsby 1982, 127). The Votadini, for a long time the allies of the Romans, had their center at Traprain, and it is difficult to see them as raiders. It is true that medieval tradition says the Votadini were removed to Wales, but the story is so full of difficulties that it cannot be used as sound evidence (Johnson 1980, 65–69).

The late evidence on the northern frontier seems to confirm the view that the Picts and Scots had not posed a great threat. There was no takeover of the military posts by them, or even any general destruction (Breeze and Dobson 1976, 232). Some forts show signs of burning, though not necessarily as a result of attacks. Recently discovered timber buildings on the site of the granaries at Birdoswald were built after coinage ceased in the fifth century (Higham 1992, 76). South Shields remained occupied until the seventh century, as did Carlisle and York. Ravenglass seems to have been deliberately dismantled. But the Yorkshire coastal fort of Huntcliffe has gruesome evidence of violence, with the severed heads of women and children.

A comparison with the transformation of North Africa after Roman rule shows an interesting number of similarities with the events in Britain, as they have come down to us through medieval historians like Gildas or through regional tradition. Britain, like Mauretania, is supposed to have been controlled by a number of local dynasties of chiefdoms that filled the frontier vacuum left by the Roman administration: the kings of Strathclyde, the kings of Galloway, the Votadini chiefs, and the Welsh kingdoms of Gwynedd and Dyfed. The famous "Hallelujah Victory" of 429 won by Saint Germanus against Saxons and Picts should be seen, says a recent study, "as the achievement of the clients and household of a member of the local aristocracy" (Higham 1992, 76).

It is difficult to separate fact from fiction but even harder to dismiss it all as pure invention. Procopius (*BVand.* 3.2.38) says that "tyrants" (the usual word for usurpers) took over from Roman rule in 411. As in Mauretania, many of these kings had what look like Latin names, some of which seem to imply that they also held Roman-style offices: Cluim (Clemens) and Cinhil (Quintilius) of

Strathclyde, Patern Pesrut (Paternus "Red Cloak") of the Votadini, Triphun (tribune?) of the Irish settlers in Dyfed. In several of the traditions Magnus Maximus seems to have been venerated as a founder, which may mean he was responsible for recognizing the federate status of the chiefdoms.[9] And as in Mauretania, the strength of Christianity in these kingdoms is striking. Saint Patrick in the later fifth century presumed to censure Coroticus of Strathclyde for his impiety, and on the basis that he was a Roman (Thomas 1979).

Although the British are said to have made a desperate appeal to the Roman general Aetius for help against sea invasions in the mid-fifth century—which, if true, shows that the severance from Rome had not been complete—the Gallic Chronicle, written in 452, records that "Britain passed into Saxon power" in the year 441–42. But it is fairly certain that Roman traditions were kept alive longer in some form by the successor kingdoms.

The Rhine Frontier

In the confused events after 407 we cannot be sure how much of the Rhine garrisons and forts remained. Jerome (*Ep.* 123) says that Strasbourg, Mainz, and Worms fell, but the pretender, Constantine III (407–11), must have partially recovered the positions, as Zosimus says (6.3.3), since Mainz, together with Kastel on the right bank, was still occupied (Petrikovits 1971, 187) and in 412 was briefly the center of a kingdom under the pretender Jovinus, supported by Burgundian and Alan federates, before it was suppressed by the Visigoths. Strasbourg shows no archaeological sign of damage (Stroheker 1975, 42), and Trier, despite being sacked a number of times, minted coins until finally taken over by the Franks (Wightman 1985, 301–3).

The astonishing success of Aetius in Gaul and Germany between 425 and 454 was due in no small part to the force of federate Huns he commanded. Part of the Rhine was restored by him in 428, and the Alaman Juthungi were defeated in Raetia in 430, followed by a victory in Noricum. In 436 he defeated the Burgundians' kingdom on the Rhine and probably used them to block the Alamans from passing through the Belfort Gap into Gaul by resettling them between Geneva and Neuchâtel, possibly in the region our sources call "Sapaudia" (James 1982, 22). In 447 or 448 he defeated the Frankish king Chlogio at *vicus Helena* near Arras. Then in 451 he was able to turn the tables and use Burgundian and Visigothic federates to defeat Attila and his Huns on the Catalaunian Plains near Troyes.[10]

But where was the frontier through all this? Can we believe the panegyricist of Aetius who gives the impression that the Rhine was now controlled by Rome again? "The Rhine," he says, "has bestowed pacts, making the wintry world Rome's servant" (Merob. *Pan.* 2). "Pacts" obviously must mean federate pacts. The archaeological evidence of federate garrisons has already been referred to, particularly that of the spectacular necropolis at Krefeld-Gellep, the Roman fort of Gelduba on the lower Rhine, not far from Cologne, which probably later became a center of the Rhineland Franks. From about the mid-fourth century the graves took on a new orientation, and some women's graves appear containing Germanic-style ornaments. They look like federates. But in about 425 the graves became much richer and some were princely, which might suggest more independent Frankish groups, only nominally serving Rome (James 1988, 56–57).

Roman policy, if such existed, followed the lead of Stilicho— to turn over the frontier forts to autonomous federates and maintain the towns by mobile *comitatenses* (James 1988, 75). But the field army too increasingly took on federate units of Huns, Alans, Burgundians and such, led by their own *reguli*, even if technically under Roman generals. It therefore becomes impossible to be sure when Roman control was genuine or only nominal. Soon after Aetius's death Sidonius proclaimed that Alamans were "drinking the Rhine from the Roman bank"; but, he adds, they dominated both sides "as either citizen or conqueror" (*vel civis vel victor; Carm.* 7.373–75). It means that federate settlers and new invaders were becoming indistinguishable. Whether leaders of invading war bands, federate princes, or Roman generals of the *comitatenses*, they became more like autonomous warlords (Bachrach 1972, 3–4). The battle was not between Romans and barbarians, and it is unclear who was now the defender of civilization.[11]

The middle and lower Rhine had benefited from long stable relations with the Romans, and they were able to profit from the chaos of central government in the fifth century to become more and more independent. Frankish federates in Upper Germany may account for the omission of Germania I on the *Notitia Galliarum* list drawn up in the early fifth century, and that may imply that the kingdom of the Salian Franks now extended from the Rhine to the Somme, as Gretgory of Tours says was the case in about 450. On the other hand, Sidonius (*Carm.* 7.372) implies that Roman control of Germania I and Belgica II was still valid when the Franks attacked in 455.

The problem is resolved if we accept the intriguing possibility that both Clovis and his father Childeric before him were recognized as Roman governors. For this there is some evidence from Childeric's grave and in a letter of Bishop Remigius of Reims (James 1988, 65; the evidence is cited later). This may also explain the interesting story told by Procopius (*BGoth.* 5.12.13–19), according to whom the last Roman soldiers on the frontiers voluntarily went over to the Franks but kept their Roman identity as units within the Frankish army.

The frontiers no longer existed after the murder of Valentinian III in 455. Alamans were infiltrating in large numbers into lower Bavaria, Switzerland, and Noricum, and in 457 a small band reached northern Italy (Sid. *Carm.* 5.373–77). Gaul and Germany had turned into a confusion of rival generals, some claiming Roman authority, others Frankish; and some both. Aegidius, father of Syagrius, was active in northern France in the name of Rome but was briefly chosen king of those Franks who formerly had supported Childeric (Greg. Tour. *HF* 2.12). Another commander, "Count" Paulus, is found leading an army of Romans and Franks against Goths and Saxons (Greg. Tour. *HF* 2.18). The descendant of the late fourth-century *magister militum,* Arbogast, was "count of Trier" in about 477, after Roman speech "had been wiped out" (Sid. *Ep.* 4.17), but still bore a Roman title, presumably with the consent of the Franks. Ragnachar, Frankish *regulus* of Cambrai, briefly allied with Clovis (Greg. Tour. *HF* 2.42). Each seems to have been master of his own enclave.

The *Life of Saint Geneviève,* like the *Life of Saint Severinus* in Noricum, gives us an inkling of what it was like in the last days of Roman rule—towns under siege and trying to carry on independently, warlords and their armies in the countryside. In 486 Syagrius, whom Gregory of Tours (*HF* 2.27) calls "king of the Romans," although he was no more than a warlord at Soissons, was defeated by Clovis, the son of his father's rival. Gregory treats it as just another episode, and it is only modern historiography that seeks to make it into a symbolic end of Roman rule (James 1988, 79).

The Danube Frontier

Upper Pannonia and Noricum became the corridor for westward movements of peoples in the fifth century; Vandals in 401, Alaric and his Visigoths in 402, and Radagaisus with his motley army in 405. Their appearance was brief but destructive. It is probably to this date we should put the sack of Vindobona (Vienna) and the large number of refugees from Illyricum (*CTh* 10.10.25 [408]). But official building was still being ordered in Lower Pannonia about the same time (*CTh* 11.17.4, 15.1.49), and recent excavations at Tokod, Scarbantia, and Heraculia suggest that the Roman population was much more stable, even in upper Pannonia, than once believed (Fitz 1984, contra Mócsy 1974b, 356).

By 407 Alaric and his Visigoths occupied the region of Noricum, and he demanded its formal cession as a federate state (Zos. 5.50); but soon after this the Visigoths moved westward to Aquitania. It is generally accepted that the *Notitia Dignitatum* lists for this area were drawn up in the early fifth century, possibly after the reorganization of Pannonia Prima, Noricum, and Raetia under the *comes Illyrici,* Generidus, in 409 (Zos. 5.46.2), showing that the frontiers were still manned (Fitz 1991, 223).

The Huns intensified their attacks on the lower Danube in 408 with their Sciri allies, though they were badly mauled and many were virtually enslaved (*CTh* 5.6.3). The *limes* was still intact, and the fleet still patrolled the river looking "for opportunities for expeditions" and supplying the forts (*CTh* 7.17.1 [412]). Sucidava on the left bank was overrun by Huns in 422 but was repaired, and Drobeta was probably similar (Torupu 1974, 79). But Hunnish pressure was increasing, and from about 420, with brief respites, large parts of Pannonia came under their control and were formally ceded by treaty in 433.

In Noricum, however, Aetius, using Hun federates, was active against the Juthungi Alamans in asserting Roman rule as late as 431 (Hydatius, *Chron.* ad 430 and 431; Sid. *Carm.* 7.233). Yet Huns and many others, such as Rugi and Gepids, probably crossed the territory on their way westward to northern Gaul, and it may be that Noricum was ceded to the Huns as part of their federate state in 433 (Wirth 1979, 227; Alföldy 1974, 214).

The archaeological evidence shows that about 441 a radical change took place on the lower Danube, where forts were destroyed, although even then they were ordered to be restored by Theodosius II until handed over to the Huns formally by treaty in 447 (cf. *NTh* 24.5 [443]). As before, the Roman emperors recognized the invader as a federate ally. Attila was given the title *magister militum,* and a demilitarized zone was established south of the Danube, over which he claimed control. In 447 we have a famous firsthand description of Attila's kingdom and its "frontiers"—really a kind of no-man's-land—extending five days travel south of the Danube, given by Priscus, the historian who accompanied a Roman mission to Attila's court north of the Danube (Prisc., fr. 11, p.243ff. Blockley).

But that was not the end of the Roman *limes.* As on the Rhine, there followed a confused history of rival powers, whose course is difficult to follow in detail. The death of Attila in 453 led to the disintegration of his kingdom into warring groups, out of which emerged successor kingdoms on the borders of the empire, the Rugi in Lower Austria, the Heruli in southern Moravia, and the Suebi, Vandals, and Alans in Pannonia. In the course of the wars many crossed or still found refuge in Roman territory as Roman federates, even if it is sometimes difficult to show exactly where that territory had its boundaries. Most prominent of these were the Ostrogoths—Valdamir's Ostrogoths in Upper Moesia, Amal Ostrogoths in Pannonia, and another group of Amal Ostrogoths in the Dobrudja and northern Bulgaria along with Alans and Sciri. It was with the Ostrogoths that the future of the Roman West lay.

By 460 the *Life of Saint Severinus* informs us that a mixed group, chiefly of Gothic Rugi, but also including Alamans, Thuringi, and Herulians, were controlling the Danube and demanding tribute from the towns (Eugip. *V. Sev.* 31). This remarkable document, written in the early sixth century by Eugippus, describes the last days of the frontier when Severinus lived there as bishop, about 467 to 482 (Lotter 1976; Thompson 1982, chap. 7). The scene is one of unpaid soldiers, with some local self-help by the towns who hired federate soldiers, but the gradual collapse of *castella*. On the other hand, the *Life* makes it very clear that Odoacer in Italy still looked upon the Danube as the formal Roman frontier, until he gave the order in 488 that the province was to be abandoned (Eugip. *V. Sev.* 44).

Even then the end did not come as a result of invasion by barbarian hordes. What we call the Roman-Rugian war of 487–88 was in reality a struggle between rival factions of Roman nobles, in which the Byzantine court was behind the Rugi (McCormick 1977). Nor was it the end of the Romans, since some forts remained occupied and in the sixth century Theodoric's outer "frontiers" extended to parts of the province.[12] But the Danube *limes* had ceased to exist.

Inland Pannonia from Lake Balaton to Sirmium more or less passed by federate treaty under the control of the Ostrogoths from 456 to 473. The victories of Theodoric, son of Thiudimir, the leader of Valdamir's Ostrogoths, against the Sarmatians in about 478 were carried out in the name of Rome, after he had been recognized as *magister militum* by the emperor Zeno. By 481 he had made himself leader of the Amal Goths and had become a Roman citizen and consul in the eastern court. In that capacity he was sent by Zeno, "until he arrived in person" (Exc. Val. 2.11.49), to set up a *praeregnum* in Italy in opposition to Odoacer the Scirian—who some sources claim was also the legitimate agent of the Roman emperor (Wolfram 1988, 278)—on the appeal of the Rugian king, whose rule Odoacer had just destroyed. It becomes more and more meaningless to talk of "barbarians," as though the frontiers of empire were the dividing line.

Although it is not really possible to detect a coherent Roman frontier on the middle Danube after about 420, there was no sudden collapse. Historians are now more inclined to stress the continuity rather than the destruction of Roman civilization (Mihäilescu-Birliba 1981). The transition took place through the growth of federate enclaves on the frontiers, through the recognition of federate kings as Roman magistrates, and through the continuity of the social and political structures of the Roman provinces. Most Roman towns, like Sirmium, carried on. Carnuntum still traded in amber. And the church in particular maintained its organization. We can see something of the process of continuity and assimilation epitomized in the last Roman emperor of the West, Romulus Augustulus. His family was Roman Pannonian, but his father, Orestes, had served as Attila's secretary and spokesman before going on to serve Rome as *magister militum*.[13]

By contrast, the lower Danube was still administered from Constantinople, despite continual raids and invasions throughout the fifth and sixth centuries by Bulgars, Slavs, and Avars. A general repair of the frontier was carried out by Anastasius in the early sixth century, followed by Justinian's new building program. Procopius the historian lists for us the sites in his book *de aedificiis,* which included some forts, like Pontes (possibly old Drobeta), on the left bank (*De aed.* 4.6). The forts appear from descriptions in the sixth century to have become islands of refuge for the countryfolk (Velkov 1977, 201–4). Inland the scene is not unlike that in Gaul, with cities maintaining their independence by local garrisons while invading "robbers" settled in the countryside (Procop. *De aed.* 4.7.13). But unlike Gaul, the central state still directed the garrisons, as we can see from the fact that Justinian had to give permission to the town of Asemus in the Thracian Chersonese when the residents wanted to raise a home guard (Theoph. Sim. 7.3.1–10).

So much for the events, insofar as they can be told. The real difficulty in such a bare narrative is to imagine what was really happening when we talk in broad terms about the collapse of the frontiers and the changes inherent in that process during the later Roman Empire. This chapter concentrates on two of those changes—in the countryside and in the army. They were, I believe, closely linked, and it was the developments that took place in these areas especially that eased the transition from the Roman Empire to the barbarian kingdoms. One of the features that has struck some modern commentators about the Frankish conquest in the West, for instance, is its relatively peaceful character.[14] Although this is controversial, I believe it is correct—not because the Franks were gentle invaders, but because out of the violence of the countryside there emerged a *modus vivendi* and a military structure that permitted Roman and invader to accommodate each other.

Military Landlords

The later Roman Empire was a period when the poor notoriously became increasingly dependent on the arbitrary will of the landed rich. It is usual, since Fustel de Coulanges, to cite as evidence disappearance of the tenancy contracts of *locatio-conductio*. In fact, some nontechnical references to land contracts do continue to appear in vulgar law in Augustine's Africa and in Byzantine Egypt as well as in Euric's Code in Gaul, and perhaps even in seventh-century Merovingian formularies.[15] Although there obviously was a diminution in the practice, I suspect that contracts were increasingly oral and that the absence of legally referable written contracts was less important than the breakdown of traditional unspoken social contracts of patronage in return for services between landowners and the poor, whether or not tenancy was involved. This breakdown was accelerated by the growth of the twin process of soldiers becoming landlords and landlords becoming soldiers.

The first part of this process—soldiers turning into landlords—is the central, though coded, message of Libanius's celebrated forty-seventh oration, which we tend to regard as a general discourse on patronage. Libanius was a fourth-century orator from Antioch who was really making an attack on military officers, particularly those of the *laterculum minus* on the frontiers, who were purchasing property from *curiales* and encouraging peasants, both tenants and free villagers, to become their *oiketai*—their "domestics" (secs. 21, 24)—turning farmers into "brigands" (sec. 6) and undermining the very structure of the empire (discussed by Carrié 1976). It was, says Libianus, like appealing to the barbarians outside the empire (sec. 20).

This was loaded language, whose technical significance becomes apparent only in the next century. *Oiketai, oikia,* and *familia* regularly signaled the presence of semiprivate armies—for instance, when Procopius describes the retinue of Belisarius (*SHist.* 4.13); brigandage was always the standard charge by the administration in legislating against such accretions, as when we find the *Theodosian Code* attacking *patrocinium*, the system of patronage, for encouraging bandits (*CTh* 1.29.8 [392]). Themistius's attack on rich aristocrats for driving peasants to seek out barbarians (*Or.* 8.115c) was, I suspect, partly a reference to the fact that barbarians were becoming the new military landlords on the Roman *limites*. More of that later.

The commentaries on Libanius's speech search, without much success, for examples of soldiers who purchased property in Syria, often called "forts" or, in Libanius's language, *pyrgoi*. There is the case of Silvanus, who possessed a property in southeastern Syria Prima, a *dux,* according to the inscription, who had taken the interesting, perhaps prudent, course for a frontier officer of marrying the daughter of Saracen *phylarchs.* [16] Another estate is identified on the Damascus-Palmyra road belonging to a Rufinus, a *dux limitis* (*CIL* 3.6660). Neither precisely proves that the officers used their position to purchase land; and that is perhaps an important reminder to us of the limitations of epigraphic evidence. But Libanius's example of his own uncle, a *strategos* who ended up with a modest estate of ten *oiketai* (*Or.* 47.28) proves that these things happened. Nor is there anything intrinsically surprising in soldiers' using their money to purchase land in the area where they served. Since some of these soldiers were of barbarian origin, who perhaps married into local families, this process helped integrate them into the imperial system.

The same development is illustrated by the Abinnaeus Archive, the dossier of a Roman officer in fourth-century Egypt. There Abinnaeus himself was becoming one of the land bosses—the *geouchoi*. In one of the papyri (*PAbin.* 61) one can even detect a formal written contract of tied labor that thus backed *patrocinium* with civil law.[17] It reads: "To Flavius Abinnaeus, *praepositus* of the camp at Dionysias etc. . . . . I, Julius, agree to act as surety for Ammonius, son of Souk of the village of Taurinon: whenever he is wanted, I myself, Julius, will produce him, as set down, and I give my consent to this under examination." If that is indeed, as it appears to be, a reference to a contract upon the person and his personal service, it is at the very least a fourth-century example of the contract known as *paramone*, that is, service as a retainer of the household—called an *oiketes* or *katadoulos pais*—which appears often in the next centuries (e.g., *POxy.* 1112; *PStras.* 40). But it is also getting close to Marc Bloch's idea that a medieval serf was essentially an *homme de corps*. a henchman bound by personal ties to a master, as opposed to the conventional theory that said he was a *serf de la glèbe*, tied to the land (Bloch 1963, 356–78; Whittaker 1989, 135). Certainly there is no mistaking the tone of this personal relationship in another document (*PAbin.* 36) from another, obviously rural, worker-peasant: "To the master of my life, to the owner of my strength, to the *praepositus* Abinnaeus: from Pallas . . . I earnestly beseech you that you . . . give my wife some sheep. . . . You know, my lord, that I have none. I am your servant forever." It is impossible to tell from the context whether Pallas was a *colonus* tenant or a free peasant, but the whole archive is nevertheless a graphic portrait of rural patronage on a desert frontier of the Fayum in the mid-fourth century.

That stimulates me to wonder about other desert frontiers in the Roman Empire, especially the Tripolitanian frontier, where we have no papyri or Libanius but certainly find many inscriptions and many fortified farmhouses, or *gsur*, mentioned earlier, which must have been very like the Syrian *pyrgoi*. Some of these were official *centenaria* of the local frontier army, the forts of the local tribunes and *principes* of the *gentiles* troops: but most we know to have been the private estates of these same military officers (Elmayer 1985). This is not a precise analogy with the Syrian or Egyptian examples, since most of the officers in Tripolitania, apart from the *praepositi limitis,* appear not to have been posted from other provinces but to have been local aristocrats, very prosperous, with large settlements attached to their farmhouses. Therefore the Tripolitanian estate owners, men like Julius Masthalul, Julius Nasif, and Flavius Isiguari (*IRT* 886—Bir ed-Dreder), illustrate both halves of the twin process, soldiers as landlords and landlords as soldiers. The evidence of the Nessana papyri in Palestine suggests that the Theodosian camel corps posted there in the sixth century also comprised local recruits who owned land (Kraemer 1958, no. 24, etc.).

When we turn to the western provinces, it is strange that we have no obvious reference at all to the Syro-Egyptian phenomenon of military landlords. But can we really believe that it did not exist?[18] More probably, in my view, the explanation lies simply in the different kinds of sources we possess. After all, even in the earlier empire it is generally believed that soldiers in Gaul bought farms in the vicinity of their camps (Drinkwater 1983, 67). There are, however, a few clues—I put it no higher than that—that the practice was becoming increasingly common in the West during the later empire. Perhaps, for instance, *patrocinium* and property lie behind the edict (*CTh* 7.1.10) addressed to Jovinus, the Gallic *magister militum* on the western front in 367, from Valentinian forbidding soldiers to take away with them freeborn men "by pretending they are *propinquitas* [relatives] or *lixae* [a word usually meaning traders attached to the army]."

Interesting in itself is the assumption of the legislation that such household retinues were large enough to create serious worries about evasion of military service, whether or not they involved *coloni.* I also believe that the legislation in 384 (*CTh* 7.1.12) complaining of soldiers "wandering through private property" when they should have been with their units could refer to men going to their own property. Later under Valentinian III soldiers of Numidia and Mauretania who "wandered away" from frontier posts were obviously landowners, since they were formally conceded a month's leave to visit their "household and land" (*familia et possessiones; NVal* 13.13 [445]).

At all events, there is a strong a priori presumption that on the Rhine-Danube front there was some growth of military landlordism. Ammianus's attack on Constantius's courtiers who were "raised at one bound from base poverty to vast riches" (22.4.3) goes on to attack those soldiers who sought "even houses of marble." But no doubt, as in Tripolitania, the situation was often confused by the presence of native *gentiles*. Where did all those Frankish and Alaman grandees who served in the Roman army have their families and land? Some, we know from Ammianus, had property beyond the frontiers (e.g., 20.4.4). But some must surely have held estates in Toxandria and the Rhine provinces under Roman control, just as we can be almost sure that the Saracen Tanukhids held Roman land in northern Syria (Shahid 1984, 545).

A number of western examples spring to mind. Charietto with his band of retainers lived around Trier and presumably had land there. The German Petulantes in the Roman army apparently had some property in the provinces, since they complained bitterly, when about to be posted away by Julian, that their families who had been freed from the Alamans would again be exposed to invasion (Amm. Marc. 20.4.10). It seems likely that the family of Arbogast, the fourth-century Frankish *magister militum,* acquired during his office the large estates on the Moselle that were occupied by his heir, the count of Trier; and Merobaudes, another *magister militum* possessed estates in Spanish Baetica and near Troyes in Gaul.[19]

These are, of course, only scraps of evidence, although, as we shall see, there is some circumstantial corroboration from archaeology that the phenomenon of military patronage was not unknown in northern Gaul and Germany. There is also a very general argument in support of the proposition. The fourth century, it is generally believed, witnessed the emergence of new landowning gentry in Gaul, consisting mainly of men who had sought and found their fortunes at the imperial court. Camille Jullian, the great historian of Roman Gaul, compared such men to the bourgeois parvenus at the courts of Henri IV and Louis XIII (Jullian 1920–26, 8:128; Stroheker 1948, 12–14; Drinkwater 1987, 254–55). It seems probable, even certain, therefore, that some would have begun as military officers. Jovinus himself, whom I mentioned earlier, seems to have had property at Reims, where he built a church and recorded his military service (*CIL* 13.3256). But unlike Syria, in Gaul for much of the fourth century emperors took up residence on the frontier and therefore military patronage vied and overlapped with court patronage, making it impossible— perhaps even pointless—to judge in which capacity the new noblesse acquired their property and powers of patronage.

In short, it is reasonable to conclude that soldiers, particularly officers, on active service became increasingly powerful locally through their attachment to the land in the regions where they served. The situation was not an invention of the later empire but the culmination of a long process, since legislation against soldiers forming local attachments had been relaxed in the second century. The change in the later empire was one of degree; properties became greater and state controls over the exercise of private patronage became weaker. And above all, there was the additional factor that the soldiers were now often men who had entered Roman service as federate leaders.

Landlords as Soldiers

The principal evidence, which we do possess, concerns the other half of the twin process: landlords turning to militarism. With the growth of huge estates and concentration of property ownership in the later empire came control of large numbers of dependents who could be mustered for military action. Again, this was not an invention of the later empire. The rebellion in Africa in 238 by the estate owners at Thysdrus against the emperor Maximinus, when rural workers—interestingly called *oiketai* by the contemporary Greek historian Herodian (7.4.5)—plus the aristocratic *iuvenes* joined forces, is an early example of how landlords could use their bands of *amici* and *clientes* forcefully in a crisis. Zosimus tells of a similar example of an estate owner at Selgeia in Pamphylia who resisted Tribigild and his Goths in 399 by calling upon his *oiketai* and farmers who, he says, "were trained in many battles with neighboring bandits" (Zos. 5.15.5). Armed battles between retainers seem to have been common, like the example of two brothers who were estate owners in Cappadocia, each with his own "army of manservants" (*stratos . . . ek tôn hypocheiriôn*; Greg. Nyss. *V. Greg. Thaumat.* [*PG* 46.925d].

From the legislation of the fourth century, however, we cannot doubt the concern of the central administration about the growing independence and inaccessibility of rich estate owners, who were recruiting soldiers from the army, offering sanctuary to deserters, and of course, in the stereotyped language of the time, aiding and abetting robbers. Hence derived their attraction to peasants unwilling or unable to pay their taxes. Egypt illustrates what this meant in personal terms. The citizens of Theadelphia in 332 protested against Eulogios, the owner of an estate in the Oxyrhinchite nome for giving protection to five taxpayers with their families; yet, they complain, "Eulogios, their landlord together with Arion the wine grower and Serapion the farmer, have prevented us with violence from approaching even the entrance of his estate" (*PThead.* 17). This does not, of course, mean that peasants and *coloni* were turning into full-time private soldiers; but landlords were using their increasing powers of patronage to bind peasants to their personal allegiance, including the use of violence if needed.

The legislation is set in more global terms. In 396 we have the well-known ban on soldiers' entering *privatum obsequium,* which the law (*CTh* 7.1.15) says had been going on for some time. Under the title *De desertoribus et occultatoribus eorum* in the *Theodosian Code* (7. 18), against estate owners who harbor deserters, the first edict is dated 365, and the laws rise to a climax in the 380s—but apparently without much effect, since they continue almost unabated into the fifth century. Obviously it was going to be difficult to maintain tight control if the authorities took such a relaxed view of military duties as is reflected in the Abinnaeus Archive. There the soldiers of the garrison in Egypt seem grossly underemployed and regularly go off on expeditions to hunt gazelle or spend time farming.

It is equally hard to be impressed by the severity of the legislation against soldiers' taking absence without leave when we read the legislation of 413: "If anyone should spend a year without leave of absence . . . in slothful ease, he shall be demoted below his next ten inferiors" (*CTh* 7.18.16). But if a year seems a long time for a soldier to be absent without leave, it is even more surprising that the legislation continues by saying that only if he is absent for four years "shall he be removed from the official register and be granted no pardon." What were soldiers *doing* for four years in slothful ease?

The language of *latrones* and deserters, native *duces* and their *servitia, rustici,* and *coloni* is also very much at the core of the scattered rural movements from the third to the fifth century in Gaul and Spain, which we call the Bagaudae (Van Dam 1985, 30), and of the circumcellions in Africa. Rightly, in my view, regarded as more than simple jacqueries, these upheavals were perhaps no more than extreme forms of local armies of dependents taking aim at the *domini curiales,* the traditional landowning classes of the *civitates.* Just as Libanius compared desertion from the patronage of local *curiales* to going over to the barbarians, so too the image of passing beyond the frontiers and going over to the barbarians was used of Gallic dissidents (Van Dam 1985, 40–42). If it is correct that the Seine and Marne were the primary regions of such disaffection,[20] we must also ask to what extent this reflected the protosettlements of Frankish war bands in just those regions.

It is not my concern here to enter the controversy about how much aid the circumcellions gave to the rebellions of Firmus and Gildo in fourth-century Africa.[21] But it is of great significance that, in addition to the support of local Mauri tribes and some regular Roman army units, there are references by Ammianus to the *satellites* and hired *plebs* plus "accompanying servants [or slaves]"— *servis comitantibus*—of Firmus (29.5.36, 39). Likewise the *Theodosian Code* cites the massive estates of Gildo and his *satellites* (*CTh* 7.8.7 [400]; 9.42.19 [405]). The language can be compared with legislation passed a few years later after the disgrace of Stilicho, when punishment was ordained for those who gave their resources *iure vel corpore* (meaning something like "by oath and personal service") to Stilicho, his son, and *ceteris satellitibus* (*CTh* 9.42.22 [408]). These words, like "companions" and *satellites,* belong, as we shall see later, to the vocabulary used of *bucellarii,* those semiprivate household retinues that became the major, mobile strike forces of the fifth century. We might note here that Gildo's rebellious retinue was defeated just one year after the edict I referred to earlier forbidding soldiers to enter into *privatum obsequium* (Diesner 1972, 324).

These men were not barbarians from the mountain or desert fringes of the empire. The House of Nubel in the Kabylie, from which Firmus and Gildo stemmed, was a world of large fortified estates, of *castella* and *centenaria* and of endemic banditry. But the builders of these *castella*—which make one think of Tripolitania again—played a dual role as Mauri chiefs and Roman officials; thoroughly absorbed into the imperial court and army, yet leaders of "tribal" bands of the local *gentes*. From the fourth to the sixth century a series of such figures pass across the scene from the *rex gentium Maurorum et Romanorum* at the old Roman fort of Altava to Koceïla, king of Awreba near Tlemcen, whose real name was perhaps Caecilius. It was these men, as I said earlier, who kept alive the Roman and the Christian name in Africa.[22]

What is important to note here, however, is how close these Roman landlords were to the world of the federate warlords. It is difficult to distinguish between a Saracen *malek* ("king") or phylarch in the service of Rome, who, like the Mauri chiefs, was settled with land on Roman territory and absorbed into the Roman administration and the Saracen warrior leader, serving Rome with his federate band but equally prepared to serve Persia. I am thinking of the chieftain commemorated in 328 on the inscription at Namara near the Druz Mountains in Syria, called "king of all the Arabs," who forced many tribal chiefs to become "phylarchs of the Romans" (Bellamy 1985; Shahid 1984, 31–53; Bowersock 1983, chap. 10), or of Mavia in the reign of Valens, the Tanukhid queen whose daughter married Victor the *magister equitum* and who fought against the Arian emperor for the right to have a Christian Catholic bishop.[23] How different were they from the phylarch Podosaces, whom Ammianus calls a *latro* because he served the Persians (Amm. Marc. 24.2.4)?

These African and Arabian examples can be likened to the various Gallic and Frankish *reguli* who kept alive the Roman name.

Men like Syagrius of Soissons—*rex Romanorum* Gregory of Tours called him—though he was a king without a kingdom (James 1988, 70–71); or Arbogast of Triers, who spoke "the true Latin of the Tiber . . . even though the Roman writ has perished at our border," says Sidonius (*Ep.* 4.17); or Childeric of Tournai. We are accustomed to think of Childeric as a Frankish invader, but he was buried with his Roman fibula of office (figs. 50, 51); and Bishop Remigius of Reims seems to imply in a letter to Clovis that Childeric had been administrator of Belgica Secunda, as was his more famous son.[24] In this last example, as we can see, the Roman landlord had merged into the federate warlord as part of the process of change.

The problem about conceptualizing this change is, as we have been reminded recently, that Gregory of Tours in the sixth century, followed by many historians since, could conceive of the Franks' entry into Gaul only as a violent barbarian invasion, culminating at Soissons, where Syagrius fell fighting symbolically as the last defender of *Romania* (James 1988, 79). In fact, the fifth century in Gaul was the culmination of a less dramatic process of integration of Germanic chiefs with their *Gefolgsleute* in the burgeoning demi-monde of estate owners surrounded by their fighting retinues. The organization of armed retinues was not simply the creation of the Germanic invaders, since we can see parallel developments in Africa and the East. It was not German federate leaders but Romano-Spanish court grandees—Veranianus, Didymus, Theodosiolus, and Lagodius, cousins of Honorius—who raised troops from the slaves and *coloni* of their Spanish domains in 408–9 in order to stop the usurpation of Constantine III.[25]

Likewise, a bishop of the church, such as Hilary of Arles, was acting as a typical Roman landlord when he raised his "armed band" as a "detestable irregular force" (*abominabilis tumultus; NVal* 17.1 [445]). Synesius's natural pride at having organized the defense of Cyrene when he "enrolled companies of officers with the resources I had at my disposal" (*Ep.* 125) is matched by the occasion when he raised a similar band of irregulars to protect his private estates at Ausamas (MacMullen 1963, 138, 140, for other references). Gregory of Tours records a long line of bishops with

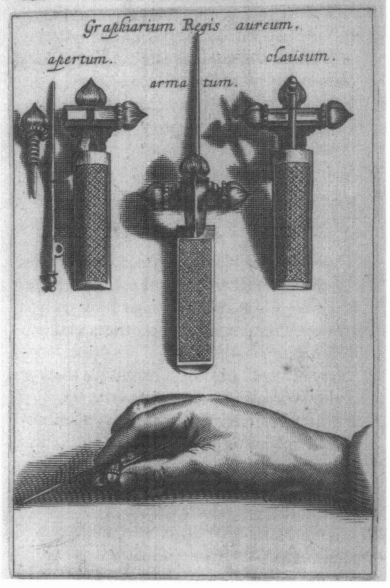

Graphiarium Regis aureum,

apertum. *clausum.*

arma tum.

Fig. 50. The grave of a famous warlord, Childeric, "king" of the Salian Franks, was discovered at Tournai, Belgium, in 1653; it contained, among many precious objects, a gold cruciform fibula of the sort used by senior Roman officers to hold their cloaks together. The brooch was stolen in 1831 and melted down, but fortunately it had been drawn by J. -J. Chiflet in 1655. Photograph of the drawing by Chiflet of the *Anastasis Childerici* by permission of the Bibliothèque Nationale, Paris.

Fig. 51. An artist's impression of what Childeric's clothing looked like when worn. Note the fibula holding together the cloak on his right shoulder. Drawing by P. Pellerin from Périn and Feffer 1987, 134. Reproduced by permission of Armand Colin Editeur, Paris.

militant bands; like Hilary of Arles or Cantinus of Auvergne (Clermont), they played havoc with the property of their neighboring brethren. Sidonius Apollinaris, as bishop of Clermont, led the defense of the city in the 470s. Indeed, one plausible reason for the conversion of Clovis, when threatened by the Alamans at Tolbiac, was that this might enable him to tap the considerable resources of the church.[26]

It might be argued that these examples of Roman estate owners and bishops are only isolated and late fifth-century examples of what was otherwise a century of general helplessness in the face of the barbarian onslaught. But that is to forget the sparseness of the sources for this period. In fact, the law codes of the later fourth century give an indication of the problem that became fully evident only when the central state armies disintegrated—a process that is itself most unclear (A. H. M. Jones 1964, 612).

The Archaeology of Change

The archaeology of Gaul provides some corroborative evidence of the naissance of warlords and their similarity to landlords. In chapter 6 I looked at the way much of the graveyard analysis from Gaul appears to confirm the generally peaceful course of integration and the "invisibility" of the barbarian invaders, just because it has been so difficult to identify them. Here I shall pick only three characteristics from what I said earlier.[27]

One of the features of the changing face of the Gallic countryside in the later empire was the growth of large estates and fortified villas. The literary references to this are well known. The villa of Pontius Leontius on the Garonne was called the *burgus*, the "chateau" with "high walls and turrets that transcend the sky" and was furnished with granaries (Sid. *Carm.* 22); or there was the chateau of Claudius Postumus Dardanus near Sisteron, which acquired new ramparts in the early fifth century (*muros et portas tuetioni omnium*) and was called for good measure Theopolis—City of God (*CIL* 12.1524; Jullian 1920–26, 8:141).

Less clear is the archaeological evidence, and whether there was greater nucleation of rural sites, as some have argued. In the central and southern regions of Gaul the abandonment of villas was less marked, and there is little doubt that many of the rural refuges, such as that at Montmaurin in Aquitania, were built by the great landowners. In the northern provinces of Germany and Belgica some cemeteries certainly grew larger in the later fourth century (like those at Eprave, Furfooz, and Homblières), although whether this reflected larger settlements is not proved. Small farms disappeared and some *vici* were abandoned when workers removed to Iron Age hilltop sites or grouped together in abandoned villas. Some large villas acquired fortifications or were associated with a *burgus* fortlet (such as those at Froitzheim and Rheinbach-Flerzheim in the Rhineland). But it has to be said that the evidence is not conclusive. It is particularly interesting, however, that on some sites of old Roman villas, among the sunken-floor huts appears a long wooden *Hallenhaus* of the sort known at Feddersen Wierde as the "manor house" of a rich man.[28]

In southern Gaul almost certainly, therefore, and perhaps in some places in the north, there was greater concentration of property holdings, increased isolation, or inaccessibility of estates and compulsion for peasants to seek refuge with the rich. It is not hard to picture what Salvian, priest of Marseilles in this period, meant when he described "those who, when driven by the terror of the enemy flee to the *castella* . . . and give themselves over to the yoke of being *inquilini*" (*De gub. Dei* 4.14).[29] An *inquilinus* was the lowest grade of tenant, who was completely tied to the service of his master.

Although Germanic-style burials were replacing many of the old Gallo-Roman interments, it is, as many archaeologists have stressed, impossible to be sure whether the men and women who used these graves were all German invaders or a frontier society. At the recently studied site of Vireux-Molhain in the Ardennes a small Roman fort opposite a *vicus* was reinforced in the mid-fourth to mid-fifth century by Germanic-looking groups, estimated at about twenty-five men and women per generation (Lemant et al. 1985; James 1988, 48). We cannot prove what the social relations with the villagers were, but these sites provide the exact setting for military, rural patronage in the style described by Libanius.

On the civil sites, as we saw, there is evidence that German over-lords with their henchmen took over Roman villas with the Gallo-Roman workers (see chap. 6, p. 237). The grave of Childeric, discovered at Tournai, is one of a type of so-called Flonheim-Gültlingen princely graves of approximately the same date; an interesting one was found at Pouan, between the rivers Aube and Seine near the presumed site of the Catalaunian Plains where Attila was defeated and where, according to one tradition, Theodoric the Visigoth fell. For that reason the tomb was for a long time identified as Theodoric's; but the name Heva appears on a golden ring, and there is no good reason, apart from the site, to date the grave precisely. All we can really say is that about this time in the mid-fifth century we find a series of princes' (or, as I prefer, warlords') graves (Périn 1980, 80, 169–70; James 1988, 76). They reflect the conditions of northern Gaul in the mid-fifth century.

Changes in the Army

It is time to return briefly to the army itself. I began by saying that frontier defense was less a problem of large pitched battles than of infiltration by small groups operating in clandestine raids—*per furta et latrocinia*. It appears that, just as the federate settlements and civilian villas were consolidating into more isolated, nucleated units, military developments were moving in the same direction. Constantine's *comitatenses,* and more particularly the regional *comi-tatenses* that had grown up with the House of Constantine, appear by the end of the fourth century to have become more and more like a static militia, based upon the cities for the purpose of supplies—a feature already evident to Ammianus (*ut commodius vescerentur;* 16.4.1; cf. 31.16.8). This tendency was perhaps encouraged by the forced cantonment of units of *laeti* and *gentiles* upon public lands attached to cities or forts. It is well known that many towns in modern France take their names from these units, such as Salmaise (ancient Sarmatia) near Langres, where the *Notitia Dignita-tum* (Oc., 42.61) locates a prefect of Sarmatian *gentiles;* in Langres itself a suburb was called Laticensis (modern Lassois), surely from a laetic unit (Bachrach 1972, 34).

That kind of degeneration of the field army was also a feature of the Byzantine army. But the corresponding evolution was a *force de frappe* in the fifth century. The force was made up overwhelmingly of "federates," a term that by the time of Honorius had lost its sense of being applied exclusively to barbarians, according to Olympiodorus (fr. 7.4, p. 158 Blockley)—who were probably often *ad hoc* irregulars—federates, but also *bucellarii*. The *bucellarii* were, again according to Olympiodorus, both Roman and foreign soldiers, defined by the scholiast on Basil (60.18.29) as "those who eat the bread of someone, on the condition of becoming his trusty." The Greek word is *paramenontes,* "those who are alongside," which is regularly used of these men in the fifth and sixth centuries and corresponds pretty closely to "gentlemen in waiting." That is the sense of the Latin word *satellites,* those who "hovered around" or, as Procopius describes them, "those who stand behind when the commander is dining" (*BVand.* 4.28).

There is no need for me to repeat all that has been said about the *bucellarii* by scholars in the past.[30] But the institution is usually discussed in terms of the army of the eastern empire, as though it postdated the collapse of the West. In fact, however, as the examples collected by Diesner's article "From Stilicho to Aetius" show (1972), it had firmly established itself in the western empire by the later fourth century. Indeed, I would argue that it is precisely through this institution that one can see most clearly the transition from the later empire to the medieval German kingdoms in the West. Titus, the leader of a unit of *bucellarii* who, according to the *Life of Daniel Styletes* (60-64), was invited to serve under Leo in the East, came from Gaul.

A good deal of the debate about *bucellarii* in the past has ranged around whether they herald the advent of feudalism by virtue of the personal oath of allegiance they gave to their leader (e.g., Bachrach 1967; Gascou 1976). But apart from the fact that medievalists now use the term "feudalism" less freely than some classical historians, most of the argument about private—as opposed to public—armies is misplaced. Procopius is clear that the private contract (of what perhaps later was called *paramone*) was supplemented by the *sacramentum* oath to the emperor (*BVand.* 4.18.6).

But obviously the public oath was of limited relevance if the patron rebelled or if imperial rule was not recognized. The loyalty of the soldiers then became private *obsequium*.

This ambiguity is well captured by Sidonius when describing the siege of Clermont in 474, at a time when the ties with an unknown western emperor were most tenuous and there was no imperial army in sight (*Ep.* 3.3) Sidonius lauds the exploits of a great landlord, Ecdicius, who with a *comitatus* of barely eighteen *sodales*—"fewer than the normal dining companions," says Sidonius—managed to cut his way through and put to flight "several thousand" Goths without loss. Gregory of Tours improves upon these incredible figures by giving Ecdicius only ten companions (*HF* 2.24). But I think we are here victims of terminology rather than rhetoric. Those who rate a mention are only the free *satellites*, the *amici* (which is the point of the reference to his table), who I think are sometimes called *clientes*. But no publicity was given to the far more numerous lesser *clientes*, *servi* and *coloni* in attendance on each companion. In the language used by the sixth-century Greek historian Procopius, we have the *doryphoroi* without the *hypaspists* (cf. Procop. *SHist.* 4.13).

Ecdicius is not unlike the example of Sarus the Goth, whom we know had two to three hundred personal followers. When he died fighting against Athaulf's army of ten thousand, however, he is said to have had only eighteen or twenty men, according to the strict account of Olympiodorus (fr. 18, p. 183 Blockley), one of whom was called Belleridus and termed a "domestic."[31] In Ammianus's account of the followers of Firmus, he distinguishes between the *plebs* whom Firmus "had hired for much pay" and the *servis comitantibus* (29.5.34–36). In the case of Ecdicius and his companions, Sidonius goes on to say that he collected "a kind of army," but it is impossible for us to be certain what kind of army this was. Was it a band of rural workers from the fields, which any patron-landlord could arm, like those noted earlier in Phrygia, "trained in many battles against bandits"? Or were they bands of private *bucellarii*, whom Delbrück compared to the *Kriegsknechte* of the Cinquecento? And was there any difference by now?

One thing that makes me think there was not much difference

is that at exactly the same time as Ecdicius was carrying out his heroic exploits at Clermont, not far south at Narbonne King Euric was passing legislation concerning the rights of *bucellarii* in relation to their private masters. But in the *antiqua* commentary (5.3.1) on *Euric's Code* the word *bucellarius* is changed to *in patrocinio constitutus*.[32] That shows how close the concept of patronage (*patrocinium*) was to the terms of service of *bucellarii*. But again I insist that it is not incipient feudalism that we detect in this relationship but something not too far from the quite separate institution of serfdom. The description of the *satellites* of Stilicho, which I cited earlier, was of those who had given themselves *iure vel corpore* to their patrons—that is, they pledged their bodies. When Marc Bloch defined the early serf as an *homme de corps*, he also believed the relationship had its origin in *patrocinium* (see above, page 259).

There is little doubt in my mind, either, that the parallels between the Byzantine *paramenontes*, "the trusted ones," and the Frankish *trustiones*, those defined in Salic law as *in truste dominica* ("in their lord's trust"), are closer than is normally recognized. Although the remnants of the Roman army continued to operate in the towns, just as in the eastern army, the countryside was controlled by these semiprivate bands. The practice of wearing exotic clothes, a characteristic of the eastern *bucellarii* (Gascou 1976, 151), is certainly matched by the description of the magnificent *comitantes* of Sigismer, one of the Rhine Franks, going to a wedding in about 469: they wore a uniform of hairskin shoes, bare lower legs and arms, and a tight-fitting multicolor garment from knee to shoulder; each carried a green mantle with crimson border, a sword hanging from the shoulder by a studded baldric, and a shield of silver with a golden boss, "the gleam from which showed their ranks and their devotion" (*censum et studium*; Sid. *Ep.* 4.20).

The central characteristic of the *bucellarii*, as we know them in the East, was their attachment to the "great houses" (*endoxoi oikoi*) as a kind of *annona* tax levy upon the estates of the rich. It was not unlike the *functio navicularia*, which was well known in the fourth century as a tax burden on the title of some estates that compelled them to provide state transport. Maintaining the *bucella-*

rii became, therefore, "a fiscalization of the *servitium militare*," a levy upon the *oikos* to provide *hospitalitas*.[33] The reform, as we see it illustrated in the Egyptian papyri, turned the estates of rich landlords, which had *de facto* become centers of military organization, into a part of the public administration.

In the West in the fifth and sixth centuries we have, as far as I know, no formal information about how the army was maintained. But it is evident from Procopius that in Gaul some units of the regular army and *laeti* continued to man the towns and forts, simply transferring their allegiance from Romans to Franks (James 1988, 83). In the sixth century there were still units of *laeti* in the Auvergne (Bachrach 1972, 14–15). That was the case also in Noricum in the fifth century, where the *Life of Saint Severinus* gives us a vivid picture of feeble units of soldiers virtually cooped up in the garrison towns, which were eventually forced to pay tribute to the Rugi.[34] In Noricum, as in Frankish Gaul, it is clear that control of the countryside was in the hands of what are called robbers. But these robbers were evidently in some cases bands under a war leader like Ferderuchus, who eventually came to control the town of Favianis (Vienna?) (*V. Severin.* 42.1).

The situation recounted in the *Life of Saint Geneviève* sounds very similar. Childeric the Frank appears to be in control of the countryside for the whole period of ten years while Geneviève was with the "Romans" holding out in Paris. In Gaul it is significant that many of the fourth- to fifth-century Frankish cemeteries of Picardy and elsewhere were rural but within a short distance of the major towns of Beauvais, Vermand, Amiens, Soissons, and so on, indicating fairly clearly the strategic points from which the various Frankish warlords came to control the *civitates* by the end of the fifth century (James 1988, 222).

Warlords in History

I have used the term "warlord" to describe some of the actors, such as federate chiefs, in the later Empire who controlled personal armies, and I have tried to separate them from landlords—although, as I have argued, the distinction became increasingly blurred as the state army declined. The word itself inevitably invites comparison with that period of Chinese history in the late nineteenth century and early twentieth that is particularly associated with warlordism, the breakdown of the Ch'ing Manchu empire and the ill-fated attempt to establish a republic after 1911. But even Chinese experts now feel the need for closer definition and analysis of the situation. Historians, complains one of them, often regard their task as merely to reproduce the chaos of their sources and not to clarify them (Lary 1980, 460). The same might be said of the later Roman Empire and its historians.

Chinese warlordism was not simply born from the extremes of regionalism and provincialism provoked by the breakdown of central administration; it was the product of two separate forces. One was a long period of organized violence throughout the nineteenth century, particularly on the fringes of the empire (Fairbank and Feuerwerker 1986, 32), where chronic banditry, rural poverty, and weak infrastructure inevitably created the natural conditions for a fragmentation of politics. For the poor, ties of kinship with the rich gentry and the protection they offered were stronger than the conflicts of class; and whole villages were often turned into protective dependencies of landlords. The system worked after a fashion as long as the "moral economy" of reciprocal benefits between rich and poor was respected. But through the nineteenth century the rich increased the pressures on the poor and reduced the conditions of tenancies to oral contracts of shorter leases, often of only one year.

The pressures developed into a series of movements of rural unrest, frequently millenary in character—like the White Wolf robber band or (later) the Spirit Boxers—culminating in the late nineteenth-century Taiping Rebellion. The upshot was the raising of local militias. The gentry selected, or themselves became, local generals, who in turn appointed lesser gentry. They with their followers created extreme factions and fictive kinship groups (Lary 1980, 460). But for all this, they were not warlords. The gentry remained loyal to the central Manchu government and bolstered it up, often themselves entering the civilian bureaus and dispatching their taxes to Beijing (Sutton 1980, 3–4).

The other force was the result of a new military class, the Ch'ing dynasty's last attempt to control from the center by modernizing the Chinese army, a central organization loyal to the Manchus—after a fashion. But when the republic after 1911 failed to unite the country, they took to direct rule in the provincial governorships. Now indeed there was not merely a loss of bureaucratic control but what has been described as a "disintegration of political authority" (Lary 1980, 448), leading to "a patchwork of local satrapies" (Sutton 1980, 6) and personal armies. Warlordism, in short, was really the phenomenon of the military specialist officer corps and included men like Sun Yat-sen and Chiang Kai-shek, who emerged as generalissimos.

Essential, however, though not fully understood, was the relationship between the two forces of landlords and warlords. In some cases it is difficult to distinguish one from the other. But in all cases it is clear that the gentry and their networks, including local bureaucrats, were necessary to the warlord for the extraction of surpluses and control of the land, including the supply of soldiers. Both parties had an interest in the union, and warlords therefore had no radical political goals. This much was clear to Mao Tse-tung when he wrote: "If the peasants do not arise and fight in the villages to overthrow the privileges of the feudal-patriarchal landlord class, the power of the warlords and of imperialism can never be hurled down root and branch" (*MTTC* 1.176).

Even the rural unrest resulted in "rebellions, not revolutions"—to use a cliché of Chinese historians; that is, the movements of religious zealots and peasant dissidents found no bridge between social banditry and political actions, and therefore they usually degenerated yet further into local militia at the disposal of warlords and gentry—as happened to the Boxers.

This very brief and probably (to the expert) simplistic summary presents a number of striking similarities with the conditions of the later Roman Empire, whatever the differences: (1) the general conditions of violence, endemic banditry, and peasant oppression; (2) the contrast between the "moral economy" of the patronage offered by the curial gentry, as presented by Libanius, and its decay owing to forces of factionalism, against which he and later Salvian protested; (3) the appearance of rural movements, frequently millenarian in aim (like the circumcellions) but without trace of real political objectives beyond those attached to the gentry; (4) the appearance of a new military elite in the intrusive *gentiles* and federates, centered on the court and intended to reinforce the imperial bureaucracy, but that disintegrated into something like local satrapies as political authority disintegrated. I am thinking of the court offices held by Childeric and Clovis (probably), by Alaric, and even by Attila the Hun.

Obviously the "fit" is not perfect, and it is possible to see many differences, not least the amount of aid from foreign powers given to the Chinese warlords, which had no equivalent in the later empire. But the similarities are enough at least to make the point that warlordism in the Roman Empire was not the simple product of rural gentry and protectionism but sprang from those factors *in combination with* the Germanic war leaders and their armies. The warlord and the landlord must be kept separate. It was the relationship between the two that created the continuity of Roman administration and law into the misnamed barbarian kingdoms.[35]

Notes

Introduction

1. Davies 1975, 6; this volume, first published in 1932, is still regarded as authoritative.
2. See, e.g., E. Birley 1956 and the criticism of Trousset 1981, 62. As I argue below, the differences between the British and the African frontiers were not as great as Trousset perhaps believes.
3. "Restituer à la Gaule les limites que la nature lui a fixées" was Richelieu's cry (Alliès 1980, 65). Foucher 1986, 101, argues that Richelieu was less concerned with natural frontiers than with how to encircle the House of Austria.
4. Turner 1893; the reference to Turner's 1894 article "Problems in American History" is reproduced in Turner 1938, 83. Lepore 1989, 66 n. 19, gives an acute and tantalizingly brief survey of Turner's comparison with the Greeks of Magna Graecia in his fine study, "La città e il suo territorio in Magna Graecia."
5. Buck 1985, 181; R. F. Berkhofer in Lamar and Thompson 1981, esp. 44; Webb 1953, 31. It is perhaps unfair to Webb not to recognize his attempt in *The Great Frontier* (1953) to enlarge his theme to include Europe, when he developed the concept of "metropolis and frontier" to describe Europe and its periphery. But the frontier in this account became almost totally subsumed under the history of imperialism and colonial expansion.
6. Hunter 1983, 58; Korinman 1990, 33, 60. Ratzel also wrote a two-

volume study of America, *Die Vereinigen Staaten von Nord-America,* which was the first such attempt by a non-American.

7. Febvre 1922, 109. Hunter argues that Semple crudely distorted Ratzel.

8. Luttwak 1976. The review of *Strategy* (Harvard University Press, 1987) is by M. Howard, *Times Literary Supplement,* 1987, 1007–8. Luttwak gives no sign of having read Ratzel. Nicolet's ingenious theory that there was a rhythm of Roman imperialism from Augustus to beyond Trajan, which alternated between expansion that led to stability and regrouping that led to expansion, is an attractive alternative to the idea that stable frontiers are a mark of weakness; Nicolet 1983, 171–73.

9. Febvre 1922, 28–30, 53, for the quotation. Mountford and Paxton in their introduction to Febvre 1932, xi–xiii, discuss Vidal de la Blache's historical perspective: "There are no necessities, everywhere possibilities." Parker 1985, 13, is surely wrong to believe Febvre was influenced by traditional French insistence on natural frontiers. Febvre is more obviously influenced by the notions developed by Lucien Gallois of *mentalités* and *milieu,* which were human cultural conditions that had evolved historically; see Baker and Gregory 1984, 11.

10. Febvre 1922, 39, 324: "Ce qui subsiste en nous, ce qui s'y est incrusté d'une façon si forte que nous ne sentons même plus ses pris, c'est une certaine conception du 'cadre naturel' des grands Etats"; cf. Alliès 1980, 30–31.

11. Lapradelle 1928, 55–57; cf. Alliès 1980, 42–43. Febvre 1922, 336: "Quand un peuple se fixe une frontière naturelle . . . c'est simplement une limite qu'il établit à l'intensité de son désir d'expansion"; see also Guichonnet and Raffestin 1974, 8, 23.

12. Hartog 1980, 207. The classic study of the development of the Greek concept of city frontiers is Vernant 1965, 97–181; cf. Foucher 1986, 67–72, for further references.

13. See the remarks in Lamar and Thompson 1981, 6–10. The editors of *Hérodote* have made more or less the same criticism of the failure of geographers to give a physical dimension to the relationship between power and knowledge on frontiers; see Foucault 1980, 63–77. Fouchet 1986 is an impressive attempt to fill the gap, though it will be evident that I do not find the brief section on Roman frontiers wholly satisfactory.

Chapter One. Space, Power, and Society

1. I am grateful to Pol Trousset (1993) for drawing my attention to this important passage, with which compare Plut. *QR* 15 and Cicero *De Rep.* 2.14; these and other references are fully discussed by Piccaluga

1974, 177–201. The traditional date is now thought to be more or less correct; see Manfredi and Piccirilli 1980 and the references given in Gabba 1983, 21. The most recent discussion on the polarities exemplified in Romulus and Numa is by Storchi Marino 1990, esp. p. 7.

2. Nicolet 1991, 70. My own translation of Nicolet's original French text would be "who in the name of 'anthropological readings' of the texts of the ancients have rather too readily set up an irreducible opposition between their conceptions and representations of space and our own."

3. Goudineau 1990, 83, with an illustration.

4. See the edition by A. Riese (1878) in the Teubner series.

5. Brunt 1978b, 169, contra Richardson 1979, 4. See below at note 12.

6. This is not the place to enter into discussion about the accuracy of Livy's account of the Treaty of Apamea. Liebmann-Frankfort 1969, 62–64, believed that Rome demanded a full-scale frontier along the Taurus-Halys line from the Mediterranean to the Black Sea; but Livy does not say so, and his account of a limited boundary has been defended (by, e.g., A. H. MacDonald, *JRS* 57 [1967]: 1–8). Will 1967 2: 255 describes the extent to which Rome "paralyzed" the Seleucid monarchs after Apamea. This was, of course, in a period when Roman hegemonial imperialism was at its height, before much direct territorial administration had begun. I doubt, therefore, whether Liebmann-Frankfort's distinction between a Roman *ligne-limite* and a *zone frontière* is relevant under such conditions.

7. Latte 1960, 41. See also Gabba 1983 for a useful summary of the history of land measurement in the republican period.

8. Dalché and Nicolet 1986, referring to the theory of Riese.

9. The alternative derivation is given by Fronto Gromaticus, which is that *arceo* means to expel and the land is that from which the original inhabitants have been expelled. See *Thesaurus Linguae Latinae*, s. v. "arcifinius" for references. For my argument here it is enough that Varro believed his own theory was plausible. A full collection of the passages referring to *ager arcifinius* is given in Botteri 1992.

10. Besnier, in Daremberg-Saglio, *Dict. Ant.,* s.v. "pomerium."

11. Ørsted 1985, 225–26; in his note Ørsted draws the parallel with the *pomerium.*

12. Trousset 1993 notes *Digest* 49. (Paulus) 15.19.3, which refers to allied kings as also within this jurisdiction "protected by public law." That seems to me a strong argument against Richardson; see above.

13. Cato's words were cited to great effect by Andrea Giardina at a recent colloquium in Rome to indicate a growing sense of Italian unity; this is not inconsistent with the view of imperial claims I have expressed here.

14. The words are those of Dyson 1986, 231.
15. Ørsted (1985, 177) puts forward the interesting idea that Augustus "took refuge in legal phraseology" when he boasted of extending the *fines* but not of creating new provinces, since the vaguer notion of tribes in terra incognita gave justification to his continued *imperium* over the unorganized territories. Certainly it is an important fact that nowhere in the *Res Gestae* does Augustus claim to have annexed any new province, which fits in with my theory that beyond the formal provinces there was an unconfined area of military power. But it does not, I think, change any of the conclusions I have suggested here about the Augustan *consilium*.

Chapter Two. Frontiers and the Growth of Empire

1. See Nicolet 1991, 38–41, for a discussion of Pompey and Caesar; the statue of Pompey in the Palazzo Spada is illustrated in his figure 9, probably the same statue that was originally in Pompey's theater, at whose feet Caesar was assassinated.
2. Further discussion of maps is in Dilke 1985, chap. 3, "Roman Mapping before Agrippa."
3. Nicolet 1991, passim. For the absolutist model, see Alliès 1980, 36, 57, etc.
4. See, e.g., Virg. *Aen.* 1.278–79; *Hor. Od.* 4.15. Further citations of poets are in Brunt 1963.
5. The Vienna cameo is illustrated and discussed by Zanker 1988, 230–31.
6. Dio 56.33.5; Tac. *Ann.* 1.11: *Addideratque consilium imperii intra terminos coercendi.*
7. Tac. *Agr.* 13; *Germ.* 37: *Tam diu Germania vincitur.* Following Ørsted's comment (1985), noted in chapter 1 (n. 15), it seems to me possible that Augustus was advising against an extension of the number of provinces, though he says nothing about the frontier.
8. Hadrian: HA *Hadr.* 5.3; Antoninus Pius: *BMC* 4. 1675; Marcus Aurelius: HA *Marc.* 24.5, 27.10; Dio (Xiph.) 71.33.4; Commodus: Hdn. 1.5.6. The Severan references are collected in Birley 1974.
9. A. R. Birley 1974 argues for Hadrian's Greek outlook. Alföldi 1952 invented the term "moral barrier," but Braund 1989b shows how far this differed from reality. Thollard 1987 discusses Strabo's adaptation of Greek ideology to Rome's more flexible civilizing mission.
10. Tacitus's disapproval of Tiberius as *princeps proferendi imperi incuriosus* (*Ann.* 4.32); Suet. *Aug.* 21.2; *Tib.* 52.2; Florus 2.30.39, 2.34.61, is discussed in Campbell 1984, 394 ff.
11. The events are described by Dio (Xiph.) 55.10a.2–3 and Tac. *Ann.*

4–44. Augustus's German policy is discussed in Wells 1972, 156–61.

12. The religious act in the annexation of space is illustrated by Tac. *Ann.* 2.22; cf. Helgeland 1978, 1503.

13. Aug. *RG* 26.4; Pliny *NH* 2.167. Strabo 7.1.4 is discussed in chapter 1.

14. Reconstruction of the Danube campaigns from inscriptions was basically the work of Syme 1934, summarized and expanded by Wilkes 1965.

15. Florus 2.28–29. Strabo 7.3.13 refers to the Mureş and Danube as being used to transport military supplies, presumably via the river Tisza, which runs into the Danube at Belgrade from the north.

16. Cadastration and road are recorded in a series of inscriptions, *CIL* 8.22786, 22789 and *ILT* 73–74, discussed by Trousset 1978.

17. Pliny should be read with the commentary by Desanges 1980.

18. On the integral role of the kings on the frontiers, see Braund 1984, 91–103. The phrase *donum p. R.* is used by Tac. *Ann.* 4.5 of Juba's kingdom in Mauretania.

19. The appeals by the British kings are recorded by Dio 60.19; cf. Aug. *RG* 32. Claudius's military glory was well publicized in Rome by a triumphal arch recording his victory over eleven British kings (*ILS* 216) and was commemorated on coins (*BMC* 1.168); cf. Dio 60.22.1.

20. Tac. *Ann.* 11.16 (Cherusci), 12.29–30 (Vannius), *Germ.* 42 (Marcomanni-Quadi). The inscription *ILS* 986 records the career of Ti. Plautius Silvanus Aelianus, who, as governor of Moesia, "brought across more than 100,000 of the Transdanubians to pay tribute along with their wives and children and their princes and kings." This was one of his many military exploits in the trans-Danube regions. He also sent to Rome a large quantity of wheat "from that province," although we do not know where it came from originally.

21. The term is used by Luttwak 1976 and discussed later in chapter 3.

22. The archaeology is discussed by Schönberger 1969, 158–61.

23. Hungarian plain: Ptol. *Geog.* 3.7.1; Dio (Xiph.) 68.10.3. Hunt's *Pridianum* is recorded in Fink 1971, 63, and discussed in chapter 4.

24. Ptol. *Geog.* 1.8.2, 10.4; cf. Pliny, *NH* 5.38. Recent pottery dates from the Libyan valleys are given by J. N. Dore in Buck and Mattingly 1985, 107–25.

25. Kolník 1990; Pitts 1989. They are discussed in more detail later.

26. References are given by Mócsy 1974b, 90, 100; cf. note 8 above.

27. The clearest study of the relation between the two walls is in Hanson and Maxwell 1983. On Carpow, see R. P. Wright in *Britannia* 5 (1974): 289–90.

28. Caucasus: Strabo 1.2.39 and Pliny *NH* 6.30; Arabia: Diod. 3.46–47. See the discussion in Braund 1986.

29. Parthian ambitions: e.g., Tac. *Ann.* 6.31.1; Jos. *AJ* 20.69.81–91. But see the reservations of Isaac 1986 and 1990, chap. 1, esp. 21 ff. Debevoise 1969 is still the standard political history of Parthia.
30. Negotiated frontiers are discussed by Crow 1986b.
31. See above, p. 27. The historian Pompeius Trogus, a freedman of Pompey the Great, says that a deal was contemplated to share the world between Parthia and Rome (Justin. 41.1.1). The negotiated treaty of 20 B.C. was celebrated in Roman poetry and iconography as the submission of the Parthians to the "right and rule of Caesar" (Hor. *Epist.* 1.12.27). See Zanker 1988, 187–92, on the iconography of the Prima Porta statue and coins showing kneeling Parthians.
32. Poidebard 1934, 21. Frézouls 1980a makes this point with great force; see esp. 370–71, where he talks of the middle Euphrates between Zeugma and the Khabur as an area that "invited" entrance and trade—a phrase reminiscent of Prescott Webb's analysis of American frontiers.
33. Recent works of research are Kennedy 1982, Mitchell 1983, Bowersock 1983, Gregory and Kennedy 1985, Freeman and Kennedy 1986, and Parker 1986a, 1987a; but above all see the excellent studies by Kennedy and Riley 1990 and Isaac 1990. They have modified much of the important pioneering studies by Poidebard and Stein.
34. A good summary of the state of play is given in Kennedy 1986.
35. Armenia: Aug. *RG* 27; Tac. *Ann.* 12.45.
36. Palmyra: *CIS* 2.3.3913, a municipal tariff of Palmyra, cites a tax law of Germanicus in A.D. 18, which Isaac 1990, 142, calls "a record of Roman interests . . . but not an indication of direct control"; cf. Matthews 1984. The best discussion of the Palmyra tariff is by Teixidor 1984, 57–90, who notes that from the first century A.D. a Roman garrison is recorded in the city. Under the emperor Tiberius, the Romans marked out the territory of the city with boundary stones, recorded by Schlumberger 1939, 61–63. Pliny (*NH* 5.88) shows that Parthia too had interests in the city. Teixidor 1984, 28–31, illustrates the ambiguity of Palmyra's position by citing the inscriptions honoring a Palmyran merchant, Soados, son of Boliades, for services to his city. He was honored by Hadrian and other Roman emperors, he built a temple to the Roman imperial cult in the Parthian city of Vologesias, and he was a man of influence in the Parthian city of Spasinou Charax. For Arab support of Palmyra, see Graf 1989b. For Hegra, see Lewin 1990.
37. Tac. *Ann.* 15.6 and 17, *Hist.* 2.6 (A.D. 69). The phrase used by Tacitus is interesting: *et quicquid castrorum Armeniis praetenditur,* with which cf. Tac. *Hist.* 2.14 (*ut. . minaci fronte praetenderetur*). The word *praetentura* is used later of a road lined with watch stations, which went

with the "non-existence of a fortified line" (Isaac 1990, 257). Contra, Mitford 1980, 1179, argues for formal recognition of the Euphrates.

38. Already stated by Chapot 1907, 147: "Resterait donc à supposer que le *limes* d'Orient n'était constitué par aucun obstacle matériel, en tant que ligne continue, et que la frontière n'était marquée que par un bornage espacé ou par quelque trace, peu accusée sur le sol." More recently, see M. P. Speidel in Mitchell 1983a, 8; Crow 1986b, 80; and Wheeler 1991.

39. Legionary bases in Cappadocia: Jos. *BJ* 7.1.3, Mitford 1980, 1186. Bases in Syria-Commagene: *ILS* 8903 (the road between Melitene and Samosata) and perhaps the Josephus reference above. Customs posts: Philostr. V. Apoll. 1.20; *ILS* 2709 (praefectus ripae); *AE* 1947, 181 (a tax officer called a *tetartones* at Palmyra).

40. See, in general, Isaac 1990, 102–3; and elsewhere in this book, p. 61, 69. Note below the point about grain supplies.

41. Caspian rock inscription: *AE* 1951, 263; Darial Pass and wall: *ILS* 8795; Gornea: *SEG* 20.110; Araxes lost inscription: Mitford 1980, 1194 (see fig. 13).

42. Roman aims are discussed by Crow 1986b and Braund 1989a.

43. Zimara: Mitford, in *JRS* 64 (1974): 171–72.

44. Examples of client kings are given by HA *Hadr.* 17 and 21.

45. Lewin 1990 gives a survey of the evidence and compares the roles of Palmyra and Hegra. Palmyran merchants are recorded at al-Karkar in the Wadi Sirhan in the later second century, showing indirect Roman control of the route (Teixidor 1984, 43).

46. Internal security is discussed by Eadie 1986 and Isaac 1986, 1990; Jos. *BJ* 2.4.3 gives an example of attacks by Jewish dissidents. But Parker 1986a, 129, and Gichon 1986 put up a strong case for the need to control (though not to exclude) nomads, which I believe to be correct. For the fort of Khan Kosseir see Rey-Coquais 1976, 70, which treats the fort as part of the *limes*. Isaac 1990, 138, thinks the enemy was internal but offers only the geographic location of the site as evidence.

47. This is the main thesis of Isaac 1990, with which it will be obvious that I am in close agreement. Note his summary: "It is easy to confuse lines of communication provided with forts for the protection of military traffic with lines of forts intended to prevent enemy movements across them."

Chapter Three. Why Did the Frontiers Stop Where They Did?

1. Cf. Buache de la Neuville, *Géographie élémentaire moderne et ancienne* . . . (1775), cited by Nordman 1979, 77. Danton is cited in Febvre

1928, 40. For the historiographic context of Danton's nationalist statement, see above, p. 4.

2. Fox 1955, esp. 279, arguing against any military function at all; now attacked by M. L. Jones 1984, 85, but largely supported by Noble 1983, 70, 91, etc., even though Noble believes the dike may have some military function at some points. The most recent work on the dike is published by Hill 1985, 140–42, although the function is not discussed.

3. Nordman 1977, 434. Febvre (1922, 331) went so far as to state that ancient *limites* were never linear and always zones; cf. Guichonnet and Raffestin 1974, 17.

4. See Luttwak 1976; reviewed or cited favorably by Brunt 1978a; Millar 1982, 2; G. D. B. Jones 1978; and Willems 1986, 219.

5. As Nicolet 1983, 163, says. The annexation of Thrace, southern Britain, and the two Mauretanias by Claudius, or the annexation of parts of Germany, including the *Agri Decumates*, and parts of Britain by the Flavians is surely more than "une portée limitée." I argued in chapter 2 for the specific need of military glory by Claudius, Nero, and Domitian as a powerful motive for expansion. Augustus's advice to keep the empire within its *termini* is discussed in chapter 1.

6. Mann 1974, 1979a; for the ideology of expansion, see A. R. Birley, 1974. The poor defensive qualities of the Scottish wall are discussed by Hanson 1989.

7. This is the theme of Isaac 1990; see especially his comprehensive critique of Luttwak 1976 in chapter 9, "Frontier Policy—Grand Strategy?" The citation is from p. 401.

8. Well documented by Millar 1982, though oddly enough he admires Luttwak's book.

9. Isaac 1990, 402–4 gives other examples of poor geographic knowledge in the East.

10. Alföldi 1952. See my comments on the "moral barrier" in Whittaker 1983, 121, and in chapter 2 above. Braund 1989b gives a good critique of the theory.

11. Porch 1986, 134; cf. Girardet 1972, 34, particularly in respect to the army of Africa.

12. Trousset 1993 discusses this point and cites *Dig.* 49.15.19.3 (Paulus), which says that allied kings were included within Roman jurisdiction for this purpose—*si in civitatem sociam amicamve aut ad regem socium vel amicum venerit, statim postliminio rediisse videtur.*

13. Noted by Dillemann 1962, 135; Isaac 1990, 396; and Trousset 1993, drawing on the article by Schlumberger 1939. See fig. 17, reproduced by Dillemann, who thinks the information dates from a period when Parthia controlled Mesopotamia. The term *arae* is puzzling—possibly,

Trousset thinks, like the *ara Philenorum* marking a provincial boundary between Tripolitania and Cyrene. Schlumberger records a number of stones marking the *fines* between Palmyra and Emesa or the Syrian province of Syria, which he notes were clearly not a *Reichgrenze*. Trousset thinks the mention of the "army" in the second reference may be an indication that from this point on the Palmyrans patrolled the region. For the problems of the Peutinger Table, see Dilke 1985, 113–20.

14. Alföldy 1971. See Hdn. 1.6.4–9; Dio (Xiph.) 72.1.1–2.
15. Schallmayer 1984, 19: "Das Prinzip . . . wie es für die nachsten zwei Jahrhunderte etwa beibehalten werden solte." Petrikovits 1980b, 79, more prudently and correctly restricts Domitian's reasons for advance to the desire for personal fame.
16. The theory of the Elbe was put forward by Rice-Holmes (see above, introduction) and developed later by Syme in the *Cambridge Ancient History*. Wells 1972, 157–59, effectively demolished the thesis, although Schutz (1985, 7) seeks to revive it by calling it a "natural consequence" of Augustan policy.
17. Febvre 1928, 32, 1922, 331. Since Febvre a number of writers have stressed the difference between administrative, political, and military frontiers; see the citations in Isaac 1990, 399, 408.
18. See, passim, Braund 1984, esp. pt. 11, sec. 3.
19. Guichonnet and Raffestin 1974, 26–27. Hanson 1989, 59, notes the "bureaucratic" character of the Miltenberg-Lorch front, drawn "without regard to topography or local tactical advantage."
20. Mann 1979a, 180: "Rome had no institute of strategic studies." The same point is now made by Isaac (1990, 337), who notes the three hundred-odd institutes of strategic studies existing today, which he thinks give the appearance of "grand strategy" with hindsight to strategic decisions.
21. Müllenhoff 1887. The citation is from Hachmann 1971, 36. For the historiographic debate, see Todd 1987, 5. Even the validity of terms like "Celtic" is now open to question; cf. N. Merrimann in Hodder, 1986.
22. Chropovský 1977, 11; cf. the remarks by Lamiová-Schmiedlova, in ibid., 205, regarding the populations on the upper Tisza, which stress the cultural "symbiosis" of the Celto-Dacian horizon, where the old herding community adapted to the intrusive warrior proto-Vandals.
23. For the middle Euphrates, see Frézouls 1980a. Teixidor 1984, 23–26, discusses the evidence of nomadic tribes and the function of the Palmyran *strategoi* and Parthian Arabarchs, who levied pasture taxes and protected the caravans between Palmyra and the Euphrates.
24. For the Nabataean road, see Eadie 1986; Gichon 1986, 584; and Isaac 1990, 119–23. Parker 1986b sums up the debate well.

25. This was the view put forward by Trousset 1974, esp. 140–41. Mattingly and Jones 1986, 89, add the new *clausurae*.
26. Higham 1986, 145–47; M. L. Jones 1984, 172. Vindolanda Tablet 23 mentions a *centurio regionarius* at Carlisle ca. A.D. 100 who may have had a command over the Scottish Lowlands beyond the wall: see Bowman and Thomas 1983.
27. G. D. B. Jones 1982, 294–95; Higham and G. D. B. Jones 1985, 74–75.
28. Most recently by Crow 1986a. Daniels 1979 makes a spirited attack on Breeze and Dobson 1976, but he himself talks not about a defensive *purpose* but about "defensive capability," "native infiltration," and the use of the wall "in time of need." This is a good example of the semantic confusion I have noted and that Daniels admits.
29. This was one of the reasons Mann 1979a attacked the theory of a grand strategy.
30. Severus had just completed a punishing invasion of the Scottish Highlands, reasserted Roman authority over the Maetae and the Caledonii, and constructed a stone depot at Carpow on the Forth far beyond the wall, quite apart from the continuing friendliness of the lowland Votadini.
31. The main advocate of the "glacis" theory is Petrikovits 1979; but see also Willems 1986, 253–55, for the ambiguous nature of the evidence on the lower Rhine. Petrikovits's theory of *militarisches Nutzland* is discussed further in chapter 4.
32. Pitts 1989, 48. Kolník in many publications has discussed the trans-Danube "villas": e.g., in Chropovský 1977, 143–71; and Kolník 1986, 1990, 1991. Most of these villas date from the later second century onward, and I discuss them in later chapters. But even at sites like that at Bratislava-Dúbravka four kilometers north of the river opposite Carnuntum, the infill dates back to the first century.
33. Curzon 1907, 25; see Dai Wenbo, "Pourquoi la muraille fut construite," in Delahaye et al. 1978, 42–51, who notes that the various walls of China were never effective against organized powers but only against nomadic pillagers.
34. Guichonnet and Raffestin 1974, 16, compare Roman and Chinese frontiers. The number of 300,000 soldiers sent to the Great Wall of China is remarkably similar to the figure usually estimated for Roman frontier troops, traveling over a distance of about six thousand kilometers in both cases.
35. Trousset 1981, 69, in a penetrating study of frontiers in Roman Africa.
36. Haselgrove, in Clack and Haselgrove 1982, 57–59; in the same volume see T. Gate, 21; contra Piggott 1958, 1. See also the studies by

Maxwell 1983, 236–37, and Bennett 1983, 215. Greene 1986, 128, provides the ecological map reproduced in fig. 21, showing higher proportions of grassland north of Hadrian's Wall. I hope this answers the criticism of Fulford 1989, 82, that Hadrian's Wall "did not obviously mark any division between intensive . . . and extensive . . . exploitation." The meaning of ecological marginality is, of course, that such divisions are not precise and hence that frontiers cannot track them.

37. Maps can be seen in Jankuhn 1976, 79–80; Petrikovits 1980b, 60; cf. Todd 1987, 96–97.
38. Schönberger 1969, 153–54. Cunliffe 1988, 174, rightly stresses that in much of free Germany the migrations had nevertheless destabilized the productive capacities of the *oppida* culture.
39. Kiechle 1962, 185 (although Kiechle thinks the Glauberg was occupied by Roman scouts); Hachmann 1971, 69. Sites like Altenburg bei Niedenstein (Hesse) in the Wetterau were abandoned a generation before Germanicus's invasion. But at Bad Nauheim La Tène burials go on until the Augustan period: Collis 1984a, 207–8; Wells 1972, 233.
40. See the maps in Pitts 1989, 56, and the distribution of German settlements in Kolník 1986, 355.
41. Poidebard 1934, 22; Parker 1986b, 637. The climatic conditions are also discussed in Banning 1987 and illustrated on the map in Gregory and Kennedy 1985. A natural desert frontier is claimed by Hodgson 1989, 178.
42. Euzennat 1985, 171. The dispute between Euzennat and Rebuffat (outlined in this article) is an extremely informative discussion of the ecological issues.
43. *ILS* 1338 records a *censito(ri) Brittonum Anavion(ensium)* (Higham and G. D. B. Jones 1985, 74–75), but see Frere, 1967, 199, for doubts about whether these people lived near the river Annan (Anava) in Dumfriesshire, which Frere questions on the grounds that southern Scotland lay outside the province. On the analogy of the Frisians, this argument is not valid.
44. Cunliffe 1988, 166, shows that Romans were drawn into lowland Scotland by economic developments but that the distributions of Roman trade goods suggests a more hierarchical and less entrepreneurial society than farther south.

Chapter Four. Economy and Society of the Frontiers

An earlier version of the ideas in this chapter in Whittaker 1983 were thoughtfully but firmly dismissed by Fulford 1989, and he deserves a considered reply.

Fulford's points are: (1) Not enough research has been done to show that Roman frontiers were located at the limits of intensive agricultural exploitation. (2) There is no way to measure interdependence between the army and local communities, since most food for Roman armies came from a long distance and there is little material evidence on native sites. (3) Transfrontier exchange cannot sensibly be measured when so few comparative data exist for goods on sites within the frontiers. But comparison of quantities of coins and pottery suggests that frontiers did have a "barrierlike" effect (with exceptions in Frisia and the *Agri Decumates*) and that symbiosis was minimal. (4) The size of the army and its centers has no evident correlation with goods crossing the frontiers, although we can see that interruptions of civil trade could cause disruption, especially to barbarian elites.

My reply is: (1) There is never enough research to know anything with certainty in ancient history. Time, as Cornford said, is always unripe, but we do the best we can, and I hope what I have said here begins to fill the gap. Fulford may have misunderstood marginality and the fact that frontiers were not at ecological *limits* but in areas of ecological ambiguity; see chapter 3 at note 36. (2) The implication of the ecological argument is not, as Fulford supposes, that the Roman army was *dependent* on local supplies for survival. It was precisely because they could not rely on supplies that they did not advance and always needed rivers to supplement their needs. But that is not to say they did not have an *interest* in what could be obtained locally (see Breeze 1989, 228). The absence of large amounts of Roman material goods on native sites may mean heavy exploitation—as is often believed to be the case in northern Britain—or exchange in perishable goods (see Breeze 1989, 230). (3) Comparison between material remains on trans-and cis-frontier sites is misconceived, since no one would argue that there were the same number of transactions. But even Fulford's distribution maps for coins show that *significant* numbers crossed the frontiers into areas of known population concentrations (Ruhr, Hessen, Mittelpfalz). No one, of course, supposes that the free German economies were monetized. If we look beyond Germany to Moravia, Slovakia or Wallachia, the evidence of transfrontier goods is even stronger. (4) The extent to which the army alone was the agent of exchange is, as Fulford rightly says, difficult to define (though see now Macinnes 1989, 114, for further evidence). It is sufficient for my argument, however, that Fulford admits that transfrontier trade of any sort existed and that its suppression could have serious consequences—a historical fact that literary sources make clear enough (see Whittaker 1983).

    1. M. I. Finley in *The Times,* 17 March 1977, review of F. Millar, *The Emperor in the Roman World* (London, 1977).

2. Bloemers 1983, 180. The problem of food for an invading army is discussed in Groenman–van Waateringe 1989.
3. Gren 1941, esp. 36–37, 104–6. Cf. Mitchell 1983b, 133–37. Ten legions (of fifty to sixty thousand men) with as many auxiliaries lived in provinces along the river that perhaps, at a guess, had a population of one to two million. Food production would have had to rise between 5 and 10 percent in a near subsistence economy.
4. Richmond 1982, 33–34, noted by Isaac 1990, 102; León in Spain, which was not on a river, was not of course a frontier fort in quite the same sense. Needless to say, I do not agree with the first part of Richmond's statement: "Not only because those rivers formed natural frontiers but . . . because water transport offered a readily accepted alternative to road traffic."
5. Crow 1986b, 79, does not quite say this but points out that the Pontic shore forts were an integrated part of the military supply line to the interior. French 1983 traces the road from Trebizond to Zimara on the upper Euphrates—not accepted by all (see Wheeler 1991, 507–8).
6. Remesal 1986, 77–79; Peacock 1978, 49–50, is more circumspect in saying there is no clear reason why sea routes or river routes should have been preferred.
7. The scale is reproduced by Fulford 1984, 134; he reckons the relative costs of transport as 1 unit by Mediterranean sea voyage = 2 units by Atlantic = 4 units by river downstream = 8 units by river upstream = about 30 units by land. From Baetica to Britain by Atlantic transport would have been about 380 units; by Mediterranean plus Rhône-Saône (upstream) plus land plus Moselle (downstream) plus Atlantic would have come to about 580 units. But to Strasbourg via the Atlantic route would have cost 700 units against 500 units via the Rhône-Saône and through the Belfort gap to the Rhine. To Mainz and to Bonn via the Rhône-Saône-Moselle, the costs would have been about equal. Cf. Tac. *Ann.* 13.53 for traffic between the Saône and Moselle, where an abortive attempt was made to dig a canal in the first century A.D.
8. E.g., *AE* 1956, 124: *Ad deducenda per Danuvium quae in annonam Pannoniae utriusque exercitum denavigarent;* cf. Laet 1949, 208. Later Empire examples are given on p. 171.
9. Mitchell 1983b documents the evidence in Asia Minor and Anatolia.
10. Ellmers 1978, 7; the Zwammerdam evidence of Celtic ship construction is discussed by M. D. de Weerd in Taylor and Cleere 1978, 15–21. The evidence of the Celtic ship found in Guernsey harbor, which has grains of wheat embedded in the pitch, has not yet been published, as far as I know.

11. Petrikovits 1979. The important study of the legionary camp at Gloucester by Hurst 1988 shows that the legion "*could* have obtained all that it required locally by controlling quite a modest amount of land." He estimates that only about ten square kilometers was required to feed soldiers, inhabitants of the *canabae,* and workers.

12. Belgica: Roymans 1983, 58; Willems 1986, 238. Bulgaria: Cicikova 1974. The production of pottery for British military sites is discussed by Darling 1977 and Hurst 1988.

13. The references to the later Empire are on p. 165. The chart of imports to London is referred to again at note 16.

14. Remesal 1986, 74–76, sets out the discussion excellently with earlier references to Mommsen and Van Berchem.

15. "Hunt's *Pridianum,*" dated early second century A.D., is reproduced in Fink 1971, no. 63. Under the heading EX EIS APSENTES ("absent from the company") are listed some soldiers whose numbers are missing *in Gallia vestitum* ("in Gaul for clothing"), *item fumi[. .]ta[.]m* (= *frumentatum?* "also to get grain").

16. The charts and maps are reproduced and discussed by Fulford 1984, 135–36.

17. Panella 1981, 76; Tchernia 1986, 136–37. The use of large storage jars or *dolia* for shipping Italian wine to Gaul, which coincides with the appearance of Dressel 2–4 amphorae, poses an archaeological problem, since wine transferred from *dolia* into perishable containers leaves no trace (Tchernia 1986, 138–39). Nevertheless, the basic fact remains that the frontiers were different from the interior, if only in respect to the containers.

18. Cerati 1975, 7–8 n. 30; cf. J. Guey, in *MEFR* 55 (1938): 56–77. This and other examples are discussed in Remesal 1986, esp. 96–99; but Remesal does not discriminate between special military officers responsible for coordinating supplies on campaign and those who actually procured supplies for frontier garrisons.

19. Gillam 1973, 55–58; Hartley 1973, 41; Williams 1977, esp. 209, for the Scottish evidence.

20. Similar tasks are recorded on other military documents; e.g., Fink 1971, no. 47: *[ad fr]ument[um compara]ndum* (1.13), *ad hordeum comparandum* (2.4). "Hunt's *Pridianum*" (fig. 41) records men who were sent *ad Haemum ad armenta addu[cenda]* . . . ("to the Balkans to fetch cattle").

21. See the excellent discussion in Breeze 1984. Examples are given in Remesal 1986, 96–99.

22. Evidence and references are given in Higham 1986, 220. The conclusion is mine, but I put it hesitantly, since a friendly archaeologist smells a rat.

23. Mitchell 1976 has the text and commentary.
24. A. R. Birley 1981, 48, gives evidence suggesting that in Pannonia the tax was as high as 12.5 percent; but Ørsted 1985, 260, rightly regards this as impossibly high. For a general discussion of the levy of *portoria* on entry to cities and camps as well as provinces, see Ørsted 1985, passim.
25. Breeze 1984, 282. Remesal 1986 gives a number of examples of marks of Spanish estates supplying specific forts on the Rhine; e.g., MALPICA predominate at Zugmantel (p. 66), CATRIA at Nijmegen and Mainz (p. 50).
26. The term is discussed by Petrikovits 1980a.
27. The date of the papyrus is now certainly established as before the annexation of Dacia; discussed by A. Rădulescu and M. Bârbulescu in *Dacia* 25 (1981): 353–58.
28. Maxwell 1983, 245; Cunliffe 1988, 167: "The overall impression given by Traprain is that it served as a major manufacturing and distribution centre throughout much of the period of Roman occupation."
29. Mócsy 1974b, 89. The buildings have been described in many publications by Kolník listed in the references.
30. Kolník 1986, 355–56. The unpublished grave is noted by Kolník 1991, 433.
31. Pitts 1989, 48, gives the inscription with references. It comes from Boldog in Slovakia and is probably early. For the prosperity of the river valleys, see Kolník 1991.
32. Coulson 1986 discusses the cavalry development. For nomadic symbiosis in Arabia, see the excellent discussion by Gichon 1986. Cf. Whittaker 1978 for Africa, where I argued that, despite the natural symbiotic exchanges between desert and sown, the balance of power shifts from farmers to nomads unless the former exercise some sort of control.
33. Jankuhn 1976, 104–6, commenting on Tac. *Germ.* 6.
34. Wightman 1970, 188 and 1985, 240, but the evidence is inconclusive.
35. Contra Thompson 1982, 12. Tacitus's words about the Hermunduri *civitas* (*Eoque solis Germanorum non in ripa commercium sed penitus atque in splendidissima Raetiae provinciae colonia*) are quite clear in the context. They were the only German people permitted to enter the province *beyond the trading posts on the frontiers*. Other Germans, says Tacitus, never saw farther than the camps under armed surveillance. That was the complaint of the Tencteri in A.D. 70 (Tac. *Hist.* 4.64), not that they were excluded from trade at Cologne.
36. See Dio 71.15.1; cf. other examples in Whittaker 1983. For the late Empire, see Velkov 1977, 180. Schlippschuh 1974, 127–28, discusses the official markets set up for barbarians alongside military camps.

37. The Latin is *burgus cui nomen commercium qua causa et factus est*. Mócsy 1974a, 194, conjectures that such *burgi* could well have been the many fortlets with landing stages found on the left bank of the Danube and the right bank of the Rhine in the later Empire.
38. Hedeager 1977, using the material recorded by Eggers 1951. Cunliffe 1988, 178–87, uses Hedeager's scheme but modifies it by adding a third "procurement zone" beyond the zone of prestige goods, where warrior societies on the extreme periphery had limited access to Roman goods.
39. Lüders 1955. Cunliffe 1988, 193–201, summarizes his model of "corridor" communities that mediated the movement of goods between the "interface" of the Roman frontier and the outer zones beyond.
40. Macinnes 1984, 189, 194; Gillam 1958, 81; Cunliffe 1988, 167, 190, detects classic signs of "administered trade."
41. Sommer 1984, esp. 39, where Sommer takes the view that there was not sufficient local production to supply army needs.
42. J. Casey, in Clack and Haselgrove 1982, 123–32. In fact, the puzzle is why the *vici* disappeared before the end of military occupation, leading to speculation about whether families moved into the camps in the later Empire; see pp. 152–53.
43. Bloemers 1983, 177. I must point out also that Bloemers's graphs for the Roman provincial sites are listed as first to third century A.D., while that for Wijster is fourth century A.D. How much this affects the conclusions I have drawn here is impossible to say on the evidence. Wijster was of course flourishing in the earlier period also and was importing Roman pottery.
44. Full references are given in Ste. Croix 1981, app. 3.

Chapter Five. The Frontiers under Pressure

1. Bowersock 1983, 96–97, 132–34; Shahid 1984, 371, 465–75. I have used "groups," not "tribes," where possible, since the concept of tribe is such a fluid one. Among Safaitic inscriptions alone there are over 140 tribal or kinship designations (Graf 1989a, 358–59). Graf 1989a, Mayerson 1986, and Isaac 1990 wrongly, in my view, play down the Saracen threat; see chapter 7, note 4.
2. Graf and O'Connor 1977. Shahid 1984, 279, argues that the term was originally confined to the nomadic Arabs, otherwise called *scenitae*—tent dwellers. This reading, I understand from experts, is highly conjectural.
3. Isaac 1990, 239–40, gives a reading of the much disputed text. The Tanukhids may have been intrusive Arabs who came to the Hauran

after helping Rome defeat Palmyra in the later third century (Graf 1989b).
4. See map in Kennedy and Riley 1990, 25.
5. Speidel 1987. Lewin 1990, 149–52, puts forward the interesting comparison with African *principes,* based on an inscription of 355 recording two men at Hegra and Teima in Saudi Arabia who are called r's, the Arabic word for *princeps.*
6. Isaac 1990, 172–73, 187. The *limites interiores* were discussed recently by Mayerson 1989.
7. Courtois 1964, 93–94. I see no evidence to confirm the view expressed by Welsby 1982, 158, that *gentiles* "were exclusively recruited from beyond the Imperial frontiers." They were units of soldiers without the personal rights of Romans who had been given *receptio* as settlers within the empire; cf. Bury 1958, 40. Demougeot 1988, 111, demonstrates their assimilation with *laeti* settlers.
8. Matthews 1976, 167 ff., gives up-to-date interpretations of the *Notitia* list.
9. Matthews 1976, 171–72, gives other examples.
10. Cagnat 1913, 687–93; Labrousse 1938. There is an excellent review of *burgi* in Isaac 1990, 178–86.
11. For the narrative, with references, see Cagnat 1913, 78–95.
12. The relative desertion of the northern part of the province of Germania Secunda and the continuity and change of settlement patterns in the later empire are studied by Ossel 1992; his conclusions are summarized on 169–74. For the excavation near Tongres and Maastricht, see Ossel 1983 and Mertens 1986.
13. Brulet 1990. Ossel 1992, 183, cites the evidence of wooden houses from Donk, Neerharen-Reken, and so on, which lie west of the Meuse. His maps 21–24 give an excellent overview of the changing scene in the fourth century, showing continuity of both Roman villa sites and settlements, but also the infiltration of squatters and Germanic-looking immigrants.
14. See Wightman 1985, 210, for some evidence of destruction layers in cities.
15. Contra Willems 1986, 452–53, who follows the thesis of Luttwak 1976.
16. Hind 1984 gives a coherent account of the evacuation.
17. Asinius Quadratus, a third-century historian, says the name derived from "men who were washed together and mixed" (fr. 21, Jacoby); HA *Prob.* 14.2 comments on the many kings and *gentes.* Cf. Stroheker 1975, 21–22.
18. Demougeot 1979, 283; but Stroheker 1975, 33, notes that the material cultural influence of Rome was far less than on the Franks. A useful

summary of the main military events can be found in Stroheker 1975 and Matthews 1989, 316–18.

19. See R. M. Swoboda, in *Limeskongress XI* 1977, 123–27.

20. Although it is difficult to know when exactly the new organization of the *comes tractus Argentoratensis* took place, whether now or after Stilicho's fall or under Aetius; see Stroheker 1975, 41, for the various propositions.

21. Petolescu 1977; cf. Velkov 1977, 141–42, but I do not understand what Velkov means when he says the Danube was now a "real frontier."

22. P. Brennan, Ph.D. thesis, Cambridge, 1972; Mann 1977, 11.

23. The trans-Danubian settlements are discussed in Kolník 1986, 1990, 1991, and Pitts 1989.

24. E.g., Mócsy 1974b, 285, but contra Kolník 1991. As noted already, Luttwak 1976, sec. 3, makes his theme Constantine's supposed development of elastic in-depth strategy after Diocletian's supposedly static perimeter defense; but neither policy stands up to detailed examination.

25. Soproni in *Limeskongress VIII* 1974, 197–203.

26. The gravestone of Bishop Amantius (*CIL* 5.1623) is the main, but uncertain evidence; discussed by Wolfram 1988, 250–51.

27. This is not the place to discuss the complex and controversial relations between Alaric and Stilicho, for which see Mazzarino 1990, 183–94, and Cameron 1970, 157–76. But Alaric was not a barbarian invading the Roman Empire; note especially the wise words of Mazzarino 1990, 183: "Il contrasto non era fra due mondi . . . avversi, ma fra un generale barbaro-romano e il governo centrale. Alarico non rappresentava un mondo nuovo, che volesse sovvrapporsi all'antico con nuovi ideali." Contrast Mazzarino's favorable view of Stilicho's policy of using federates to save the empire with Liebeschuetz 1991, 35: "a disastrous innovation."

28. Soproni 1986. Liebeschuetz 1991, 36 and 42, notes how much recruiting of irregular federates within the empire took place after Adrianople.

29. A recent synthesis of the evidence is in Heather and Matthews 1991, chap. 3.

30. No doubt the presence of Goths in the Roman province was the reason legislation was passed threatening death to all collaborators (*CTh* 7.1.1 [323]), which is an interesting commentary on the attitude of many in the frontier provinces.

31. Heather and Matthews 1991, 134, citing the earlier work of E. A. Thompson.

32. Ladner 1976 discusses Ammianus's view in the light of traditional

Roman ideology; but there did exist an alternative, more construc-
tive attitude toward foreigners, which is evident in the reign of Constantius II and later under Theodosius; Ladner 1976, 20; Frézouls
1983.
33. Wolfram 1988, 133, gives what details are known. See Liebeschuetz
1991, 36–38, for the very large number of Goths employed as federates in the later fourth century.
34. Ladner 1976, 8–10, gives a useful summary of the historiographic
debate about the meaning of the term *foederati* since Mommsen.
35. Vasić 1991. Cf. also Vasić in *Limeskongress XIV* 1990, 897–911.
36. Mazzarino 1990, chap. 7; but against any idea of cooperation, see
Cameron 1970, 157–87. Cf. note 25 above.

Chapter Six. The Collapse of the Frontiers

1. CTh 9.14.2; cf. Paschoud's comments ad loc. in his edition of *Zosime*
(Belles Lettres, 1979).
2. Zos. 3.7; cf. *PLRE,* vol. 1, s.v. "Charietto" for references.
3. Thompson 1982, 230: "We have to look at these 'barbarians' from
the outside."
4. Giardina 1989, xxiii–xxxvii. On the entirely negative attitude toward
barbarians, see Jouffroy 1991, although I disagree with Jouffroy's
view that *De rebus bellicis* puts forward a serious military strategy.
5. Doubted by Thompson (above) but defended by Blockley 1983, ad
loc.
6. *CIL* 3.6151; this is a formulaic inscription, repeated on other buildings
(cf. note 13 below). Compare also the fourth-century repairs to forts
in Tunisia, described as *propugnacula* (*CIL* 8.22766–67), which were
not part of the *fossatum.*
7. Cited in Alföldi 1952, 4, with references; Alföldi regards such expres-
sions as no more than "euphemisms," but see Wolfram 1988, 137–
38. They follow in the same tradition of the civilizing mission of
Rome as Strabo; see Thollard 1987, 39.
8. See Isaac 1988 for the previous literature. Other references are cited
below.
9. E.g., Ps-Boethius, probably fifth century A.D., in *Grom. Vet.* (Lach.
401.8): *viae militares finem faciunt.*
10. See p. 61; Velkov 1977, 141. Ørsted 1985, 271–72, has interesting
comments about the term *ripa* meaning a borderland, over which
portoria were levied.
11. Although this is disputed by Mann 1977, 11, who thinks they were
two separate grades of soldiers.
12. E.g., Am. Marc. 28.2.1 for the period of Valentinian.

13. In 316, for instance, Constantine and Licinius are recorded as having built forts in the Dobrudja some thirty kilometers behind the line of the lower Danube River frontier, but *ad confirmandum limitis tutelam* (*CIL* 3.13734). Likewise the fort at Tabalati on the Tripolitanian front, headquarters of the *limes Tablatensis* (see previous chapter), was about twenty kilometers behind the stretch of *fossatum*. By contrast, Tisavar was some fifty kilometers in front of the same wall-and-ditch system and clearly was intended to control the routes of penetration from the desert; Trousset 1974, 93.

14. Isaac 1988. Isaac has suggested to me orally that *limes* came to mean something like the English term "command," as in "Northern Command"—an area of military action. In the *Notitia Dignitatum* a number of *limites* are listed, clearly referring to sectors of the frontier, over which a *praepositus* was placed in charge. The special conditions are discussed in chapter 5.

15. Malalas, *Chron.*, p. 448 Dindorf; discussed by Mayerson 1989. However one understands the passage, it is clear there was first a line that marked the territory administered by Rome, followed by a vaguer region over which Rome claimed control.

16. Collected in *Geographici Latini minores* (ed. Riese); the best discussion of these texts is Dalché and Nicolet 1986; see chapter 1.

17. This theme has been ingeniously developed by Brennan, 1972. Cf. Mann 1977, 11.

18. Soproni 1974, 1977.

19. R. M. Swoboda in *Limeskongress XI* 1977, 123–27.

20. The quotation is from Frézouls 1983, 186.

21. Soproni 1974. This is one of many such sites. In general, see Mócsy 1974b, 269–71: "an entirely new measure in the field of foreign and military policy . . . the partial occupation of Sarmatian territory."

22. See chapter 5, p. 86, for the discussion.

23. Constantius: Frézouls 1983; Stilicho: see note 24.

24. Ruggini 1961; Matthews 1975, 270. On Alaric's supposed barbarism, see Mazzarino's comment quoted in chapter 5, note 27.

25. E.g., Luttwak 1976, 130–31, and often since repeated.

26. A.H.M. Jones 1964; app. 2 presents his calculations. MacMullen 1980 reaches a lower total. For the quality of *limitanei*, see A.H.M. Jones 1964, 649–52.

27. The best argument I know for this is in Brennan 1972, which remains unpublished, since some of his independent conclusions were anticipated by Hoffmann 1969–70; cf. Petrikovits 1971, 181, which recognizes the political factor.

28. The debate is set out with the names of its protagonists in F. Paschoud's edition of Zosime, *Histoire nouvelle* (1971), 1:235.

29. Petrikovits 1971, 205, although he does think regional directives were probable. Johnson 1983, 63–64, 114, gives examples of some imperial aid to cities for rebuilding and groups the walls of cities by type regionally.

30. Recognized by Luttwak 1976, 131–32, but not on the Arabian front, for which see above at note 28. For the *Langmauer,* see Gilles 1985. Bogaers 1971, 79, shows that the use of a town like Cuijk on the Maas for military purposes, well behind the front line of the Rhine, had taken place long before the fourth century—so this was no new strategy. Johnson 1983, 246, suggests that unrest among foreign settlers led to fortified sites. Ossel 1992, 158–59, discusses the relationship between *burgi* and granary "silo towers" in Gaul; not all towers were *burgi,* but all *burgi* were probably granaries.

31. Goffart 1980, 4; see also the excellent introduction by Wolfram 1988, esp. 7–8.

32. The debate about whether these "bandits" were internal or external is given below.

33. The ancient sources are Vic. Vit. 1.1; cf. Procop. *BVand.* 3.5.18. A.H.M. Jones 1964, 195, believes the figure; but see Goffart 1980, 231–32.

34. For the demythologizing of "tribes," see Wolfram 1988, 40–42. The quotation is from James 1988, 57.

35. Wolfram 1988, 66–67, plays down the conspiracy, although the author goes on to say that this does not mean there was no development toward greater unity.

36. Goths: Wolfram 1988; for references on the British conspiracy, see chapter 5.

37. Isaac 1990, chap. 1, esp. 52, although underestimating the Saracen threat (72–74); see chapter 5, note 1.

38. Graf 1989a; see my comments in chapter 5, p. 137.

39. For a full discussion, see Shahid 1984, chap. 7.

40. Mayerson 1986, 39: "The borders were meaningless when the 'enemy' lived and freely moved within them."

41. Jankuhn 1976, 97, quoting figures from Harnaagel.

42. For the Rhine, see Schmid 1978, 137; Zimmermann 1974, 69. For the Danube, see Heather and Matthews 1991, 78–79.

43. Christlein 1978, 28–29, quotes a number of other examples, although he argues there was little continuity from early to late Empire.

44. Demougeot 1979, 281. Cunliffe 1988, 187–88, argues that Vandals and Burgundians were historical manifestations of the Oksywie and Przeworsk cultures in central Europe, whose demand for prestige goods caused migrations in the late second and early third centuries, thereby destabilizing peoples to the south.

45. See chapter 5, p. 155.
46. Mattingly 1983; the quotation is from Guey 1939, 231.
47. Graf 1989a believes in inverse transhumance, but his evidence could as easily indicate movements in both directions, as is usual in transhumant societies.
48. Discussed most recently by Kuhnen 1991, which puts forward the interesting idea that it was the combination of horse and camel that provided the mobility for true nomadism. Graf 1989a is skeptical about similar theories in the past.
49. Discussed, with references to earlier literature, in Gichon 1986, 585; Graf 1989a, 371; and Isaac 1990, 239.
50. The example with references is provided by Wolfram 1988, 103.
51. Discussed in chapter 5, p. 179 f.
52. Although the contrary is asserted by Demougeot 1979, 191–92, and Willems 1986, 249, 429.
53. For the term *arcani* or *areani,* see Salway 1981, 312–13. Alföldy 1968, 79, gives two or three other examples in the third century. But not all scouts were natives.
54. If A.H.M. Jones 1964, 652–53, is right that the transfer of African *limitanei* to the *comitatenses* took place under Honorius, the third legion must have been on the frontier throughout the fourth century.
55. *PLRE,* vol. 1, s.v. "Magnentius," gives the conflicting references about his laetic status.
56. Brennan (see note 27 above) gives an account of the changes.
57. Hoffmann 1969–70, 150–52. Liebeschuetz 1991, 32–35, notes a number of times when ad hoc allied (federate) troops were recruited alongside regular army units, often from the same ethnic background.
58. References in *PLRE,* vol. 1, s.v. "Vadomarius."
59. See Graf 1989a, 348–49, for the literature and the problems of chronology, which are unimportant here. Mavia's ambiguous position is no more "incredible," pace Graf, than that of Vadomar or of Aspebetos in 432, a former Persian ally, then a Roman phylarch, and finally a bishop; see Isaac 1990, 246, for references.
60. This is one of many examples in Lieu 1986, on whom I have shamelessly drawn; his is a fascinating study of Roman-Persian cross-border exchanges of all sorts. Some of the sources for these examples are given in Dodgeon and Lieu 1991.
61. Toropu 1974, notes the coins in Oltenia.
62. Johnson 1980, 56–57, describes the belt fittings as "of Gothic or Germanic character," but they could easily have been worn by Romans.
63. Whittaker 1983. For the East, see Isaac 1990, 146. The celebrated

case of drought that drove Saracens into Commagene in 484 is cited by Parker 1986a, 150.

64. Ste Croix 1981, app. 3, collects most of the references.

65. Whittaker 1982. The Hunnish Skiri, noted earlier, were expressly excluded from the Thracian diocese.

66. Mertens 1986, 196, citing the earlier work by R. de Maeyer; Wightman 1985, 244. Ossel 1992 provides an important catalog of the recent evidence and the problems of the evidence (e.g., 67): most sites in the northern Rhine frontier provinces are "mute," pending proper investigation; only 25 percent of the total rural sites can be *proved* to have survived into the fourth century; but the survival rate is 83 percent if one confines oneself to the datable evidence.

67. See the problem in Agache 1977; the author thinks the village of Laboisière could be a laetic settlement. But even this example is now discounted in the absence of any datable fourth-century evidence. Discussion of laetic settlements is summed up by James 1988, 45–48. Ossel 1983 now believes it may be possible to identify Franks in Toxandria, but with little certainty. Ossel 1992, 125, discusses the evidence of sunken wooden houses at old villa sites like Lixhe (Liège) in Belgium and Haarf (Erftkreis) in the northwestern Rhineland, which may indicate *laeti,* he thinks, because the buildings contain no Germanic-looking objects.

68. Summaries of the evidence are in Périn and Feffer 1987, 64–72, and James 1988, esp. 19–28. Périn 1980 gives the history of research and evidence. See also Böhme 1978, 30; Böhme's article is a French résumé of his longer *Germanische Grabfunde des 4 bis. 5 Jahrhunderts zwischen unterer Elbe und Loire* (1974). Ossel 1992, 165–68, makes a prudent study of these "Germanic" objects, which he believes are signs of militarization and genuine Germanization but not necessarily of Germans.

69. Périn 1980, 79–80, notes Böhme's tendency to classify graves as "German" too readily from the artifacts. See Wightman 1985, 250. Ossel 1992, 101–4, discusses the frequent difficulty in linking the necropoles to the habitations; broadly speaking most "Germanic" burial goods are found in western France north of the Seine-Oise and in Belgium, whereas the burials between Trier and Cologne remain firmly Gallo-Roman. Nico Roymans with the Amsterdam Pionier project is attempting a multifaceted study of Celto-German societies, including graves, which when published will probably alter many of our views.

70. James 1988, 46; Böhme 1978, 25, 36–37; Christlein 1978, 72. Périn advises caution in dating by the evolution of art forms.

71. Simpson 1976, 192–206; Böhme 1978, 31. For the Gothic fibulae, see Heather and Matthews 1991, 78–79.

72. Gilles, 1985, 288–91, identifies the pottery as coming from the mouth of the Elbe. Map 29 in Ossel 1992 shows the bunching of this kind of material around Trier and Cologne, as one might expect from German units protecting these centers.

73. James 1988, 56, 90; Périn 1980, 117. The enormous work of publication of the Krefeld-Gellep necropolis has been done by Pirling 1966–79, summarized in Pirling 1978, 59–68.

74. Cleary 1989, passim, esp. 188–97. Hawkes 1989. The most extreme case for discontinuity between Romano-British and Anglo-Saxons is in Welch 1992, 97–107. For a less radical view, see Johnson 1980, 141–43. The most recent attempt to synthesize the controversial evidence is by Higham 1992, especially 168–88, on the "archaeology of *adventus*."

75. The quotation is from Drewett, Rudling, and Gardiner 1988, 252. Cleary 1989, 173–84, describes the evidence of the post-Roman culture of the fifth century. Even Welch (previous note) concedes that pollen analysis indicates no change in land use or abandonment of land, suggesting that the Anglo-Saxons settled in easily with the Romano-British. Higham 1992, 113–19, regards the invasions as small scale, which therefore implies continuous use of native rural labor.

76. Böhme 1974, 306, 1978, 32. For Frénouville, see Pilet 1980 and James 1988, 110–11.

77. See chapter 5, p. 161.

78. Ossel 1992, 104, is critical of Wightman's thesis that there was growing nucleation and new "villages of workers," because it uses the evidence of large necropoles but ignores the many smaller graveyards and settlements. But Ossel 1992, 163–65, does concede that there were some large fortified rural sites, although whether military or civil is not easy to say. Perhaps the distinction was blurred. See Drewett, Rudling and Gardiner 1988, 224–26, for the recent studies at Bignor villa in Britain.

Chapter Seven. Warlords and Landlords in the Later Empire

1. The example is drawn from Isaac 1990, 236. I make no apologies for repeating here a part of my review of Isaac's excellent book in *TLS*, 22 March 1991.

2. A summary of later Roman-Saracen relations can be found in Isaac 1990, 235–49. Parker 1986a, 149–54, gives a more catastrophic

historical narrative. On Christianity among the Tanukhids, even under early Islam, see Shahid 1984, 455–56.

3. Graf 1989a, 349, accepted by Isaac 1990, 76. I find the suggestion implausible.

4. Mayerson 1986; but Gatier 1989, 509, and Whittaker, *TLS*, 22 March 1991, think Isaac and Mayerson underestimate the threat.

5. See especially *CJ* 1.27.2.4: *usque ad illos fines provincias Africanas extendere ubi ante invasionem Vandalorum et Maurorum respublica romana fines habuerat.* Trousset 1985 notes that in Justinian's description the *limes* west of Sétif seems to have retreated far to the north, corresponding, in his view, to what had happened before the end of Valentinian III's rule.

6. Decret 1985 believes these *gentes* were rebels formerly within the empire, but Kotula's comment on the article is skeptical.

7. Courtois 1964, 338, discusses the date, which may be either fifth or sixth century.

8. Coins: Kent 1979, 21; pottery: Fulford 1979.

9. Frere 1967, 360–62. I am impressed by the continuity of the Roman legal tradition of landholding revealed in medieval documents of southeastern Wales; see Davis 1979, 153–73. Higham 1992, 94–97, describes the material evidence of this sub-Roman society of patrons and warriors.

10. *PLRE*, vol. 2, s.v. "Aetius 7," for references.

11. Cf. Wolfram 1988, 186, discussing the relations between Aetius and the Visigoths.

12. Eckhart 1977; Wolfram 1988, 316, makes a good study of Theodoric's frontiers.

13. See *PLRE*, vol. 2, "Orestes 2," for references.

14. Wallace-Hadrill 1962, 3. James 1988 agrees with this verdict. A number of papers at the recent conference titled "Fifth Century Gaul: A Crisis of Identity?" stress the dislocation of the period more than I have done here. I am grateful to John Drinkwater for allowing me to see these papers before publication; they have now been published, but too late for me to comment on them in detail; see Drinkwater and Elton 1992. Suffice it to say that the misery and dangers of the period when Roman central authority was crumbling do not in themselves prove there was chaos and military anarchy everywhere—largely because, as I argue here, of local protection agencies.

15. See Levy 1951, 62, 90–93. The African example reads *locata est enim tibi domus . . . non donata,* which refers to an *inquilinus* (Aug. *Enn. in Ps. 148*.11 [*PL* 37.1945]). Some examples from Byzantine Egypt can be seen in *PLond.* 1695 (531), *PRG* 3.39 (584)—the first a five-year

contract and the second a protest at the termination of a contract. Note Levy's comment about Euric's Code (*lex* 12)—"a contract about equivalent to . . . *locatio-conductio rei*"—and his citation of a reference even in Merovingian *formulae*.

16. Harmand 1955, 155. I assume the plural means a long line; for references, see *PLRE*, vol. 2, s.v. "Silvanus 8."

17. Rémondon 1965, 142. The text of the Abinnaeus Archive is published in Bell et al. 1962.

18. As Carrié thinks (1976, 175).

19. For references, see *PLRE*, vol. 2, s.v. "Arbogast," "Merobaudes."

20. Drinkwater 1984. It is only proper to point out that Drinkwater strongly disagrees with Van Dam's (and my) interpretation of the Bagaudae, most recently in Drinkwater 1989. His main arguments are (1) it is impossible to identify any known prominent landowner associated with the Bagaudae movement; (2) there was no continuity of Gallic elites from early to late Roman periods. To which I respond: (1) we know so little of later Gallic elites that I have no confidence in the argument from silence. In Africa, by way of comparison, we know nothing about the origins of the House of Nubel before the fourth century, although they were obviously massive landowners; (2) a change of elites during the disturbances of the third century does not preclude continuity of conditions of extreme rural dependence associated with early Gallic nobles. In a recent publication (referred to in note 14) Drinkwater develops the interesting idea that the fifth-century movement was caused by refugees from the barbarian invasions putting unacceptable pressure upon land in southern Gaul.

21. Recently played down by Gabbia 1988.

22. Camps 1985; cf. above, p. 247. It may not be too fanciful to note here a further parallel with the Bagaudae, whose leaders Amandus and Aelianus were also called native usurpers but were regarded as local heroes of Christianity in the fifth century. Later medieval tradition associated Saint-Maur-des-Fossés with a place called *castrum Bagaudarum* and viewed the rebel *latrones* as *custodes* of the Christian faith; see Jullian 1920–26, 8:14; Giardina 1983, 383–85; Van Dam 1985, 54.

23. For references, see *PLRE*, vol. 1, s.v. "Mavia"; Shahid 1984, 142–52; Bowersock 1980.

24. James 1988, 78; cf. above, p. 252. Périn and Feffer 1987, 119–34, describe the burial and grave goods.

25. For references, see *PLRE*, vol. 2, s.v. "Veranianus." Wolfram 1988, 239–40, discusses the difference between Roman and Gothic "retainership," the latter influenced by the former.

26. Bachrach 1972, 7–8; *Lib. Hist. Franc.* 15 (Krusch) (*MGH* [*SSRM*] II).

Procopius B *Goth.* 5.12.15 ff. says Roman soldiers were willing to surrender to Christian Germans but not to Arian Goths.

27. See chapter 6, pp. 214–22.

28. Wightman 1981, 1985, 246–50, makes confident statements about nucleation and more concentrated villages in the north, which Ossel 1992, esp. 104–5, 163–65, has challenged, although he does concede that some of the evidence is ambiguous. For the *Hallenhaüser*, see Ossel 1992, 125. A more general survey of fortified villas and refuges is given in Ferdière 1988, 2:212–22.

29. Whittaker 1989, chap. 4, discusses the situation on the land in more detail.

30. The bibliography runs from Mommsen 1889 to Liebeschuetz 1986, 1991; the latter collects the references. See also Wolfram 1988, 139–40, for the different grades of dependence; the *bucellarii* were more free than the *saiones* in early Gothic law and correspond well with the difference I have underlined between *satellites* and *servi*.

31. For references, see *PLRE*, vol. 2, s.v. "Sarus."

32. Delbrück 1990, 390. Cf. Wolfram 1988, 240, for references in Euric's Code and later.

33. Gascou 1976, 151; *POxy.* 156, for instance, directs others in the Oxyrhinchite nome to enroll two men as *bucellarii* and provide them with *annona*.

34. See Thompson 1982, chap. 7, "The End of Noricum."

35. I must express my thanks to Wolf Liebeschuetz and John Drinkwater for the comments they offered on an earlier draft of part of this chapter. I hope I have repaid their care by explaining or correcting the points they raised.

References

Abbreviations of journals as far as possible follow the index of *L'Année Philologique*. Otherwise they are self-evident.

Agache, R. 1977. La marque de Rome dans le paysage du nord de la France. In *Influence de la Grèce et de Rome sur l'occident moderne*, ed. R. Chevallier, 375–82. Paris.

———— 1981. Le problème des fermes indigènes pré-romaines et romaines en Picardie. In *Les structures d'habitat à l'âge du fer en Europe tempérée: L'évolution de l'habitat en Berry*, ed. O. Buchsenschutz, 45–50. Paris.

Alföldi, A. 1952. The moral frontier on Rhine and Danube. In *Limeskongress I*, 1–16.

Alföldy, G. 1968. *Die Hilfstruppen der römischen Provinz Germania Inferior*. Düsseldorf.

———— 1971. Der Friedenschluss des Kaisers Commodus mit den Germanen. *Historia* 20:84–109.

———— 1974. *Noricum*. Trans. A. Birley. Boston.

Alliès, P. 1980. *L'invention du territoire*. Grenoble.

Anderson, J. G. C. 1938. *Cornelii Taciti: De origine et situ Germanorum*. Oxford.

ANRW = *Aufstieg und Niedergang des römischen Welts*, ed. H. Temporini. Tübingen.

Arnaud, P. 1989. Pouvoir des mots et limites de la cartographie dans la géographie grecques et romaines. In *Espace, paysages, histoire, antiquité*,

9–29. Dialogues d'histoire ancienne, Centre de Recherches d'Histoire Ancienne, vol. 87, Ann. Litt. Univ. Besançon 395. Paris.

Bachrach, B. S. 1967. Was there feudalism in Byzantine Egypt? *JARCE* 6: 163–66.

——— 1972. *Merovingian military organization, 481–551.* Minneapolis, Minn.

Baker, A. R. H., and D. Gregory. 1984. *Explorations in historical geography.* London.

Banning, E. B. 1986. Peasants, pastoralists and *Pax Romana*: Mutualism in the southern highlands of Jordan. *BASO* 261:25–50.

——— 1987. *De bello paceque*: A reply to Parker. *BASO* 265:52–54.

Barker, G. W. W., and G. D. B. Jones. 1982. The UNESCO Libyan Valleys Survey, 1979–81. *Libyan Studies* 13:1–34.

Barnea, I., and G. Ştefan. 1974. Le limes Scythicus. In *Limeskongress IX,* 15–25.

Barnes, T. D. 1981. *Constantine and Eusebius.* Cambridge, Mass.

Barrett, J. C., A. P. Fitzpatrick, and L. Macinnes. 1989. *Barbarians and Romans in northwest Europe.* BAR S471. Oxford.

Bartel, B. 1980–81. Colonialism and cultural responses: Problems related to Roman provincial analysis. *World Arch.* 12:11–26.

Bell, H. I., V. Martin, E. G. Turner, and D. van Berchem. 1962. *The Abinnaeus Archive: Papers of a Roman officer in the reign of Constantius II.* Oxford.

Bellamy, A. 1985. A new reading of the Namarah inscription. *JAOS* 105:31–48.

Bennett, J. 1983. The end of Roman settlement in northern England. In Chapman and Myrtum 1983, 205–32.

Berchem, D. van. 1937. L'annone militaire dans l'empire romaine au IIIe siècle. *Mem. Soc. Nat. Ant. France* 10:117–202.

——— 1971. L'occupation militaire de la haute Egypte sous Dioclétian. In *Limeskongress VII,* 123–27.

Birley, A. R. 1974. Roman frontiers and Roman frontier policy. *Trans. Architect. Arch. Soc. Durham Northumberland* 3:13–25.

——— 1981. The economic effect of Roman frontier policy. In *The Roman West in the third century,* ed. A. King and M. Henig, 39–53. BAR S109. Oxford.

Birley, E. 1956. Hadrianic frontier policy. In *Carnuntina,* ed. E. Swoboda, 25–33. Graz-Cologne.

Blagg, T. F. C, and A. C. King, eds. 1984. *Military and civilian in Roman Britain.* BAR 136. Oxford.

Bloch, M. 1963. *Mélanges historiques.* Paris.

Blockley, R. C. 1983. *The fragmentary classicizing historians of the later*

Roman Empire: Eunapius, Olympiodorus, Priscus and Malchus. Vol. 2. Text. Liverpool.

——— 1987. The division of Armenia between the Romans and Persians at the end of the fourth century. *Historia* 36:222–34.

Bloemers, J. H. F. 1983. Acculturation in the Rhine-Meuse basin in the Roman period: A preliminary survey. In Brandt and Slofstra 1983, 159–210.

Bogaers, J. E. 1971. The limes of Germania Inferior. In *Limeskongress VII,* 71–87.

Böhme, H. W. 1974. *Germanische Grabfunde des 4. bis 5. Jahrhunderts zwischen unterer Elbe und Loire.* 2 vols. Munich.

——— 1978. Tombes germanique des IVe et Ve siècles en Gaule du nord: Chronologie, distribution et interprétation. In Fleury and Périn 1978, 21–38.

Bökönyi, S. 1974. *History of domestic mammals in central and eastern Europe.* Trans. L. Halápy. Budapest.

——— 1988. Animal breeding on the Danube. In *Pastoral economies of classical antiquity,* ed. C. R. Whittaker, 171–76. Cambridge.

Boon, G. C. 1975. Segontium fifty years on. *Arch. Cambrensis* 124:52–57.

Botteri, P. 1992. La définition de l'ager occupatorius. *Cah. Centre Glotz* 3:45–55.

Bouché-Leclerq, A. 1882. *Histoire de la divination dans l'antiquité.* Vol. 4. *Divination italique.* Paris.

Bowersock, G. W. 1980. Mavia, queen of the Saracens. In *Studien zur antiken Sozialgeschichte: Festschrift F. Vittinghoff,* 477–95. Cologne.

——— 1983. *Roman Arabia.* Cambridge, Mass.

Bowman, A. K., and J. D. Thomas. 1983. *Vindolanda: The writing tablets.* Britannia, Monograph 4.

Brandt, R., and J. Slofstra, eds. 1983. *Roman and native in the Low Countries.* BAR S184. Oxford.

Braund, D. C. 1984. *Rome and the friendly king.* London.

——— 1986. The Caucasian frontier: Myth, explanation and the dynamics of imperialism. In Freeman and Kennedy 1986, 31–49.

——— 1989a. Coping with the Caucasus: Roman responses to local conditions in Colchis. In French and Lightfoot 1989, 31–43.

——— 1989b. Ideology, subsidies and trade: The king on the northern frontier revisited. In Barrett, Fitzpatrick, and Macinnes 1989, 14–26.

Breeze, D. J. 1977. The fort at Bearsden and the supply of pottery to the Roman army. In *Roman pottery studies in Britain and beyond,* ed. J. Dore and K. Greene, 133–45. BAR S30. Oxford.

——— 1984. Demand and supply on the northern frontier. In Micket and Burgess 1984, 264–86.

———— 1989. The impact of the Roman army on north Britain. In Barrett, Fitzpatrick, and Macinnes 1989, 227–34.

Breeze, D. J., and B. Dobson. 1976. *Hadrian's Wall*. London.

Brennan, P. 1972. The dispositions and the interrelation of Roman military units in provincial field armies in the late third and early fourth centuries. Ph.D. thesis, Cambridge University.

———— 1980. Combined legionary detachments as artillery units in late Roman Danubian bridgehead dispositions. *Chiron* 10:553–67.

Brulet, R. 1977. La tour de garde du Bas-Empire romain de Moranwelz. In *Limeskongress X*, 109–14.

———— 1989. The Continental *Litus Saxonicum*. In Maxfield 1989, 45–77.

———— 1990. La chronologie des fortifications du Bas-Empire dans l'hinterland de la Gaule septentrionale. In *Limeskongress XV*, 301–9.

———— 1991. Le litus Saxonicum continental. In *Limeskongress XV*, 155–69.

Brunt, P. A. 1963. Review of H. G. Meyer, *Die Aussenpolitik des Augustus und die augusteische Dichtung*. *JRS* 53:170–76.

———— 1978a. Review of Luttwak 1976. *Times Literary Supplement*, 154.

———— 1978b. *Laus imperii*. In *Imperialism in the ancient world*, ed. P. D. A. Garnsey and C. R. Whittaker, 159–91. Cambridge.

Buck, D. J. 1985. Frontier process in Roman Tripolitania. In Buck and Mattingly 1985, 179–90.

Buck, D. J., and D. J. Mattingly, eds. 1985. *Town and country in Roman Tripolitania*. BAR S274. Oxford.

Bulliet, R. W. 1975. *The camel and the wheel*. Cambridge.

Burns, J. R., and B. Denness. 1985. Climate and social dynamics: The Tripolitanian example, 300 B.C.–A.D. 300. In Buck and Mattingly 1985, 201–25.

Bury, J. B. 1958. *History of the later Roman Empire*. 2 vols. Reprint New York.

Cagnat, R. 1882. *L'étude historique sur les impôts indirects chez les Romains*. Paris.

———— 1913. *L'armée romaine de l'Afrique*. Paris.

Cameron, A. 1970. *Claudian: Poetry and propaganda at the court of Honorius*. Oxford.

Campbell, J. B. 1984. *The emperor and the Roman army, 31 B.C.–A.D. 235*. Oxford.

Camps, G. 1985. De Masuna à Koceila: Les destinées de la Maurétanie aux VIe et VIIe siècles. In Lancel 1985, 307–25.

Carrié, J.-M. 1976. Patronage et propriété militaires au IVe siècle. *BCH* 100:159–76.

Carrington, C. 1970. *Rudyard Kipling: His life and works*. London.

Casey, P. J. 1978. Constantine the Great in Britain: The evidence of coinage of the London mint, A.D. 312–14. *LMAS* special paper no. 2:181–83.

———, ed. 1979a. Magnus Maximus in Britain: A reappraisal. In Casey 1979b, 181–83.

——— 1979b. *The end of Roman Britain.* BAR 71. Oxford.

Cerati, A. 1975. *Charactère annonaire et assiette de l'impôt foncier au Bas-Empire.* Paris.

Champion, T. C., et al. 1984. *Prehistoric Europe.* London.

Chapman, J. C., and M. C. Myrtum, eds. 1983. *Settlement in North Britain, 1000 B.C.–A.D. 1000.* BAR 118. Oxford.

Chapot, V. 1907. *La frontière de Euphrate de Pompée à la conquête arabe.* Paris.

Christ, K. 1957. Die antiken Münzen als Quelle der westfälischen Geschichte. *Westfalen* 35:1–32.

Christie, N. 1991. The Alps as a frontier (A.D. 168–774). *JRomArch* 4:410–30.

Christlein, R. 1978. *Die Alamannen.* Stuttgart.

Christlein, R., and O. Braash. 1982. *Das unterirdische Bayern.* Stuttgart.

Chropovský, B., ed. 1977. *Symposium Ausklang der Latène-Zivilisation und Anfänge der ger. Besiedlung im mittleren Donaugebiet.* Veda.

Cicikova, M. 1974. "Firmalampen" du limes danubien en Bulgarie. In *Limeskongress IX*, 155–65.

Clack, P., and S. Haselgrove, eds. 1982. *Rural settlement in the Roman north.* CBA Report 3. Durham.

Claval, P. 1978. *Espace et pouvoir.* Paris.

Cleary, A. S. E. 1989. *The ending of Roman Britain.* London.

Collis, J. 1972. The Dacian horizon—settlements and chronology. *Slovenskà Arch.* 20:313–16.

——— 1984a. *Oppida: Earliest towns north of the Alps.* Huddersfield, Eng.

——— 1984b. *The European Iron Age.* London.

Coulson, J. C. 1986. Roman, Parthian and Sassanid tactical developments. In Freeman and Kennedy 1986, 59–77.

Courtois, C. 1964. *Les Vandales et l'Afrique.* Paris. First published 1955.

Crow, J. G. 1986a. The function of Hadrian's Wall and the comparative evidence of late Roman long walls. In *Limeskongress XIII*, 724–29.

——— 1986b. A review of the physical remains of the frontiers of Cappadocia. In Freeman and Kennedy 1986, 77–91.

Cunliffe, B. 1977. The Saxon Shore—some problems and misconceptions. In Johnston 1977, 1–6.

——— 1988. *Greeks, Romans and barbarians: Spheres of interaction.* London.

Cunliffe, B., and T. Rowley. 1978. *Lowland Iron Age communities in Europe.* BAR S48. Oxford.

Curzon, Lord. 1907. *Frontiers*. Romanes Lecture. Oxford.

Dalché P. G., and C. Nicolet. 1986. Les "quatres sages" de Jules César et la mesure du monde, selon Julius Honorius: Réalité antique et tradition médiévale. *JS* 157–218.

Daniels, C. M. 1968. Garamantian excavations: Zinchecra, 1965–67. *LibAnt* 5:113–94.

———— 1979. Fact and theory on Hadrian's Wall. *Britannia* 10:357–64.

———— 1980. Excavations at Wallsend and fourth century barracks on Hadrian's Wall. In *Limeskongress XII*, 173–94.

Daremberg, C., and E. Saglio. 1877–1919. *Dictionnaire des antiquités.* Paris.

Darling, M. J. 1977. Pottery from early military sites in western Europe. In *Roman pottery studies in Britain and beyond*, ed. J. Dore and K. Greene, 57–100. BAR S30. Oxford.

Dasnoy, A. 1978. Quelques tombes du cimitière de Pry (IVe–VIe s.) (Belgique, Namur). In Fleury and Périn 1978, 69–70.

Dauge, Y. A. 1981. *Le Barbare: Recherches sur la conception romaine de la barbarie et de la civilisation.* Coll. Latomus 176. Brussels.

Davies, C. C. 1975. *The problem of the North-West Frontier, 1890–1908.* Reprint Oxford.

Davies, R. W. 1981. The Roman military medical service. *Saalburg-Jahrbuch* 27 (1970): 84–104. Reprinted in *Service in the Roman army*, 209–36. Edinburgh.

Davis, W. 1979. Roman settlement and post-Roman estates in south-east Wales. In Casey 1979b, 153–73.

Debevoise, N. C. 1969. *A political history of Parthia.* Reprint Chicago.

Decret, F. 1985. Les *gentes barbarae* asservies par Rome dans l'Afrique du Ve siècle. In Lancel 1985, 265–71.

Delahaye, H., et al. 1978. *La Grande Muraille.* Paris.

Delbrück, H. 1920. *Geschichte der Kriegskunst im Rahmen der politischen Geschichte.* Vols. 1–2. 3d ed. Berlin. (All citations are from the English translations listed below.)

———— 1990. *History of the art of war within the framework of political history.* Trans. W. J. Renfroe. Vol. 1, *Warfare in antiquity.* Vol. 2, *The barbarian invasions.* Lincoln, Nebr.

Demougeot, E. 1979. *La formation de l'Europe de les invasions barbare.* Vol. 2. *De l'avènement de Dioclétien an début du VIe siècle.* Paris.

———— 1983. Constantin et Dacie. In Frézouls 1983, 91–112.

———— 1988. *L'Empire romain et les barbares d'Occident (IVe–VIIe siècle): Varia Scripta.* Paris.

Desanges, J. 1980. *Pline l'ancien: Histoire naturelle. Bk. 5, 1–46, L'Afrique du Nord.* Text and commentary. Paris.

Diesner, H. J. 1972. Das Bucellarietum von Stilicho und Sarus bis auf Aetius, 454–55. *Klio* 54:321–50.

Dilke, O. A. W. 1971. *The Roman land surveyors: An introduction to the agrimensores.* Newton Abbot.

——— 1985. *Greek and Roman maps.* London.

Dillemann, L. 1962. *Haute Mésopotamie orientale et pays adjacents: Contributions à la géographie historique de la région, du Vème siècle av. Chr. au VIème siècle de cette ère.* Paris.

Dion, R. 1977. *Aspects politique de la gèographie.* Paris.

Dobrawa, E. 1986. The frontier in Syria in the first century A.D. In Freeman and Kennedy 1986, 93–100.

Dodgeon, M. H., and S. N. C. Lieu. 1991. *The Roman eastern frontier and the Persian wars, A.D. 226–363. A documentary history.* London.

Drewett, P., D. Rudling, and M. Gardiner 1988. *A regional history of England: The South East to A.D. 1000.* New York.

Drinkwater, J. F. 1983. *Roman Gaul.* London.

——— 1984. Peasants and Bagaudae in Roman Gaul. *Classical Views/ Echos du Monde Classique* 3:349–71.

——— 1987. *The Gallic empire: Separatism and continuity in the northern western provinces of the Roman Empire A.D. 260–274.* Historia Einzelschriften 52. Tübingen.

——— 1989. Patronage in Roman Gaul and the problem of the Bagaudae. In *Patronage in ancient society,* ed. A. Wallace-Hadrill. London.

Drinkwater, J. F., and H. Elton, eds. 1992. *Fifth century Gaul: A crisis of identity?* Cambridge.

Dumézil, G. 1966. *La religion romaine archaïque.* Paris.

Dyson, S. L. 1986. *The creation of the Roman frontier.* Princeton, N.J.

Eadie J. 1986. The evolution of the Roman frontier in Arabia. In Freeman and Kennedy 1986, 243–52.

Eckhart, L. 1977. Der Tod der Antike in Ufernoricum, etc. In *Limeskongress X,* 219–24.

Eggers, H. 1951. *Der römische Import im freien Germanien.* Hamburg.

Ellmers, D. 1978. Shipping on the Rhine during the Roman period: The pictorial evidence. In Taylor and Cleere 1978, 1–14.

Elmayer, A. F. 1985. The *centenaria* of Roman Tripolitania. *Libyan Studies* 16:77–84.

Erison, V. 1978. La tombe de guerrier de Landifay (Aisne). In Fleury and Périn 1978, 39–40.

Ettlinger, E. 1977. Aspects of amphorae typology—seen from the North. In *Methodes classiques et méthodes formelles dans l'étude des amphores,* 9–16. Coll. EFR, 32. Rome.

Euzennat, M. 1984. Le limes de Sebou. In Picard 1984, 371–81.
—— 1985. L'olivier et le limes: Considérations sur la frontière romaine de Tripolitaine. In Lancel 1985, 161–71.
—— 1989. *Le limes de Tingitane.* Paris.
Fahd, T., ed. 1989. *L'Arabie préislamique et son environment historique et culturel.* Actes Colloque Strasbourg, 1987. Leiden.
Fairbank, J. K., and A. Feuerwerker, eds. 1986. *The Cambridge History of China.* Vol. 13, *Republican China*, 1912–49, pt. 2. Cambridge.
Febvre, L. 1922. *La terre et l'evolution humaine.* Paris. (All citations are from the reprint of 1970. Note also the English translation by E. G. Mountford and J. H. Paxton, *A geographical introduction to history.* London, 1932.)
—— 1928. Frontière. *Rev. Synth. Hist.* 45:31–44.
Ferdière, A. 1988. *Les campagnes en Gaule romaine.* 2 vols. Paris.
Fink, R. O. 1971. *Roman military records on papyrus.* Ann Arbor, Mich.
Fitz, J. 1984. La sopravivenza della civiltà classica nella provincia Valeria. In *Il crinale d'Europa: L'area illirico-danubiana nei suoi rapporti con il mondo classico*, 139–53. Rome.
—— 1991. Neue Ergebniss in der Limesforschung des Donaugebiets. In *Limeskongress XV*, 219–24.
Fleury, M., and P. Périn. eds. 1978, *Problèmes de chronologie relative et absolue concernant les cimitières mérovingiens d'entre Loire et Rhin.* Colloque 1973. Paris.
Foucault, M. 1980. *Power/knowledge: Selected interviews and other writings, 1972-77.* Ed. C. Gordon. New York.
Foucher, M. 1986. *L'invention des frontières.* Paris.
Fox, C. F. 1955. *Offa's Dyke.* London.
Frank, R. I. 1969. *Scholae palatinae: The palace guards of the later Roman Empire.* Papers of the American Academy. Rome.
Freeman, P., and D. L. Kennedy, eds. 1986. *The defence of the Roman and Byzantine East.* BAR S297. Oxford.
French, D. H. 1983. New research on the Euphrates frontier. In Mitchell 1983a, 71–101.
French, D. H., and C. S. Lightfoot, eds. 1989. *The eastern frontier of the Roman Empire.* BAR S553. Oxford.
Frere, S. S. 1967. *Britannia.* London.
Frézouls, E. 1980a. Les frontières du Moyen-Euphrate à l'époque romaine. In *Le moyen Euphrate: Zones de contacts et d'échanges*, ed. J.-C. Margueron, 355–86. Act. Coll. Strasbourg 1977. Leiden.
—— 1980b. Rome et la Maufetanie Tingitane: Un constant d'échec. *Ant. Afr.* 16:65–94.
—— 1983. Les deux politiques de Rome face aux barbares d'après

Ammien Marcellin. In *Crise et redressement dans les provinces européennes de l'empire*, ed. E. Frézouls, 175–97. Strasbourg.

Fulford, M. G. 1979. Pottery production and trade at the end of Roman Britain: The case against continuity. In Casey 1979b, 120–32.

———— 1981. Roman pottery: Towards the investigation of social and economic change. In *Production and distribution: A ceramic viewpoint,* ed. H. Howard and E. L. Morris, 195–208. BAR S120. Oxford.

———— 1984. Demonstrating Britannia's economic dependence in the first and second centuries. In Blagg and King 1984, 129–42.

———— 1985. Roman material in barbarian society c. 200 B.C.–C. A.D. 400. In *Settlement and society: Aspects of west European prehistory in the first millennium B.C.,* ed. T. C. Champion and J. V. S. Megaw, 91–108. Leicester.

———— 1989. Romans and barbarians: The economy of Roman frontier systems. In Barrett, Fitzpatrick, and Macinnes 1989, 81–95.

Gabba, E. 1983. Per un'interpretazione storica della centurazione romana. In *Misurare la terra: Centurazione e coloni nel mondo romano,* ed. R. Bussi. Modena.

Gabbia, C. 1988. Ancora sulle "rivolte" di Firmo e Gildone. *L'Africa Romana* 5:117–29.

Gabler, D. 1977. Untersuchungen am oberpannonischen Donau limes. In *Limeskongress X,* 297–312.

———— 1980. The structure of the Pannonian frontier on the Danube and its development in the Antonine period. In *Limeskongress XII,* 637–54.

Garnsey, P. D. A. 1978. Rome's African empire under the principate. In *Imperialism in the ancient world,* ed. P. D. A. Garnsey and C. R. Whittaker, 223–54. Cambridge.

Garnsey, P. D. A., and C. R. Whittaker, eds. 1983. *Trade and famine in classical antiquity.* Cambridge.

Gascou, J. 1976. L'institution des bucellaires. *Bulletin de l'Institute Française de l'Archéologie Orientale* 76:143–56.

Gatier, P.-L. 1989. Les traditions et l'histoire du Sinaï de IVe au VIIe siècle. In Fahd 1989, 499–523.

Gautier, E. F. 1952. *Le passé de l'Afrique du Nord.* Paris.

Giardina, A. 1983. Banditi e santi: Un aspetto del folklore gallico tra tarda antichità e medioevo. *Athenaeum* 61:374–89.

————, ed. 1989. *De rebus bellicis.* Rome.

Giardina, A., and A. Schiavone, eds. 1981. *Società romana e produzione schiavistica.* 3 vols. Bari.

Gichon, M. 1986. Who were the enemies of Rome on the Limes Palestinae? In *Limeskongress XIII,* 584–92.

Gillam, J. P. 1958. Roman and native A.D. 122–197. In Richmond 1958, 60–90.

——— 1973. Sources of pottery found in northern military sites. In *Current research in Romano-British coarse pottery*, ed. A. Detsicas, 53–62. CBA Report 10. London.

Gillam, J. P., and K. Greene. 1981. Roman pottery in the economy. In *Roman pottery research in Britain and north-west Europe*, ed. A. C. Anderson and A. S. Anderson, 1–24. BAR S123. Oxford.

Gilles, K.-J. 1985. Landmauer and Germanen im Trierer Land. In *Trier Kaiserresidenz und Bischofssitz: Die Stadt in spätantiker und frühchristlicher Zeit*, 288–91, 335–51. Catalog of exhibition. Mainz.

Girardet, R. 1972. *L'idée coloniale en France de 1871 à 1962*. Paris.

Goffart, W. 1980. *Barbarians and Romans, A.D. 418–584: The techniques of accommodation*. Princeton, N.J.

Goodburn, R., and P. Bartholomew, eds. 1976. *Aspects of the Notitia Dignitatum*. BAR S15. Oxford.

Goodchild, R. G. 1976. The Roman and Byzantine *limes* in Cyrenaica. *JRS* 43 (1953):65–76. Reprinted in *Libyan Studies*, ed. J. Reynolds, 185–209. London.

Goudineau, C. 1980. *Histoire de la France urbaine*. Gen. ed. G. Duby. Vol. 1, *La ville antique des origines au IXe siècle*. Paris.

——— 1990. *César et la Gaule*. Paris.

Graf, D. F. 1989a. Rome and the Saracens: Reassessing the nomad menace. In Fahd 1989, 341–400.

——— 1989b. Zenobia and the Arabs. In French and Lightfoot 1989, 143–67.

Graf, D. F., and M. O'Connor. 1977. The origin of the term Saracen and the Rawwafa inscriptions. *ByzStud* 4:52–66.

Greene, K. 1979. *The pre-Flavian fine wares*. Report on the excavations at Usk, 1965–76. Cardiff.

——— 1984. The Roman fortress at Usk, Wales, and the processing of Roman pottery for publication. *JField Arch.* 11:405–12.

——— 1986. *The archaeology of the Roman economy*. London.

Gregory, D., and D. Urry. 1985. *Social relations and spatial structures*. London.

Gregory, S., and D. L. Kennedy. 1985. *Sir Aurel Stein's limes report*. BAR S272. Oxford.

Gren, E. 1941. *Kleinasien und der Ostbalkan in der wirtschaftlichen Entwicklung der röm. Kaiserzeit*. Uppsala.

Grey, E. W. 1973. The Roman eastern *limes* from Constantine to Justinian. *PACA* 12:24–44.

Groenman–van Waateringe, W. 1980. Urbanization and the north west frontier of the Roman Empire. In *Limeskongress XII*, 1037–44.

—— 1986. The horrea of Valkenburg ZH. In *Limeskongress XIII*, 159–68.

—— 1989. Food for soldiers, food for thought. In Barrett, Fitzpatrick, and Macinnes 1989, 96–107.

Gsell, S. 1903. Observations géographiques sur la révolte de Firmus. *Rec. Not. Mem. Soc. Arch. Constantine* 37:21–45.

Guey, J. 1939. Note sur le limes romaine de Numidie et le Sahara au IVe siècle. *MEFR* 56:178–248.

Guichonnet, P., and C. Raffestin. 1974. *Géographie des frontières*. Paris.

Hachmann, R. 1971. *The German peoples*. Trans. J. Hogarth. London.

Hachmann, R., G. Kossack, and H. Kuhn. 1962. *Völker zwischen Germanen und Kelten*. Neumünster.

Hanson, W. S. 1989. The nature and function of Roman frontiers. In Barrett, Fitzpatrick, and Macinnes 1989, 55–63.

Hanson, W. S., and G. S. Maxwell. 1983. *Rome's north west frontier: The Antonine Wall*. Edinburgh.

Harley, J. B., and David Woodward, eds. 1987. *The history of cartography*. Vol. 1. *Cartography in prehistoric, ancient, and medieval Europe and the Mediterranean*. Chicago.

Harmand, L. 1955. *Libanius: Discours sur les patronages*. Paris.

Harrison, R. M. 1974. To Makron Teichos: The long wall in Thrace. In *Limeskongress VIII*, 244–48.

Hartley, K. F. 1973. The marketing and distribution of mortaria. In *Current research in Romano-British coarse pottery*, ed. A. Detsicas, 39–43. CBA Report 10. London.

Hartog, F. 1980. *Le miroir d'Hérodote: Essai sur la réprésentation de l'autre*. Paris.

Hassall, M. W. C. 1977. The historical background and military units of the Saxon Shore. In Johnston 1977, 7–10.

Hawkes, S. C. 1989. The South-east after the Romans: The Saxon settlements. In Maxfield 1989, 78–95.

Heather, P., and J. Matthews. 1991. *The Goths in the fourth century*. Liverpool.

Hedeager, L. 1977. A quantitative analysis of Roman imports in Europe north of the limes. In *New directions in archaeology*, ed. K. Kristiansen and D. Paludan-Müller, 191–216. Copenhagen.

—— 1987. Empire, frontier and the barbarian hinterland: Rome and northern Europe from A.D. 1–400. In *Centre and periphery in the ancient world*, ed. M. Rowlands et al., 125–40. Cambridge.

Helback, H. 1964. The Isca grain: A Roman plant introduction in Britain. *New Phytologist* 63:158–64.

Helgeland, J. 1978. Roman army religion. *ANRW* II. 16:1470–505.

Higham, N. 1986. *The northern counties to A.D. 1000*. New York.

———— 1992. *Rome, Britain and the Anglo-Saxons*. London.

Higham, N., and G. D. B. Jones. 1985. *The Carvetii*. Gloucester.

Hill, D. 1985. The construction of Offa's Dyke. *Antiquaries Journal* 65:140–42.

Hind, J. G. F. 1984. Whatever happened to the Agri Decumates? *Britannia* 15:187–92.

Hinrichs, F. T. 1989. *Histoire des institutions gromatiques*. Paris.

Hodder, I. 1986. *The archaeology of contextual meaning*. Cambridge.

Hodgson, N. 1989. The East as part of the wider Roman imperial frontier policy. In French and Lightfoot 1989, 177–89.

———— 1991. The *Notitia Dignitatum* and the later Roman garrison of Britain. In *Limeskongress XV*, 84–92.

Hoffmann, D. 1969–70. *Das spätrömischen Bewegungsheer und die Notitia Dignitatum*. 2 vols. Düsseldorf.

Holdich, T. 1916. *Political frontiers and boundary making*. London.

Hopkins, K. 1983. Models, ships and staples. In Garnsey and Whittaker 1983, 84–109.

Horedt, K. 1977. Die siebengebürgische Limesstrecke Dakiens. In *Limeskongress X*, 331–38.

Hunter, J. M. 1983. *Perspectives on Ratzel's political geography*. New York.

Hurst, H. R. 1988. Gloucester (Glevum). In *Fortress into city: The consolidation of Roman Britain in the first century A.D.*, ed. G. Webster. London.

Isaac, B. 1986. Reflections on the Roman army in the East. In Freeman and Kennedy 1986, 383–94.

———— 1988. The meaning of *limes* and *limitanei* in ancient sources. *JRS* 17:125–47.

———— 1990. *The limits of empire: The Roman army in the East*. Oxford.

James, E. 1977. *The Merovingian archaeology of south-west Gaul*. BAR S25. Oxford.

———— 1982. *The origins of France*. London.

———— 1988. *The Franks*. Oxford.

Jankuhn, H. 1961–63. Terra . . . silvis horrida: Zu Tacitus, Germania cap. 5. *Archaeologia Geographica* 10–11:19–38.

———— 1976. Siedlung, Wirtschaft und Gesellschaftsordnung der germanischen Stämme in der Zeit der röm. Angriffskriege. *ANRW* II. 5:65–126.

Jobey, G. 1966. Homesteads and settlements on the frontier area. In *Rural settlement in Britain*, ed. C. Thomas, 1–13. CBA Report 7. London.

———— 1982. Between Tyne and Forth: Some Problems. In Clack and Haselgrove 1982, 7–20.

Johnson, H. B. 1976. *Order upon the land*. New York.

Johnson, S. 1980. *Later Roman Britain*. London.

———— 1983. *Late Roman fortifications*. London.

Johnston, D. E., ed. 1977. *The Saxon Shore*. CBA Report 18. London.

Jones, A. H. M. 1964. *The later Roman Empire*. Oxford.

——— 1968. Frontier defense in Byzantine Libya. In *Libya in history*, 289–97. Historical Conference, University of Libya. Beirut.

Jones, G. D. B. 1978. Concept and development in Roman frontiers. *Bull. J. Rylands Library* 61:115–44.

——— 1982. The Solway frontier. *Britannia* 13:282–97.

——— 1984. "Becoming different without knowing it": The role and development of *vici*. In Blagg and King 1984, 75–91.

Jones, M. L. 1984. *Society and settlement in Wales and the Marches 500 B.C. to A.D. 1100*. BAR 121. Oxford.

Jouffroy, H. 1991. La défence des frontières: Le point du vue de *rebus bellicis*. In *Limeskongress XV*, 373–75.

Jullian, C. 1920–26. *Histoire de la Gaule*. 8 vols. Paris.

Kennedy, D. L. 1979. Ti: Claudius Subatianus Aquila, "first prefect of Mesopotamia." *ZPE* 36:255–62.

——— 1982. *Archaeological explorations on the Roman frontier in northeast Jordan*. BAR S134. Oxford.

——— 1986. Rome's eastern frontier. *Popular Archaeology*, March 2–9.

Kennedy, D. L., and D. Riley. 1990. *Rome's desert frontier*. London.

Kent, J. P. C. 1979. Late Roman Britain: The literary and numismatic evidence reviewed. In Casey 1979b, 15–27.

Kiechle, F. 1962. Die giessener Gräberfeld und die Rolle der Regio Translimitana in röm. Kaiserzeit. *Historia* 11:171–91.

Kirk, W. 1979. The making and impact of the British imperial North-West Frontier in India. In *Invasion and response*, ed. B. C. Burnham and H. B. Johnson, 39–55. BAR 73. Oxford.

Knights, B. A., et al. 1983. Evidence concerning the Roman military diet at Bearsden, Scotland in the 2nd century A.D. *Journ. Arch. Science* 10, no. 2:139–52.

Kolník, T. 1986. Neue Ergebnisse der Limesforschung in der CSSR. In *Limeskongress XIII*, 355–61.

——— 1990. Villae rusticae in nordpannonischen Limesvorland? In *Limeskongress XIV*, 779–87.

——— 1991. Römer und Barbaren im nördlichen Mitteldonaugebiet. In *Limeskongress XV*, 432–34.

Kopytoff, I. 1987. *The African frontier: The reproduction of traditional African society*. Indianapolis.

Korinman, M. 1990. *Quand l'Allemagne pensait le monde*. Paris.

Kotula, T. 1985. Thèmes de la propagande impériale à travers les inscriptions africaines du Bas-Empire romain. In Lancel 1985, 257–62.

Kraemer, C. 1958. *Excavations at Nessana*. Vol. 3, *Non-literary papyri*. Princeton, N.J.

Kuhnen, H.-P. 1991. Der Sarazensattel: Zu den Voraussetzungen der Sarazeneneinfälle am Limes Arabiae. In *Limeskongress XV*, 326–34.

Kunow, J. 1987. Das Limesvorland der südlichen Germania inferior. *BJ* 187:63–77.

Labrousse, M. 1938. Les *burgarii* et le *cursus publicus*. *MEFR* 55:151–67.

Ladner, G. B. 1976. On Roman attitudes towards the barbarians in late antiquity. *Viator* 7:1–26.

Laet, S. J. de. 1949. *Portorium*. Brugge.

Lamar, H., and L. Thompson, eds. 1981. *The frontier in history: North America and southern Africa compared*. New Haven, Conn.

Lancel, S., ed. 1985. *Actes du IIe colloque international sur l'histoire et l'archéologie de l'Afrique du Nord, 1983*. *BCTH* 19 B. Paris.

Lapradelle, A. G. de. 1928. *La frontière; Etude du droit international*. Paris.

Lary, D. 1980. Warlord studies. *Modern China* 6:439–70.

Lassère, F. 1983. Strabon devant l'Empire romain. *ANRW* II.30:867–96.

Latte, K. 1960. *Römische religionsgeschichte*. Mochen.

Lattimore, O. 1940. *Inner Asian frontiers of China*. New York.

——— 1962. *Studies in frontier history*. London.

Laur-Belart, R. 1952. The late *limes* from Basel to the Lake of Constance. In *Limeskongress I*, 55–76.

Lefebvre, H. 1976. Reflections on the politics of space. *Antipode* 8, no. 2:30–37.

Lemant, J.-P., et al. 1985. *Le cimitière et la fortification du Bas-Empire de Vireux-Molhain (Ardennes)*. Mainz.

Lentacker, F. 1974. *La frontière franco-belge: Etude gèographique des effets d'une frontière internationale sur la vie de relations*. Lille.

Lepore, E. 1989. *Colonie greche dell'Occidente antico*. Rome.

Levy, E. 1951. *West Roman vulgar law*. Philadelphia.

Lewin, A. 1990. Dall'Eufrate al Mar Rosso: Diocleziano, l'esercito e i confini tardo antichi. *Athenaeum* 78:141–65.

Lidner, P. P. 1981. Nomadism, horses and Huns. *Past and Present* 92:3–19.

Liebeschuetz, J. H. W. 1986. Generals, federates and bucellarii. In Freeman and Kennedy 1986, 463–74.

——— 1991. *Barbarians and bishops: Army, church and state in the age of Arcadius and Chrysostom*. Oxford.

Liebmann-Frankfort, T. 1969. *La frontière orientale dans la politique extérieure de la République romaine depuis la traité d'Apamée jusqu'à la fin des conquêtes asiatiques de Pompée (189–63)*. Brussels.

Lieu, S. N. C. 1986. Captives, refugees and exiles: A study of cross-frontier civilian movements and contacts between Rome and Persia from Valens to Jovian. In Freeman and Kennedy 1986, 475–505.

Lightfoot, C. S. 1983. The city of Bezabde. In Mitchell 1983a, 189–204.

Limeskongress I. 1952. *The congress of Roman frontier studies, 1949*. Durham.

Limeskongress II. 1956. Carnuntina: Ergebniss der Forschung über die Grenz-provinzen des röm. Reiches, 1955. Graz.

Limeskongress III. 1959. Limes-Studien: Vorträge des 3 internationale Limes-kongresses in Rheinfelden, Basel, 1957. Basel.

Limeskongress. V. 1963. Quintus Congressus Internationalis Limitis Romani Studiosorum, 1961. Zagreb.

Limeskongress VI. 1967. Studien zu den Militärgrenzen Roms: Voträge des 6 internationale Limeskongresses in Süddeutschland, 1964. Cologne.

Limeskongress VII. 1971. Roman frontier studies: The proceedings of the seventh international congress, Tel Aviv, 1967. Tel Aviv.

Limeskongress VIII. 1974. Roman frontier studies: Eighth international congress of Limesforschung, Cardiff, 1969. Cardiff.

Limeskongress IX. 1974. Actes du IXe congrès international d'études sur les frontières romaines, Mamaia, 1972. Bucharest.

Limeskongress X. 1977. Studien zu den Militärgrenzen Roms II. Vorträge des 10. internationalen Limeskongresses in der Germania Inferior, 1974. Cologne.

Limeskongress XI. 1977. Limes: Akten des XI internationalen Limeskongresses, Székesfehérvar, 1976. Budapest.

Limeskongress XII. 1980. Hanson, W. S., and L. J. F. Keppie, Roman frontier studies XII, 1979. BAR S71. Oxford.

Limeskongress XIII. 1986. Studien zu den Militärgrenzen Roms III, 13 interna-tionalen Limeskongresses, Aalen, 1983. Stuttgart.

Limeskongress XIV. 1990. Akten des 14 internationalen Limeskongresses in Bad Deutsch–Altenberg/Carnuntum. Ost. Akad. Wissensch.

Limeskongress XV. 1991. Roman frontier studies, 1989: Proceedings of the fifteenth international congress of Roman Frontier studies. Exeter.

Lotter, F. 1976. Severinus von Noricum: Legende und historische Wirklichkeit. Stuttgart.

Lüders, A. 1955. Eine kartographische Darstellung der römischen Münzschatze im freien Germanien. Arch. Geographica 2:85–89.

Luttwak, E. N. 1976. The grand strategy of the Roman Empire. Baltimore.

McCormick, M. 1977. Odoacer, the emperor Zeno and the Rugian victory legation. Byzantion 47:212–22.

MacDonald, G. 1921. The building of the Antonine Wall: A fresh study of the inscriptions. JRS 11:1–24.

Macinnes, L. 1984. Settlement and economy: East Lothian and the Tyne-Forth province. In Micket and Burgess 1984, 176–98.

———— 1989. Baubles, bangles and beads: Trade and exchange in Roman Scotland. In Barrett et al. 1989, 108–16.

MacMullen, R. 1963. Soldier and civilian in the later Roman Empire. Cam-bridge, Mass.

———— 1980. How big was the Roman army? *Klio* 62:451–60.

———— 1986. Judicial savagery in the Roman Empire. *Chiron* 16:43–62.

Manfredi, M., and L. Piccirilli. 1980. *Plutarco: Le vite di Licurgo e di Numa.* Rome.

Mann, J. C. 1974. The frontiers of the principate. *ANRW* II. 1:508–31.

———— 1977. Duces and comites in the fourth century. In Johnston 1977, 11–14.

———— 1979a. Power, force and the frontiers of the empire. *JRS* 69:175–83.

———— 1979b. Hadrian's Wall: The last phase. In Casey 1979b, 144–51.

Marichal, R. 1979. Les ostraca de Bu Ngem. *CRAI*, 436–52.

Matthews, J. 1975. *Western aristocracies and imperial court* A.D. *364–425.* Oxford.

———— 1976. Mauretania in Ammianus and the Notitia. In Goodburn and Bartholomew 1976, 157–88.

———— 1984. The tax law of Palmyra: Evidence for economic history in a city of the Roman East. *JRS* 74:157–80.

———— 1989. *The Roman Empire of Ammianus.* Baltimore.

Mattingly, D. J. 1983. The Laguatan: A Libyan tribal federation. *Lib. Stud.* 14:98–108.

———— 1985. Olive oil production in Roman Tripolitania. In Buck and Mattingly 1985, 27–46.

———— 1987. Libyans and the "limes": Culture and society in Roman Tripolitania. *Ant. Afr.* 23:71–94.

Mattingly, D. J., and G. D. B Jones. 1986. A new Tripolitanian *clausura. Lib. Stud.* 17:87–96.

Maxfield, V. A., ed. 1989. *The Saxon Shore.* Exeter Studies in History 25. Exeter.

Maxwell, G. 1983. "Roman" settlement in Scotland. In Chapman and Myrtum 1983, 233–61.

Mayerson, P. 1986. The Saracens and the *limes. BASO* 262:35–47.

———— 1989. Saracens and Romans: Micro-macro relationships. *BASO* 274:71–79.

Mazzarino, S. 1990. *Stilichone: La crisi imperiale dopo Theodosio.* reedition of 1942 by A. Giardina. Rome.

Mertens, J. 1983. Roman settlements in Belgium. In *Rome and her northern provinces,* ed. B. Hartley and J. Wacher, 153–68. Gloucester.

———— 1986. Recherches récentes sur le-Bas Empire romain en Belgique. In *Limeskongress XIII,* 192–99.

Micket, R., and C. Burgess, eds. 1984. *Between and beyond the walls: Essay on the prehistory and history of northern Britain in honour of G. Jobey.* Edinburgh.

Middleton, P. 1979. Army supply in Roman Gaul. In *Invasion and response: The case of Roman Britain*, ed. B. C. Burnham and H. B. Johnson, 81–97. BAR S73. Oxford.

Mihäilescu-Birliba, V. 1981. Review of H. Wolfram and F. Dain, *Die Völker an der mittleren Donau*. *Dacia* 25:412–13.

Millar, F. 1982. Emperors, frontiers and foreign relations, 31 B.C. to A.D. 378. *Britannia* 13:1–23.

Mitchell, S. 1976. Requisitioned transport in the Roman Empire: A new inscription from Pisidia. *JRS* 66:106–31.

———, ed. 1983a. *Armies and frontiers in Roman and Byzantine Anatolia*. BAR S156. Oxford.

——— 1983b. Balkans, Anatolia and Roman armies across Asia Minor. In Mitchell 1983a, 131–50.

Mitford, T. B. 1980. Cappadocia and Armenia Minor: Historical setting of the *limes*. *ANRW* II. 7.2:1170–1227.

Mócsy, A. 1974a. Ein spätantiken Festigungstyp am linken Donau. In *Limeskongress VIII*, 191–96.

——— 1974b. *Pannonia and upper Moesia*. Trans. S. Frere. London.

Mócsy, A., and D. Gabler. 1986. Alte und neue Probleme am Limes von Pannonien. In *Limeskongress XIII*, 369–76.

Mommsen, T. 1889. Das römische Militarwesen seit Diokletien. *Hermes* 24:206–83. Reprinted in *Gesammelte Schriften* (1905–13), vol. 6, chap. 13.

——— 1976. *Römische Geschichte*. 8 vols. DTV-Bibliothek Lit. Philos. Wiss. Munich.

Moynihan, R. 1986. Geographical mythology and Roman imperial ideology. In *The age of Augustus*, ed. R. Winkes, 149–61. Providence, R. I.

MTTC = Mao Tse-tung. 1913. *Chi-ch'u chan-shu* (Basic tactics). Hankow.

Müllenhoff, K. 1887. *Deutsche altertume Kunde*. Vol. 2. Berlin.

Nagy, T. 1974. Drei Jahre Limesforschungen in Ungarn. In *Limeskongress IX*, 27–37.

Napoli, J. 1989. Signification des ouvrages linéaires romains. *Latomus* 98:823–34.

Nicolet, C. 1983. L'Empire romain: Espace, temps et politique. *Ktema* 8:163–73.

——— 1988. *L'inventaire du monde: Géographie et politique aux origines de l'Empire romain*. Paris.

——— 1991. *Space, geography, and politics in the early Roman Empire*. Trans. H. Leclerc. Ann Arbor, Mich.

Noble, F. 1983. *Offa's Dyke reviewed*, ed. M. Gelling. BAR 114. Oxford.

Nordman, D. 1977. Géographie ou histoire d'une frontière: La frontière franco-belge. *Annales (ESC)* 3:433–44.

——— 1979. L'idée de frontière fluviale en France. In *Frontières et con-*

References

tacts de civilisation, 76–89. Colloque Université Franco-Suisse. Neufchâtel.

——— 1980. Problematique historique: Des frontières de l'Europe aux frontières du Maghreb (19e siècle). Pluviel 30:17–29.

Oelmann, F. 1952. The Rhine limes in late Roman times. In Limeskongress I, 85–96.

Ørsted, P. 1985. Roman imperial economy and romanization. Copenhagen.

Ossel, P. van. 1983. L'établissement romain de Loën à Lixhe et l'occupation rurale au Bas-Empire dans la Hesbaye liégoise. Helinium 23:143–69.

——— 1992. Etablissements ruraux de l'antiquité tardive dans le nord de la Gaule. Gallia, suppl. 51. Paris.

Panella, C. 1981. La distribuzione e i mercati. In Giardina and Schiavone 1981, 2:55–80.

Parker, G. 1985. Western geopolitical thought in the twentieth century. Beckenham.

Parker, S. T. 1986a. Romans and Saracens: A history of the Arabian frontier. Ph.D. Diss. Series. 6, ASOR.

——— 1986b. Retrospective on the Arabian frontier after a decade of research. In Freeman and Kennedy 1986, 634–47.

——— 1987a. The Roman frontier in central Jordan. BAR S340. Oxford.

——— 1987b. Peasants, pastoralists and the Pax Romana. BASO 265:35–51.

——— 1990. New light on the Roman frontier in Arabia. In Limeskongress XIV, 215–30.

——— 1991. The nature of Rome's Arabian frontier. In Limeskongress XV, 498–504.

Parker-Pierson, M. G. 1984. Death, society and social change: The Iron Age of S. Jutland, 200 B.C.–600 A.D. Diss., Cambridge University.

Peacock, D. P. S. 1978. The Rhine and the problem of Gaulish wine in Roman Britain. In Taylor and Cleere 1978, 49–57.

——— 1982. Pottery in the Roman world. New York.

Peacock, D. P. S., and D. F. Williams. 1986. Amphorae and the Roman economy. New York.

Périn, P. 1980. La datation des tombes mérovingiennes. Geneva.

Périn, P. and L.-C. Feffer. 1987. Les Francs. Paris.

Petolescu, C. C. 1977. Données inédites sur la legio II Italica en Dacie. In Limeskongress XI, 297–302.

Petrikovits, H. von. 1971. Fortifications in the north-western Roman Empire from the third to the fifth centuries A.D. JRS 61:178–218.

——— 1979. Militarisches Nutzland in dem Grenzprovinzen des römischen Reichs. In Acts VIIe Congrès internationale d'Epigraphie Grecque et Latine, Constanza, 1977, 229–42. Bucharest.

———— 1980a Lixae. In *Limeskongress XII*, 1027–35.

———— 1980b. *Die Rheinlande in römischer Zeit.* Düsseldorf.

Petrović, P. 1977. Forteresse romaine à l'embouchure de la rivière Porečka dans les Portes de Fer. In *Limeskongress XI*, 259–75.

Picard, G. C. 1984. *Actes du Ière colloque international sur l'histoire et archéologie de l'Afrique du Nord, 1981.* BCTH 17 B. Paris.

Piccaluga, G. 1974. *Terminus: I segni di confine nella religione romana.* Rome.

Piggott, S. 1958. Native economies and the Roman occupation of North Britain. In Richmond 1958, 1–27.

Pilet, C. 1980. *La nécropole de Frénouville.* BAR S83. Oxford.

Pirling, R. 1966–79. *Das römisch-fränkische Gräberfeld von Krefeld-Gellep.* 4 vols. Berlin.

———— 1978. Chronologie du cimitière de Krefeld-Gellep (Rép. Fed. allemande, Nordrheinland-Westfalen). In Fleury and Périn 1978, 59–68.

Pitts, L. F. 1989. Relations between Rome and German "kings" on the middle Danube in the first to fourth centuries A.D. *JRS* 7:45–58.

Planck, D. 1985. Die Viereckschanze von Fellback-Schmiden. In *Der Keltenfürst von Hochdorf: Methoden und Ergebnisse der Landesarchäologie,* ed. D. Planck, 340–54. Stuttgart.

PLRE = *The prosopography of the later Roman Empire.* Ed. A. H. M. Jones, J. R. Martindale, and J. Morris. Vol. 1 (1971), A.D. 260–395. Vol. 2 (1980), A.D. 395–527. Cambridge.

Poidebard, A. 1934. *La trace de Rome dans le désert de Syrie.* 2 vols. Paris.

Porch, D. 1986. *The conquest of the Sahara.* Oxford.

Powell, P. W., et al., eds. 1983. *Essays on frontiers in world history.* Austin, Tex.

Price, R. M. 1976. The limes of lower Egypt. In Goodburn and Bartholomew 1976, 143–51.

Raschke, M. G. 1978. New studies in Roman commerce with the East. *ANRW* II. 9:604–1361.

Rebuffat, R. 1977. Une zone militaire et sa vie économique: Le limes de Tripolitanie. In *Armée et fiscalité dans le monde antique,* 395–417, ed. A. Chastagnol et al. Colloques CNRS 936. Paris.

———— 1982. Au-delà des camps romains d'Afrique mineure: Renseignement, controle, pénétration. *ANRW* II. 10.2:474–513.

Reddé, M. 1991. A l'ouest du Nil: Une frontière sans soldats, des soldats sans frontière. In *Limeskongress XV*, 483–93.

Remesal Rodriguez, J. 1986. *La annona militaris y la exportación de aceite betico a Germania.* Madrid.

Rémondon, R. 1965. Militaires et civiles dans une campagne égyptienne au temps de Constance II. *JS*, 132–43.

References

Rey-Coquais, J.-P. 1976. Syrie romaine de Pompée à Dioclétien. *JRS* 66:44–73.

Rice Holmes, T. 1928–31. *The architect of the Roman Empire*. 3 vols. Oxford.

Richardson, J. S. 1979. Polybius' view of the Roman Empire. *PBSR* 47:1–11.

Richmond, I. A., ed. 1958. *Roman and native in north Britain*. Edinburgh.

———— 1982. *Trajan's army on Trajan's Column*. London.

Rivet, A. 1976. The Notitia Galliarum: Some questions. In Goodburn and Bartholomew 1976, 119–41.

Romanelli, P. 1959. *Storia delle provincie romane dell'Africa*. Rome.

Roques, D. 1987. *Synésios de Cyrène et la Cyrénaïque du Bas-Empire*. Paris.

Rostovtzeff, M. 1957. *Social and economic history of the Roman Empire*. 2d ed. Oxford.

Roymans, N. 1983. The North Belgic tribes in the first century B.C.: A historical-anthropological perspective. In Brandt and Slofstra 1983, 43–69.

Ruggini, L. Cracco. 1961. *Economia e società nell' "Italia annonaria": Rapporti fra agricoltura dal IV al VI secolo*. Milan.

Sacks, R. D. 1986. *Conceptions of space in social thought*. London.

Salama, P. 1954. A propos d'une inscription maurétanienne de 346 après J. C. *Libyca* 2:205–29.

———— 1966. Occupation de la maurétanie Césarienne occidentale sous le Bas-Empire. *Mélanges Piganiol* 3:1291–1311.

———— 1977. Les déplacements sucessifs du limes en Maurétanie Césarienne. In *Limeskongress XI*, 577–95.

———— 1980. Les voies romaines de Sitifis à Igilgili. *AntAfr*. 16:101–33.

Salamon, A., and I. Lengyel. 1980. Kinship interrelations in a fifth-century "Pannonian" cemetery, etc. *World Arch*. 12:93–104.

Saller, R. P., and B. D. Shaw. 1984. Tombstones and Roman family relations in the principate: Civilians, soldiers and slaves. *JRS* 74:124–56.

Salway, P. 1981. *Roman Britain*. Oxford.

Sarnowski, T. 1990. Die Anfänge der spätrömanischen Militärorganisation des unteren Donauraumes. In *Limeskongress XIV*, 855–61.

Schallmayer, E. 1984. *Der Oldenwaldlimes: Vom Main bis an den Neckar*. Stuttgart.

Schlippschuh, O. 1974. *Die Händler im römischen Kaiserreich in Gallien, Germanien und den Donauprovinzen Rätien, Noricum und Pannonien*. Amsterdam.

Schlumberger, D. 1939. Bornes frontières de la Palmyrène. *Syria* 20:43–73.

Schmid, P. 1978. New archaeological results of settlement structures

(Roman Iron Age) in the north west German coastal area. In Cunliffe and Rowley 1978, 123–46.

Schönberger, H. 1969. The Roman frontier in Germany: An archaeological survey. *JRS* 59:144–97.

Schutz, H. 1983. *The prehistory of Germanic Europe*. New Haven, Conn.

——— 1985. *The Romans in central Europe*. New Haven, Conn.

Scorpan, C. 1980. *Limes Scythiae*. BAR S88. Oxford.

Shahid, I. 1984. *Byzantium and the Arabs of the fourth century*. Washington, D.C.

Sidebotham, S. E. 1991. A limes in the eastern desert of Egypt: Myth or reality? In *Limeskongress XV*, 494–57.

Simpson, C. J. 1976. Belt buckles and strap ends of the later empire. *Britannia* 7:192–206.

Snape, M. E. 1991. Roman and native: Vici on the north British frontier. In *Limeskongress XV*, 468–71.

Soja, E. W. 1985. The spatiality of social life. In Gregory and Urry 1985, 90–127.

Sommer, C. S. 1984. *The military vici in Roman Britain*. BAR 129. Oxford.

——— 1991. Life beyond the ditches: Housing and planning of the military vici in Upper Germany and Raetia. In *Limeskongress XV*, 472–76.

Soproni, S. 1974. Ein spätromische Militärstation im sarmatischen Gebiet. In *Limeskongress VIII*, 197–203.

——— 1977. Contra Acinco e Bononia: Bermerkungen zu den Fasti des Hydatius. In *Limeskongress X*, 393–97.

——— 1986. Nachtvalentinianische Festungen am Donaulimes. In *Limeskongress XIII*, 409–15.

Speidel, M. 1975. The rise of ethnic units in the Roman imperial army. *ANRW* II. 3:202–31.

——— 1987. The Roman road to Dumnata (Jawf in Saudi Arabia) and the frontier strategy of *praetensione colligare*. *Historia* 36:211–21.

Ste Croix, G. E. M. de. 1981. *The class struggle in the ancient Greek world*. London.

Storchi Marino, A. 1990. *Caio Marcio Censorino, la lotta politica interno al pontificato e la formazione della tradizione zu Numa*. Naples.

Stroheker, K. F. 1948. *Der senatorische Adel in spätantiken Gallien*. Tübingen.

——— 1975. Die Alamannen und der spätrömische Reich. In *Zur Geschichte der Alamannen*, ed. W. Müller, Wege der Forschung, Vol. C, 20–48. Darmstadt.

Sutton, D. S. 1980. *Provincial militarism and the Chinese Republic: The Yunnan army, 1905-25*. Ann Arbor, Mich.

Syme, R. 1934. *The Cambridge ancient history.* Vol. 10, chap. 22. Cambridge.

Taylor, J. du Plat, and H. Cleere, eds. 1978. *Roman shipping and trade: Britain and the Rhine provinces.* CBA Report 24. London.

Tchernia, A. 1986. *Le vin de l'Italie romaine.* Rome.

Teillet, S. 1984. *Des Goths à la nation gothique: Les origines de l'idée en Occident de nation du Ve au VIIe siècle.* Paris.

Teixidor, J. 1984. *Un port romain du désert: Palmyre.* Semitica, vol. 34. Paris.

Ternes, L. M. 1972. *La vie quotidienne en Rhenanie romaine (Ier-IVe s.).* Paris.

Thollard, P. 1987. *Barbarie et civilisation chez Strabon.* Ann. Lit. Univ. Besançon 365. Paris.

Thomas, C. 1979. Saint Patrick and fifth century Britain. In Casey 1979b, 81–101.

Thompson, E. A. 1980. Barbarian invaders and Roman collaborators. *Florilegium* 2:71–88.

———— 1982. *Romans and barbarians: The decline of the western empire.* Madison, Wisc.

Todd, M. 1987. *The northern barbarians 100 B.C.–A.D. 300.* Rev. ed. Oxford.

Tomlin, R. S. O. 1974. The date of the barbarian conspiracy. *Britannia* 5:303–9.

———— 1976. Notitia Dignitatum omnium, tam civilium quam militarium. In Goodburn and Bartholomew 1976, 189–210.

Toropu, O. 1974. La frontière nord-danubienne de la Dacie Ripensis depuis l'abandon de la Dacie traiane jusqu'aux invasions hunniques. In *Limeskongress IX,* 71–81.

Trousset, P. 1974. *Recherches sur le limes Tripolitanus.* Paris.

———— 1978. Les bornes du Bled Segui: Nouveau aperçus sur la centuriation romaine du sud Tunisien. *AntAfr.* 12:125–77.

———— 1980. Signification d'une frontière: Nomades et sedentaires dans la zone du limes d'Afrique. In *Limeskongress XII,* 931–42.

———— 1981. L'idée de frontière au Sahara et les données archéologiques. In *Enjeux Sahariens,* 47–78. Table Ronde, CRESM.

———— 1984. Note sur un type d'ouvrage linéaire du limes d'Afrique. In Picard 1984, 383–98.

———— 1985. Les "fines antiquae" et la reconquète Byzantine en Afrique. In Lancel 1985, 361–76.

———— 1987. Limes et "frontière climatique." In *Actes du IIIe colloque international sur l'histoire et archéologie de l'Afrique du Nord, Montpellier, 1985,* 55–84. Paris.

———— 1993. La frontière romaine et ses contradictions. In *Travaux de la Maison de l'Orient (Lyon).* Forthcoming.

Tuan, Y.-F. 1987. *Space and place*. London.

Turner, F. J. 1893. The significance of the frontier in American history. *Ann. Report Am. Hist. Assoc.*, 199–207.

—— 1938. *The early writings of Frederick Jackson Turner*. Madison, Wisc.

Van Dam, R. 1985. *Leadership and community in late antique Gaul*. Berkeley and Los Angeles.

Van Es, W. A. 1967. *Wijster: A native village beyond the imperial frontier, 150–425 A.D.* Gröningen.

Vasić, M. 1991. L'architecture à l'intérieur des camps des Portes de Fer au Ière et Vème siècle. In *Limeskongress XV*, 308–19.

Vasić, M., and V. Kondić. 1986. Le limes romain et paléobyzantin des Portes de Fer. In *Limeskongress XIII*, 542–60.

Velkov, V. 1977. *Cities in Thrace and Dacia in late antiquity*. Amsterdam.

Vernant, J.-P. 1965. *Mythe et pensée chez les Grecs*. Paris.

Vittinghoff, K. 1976. Die politische Organization der röm. Rheingebiete in der Kaiserzeit. *Atti Conv. Lincei* 23:73–94.

Vulpe, R. 1974. Les valla de la Valachie, de la Basse-Moldavie et de Boudjak. In *Limeskongress IX*, 267–76.

Wacher, J. 1974. *The towns of Roman Britain*. London.

Wachtel, K. 1977. Das Kastell Iatrus und die spätantiken Limesbauten an der unteren Donau. In *Limeskongress X*, 405–9.

Wallace-Hadrill, J. M. 1962. *The long-haired kings*. London.

Warmington, B. H. 1976. Objectives and strategy in the Persian war of Constantius II. In *Limeskongress XI*, 509–20.

Webb, W. P. 1931. *The Great Plains*. Boston.

—— 1953. *The great frontier*. Austin, Tex.

Weisgerber, J. L. 1968. *Die Namen der Ubier*. Cologne.

Welch, M. G. 1992. *Anglo-Saxon England*. London.

Wells, C. M. 1972. *The German policy of Augustus*. Oxford.

Wells, P. S. 1980. *Culture, contact and culture change: Early Iron Age central Europe and the Mediterranean*. Cambridge.

Welsby, D. A. 1982. *The Roman military defence of the British provinces in the later phases*. BAR 101. Oxford.

Wheeler, E. L. 1991. Rethinking the upper Euphrates: Where was the western border of Armenia? In *Limeskongress XV*, 505–11.

Whittaker, C. R. 1978. Land and labour in North Africa. *Klio* 60:331–62.

—— 1982. Labour supply in the later Roman Empire. *Opus* 1:161–70.

—— 1983. Trade and frontiers of the Roman Empire. In Garnsey and Whittaker 1983, 110–25.

—— 1989. *Les frontières de l'Empire romain*. Ann. Litt. Université de Besançon. Paris.

Wieczynski, J. L. 1976. *The Russian frontier: The impact of borderlands upon the course of Russian history.* Charlottesville, Va.

Wightman, E. M. 1970. *Roman Trier and Treveri.* London.

———— 1978. Cultural frontiers within a Roman province. *Comparative frontier studies.* 10, 3. Norman: University of Oklahoma.

———— 1981. The fate of the Gallo-Roman villages in the third century. In *The Roman West in the third century* A.D., ed. A. King and M. Henig, 235–43. BAR S109. Oxford.

———— 1985. *Gallia Belgica.* London.

Wilkes, J. J. 1965. The military achievement of Augustus in Europe with special reference to Illyricum. *Univ. Birmingham Hist. Journ.* 1–27.

———— 1977. The Saxon Shore—British anonymity in the Roman Empire. In Johnston 1977, 76–80.

Will, E. 1967. *Histoire politique du monde hellenistique.* Nancy.

Willems, W. J. H. 1986. *Romans and Batavians: A regional study in the Dutch Eastern River area.* Amsterdam.

Williams, D. F. 1977. The Romano-British Black-Burnished industry: An essay on characterization by heavy mineral analysis. In *Pottery and early commerce*, ed. D. P. S. Peacock. New York.

Williams, D. F., and D. P. S. Peacock. 1983. The importation of olive oil in Iron Age and Roman Britain. In *Producción y comercio del aceite en la antigüedad*, ed. J. M. Martinez Blàquez and J. Remesal Rodriguez, 263–80. Madrid.

Wirth, G. 1979. Anmerkungen zur Vita des Severin von Noricum. *Quad. Catanesi* 1:217–66.

Wolfram, H. 1988. *History of the Goths.* Trans. T. J. Dunlap. London.

Ypey, J. 1978. La chronologie du cimitière Franc de Rhenen (Pay-Bas, Utrecht). In Fleury and Périn 1978, 51–58.

Zahariade, M. 1991. An early and late Roman fort on the lower Danube limes: Halmyris (Independenta, Tulcea County, Romania). In *Limeskongress XV*, 311–17.

Zanker, P. 1988. *The power of images in the age of Augustus.* Trans. A. Shapiro. Ann Arbor, Mich.

Zimmermann, W. H. 1974. A Roman Iron Age and early migration settlement at Flögeln, Kr. Wesermund, Lower Saxony. In *Anglo-Saxon settlement and landscape*, ed. T. Rowley, 56–73. BAR 6. Oxford.

Index

Page numbers in italics refer to illustrations.

ANCIENT SOCIETY AND HISTORY

The series Ancient Society and History offers books, relatively brief
in compass, on selected topics in the history of ancient Greece and
Rome, broadly conceived, with a special emphasis on comparative
and other nontraditional approaches and methods. The series,
which includes both works of synthesis and works of original schol-
arship, is aimed at the widest possible range of specialists and
nonspecialist readers.

4852013

Made in the USA
Lexington, KY
08 March 2010